ACTIVEXPERT

ActiveXpert

Tom Armstrong

with Jim Crespino and Rob Alumbaugh

McGraw-Hill
New York • San Francisco • Washington, D.C. • Auckland • Bogotá
Caracas • Lisbon • London • Madrid • Mexico City • Milan
Montreal • New Delhi • San Juan • Singapore
Sydney • Tokyo • Toronto

CONTENTS

Contents

ACKNOWLEDGMENTS

There was a lot of effort behind the creation of this book, and everyone involved deserves much praise. I'd like to first thank my editor, Judy Brief, for hanging in there and pushing me to get this book finished. The book was late through no fault of hers. As a new author, I thought I could handle two concurrent book projects, and I was wrong. Thanks also to my copy editor, Wayne Coleson, for cleaning up my run-on sentences, dangling participles, and so on. To this day, I don't even know what a participle is.

To Rob Alumbaugh and Jim Crespino—two gifted developers who helped me complete this book. Thanks guys, I owe you. Thanks to Chuck Reeves, also a gifted developer, who provided the cool math control example in Chapter 8. Rob actually developed the control in Chapter 8, but it is based on Chuck's original C++ design. Check the Website for Chuck's C++ and Java versions of the control.

This book has also benefited through the help of Don Weiss and Bill Radford of Step 1 Training, Inc. Don and Bill introduced me to the world of developer training, and I love it. The classes I teach at Step 1 provide a medium to "test" the organization and presentation of difficult topics such as COM- and ActiveX-based development. Thanks for the opportunity.

Thanks to Steve Vaughan and Lane Culvert. I recently changed groups at DST, and these guys now control my time. Thankfully, they have allowed me to pursue writing and to routinely take time off to teach. Without such freedom, I wouldn't get to enjoy life nearly as much as I do.

Finally, I must thank my beautiful wife, Nicole, and my wonderful children, Eric and Jessica—each of whom adds focus, clarity, and love to everything I do.

INTRODUCTION

On March 12, 1996, the computer world shook as Microsoft unveiled its strategy to integrate its products and technologies with the increasingly popular Internet. It was just a tremor at the time, just a series of announcements with no real products or software to back it up. Today, however, the tremor has turned into a high-magnitude quake. Microsoft has made good on its promise to radically change its focus, and by all accounts has succeeded in embracing this new entity called the World Wide Web. Microsoft has succeeded in implementing this grand vision—based on a thing called *ActiveX*.

Microsoft coined ActiveX to described its extreme shift in focus, from the isolated desktop to an Internet-aware world, where each desktop is connected to the Web. ActiveX is a broad term that describes a whole slew of new technologies. New languages such as VBScript, JavaScript, and Java. New Windows operating system features such as Internet Information Server and Internet Explorer. New Web-aware products such as Office 97, FrontPage 97, and the Windows operating system itself. New Web-based technologies such as ActiveX controls, URL Monikers, Active Scripting, and Active Server Pages. Everything, it seems, that Microsoft produces has something to do with the Web.

Microsoft's comprehensive shift to incorporate the Web into everything it produces is having—and will continue to have—a profound effect on software developers, not just the typical Windows-application developer, but also a new group of developers and designers who create Websites using HTML, JavaScript, and Perl. Because of its dominance of the client operating system, Microsoft's ActiveX strategy will affect areas previously untouched: Web servers, client browsers, transaction services, and so on. Microsoft now has ActiveX-based products covering every aspect of the Web. If you develop Windows software or develop Websites, you need to understand what ActiveX is all about.

Windows and Website Developers

Microsoft's adoption of the Web as its primary focus is having a dramatic effect even on those developers that do not directly develop software for the Web environment. ActiveX technologies permeate the whole of Microsoft's applications and tools. For example, HTML (Hypertext Markup Language) is the primary language for Website developers today. However, Microsoft has adopted HTML as its own "rich data type." As the browser is integrated directly into the Windows shell, HTML becomes the language for describing GUI (graphical user interface) elements. HTML is now the language of Microsoft's WinHelp system. Previous Web-only languages such as JavaScript and VBScript can now be used to write scripts in the Windows environment. The JavaScript language can easily be integrated into *your* application, even if it has absolutely nothing to do with a Web-type environment.

The examples are numerous. Windows developers today must become familiar with these new languages, technologies, and tools. They have no choice. Microsoft's grand vision is to make the Windows operating system the very best "client" or browser for the Web environment, and in doing so is radically changing what it means to develop for the Windows platform.

Beyond these facts, the Web itself is becoming the target platform. As Web and desktop technologies converge, the concept that developing for one or the other disappears. Windows-application developers are really Web-based developers and vice versa. The skills necessary to build a good Windows application can be used to build a nice Website, and so on. This is one of Microsoft's strategies, to make its existing languages, tools, and technologies "work" in the Web environment. If you're an existing Visual Basic developer, you can now use your knowledge to develop a Website using VBScript and ActiveX controls, two concepts that you may already understand. Differences between the Web and a Windows application are beginning to shrink, and will continue to do so.

If your primary focus today is building Websites, ActiveX is just as important for either Internet or intranet environments. As Microsoft moves to embrace the Web, understanding how to use these new technologies in your Websites is important. As previously stated, the Web and the Windows environments are merging quickly, and the Window operating system can easily represent 80 percent of the visitors to your site. There is no doubt that your site needs to demonstrate that it can effectively cater to these visitors.

The Goal

Our goal, then, is to provide you, the developer, with a broad understanding of Microsoft's ActiveX-based technologies—to detail what ActiveX is all about and how you can use it effectively.

Chapters 1 through 3 get things started. Chapter 1 covers the basic technologies that enabled the development of the World Wide Web, and argues for developers to investigate, understand, and apply these technologies in their applications today. Chapter 2 then goes into Microsoft's ActiveX technologies. It presents, with a broad brush, what Microsoft's vision is and how it affects you as a developer. Chapter 3 covers the primary language of the Web, HTML, and then covers a new Web page standard, Cascading Style Sheets. We mentioned earlier why this is important: HTML is now as important to Windows development as the dialog editor was before the advent of ActiveX. It is the new Windows rich data type.

Chapter 4 introduces the new Active Scripting languages: JavaScript and VBScript. An example is created using both languages, and comparisons are made. Chapter 5 covers the use of ActiveX controls both in Web pages as well as in Visual Basic and Visual C++ applications. A full-function browser is developed.

ActiveX is based on Microsoft's Component Object Model (COM), which is a system-level, object-oriented technology on which most of Microsoft's new technologies are based. Chapter 6 covers COM in good detail, and several examples are developed using Visual C++ and the Active Template Library. Chapters 7 and 8 cover the development of ActiveX controls in detail from a Visual C++ with ATL, and a Visual Basic perspective.

Chapter 9 covers Active Scripting. Scripting is becoming an important aspect of application development. Internet Explorer 4.0 adds JavaScript and VBScript support directly to the Windows shell. Using Active Scripting it is easy to add VBScript and JavaScript support to your Windows applications. Chapter 10 provides an introduction to Java for the Windows developer and then proceeds into a discussion of Microsoft's Visual J++ development tool and how ActiveX is a major part of Microsoft's Java strategy.

After finishing this book, you should definitely be an expert on Microsoft's ActiveX vision. You can then choose to apply some or all of these techniques within your applications and Websites. Remember, however, that the difference between the two is getting smaller every day.

Comments and Bug Reports

We welcome and encourage comments, suggestions, and bug reports at the email address provided here. Languages—particularly tools—change all the time, and it is difficult to release a book that has completely up-to-date examples. As things change, we will keep the examples updated and available. You can contact me via email or through WidgetWare.com. WidgetWare.com contains ActiveX-based FAQs, pointers to other developer-oriented sites, and lots of examples. WidgetWare.com gets over 2,000 page hits every day from developers like you. Stop by and see why.

email: tom@WidgetWare.com

URL: http://www.WidgetWare.com/

ACTIVEXPERT

Software Development and The Web

Unless you've been living in a cave for the last year or so, you've undoubt-edly heard about the explosive growth of the Internet. In fact, as a soft-ware developer you probably use the Internet on a daily basis. These uses typically involve product support from vendors, cruising the newsgroups looking for help with a particular development problem, corresponding with friends and co-workers via email, and so on. Personally, I spend at least three hours a day doing these various things.

Is all of the media attention and hype concerning the Internet, the World Wide Web (hereafter I use the term *Web*), and corporate intranets justified? Probably not; but there is no doubt in my mind that the Web is radically changing the way we work as well as the way we live. In this chapter, we quickly introduce and explain some of the Web-oriented ter-minology, and from there we work our way through the hype and try to understand some of the potential of the Web. From there, we discuss some ways that software developers can harness these new Web-based technologies.

The World Wide Web

Commercial use of the Internet has grown enormously within the last few years and continues to grow at a tremendous rate. The primary impe-tus for this growth was the development of the HTTP protocol by Tim Berners-Lee of CERN Laboratories. The development of a standard pro-tocol, coupled with the creation of graphical content browsers such as Netscape's Navigator and Microsoft's Internet Explorer, allowed the aver-age computer user to harness the capabilities and resources of the Inter-net. This has led to a nearly exponential increase in the number of producers and consumers of Internet-based resources, primarily through the proliferation of HTML-based Web pages.

Today, most client-side Web applications are based on the HTML lan-guage. HTML is a simple document-specification language that describes how textual and graphical documents appear within Web-based browsers. The content can be as simple as a text-based description of a product, or as complex as a large multimedia-based presentation of a major publication such as *USA Today*. HTML's ease of use and its ability to provide platform-independent content has made the Web what it is today.

While Web content based on HTML has provided a new and fasci-nating aspect to software development, it is only the beginning. Static, HTML-based documents are quickly giving way to a more powerful and dynamic type of application. These newer Web-based applications provide dynamic interaction with the user. Instead of just viewing content, these applications provide the user with everything that a typical desktop application does: Real-time updating of data such as stock quotes; multimedia applications that use voice and video; desktoplike applications such as word processing; and even distributed client-server applications. The Web has fundamentally changed the way in which software is being developed, marketed, and delivered.

WEB RESOURCES:

URL	Description
http://www.devry-phx.edu/webresrc/webmstry/wwwintro.htm	A list of documents and sites that provide good introductory material on the World Wide Web.
http://www.wdvl.com/	The Web Developer's Virtual Library. Lots of introductory Web material.

Why All the Hype?

There is a tremendous amount of hyperbole surrounding the Internet and the World Wide Web. I'm sure not all of it is justified, but I do know that it has had a major effect on my work life, and my home life too.

The Web has changed how we software developers do our jobs. The Web makes accessing developer-oriented information a lot easier. When you have a development problem, more often than not you can get help from others on the Web. You can search Microsoft's developer knowledge base and probably download sample code that helps solve your problem. If not, go to one of the newsgroups and ask for some help with your problem. This is just the start of how the Web affects the field of software development; it will also profoundly affect the architecture of future applications.

The Web has made communication between authors and readers much easier. By maintaining a Website with book material, we can keep you all updated with the latest sample programs. The Website that I maintain currently gets several hundred hits a day from readers and software developers. I get email from Russia, Japan, Israel, Australia—basically anywhere in the world that has access to the Web. The Web makes communication with one another nearly effortless and for a very low cost.

The Web is going to have a major impact on several areas of our daily lives. I've chosen a few here to take a look at: The software industry itself, marketing, and the broader subject of human interaction.

A Vast Change in the Software Industry

The Web has already significantly changed the software industry—but this is only the beginning. The design and development of software will itself change as products are developed with the new "Web" architecture in mind. Development companies, such as Microsoft, Sun, and Oracle, will change the face of software by the tools that they produce, and it is happening fast. Software is now developed and delivered using "Internet years." *Internet years* are much shorter than the 365 days that we're used to. They're more similar to dog years, seven of which the Earth takes to circumscribe the sun.

The Web is drastically changing the way software products are supported. Web-based product support systems will soon be the norm rather than the exception. Companies must move their support departments closer to the Web and use Web-based products and tools to quickly publish support information. Microsoft does a good job of this. It publishes a product support knowledge base for each of its software products and development tools. You can search the knowledge base to quickly find articles that can help you with your problems. This provides an inexpensive solution for those customers that take the time to find solutions to their problems. If this doesn't appeal to a customer, the old technical support method—the phone—is still available, but at a much higher cost.

The Web also makes it easier to market software products directly. Software producers no longer need a retail presence to get started. Marketing, delivering, and supporting your software is much easier and less expensive now that the Web is here. The only problem is that Web users expect to get almost everything for free, especially a new product, so you still have to work extra hard.

Marketing and the Web

Some pundits have hypothesized that the Web will radically change the delivery of marketing-type information, and I agree. Individuals can now go after the marketing information they need, and do so quickly. If I'm interested in buying a new car, I can research all of the makes and models from the comfort of my own home. I'm pretty certain that if I type www.ford.com into my browser, I'll find all kinds of information on Ford products (see Fig. 1.1). After I've read what Ford has to say, I'll go over to www.edmunds.com and get some unbiased information as well. Later, when I do go down to my local dealer to look at buying that new car, I'll be a very informed buyer. The process has changed from passive to active. Of course, I could have been such a smart buyer before the coming of the Web, but with the Web it is much easier. If it's easier, I'm much more inclined to actually do it.

There's no longer a need to leaf through a magazine looking for that advertisement of a software product that I'm interested in. Instead I jump on the Web, go to one of the search engines, and start looking from there. There's no doubt I'll find a whole lot more information than I would find in a magazine advertisement or a 30-second spot on television. I'll find links to reviews of the product, a link to the providing company's Website, and so on.

The Web also provides one of the biggest and most diverse markets in the world. Nearly every country in the world is linked to the Web, and

Figure 1.1
Ford's Website.

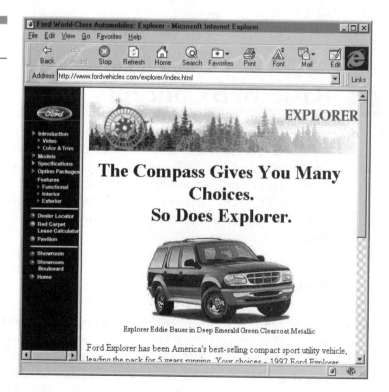

their populations are beginning to use the Web as we do here in the United States. One study even suggests that everyone in the world will have an email address by the year 2000. I think this is rather optimistic, but at least it gives you an idea of how big the Web could eventually become. Imagine what the world would be like if we could email anyone (or everyone!) in the world for virtually no cost.

Potentially a Vast Shift in the Way Humans Interact

By some accounts, thanks to the Web, the existence of governments may be in jeopardy. With the advent of technology that allows a true democracy, instead of the current *representative* democracy, the whole governing process could very well change, dramatically if not drastically. If such large institutions are in jeopardy, just imagine what the Web would do to smaller entities such as software development companies.

Of course, the Web won't change every aspect of our lives. It still can't clean our teeth like a good dental hygienist. Enough speculation—let's get into how we can harness this thing called the Web. Before we start though, let's review some basic Web concepts.

Basic Web Concepts

One of the reasons the Web has grown so fast is that many of its concepts are simple. The Web also uses many technologies that have been around for several years—technologies that have been well tested in the largest networked environment in the world, the Internet.

Before we go any farther in this chapter, let's stop and take a quick look at the primary technologies and terms used in the Internet and Web environment.

Networks

The Internet is a loosely coupled, heterogeneous network comprised of many different computer types. There are large mainframe computers (e.g., IBMs running MVS); midrange minicomputers (e.g., Digital VAXes running VMS or UNIX); and, of course, thousands of microcomputers running some variation of UNIX, Windows NT, or Macintosh System 7.

All of these machines are physically connected, typically through some form of telephone line or cable. The machines form a useful network because they are all connected and communicate using a similar language or protocol.

NOTE: *In a networked environment, it is important that each machine have its own unique and relatively permanent address. A unique address facilitates communication between thousands or millions of different resources in a large networked environment. The Internet uses an addressing scheme specified by the TCP/IP protocol, which we discuss in a moment.*

Protocols

In a network consisting of hundreds of different computer types—where some encode their data using ASCII and others use EBCDIC; where most use stack-based architectures, and some don't; where many run UNIX and the others run one of a hundred different operating systems—it is important that all of them speak a common, well-understood protocol. It is this common protocol that makes a network such a powerful entity. Without the protocol, there would be no network.

A *protocol* specifies a well-defined technique of communication. A protocol is established and must be honored by all involved parties for communication to take place. As individuals, we have a speaking protocol. When interacting, we don't all speak at the same time; one person speaks and when that person stops speaking, another speaks. If someone has something very important to say, he or she may interrupt the current speaker, who then stops, and the person with the important information speaks, and so on. Computer-based protocols are no different. The primary Internet protocol is TCP/IP.

TCP/IP

Transmission Control Protocol/Internet Protocol (TCP/IP) is the protocol used in the Internet and Web environments. TCP/IP has been around for a number of years and is supported by all major operating systems. TCP/IP specifically defines how data is transferred between machines. Thanks to the TCP/IP standard, machines that are vastly different, both in architecture and operating system, can easily transfer information.

Actually, TCP and IP are two different protocols. IP is a lower-level protocol, the purpose of which is to ensure that small data packets in a network can be successfully transferred between machines. Each pack is independent and stateless. TCP works at the next level; it uses the packet-level services provided by IP to create a stream-based, connection-oriented protocol, which basically means that the TCP provides a context or "state" for the stateless IP packets. Once a common protocol is established, processes on disparate machines can communicate. There are two basic process types: the client and server.

Clients and Servers

Protocols such as TCP/IP use the concept of client-server interaction. In order for information transfer to occur, there must be at least two software entities, and in a networked environment the communicating processes will typically reside on separate networked machines.

In the simplest case, where there are two entities communicating, we can establish a client-server relationship. The client process will initiate a session with a server, who typically provides some service to the client. The server is always there waiting (or is launched by request) for a client to use its services. The client uses these services to perform some action, usually at the request of a user.

Figure 1.2 depicts a simple example where an Intel PC running Windows 95 is retrieving data from a server that is a Digital Alpha running UNIX. Most machine relationships are similar to the simple one shown in Fig. 1.2. Once simple, interprocess communication is available (through

Figure 1.2
Client-Server interaction.

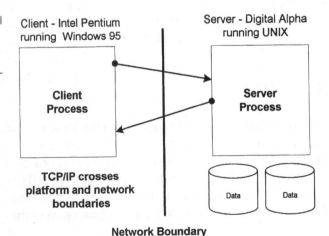

TCP/IP), higher-level software services can be built. The Web itself was built using a simple high-level application protocol called *Hypertext Transfer Protocol* (HTTP).

HTTP

Once you have all these machines connected and communicating with a standard protocol, the next step is to develop higher-level protocols and applications that realize the potential of such a large network of machines. Tim Berners-Lee did this with the creation of the Hypertext Transfer Protocol (HTTP) in 1990. The specification of HTTP, along with HTML, allowed the creation of the Web as we know it today. Here's a snippet from the HTTP specification:

> The Hypertext Transfer Protocol (HTTP) is an application-level protocol with the lightness and speed necessary for distributed, collaborative, hypermedia information systems. It is a generic, stateless, object-oriented protocol which can be used for many tasks, such as name servers and distributed object management systems, through extension of its request methods (commands). A feature of HTTP is the typing and negotiation of data representation, allowing systems to be built independently of the data being transferred.

HTTP is your typical client-server protocol. The client sends a request and waits for the response from the server. The server provides information based on the request from the client. HTTP is connectionless and stateless. In other words, each client request is independent of any other. The server will not maintain any contextual information between client requests.

An HTTP client process will request data from the server using one of three primary HTTP methods: The *GET method* retrieves a Web-based document; the *HEAD method* retrieves information about a document; and the *POST method* can be used to transfer information from the client to the server. After receiving the request from a client process, the HTTP server will pass back its *response* message. In the Web environment, this client that we're referring to is the browser.

The Browser (or the Ultimate Client)

A *browser* is a client application that uses the HTTP protocol to retrieve and display HTML-based Web documents. (We cover HTML shortly.) The server application passes data to the browser, which then parses it and finally renders the output on the client workstation.

One of the important features here is that the document data is platform independent. Of course, the browser must be written to work on the client platform's architecture (e.g., Intel, Windows, Macintosh). However, the server application couldn't care less. It speaks the HTTP protocol and can execute on whatever platform desired (e.g., Sun Sparcstations running UNIX, Intel running Windows NT, and so on). Platform independence is provided by the Web protocols: TCP/IP, HTTP, and HTML.

The scenario just described was the initial purpose of the browser and is what initially created the Web environment. Today, however, the browser is undergoing radical changes. Client-side technologies, such as ActiveX controls, JavaScript, Java applets, and so on, are transforming the browser into a true development environment. At the same time, the major browser vendors are integrating the browser directly into the operating system. The next version of Internet Explorer as well as Netscape's Communicator product are integrating the browser into the operating system shell. We have more to say about this in the coming chapters.

Web Servers

A Web server is a machine running one of several different operating systems (e.g., UNIX, Windows NT), supports TCP/IP, and is physically part of the Internet network that we previously described. It has an explicit Web address, and should be running 24 hours a day so that it is always available for any clients that might request information. The other characteristic that makes an Internet-based server a true Web server is the fact that it supports the HTTP protocol—the Web protocol.

There are a number of vendors that supply Web server software. Microsoft has written Internet Information Server (IIS) that runs on the Windows NT Server platform. Netscape has a comprehensive server suite that runs on several platforms, including Windows NT. Once all of this is set up, the primary purpose of a Web server is to provide a static location for a collection of HTML-based documents—in other words, a Web *site*.

HTML

HTML is a page description language. HTML uses a simple and standard way to describe how text and images should appear when viewed by a

Figure 1.3
A simple HTML-based
document.

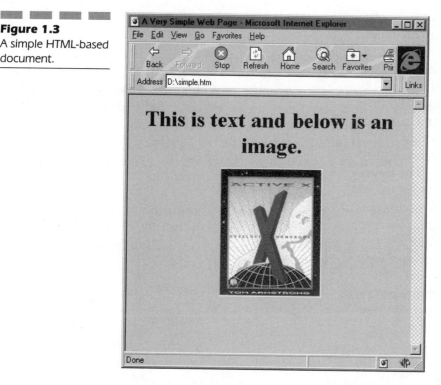

browser. The browser parses the HTML-based text and renders it for the user to view. For example, following is a complete HTML document that displays some simple text over an image in the browser window. See Fig. 1.3.

```
<HTML>
<HEAD>
<TITLE>A Very Simple Web Page</TITLE>
</HEAD>
<BODY>
<CENTER>
<H1>This is text and below is an image.</H1>
<IMG SRC=xpert.gif>
</CENTER>
</BODY>
</HTML>
```

We cover HTML in detail in Chapter 3, but the gist of HTML is that it provides a platform-independent way of describing text and images. HTML also has been recently extended to provide more interactive techniques as well. As you come to see throughout this book, HTML is just the start: With the addition of rich data types (e.g., sound, video), scripting, and the embedding of software components, the HTML-based browser has become a full-blown application environment.

HyperText

One of the most important features of HTML is the concept of a hyperlink. A *hyperlink* allows a page developer to embed links to other documents or resources directly in a page. The user can then link or jump directly to the embedded resource with one mouse click. It is this aspect that makes the Web such a compelling technology.

Actually, hyperlinks are what gave the Web its name. Just imagine what fifty million Web pages, each with five or six links to other Web pages, would look like if we could somehow depict such a large interconnection of resources.

The concept of providing links to information has created whole businesses. Yahoo, a major Website, basically provides a catalog of links to other sites. It doesn't actually produce any content; it only categorizes it (of course, this is also content, but you get the idea).

WEB RESOURCES:

URL	Description
http://www.asiapac.com/Hypertext/ HypertextPublishingKED.html	*Hypertext Publishing and the Evolution of Knowledge*—A 1987 article from *Social Intelligence* that describes and argues cogently for a hypertext-based publishing system. We now have it.
http://www.isg.sfu.ca/duchier/misc/ vbush	*As We May Think*—An article from the July 1945 issue of *The Atlantic Monthly.* Author Vannevar Bush describes the Web long before its time.

The Shift from Static to Dynamic Pages

The first major benefit of the Web was that it allowed easy access to information. In today's world, the right information at the right time can help enormously. Tim Berners-Lee's initial vision of the HTTP protocol was to provide a way for academicians to access each other's work across the Internet. Today, of course, the Web, which is based on the work of Berners-Lee, has become something much larger. As we described earlier, the client side of the equation is the browser. Initially, the browser was a rather simple entity that would blindly parse and display text and images described using the HTML language.

The idea of such a simple browser is gone. Thanks to the growing popularity of the Web and because of its perceived potential, massive enhancements are being made to the browser. Changes are being made to the server-side as well, but we focus mostly on browser-side enhancements in this book.

Recently, basic Web technologies have been enhanced to provide a very effective client-server development environment. The browser has evolved into a powerful client through such improvements as platform independence (through Java), robust client-side programmability (through Java-Script), and complete access to the client-side environment (through ActiveX).

Two Major Web Development Areas

The Web technologies that we've discussed so far, and those discussed throughout this book, are used in two broad areas: the commercial Web environment and a new area called the intranet.

The Commercial Web Environment

The commercial Web is part of the larger Internet environment. The Internet was initially funded by the U.S. government and consisted of a network of Department of Defense and university-based computers. The Internet was used primarily for the exchange of research and other academic-type information.

Today, of course, all this has changed. The majority of Web (and, thus, Internet) traffic is commercial. The major Web backbones are financed by individuals and corporations that use the Web as part of their daily activities. The Web is open to anyone with a telephone line and a few dollars to spend each month. The commercial Web is here to stay, and will probably change significantly as more and more people get their own Web accounts. However, there is an equally important development in the corporate world—the rise of corporate intranets.

Corporate Intranets and Extranets

While most of the interest in the Web is based on its commercial and consumer-oriented potential, another important aspect of the Web has received little attention: corporate intranets. The Web has provided a very rich environment that provides easy distribution of information. Today's corporate environments rely heavily on the ability to disseminate information quickly. Groupware products such as Lotus Notes provide a proprietary method of solving the problem of information distribution (although it is becoming less proprietary and embracing Web standards).

The Web provides an alternative to these products. Because of the tremendous amount of interest in the Web, software vendors are spending their time, energy, and money developing truly great tools for Web-based environments. These development tools, technologies, and products provide a high-quality yet inexpensive way to implement an effective, companywide groupware environment without the cost of using a proprietary product like Lotus Notes. The corporate intranet market may already be as large (at least in dollars) as the consumer-oriented Web that we read about constantly. Plus, the number of corporate intranets is doubling every six months. One study estimates that 80 percent of Web-based development is specifically for corporate intranets.

Once a corporation sets up an internal intranet, the next phase can begin, namely, the creation of cooperative, interconnected intranets called extranets. An *extranet* is a series of connected corporate intranets. Typically an intranet mostly comprises internal, company-specific information. However, some of this information can be of great value to corporate partners or clients, and so it needs to be somewhat "public." Independent companies that rely on each other (e.g., General Motors and its parts suppliers) may find it beneficial to connect their intranets to form data-sharing extranets to allow efficient transfer of information.

What Should I Do as a Developer Today?

As we've stated throughout this first chapter, the Web will affect the work of a software developer significantly. As such, you should begin now learning how to use the tools and techniques of the Web. Very soon now, the Web and the software you currently develop will become inseparable. Microsoft is moving quickly to merge most of the Web technologies directly into its products and tools.

For example, as a developer you're probably familiar with building dialog and related resources for Windows-based applications. You understand the contents of a Windows resource definition (.RC) file. Well, guess what: Windows resource files may soon become HTML documents! You're going to need to understand HTML just to write regular Windows applications. HTML is Microsoft's new rich data type. Knowledge of HTML is becoming a requisite for Windows development.

You should begin now to understand all of the new technologies spawned by the Web. Here are some things you should consider doing.

Make Your Applications Internet-Aware

If you develop workstation-based software, one of the first things you should consider is making your application Internet-aware. Of course, what Internet-aware means to your application depends on what it currently does. If it deals with documents, you might want to add Internet-type email capability. Adding SMTP (Simple Mail Transport Protocol) support to a text-oriented application isn't difficult thanks to several ActiveX technologies. You can use an SMTP ActiveX control to do this with very little coding. After reading through this book, you should certainly have several new concepts that you can apply to your development projects.

Understand Component-Based Development

Component-based software development has become very popular in the last few years. With the popularity of component-based tools (e.g., Microsoft's Visual Basic, Borland's Delphi, Microsoft's Visual J++) continuing to rise, this trend should continue. The increasing popularity of Web-based environments will add even more fuel to this new development model because the Web uses the concept of a software component just about everywhere.

A software component in Web terms is an applet. *Applets* are small, mostly self-contained applications that initially reside on a server, but are executed on the client within the browser. An applet has to be small because it has to be downloaded to the client machine before it can be used. In a Web environment, where the bandwidth is typically low, the smaller the size the better.

There are several ways to develop Web-based components. You can write them in Java, which provides nice platform-independent code; you can develop Netscape plug-ins; and you can develop ActiveX controls. We discuss component-based development in Chapter 6, and cover developing ActiveX controls in Chapters 7 and 8.

Learn the Java Language

Sun's Java language has caused hysteria in the software industry. Java appears to be the language that will solve many of the software industry's problems. Java is basically C++ with the sharp edges rounded off. Java incorporates all of the object-oriented features of C++, but leaves out those things that can cause problems. (For example, Java does not support the concept of pointers.)

However, Java is just a language. It is not a comprehensive group of technologies for solving problems, but Sun is doing its best to use the Java hysteria to create a number of Java-based products. Sun has joined ranks with other companies, such as Oracle, to promote the idea of Network Computers (NCs). Sun's JavaStation is an entry in this new field.

Independent of what happens with the Network Computer concept or ActiveX, Java is a viable language that software developer's should at least evaluate and become familiar with. We take a look at Java in Chapter 10.

Understand Microsoft's Component Object Model

Microsoft's ActiveX technologies are based on another technology called the Component Object Model, or COM. COM is the foundation for all new Windows-based software technologies. If you're a Windows software developer, you need to understand what COM is and how it is used when developing Windows-based software. ActiveX, which basically used to be termed "OLE," uses COM throughout its implementation. We cover the particular features and relationships between COM, OLE, and ActiveX in Chapter 6.

Set Up a Website

One very good way to learn about the Web and its various technologies is to set up your own Website. You'll learn a lot as you grapple with writing you first HTML-based pages, set up a hierarchy for your site, and start publishing whatever material you feel is beneficial. The cost is low and all the good Internet Service Providers (ISPs) allow you to create your own Web pages.

Setting up a Website for my first book, *Designing and Using OLE Custom Controls,* taught me a lot, and propelled me to learn more. I started small by adding an FAQ (Frequently Asked Questions) section for ActiveX controls (they were called OLE controls at the time). I answered a few questions in the newsgroups with pointers to the FAQ, and from there the site has grown, day by day. So much so, that it now gets over 2,000 page hits every day. Of course, it is a lot of work, but the thankful emails from all over the world make it worthwhile.

As developers we all spend a considerable amount of time learning and applying new technologies. As we learn, why don't we go ahead and publish the information for others to use. Visit the newsgroups on the Web, answer questions, ask questions, and when you have something to contribute, publish it. If you need help, stop by my Website or send me an email. I'll do my best to help you out.

In the end, no matter how you look at it, the Web is having and will continue to have a major impact on our lives. The purpose of this book is to help software developers exploit to its fullest all of this technology.

Summary

In 1991, the Web started as a way to distribute academic information on the Internet. Since then, the Web has grown far beyond what its original designer, Tim Berners-Lee, had imagined. Today, through all the hype, most see the true potential of the Web. Not only is the Web going to have a major impact on our jobs as software developers, but it will affect nearly every aspect of our lives.

The Web is built using Internet-based technology. The Internet is a large collection of disparate computer systems networked together using well-tested technologies such as TCP/IP. HTTP is the protocol of the Web and is built on top of TCP/IP. A browser is a client application that communicates with a Web server using the Hypertext Transfer Protocol (HTTP). The browser's primary purpose is to render HTML-based documents that are passed to it from a Web server. HTML is a page description language that provides a platform-independent way to describe textual and image data.

There are two major areas where Web technology is being put to use: (1) The commercial Web environment that basically connects millions of worldwide computers into a cohesive network that most use on a daily basis. (2) Corporate intranets—based on the same Web technologies— used to build information-sharing environments within a corporation; in other words, they are private.

The Web is having a major impact on how we software developers do what we do. Web-based technologies and architectures will eventually become the standard for all new application development. As a developer you should do several things to exploit these shifts in the software industry. Start by making your existing applications Internet-aware. Then go about understanding the component-based development model, learn the Java language, investigate Microsoft's Component Object Model, and finally, set up your own Website.

CHAPTER **2**

Microsoft's ActiveX-Based Technologies

In this chapter we take a look at Microsoft's ActiveX technologies. Since Microsoft announced the ActiveX framework on March 12, 1996, it has been working feverishly to implement this grand ActiveX vision—quite successfully, too, by nearly all accounts. However, it has left the average software developer in a state of extreme confusion. Microsoft seems to release a new ActiveX-based product every week. As software developers who have to learn continually just to keep up with our current projects, Microsoft's pace makes it impossible to maintain a sense of total understanding. Thankfully, with new tools like to the Web to help, we can usually find the information when we need it. The Web is a great resource, but the information is hard to find and is scattered everywhere. One of the purposes of this chapter is to present a broad view of Microsoft's ActiveX-based products.

Microsoft's ActiveX Technologies

The major focus of this book is on using Microsoft's ActiveX technologies to develop client-side, Web-based software. As we review the ActiveX technologies, we discuss how they relate to each other, and in what areas of software development they can be used. The chapters comprising the rest of the book focus on several of these technologies in detail. Our focus is on ActiveX, but this focus also includes using other technologies, such as Java and JavaScript, when appropriate.

There are a number of technologies, tools, and products available that support Web-based software development. The market potential for Web-based development tools and technologies is tremendous. This is demonstrated by the number of companies vying for your mind-share and development dollars. Sun, Netscape, IBM, Microsoft, and others are working day and night to produce the best and most effective Web-based solutions. Who knows who will win in the end? Probably not all of them, but I'm certain that Microsoft will be one of the major players.

Why ActiveX Is a Major Player

As I write this there is a lot of consternation concerning the "battle" between Microsoft, Sun, and Netscape for control of the Web. Many feel that Microsoft will lose this battle because it doesn't support very many operating platforms. Their argument goes something like this: Microsoft's idea of multiplatform browser support basically means it supports Windows 3.1, Windows 95, and Windows NT. If it doesn't support the other major platforms, UNIX, OS/2, Macintosh, and so on, it will fail. Success on the Web requires that you program for all of the possible platforms, and Microsoft has offered only half-hearted support for non-Microsoft platforms.

This argument misses on at least two points. Microsoft has smelled the Internet coffee (including Java), and support for these other operating systems is quickly forthcoming. Another major factor is the market for *intranets* is 5 to 10 times larger that the commercial Internet-Web market. Microsoft's strength is in this much larger market. Corporate LAN environments are much more structured and proprietary than the heterogeneous Internet. In other words, in corporate intranet environment, the client operating system and browser can be specified. As we discussed in Chapter 1, the corporate intranet (and now extranets) is by far the largest Web-based market.

Oh, there's one other reason. Microsoft succeeds because it provides the best *tools* to get the job done. Microsoft's underlying technology may not always be the best, but it works hard at making it easy for developers to quickly *implement* their technologies. What good is a technology if it's difficult to implement? (Take a look at the history of CIL's OpenDoc technology.) Microsoft's Component Object Model, on which ActiveX is based, is a good technology, and Microsoft is backing it up with great tools that make Web-based development easy. This is also a major factor.

Java or ActiveX?

But what about Java—isn't it easy to use, too? Yes, but Java is just a language, not a comprehensive technology (although Sun is doing its best to make it one). Java is a good Web-based development language, and in many ways its design is superior to other languages (e.g., C++). Microsoft fully supports the Java language within its tools (e.g., Visual J++) and products (e.g., Internet Explorer), but it has also established a major effort to apply their Windows-oriented software development standards to Web-based development.

The Java language is based on C++, but removes some of the esoteric constructs that make C++ difficult to learn and use. Even so, many still feel that Java is too difficult for an average Web developer to utilize effectively. Microsoft has based its ActiveX technology on existing Windows-based technologies (e.g., The Component Object Model, Visual Basic), which will make Web development more accessible to the large number of Windows developers. This is the key to Microsoft's strategy.

NOTE: *Sun's slogan for Java is "Write it once, run it anywhere." Microsoft's motto has always been "Windows everywhere." One of the more intriguing developments is that Microsoft has recently stated that it may port the Win32 API to Java. If Microsoft actually does the port, it may achieve its long-term vision because everywhere that Java runs, the Windows operating environment may run as well.*

ActiveX as an Evolutionary Approach to the Web

Microsoft's Internet strategy is grounded in its current Windows-based technologies. Dynamic client-side and server-side content is developed with a derivative of Visual Basic called VBScript. Small, client-side applets are developed using a new lightweight ActiveX Control specification. Browser technology is based on a revised OLE Document standard, called *ActiveX documents*, that provides features needed within the dynamic Web environment. Server-side Web development is handled through Microsoft's new ISAPI (Internet Services API) and Server-side scripting (ASPs), and through Web server software hosted—and provided free—on Windows NT Server.

Compared to Java-based methods, Microsoft's OLE- and Visual Basic—centered approach (embodied in ActiveX) to Web development is more accessible to the average developer. Visual Basic developers outnumber C++ developers by at least an order of magnitude. Microsoft estimates the number of Visual Basic developers at three million. VBScript and the associated ActiveX control technologies are already being used by hundreds of thousands of developers. This massive installed base will provide the force by which Microsoft will achieve a major Web presence, and ActiveX is at the very center of this momentum.

Microsoft's approach, then, is evolutionary. It builds on the existing strengths of millions of software developers. It does not require them to learn a new language, although they can if they feel it is necessary. ActiveX builds on existing Windows concepts, which are very widely known. Also, there are tens of millions of machines sitting on desktops today that can take advantage of this new technology, each with a significant amount of built-in capability.

This built-in capability is the Windows API. Most of ActiveX builds upon existing capabilities provided by the Windows operating system. This, of course, makes ActiveX less portable, but we must agree that Microsoft's ultimate goal is "Windows on every desktop." Microsoft is walking a fine line with ActiveX, but that's what makes this stuff interesting.

ActiveX-Based Technologies and Tools

ActiveX is a new moniker for what Microsoft previously called its OLE technologies. Microsoft also uses the term "Active" to describe a number of its Internet-based technologies, reflecting the shift from static to "active" or dynamic Web content. If it all seams a bit confusing, don't worry—it is. The first thing to understand is that the majority of this technology is based on Microsoft's component-based system technology: COM. From there, we have Microsoft-based technologies that propel the development of effective, Web-based applications. Microsoft's goal is to provide developers with the technologies, tools, and products to make the Windows operating system the very best Web platform.

The Component Object Model

The Component Object Model (COM) is at the center of every tool, technology, and product that Microsoft produces. *COM* is Microsoft's system technology that provides support for software components. In the past, Microsoft would publish new APIs whenever it added additional functionality to the Windows operating system. Now, Microsoft bases new functionality on the Component Object Model.

One of COM's purposes is to provide a binary standard for software components. A binary standard, in a software sense, provides the means by which objects and components, developed with various languages, from disparate vendors, running on heterogeneous platforms, can *interoperate* without any changes to the binary or executable code. This is a major goal of COM and is one that the software development community desperately needs.

Once you have COM in place, you can begin building higher-level, component-based technologies that use COM's services. OLE and ActiveX are examples of such higher-level services. If you're going to develop Windows-based software you need to understand what COM is all about. We cover COM in detail in Chapter 6. I've mentioned COM here because it is the basis of what we cover in this chapter, ActiveX. Since ActiveX is built using COM, all ActiveX technologies use COM as well.

Client-Side Technologies (The Active Desktop)

Microsoft's client-side technologies are provided primarily by the browser environment. Currently, the browser that implements most of these new technologies is Microsoft's Internet Explorer. The Active Desktop platform is comprised of several client-side technologies, including a rich HTML; language-independent scripting environment; and support for client-side components, such as ActiveX controls and Java applets. Netscape has announced that it will support ActiveX-based technologies, but to what extent remains to be seen.

Server-Side Technologies (The Active Server)

Microsoft's server-side technologies are provided by Internet Information Server, Microsoft's Web server software that runs on Windows NT Server. IIS provides support for all of the major Web protocols, such as HTTP. However, IIS also provides a number of other, ActiveX-based technologies, that make Web-server-based application programming easier. Server-side scripting (ASPs) and Active Data Objects provide efficient ways to build dynamic HTML-based Web pages.

Development Tools

Microsoft provides a number of developer-oriented tools for developing Web-based applications. The older tools, such as Visual Basic and Visual C++, have been enhanced to work with all of the new ActiveX-based technologies. Remember, everything ActiveX is based on COM, and Microsoft has provided support to build COM-based applications for a long time. Visual Basic, Visual C++, and the new Visual J++, all provide effective environments for building Web-based applications. Additional tools, such as the Microsoft Foundation Libraries (MFC) and the Active Template Library (ATL), also support the process of building Internet-aware applications.

Web-Based Products

Microsoft also has a number of products that are based on, or target, the Web environment. As we discussed in Chapter 1, when we use the term *Web* we mean both the Internet as well as the corporate intranet environment. Since the intranet market is a major one, many of Microsoft's products are actually targeted toward the intranet developer. When you see the term *Web-based* throughout this book, it pertains to *all* environments that use Web-based technologies.

The rest of this chapter provides a quick introduction to several of Microsoft's ActiveX-based technologies, tools, and products. The overview starts with a look at client-side technologies; then a look at the server side; next a brief look at Microsoft's development tools; and finally, a look at Microsoft's Web-based products.

Client-Side Technologies (The Active Desktop)

A major portion of Microsoft's Internet strategy pertains to the client side of the equation. By client, we basically mean the end-user workstation, which in most cases is an Intel PC running some version of Microsoft Windows, probably Windows 95. The majority of all workstations run Microsoft Windows, so Microsoft has a firm hold on the client-side platform and it is doing its best to maintain control of this aspect of the Web. Client-side development using ActiveX is the primary focus of this book, and the next few sections introduce the various technologies.

Internet Explorer

Microsoft's *Internet Explorer* embodies Microsoft's client-side technologies. In the Web environment, the user's browser provides virtually all of the perceived functionality. This is exactly why vendors such as Sun Microsystems feel that they can replace the Windows operating system with a Java-based browser. "Who needs an operating system when you have a fully functional browser?" or so the theory goes.

However, when you get down to it, a browser depends heavily on the underlying functionality provided by the operating system. Microsoft understands this and is moving quickly to merge the functionality typically provided by a browser into the operating system itself. Once this occurs (and it will with the release of Internet Explorer 4.0), all of the client-side ActiveX technologies described here will be part of the Windows shell. Browsing the Web will be as simple as using the Windows 95 Explorer.

Anyway, Internet Explorer provides the environment in which most of the client-side technologies can be used. It is the Web-based application execution environment. The browser is responsible for parsing and displaying HTML-based Web pages. It supports the latest HTML standards, executes VBScript, is a great ActiveX control container, and supports Active documents—face it, it *is* the application. Nearly all of the following client-side techniques will typically be used within a browser that supports ActiveX, such as Internet Explorer. However, as the ActiveX technologies are integrated into the Windows shell, they will be accessible directly from the Windows desktop.

The ActiveX SDK (A Subset of the Platform SDK)

The *ActiveX Software Development Kit* (SDK) provides C/C++ header files, library files, redistributable components, examples, and extensive documentation of many of the ActiveX technologies. The primary focus of the SDK is on client-side ActiveX technologies, such as ActiveX Controls, Active Documents, Internet Explorer HTML support, and so on.

NOTE: *The ActiveX SDK is included as part of Microsoft's comprehensive Platform SDK. All of Microsoft's SDKs are available as part of the Microsoft Developer Network (MSDN) subscription service. For details check out http://www.microsoft.com/msdn.*

ActiveX Controls

ActiveX controls are at the center of Microsoft's Internet strategy. Initially called OLE controls, *ActiveX controls* are small software components that can provide significant functionality. They are backed by a well-defined, published standard. ActiveX controls are built upon Microsoft's Component Object Model and can be plugged in to Visual Basic, Visual C++,

Borland's Delphi, and Visual J++ development tools, as well as many others. ActiveX controls can also be embedded directly within HTML-based Web pages. This allows a Web-page developer to add significant new functionality to previously static Web pages.

An ActiveX control adds functionality to Web pages in the same way that Java applets do. However, because an ActiveX control gives the developer complete access to the Win32 API, it has access to a tremendous amount of existing functionality. Anything that you can do with a normal Windows application, you can also do with an ActiveX control. This cannot be said for a typical Java applet, primarily because a Java applet has very restricted access to the local machine. Figure 2.1 shows Internet Explorer displaying a page with several ActiveX controls.

Web Design-Time Controls

Normal ActiveX controls work in two different modes: design-time and run-time. A control behaves quite differently at design-time than it does at

Figure 2.1
ActiveX controls in
Internet Explorer.

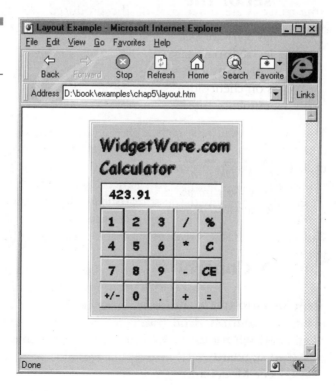

run-time. At *design-time* the control's main purpose is to allow the user to set its characteristics, such as color, font, and so on. The functionality of the control, such as playing an AVI file, isn't used at design-time. Design-time is typically the period where the software or Web-page developer sets everything up.

The term *run-time* describes the period when a control is actually executing and providing its functionality. In our AVI example, at run-time the control would load and play the AVI file. Microsoft has enhanced the ActiveX control standard to include a new type of control, the design-time control. Design-time controls provide their functionality only during the design phase of Web-page development and are used in tools such as FrontPage and Visual InterDev.

For example, a design-time control could be written to write HTML-based text to a Web page each time the document is "saved" using the tool. This could provide a "last update" date for the page. The control's purpose is to assist the Web-page design tool. Design-time controls are used in this way to provide plug-in functionality. A tool such as Visual InterDev can be enhanced with third-party design-time controls just as Visual Basic is enhanced by third-party ActiveX controls. The difference is that design-time controls are never part of the produced Web page; they are used only by the Web-page development tool to facilitate the production of Web documents.

Active Documents

The Active Document technology is an enhancement of the familiar OLE Document technology. OLE Document technology allows Windows users to embed documents created with one application within another application. For example, you can create a spreadsheet with Microsoft Excel and then embed the spreadsheet within a Microsoft Word document. Then, by double-clicking on the spreadsheet within Word, Excel will take over Word's menus, and the user has full Excel functionality within Word.

The Active Document standard takes this concept to the next level. OLE Documents must operate within a one-page or smaller area of the client application, and must negotiate menu space as well. Active documents on the other hand have access to the complete frame area of the client application and can be multiple-page documents. Figure 2.2 shows a word document hosted in Internet Explorer.

Active Scripting—JavaScript and VBScript

Active Scripting is a technology that allows an application to provide script-like services. A scripting language is typically interpreted at run-time, and operates on application-specific objects or components. For example, Microsoft's Office 97 products include Visual Basic for Applications (VBA) as their scripting language. With VBA, a user can "script" the behavior of the application. VBA becomes a macrolanguage for describing high-level application behavior.

Prior to Microsoft's release of its Active Scripting implementation, VBA was a proprietary technology. Now, however, VBA can be licensed by other software vendors for inclusion in their products. Active Scripting supports any scripting language that a vendor might implement. Microsoft has provided, as part of the implementation, the VBScript and JScript languages. As a software vendor, you can now incorporate VBScript or JScript into your application for free. This is an exciting development, which we cover

Figure 2.2
A Word document in
Internet Explorer.

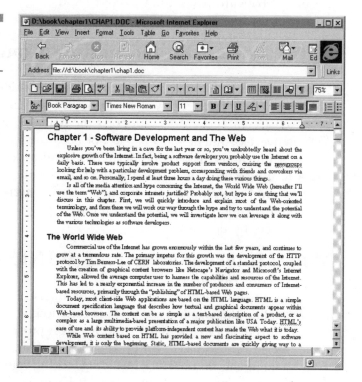

in Chapter 9. VBScript is now poised to become a universal macrolanguage.

VBScript is a subset of both Visual Basic and Visual Basic for Applications. Since VBScript is designed to be used in Web-based documents and applications, those features (e.g., *CreateObject*) that might compromise the local machine environment have been removed.

JScript is Microsoft's Implementation of JavaScript. JavaScript is not related to Java, and was initially developed by Netscape for inclusion in its browser products. However, only recently was the specification made public by Netscape. Microsoft had to reverse engineer JavaScript in order to include support for it in Internet Explorer. Recently, Netscape passed control of the JavaScript specification to a standards body in Europe. This should eventually eliminate the implementation differences in the major browsers.

Active Scripting is used heavily by Internet Explorer to provide client-side scripting support through JScript and VBScript. However, Active Scripting is both a client-side and server-side technology, as it is used extensively on the server side as part of Active Server Pages. We talk more about VBScript and JScript in Chapters 4 and 9.

ActiveMovie SDK and ActiveX Control

ActiveMovie is a technology that provides the client-side application with the ability to render and play streaming video and audio from local files or a Web server. ActiveMovie supports the MPEG, QuickTime, AVI, and WAV standards. Most developers will not need the services of the Active-Movie SDK, because Microsoft's ActiveMovie ActiveX control provides an easier to use method of harnessing the functionality. However, the SDK does provide complete documentation for the ActiveMovie standards, controls, and concepts, which is very useful.

Win32 Internet Functions (WININET.DLL)

The ActiveX SDK describes a number of Internet functions that have been added to the Windows API. These functions are provided by a new DLL: WININET.DLL. The Win32 Internet APIs provide support for three basic Internet services: HTTP, FTP, and Gopher. Using the HTTP services you can do just about anything, including writing your own Web browser. The FTP functions can be used to provide FTP services within your own applications or for writing your own FTP software. Gopher is an older Internet standard that provides capabilities similar to HTTP; however, it's not used that much today.

WebPost

The WebPost SDK is part of the ActiveX SDK. *WebPost* is a set of Win32 API functions that can be used by authoring tools (e.g., HTML editors) to post Web pages to an Internet Server Provider's server. There are number of options available to the API user, including the option to display a Wizard-like application to step the user through the publishing process. The SDK provided WEBPOST.DLL file provides support for some Web servers. ISPs that run other server software may have to provide specific information about their site in a posting information file. See the SDK for more details.

WEB RESOURCES:

URL	Description
http://www.microsoft.com/activex	ActiveX SDK.
http://www.microsoft.com/intdev/ sdk/dtctrl	Web Design-time Controls SDK.
http://www.microsoft.com/jscript	JScript information.
http://www.microsoft.com/imedia	ActiveMovie and related information.
http://www.microsoft.com/vbscript	VBScript information.

Server-Side Technologies (The Active Server)

Although the client side of the Web equation is changing drastically, it isn't any slower on the server side. Browser technologies are becoming a commodity and large software vendors, such as Microsoft, Netscape, Oracle, Sun, and IBM, know that the real money to be made is on the server side. Microsoft has created several server-side technologies, most of which are implemented within its Internet Information Server (IIS) product.

Internet Information Server

Internet Information Server (IIS) is Microsoft's Web server. It runs only on the Windows NT Server platform but provides a number of features. The primary component of a Web server is its HTTP engine. As we discussed in the last chapter, HTTP is *the* protocol in the Web environment. Microsoft's IIS provides a very efficient HTTP engine, but this is just the start. IIS provides a number of other new technologies that make Web server-side development more effective: Server side scripting, ISAPI, and Active Data Objects.

Server-Side Scripting or Active Server Pages

Traditional Websites use the Web model of building and publishing a hierarchy of HTML-based documents. The content of the site is contained in these rather static documents. Server-side scripting provides a mechanism where HTML-based documents can be generated and passed back to the browser dynamically. This is similar to the CGI capability provided by writing complicated Perl or C scripts on the server. However, server-side scripting is somewhat easier to use.

IIS's server-side scripting technology is also called Active Server Pages for the file extension used by the scripts (.ASP). Active Server Pages are written using a combination of HTML, Java, Visual Basic, Visual C++, JavaScript, VBScript, and virtually any other server-side component. The gist of server-side scripting is that you develop scripts that execute on the server that dynamically create the HTML-based document that is returned to the client browser. It is not a static document file (e.g., INDEX.HTML) stored in some directory structure; each page is generated specifically for each client request.

Internet Services API (ISAPI)

Internet Information Server provides the Internet Services API (ISAPI). *ISAPI* provides CGI-like capabilities under those Web server products that support ISAPI. CGI provides server-side scripting using languages such as Perl. CGI scripts allow Web developers to create dynamic HTML-based pages on the server, which are then passed back to the browser through HTTP. ISAPI provides identical functionality, but does so using a completely different architecture. CGI is an older, UNIX-based architecture;

ISAPI is tuned to work with Windows NT. With ISAPI, instead of writing Perl scripts, you write Windows DLLs. However, much of what you can achieve using ISAPI, you can also achieve with the newer Active Server Page approach.

Microsoft Transaction Server

Microsoft Transaction Server is a component-based tool that speeds development of transaction-based client and server software. Transaction Server provides a basic API that is implemented using COM-based services. The developer implements the transaction components using tools that support the creation of COM in-process server components, tools such as Visual Basic, Visual C++, and Visual J++.

Transaction server provides a high-level, transaction-based business-rule environment, where the developer doesn't have to worry about implementing the difficult aspects of server-side, middle-tier development. Items such as resource pooling, context management, threading, and other complex issues are handled by MTS.

Active Data Object (ADO)

The Active Data Object (ADO) programming model combines many of Microsoft's previous database interaction APIs, such as Remote Data Objects (RDO) and Data Access Objects (DAO). *ADO* combines the best of these previous models and provides a comprehensive way of accessing external data sources with server-side scripts. ADO is built, as are most of Microsoft's new technologies, using the Component Object Model. ADO's services are exposed through a set of COM-based interfaces. The ADO programming model is supported in IIS 3.0 Active Server Pages. ADO makes it easy to retrieve data from disparate data sources when building dynamic Web pages.

WEB RESOURCES:

URL	*Description*
http://www.microsoft.com/iis	Internet Information Server site.
http://www.microsoft.com/ado	Active Data Object information.

http://www.microsoft.com/
    transaction/default.asp
	Microsoft Transaction Server (MTS)
	    information.

Development Tools

Okay, we've discussed several of Microsoft's ActiveX-based technologies. Now, what tools are available that help developers take advantage of them? In the next few sections we look at Internet Explorer, Visual C++, the Microsoft Foundation Class libraries, the Active Template Libraries, Visual Basic, and Visual J++.

Internet Explorer (with Script Debugger)

Internet Explorer itself is quite a development environment now that it has an add-on debugger. Microsoft's *Script Debugger* allows you to debug JScript- and VBScript-based scripts directly in Internet Explorer. You can set breakpoints, view the call stack, view the contents of variables, basically everything that you can do with a normal language-based debugger.

Figure 2.3
Microsoft's Script Debugger.

We use the Script Debugger in later chapters. Figure 2.3 shows the debugger in action.

Visual C++

Visual C++ is Microsoft's C++ development tool. It has a great integrated development environment (IDE), called Developer Studio. One of the most powerful features of Visual C++ is its integration with Microsoft's Windows-based application framework, the Microsoft Foundation Class libraries. Visual C++ provides an application called AppWizard that creates a skeletal application based on several parameters supplied by the developer. Once an application is created, Visual C++'s ClassWizard and Component Gallery make it easy to add MFC-based functionality to the application.

On the COM, OLE, and ActiveX front, Visual C++ provides a number of features to help in this area. However, they are provided mostly through the two included application frameworks: MFC and ATL.

The Microsoft Foundation Classes

The MFC libraries can be described as an application framework. An *application framework* provides an abstracted, high-level view of the underlying operating system, or application environment (e.g., Windows). The primary purpose of application frameworks is to make a software developer more productive. An application framework's goals are similar to those of C++: Hide the mundane details of programming within class libraries so developers do not have to continually deal with the trivial.

MFC's implementation provides a *thin* layer of abstraction above the Windows API. In other words, each MFC class closely mirrors a Windows programming construct. For example, the MFC CWnd class provides access to a Windows window. Each window API function is mapped one-to-one to the CWnd class. So, the SetWindowText API function has a direct analog, CWnd::SetWindowText, in the CWnd class. When first introduced to MFC, this aspect makes using MFC easy for those with Windows API experience, but difficult for those that don't.

MFC not only encapsulates the Windows API, but provides a number of other classes as well, many of which are useful to a Web-based developer. Through its support for COM, OLE, and ActiveX, MFC provides classes for building and using ActiveX controls, Active Documents, ISAPI programming, and Asynchronous Monikers. We use the MFC libraries for several of our examples in this book.

The Active Template Library

MFC provides a tremendous amount of functionality, most of which is focused on encapsulating the GUI portion of the Windows API. In many cases, developers may not need all of this functionality for their project. If you're developing a COM-based server, you may not need any GUI services at all. In this case, the Active Template Library (ATL) may be all that you need.

The ATL is a template-based, C++ framework that facilitates the creation of small, COM applications such as ActiveX controls. There are classes for creating COM-based servers, managing the Windows registry, and so on. When developing applications in the Web environment, your application should be as small as possible. The ATL allows you to build small, yet highly functional COM components. We discuss the ATL in detail in Chapters 6 and 7.

Visual Basic

Visual Basic has been around since 1991 and has grown into one of the most popular Windows development environments. With the release of Visual Basic 5.0, it provides just about everything a developer needs to develop regular applications or applications for Internet and intranet environments. In particular, Visual Basic now supports the creation of ActiveX controls. We cover this aspect of Visual Basic in Chapter 8.

Java and Visual J++

Visual J++ is Microsoft's Java development environment. Visual J++ uses the same IDE used by Visual C++. Visual J++ also has wizards, such as the Applet Wizard, similar to those provided by Visual C++. COM, OLE, and ActiveX support is also provided with Microsoft's implementation of Java. Visual J++ supports native use of ActiveX controls, programming of external applications through Automation, and the building of COM-based components such as ActiveX controls.

Java is an important new language, and Visual J++ supports all of its features and more. It won't be long before straight Windows-based applications will be built with Java. We discuss Java and Visual J++ in detail in Chapter 10.

The Application Foundation Classes

Microsoft has recently released a set of Java class libraries called the Application Foundation Classes. The basic GUI classes (via the AWT) provided by the Java SDK give the developer only minimal presentation capabilities. The GUI library that is part of the AFC provides rich, full-featured GUI controls like those found in Windows 95 (e.g., List View, Tree View, and so on). In other words, you can now build Java applications that have the look and feel of a real Windows application. One of the more exciting aspects of the AFC it that is directly portable to other operating environments. In other words, you can build an application with the universally accepted Windows 95 look, and run it on a Macintosh, or on a UNIX X station. Microsoft has given us the ability to write portable Windows software.

WEB RESOURCES:

URL	Description
http://www.microsoft.com/vbasic/controls	Visual Basic Control Creation Edition information.
http://www.microsoft.com/visualc	Visual C++ information.
http://www.microsoft.com/vbasic	Visual Basic information.
http://www.microsoft.com/visualj	Visual J++ information.
http://www.microsoft.com/java	Java SDK, VM, and AFC information.

Other Microsoft Web-Based Products

Since early 1996, Microsoft has developed and delivered a bevy of products for Web environments. Some of the products are available for free at Microsoft's Website and the rest are available through either an MSDN subscription or other retail software outlet.

We've divided the development tool and product area into two sections in this chapter, but many of the products in this section could be classified as development tools as well. The previous section described those tools that are used to develop low-level software components, such as ActiveX controls, Java applets, and so on. The products in this section typically provided some ability to *use* the Web-based components; in other words, they are higher-level development tools. Other products described here provide Web-based services for Web developers or administrators.

ActiveX Control Pad

Microsoft's *ActiveX Control Pad* is a simple HTML editor that does not provide WYSIWYG-like capabilities. Its primary purpose is to facilitate embedding ActiveX controls and script into HTML-based pages. ActiveX Control Pad supports Microsoft's Layout ActiveX control, which allows finer control over the placement of text and images than that provided by straight HTML. The ActiveX Control Pad also has a built in Script Wizard that makes it easier to add VBScript or JScript to your Web pages. ActiveX Control Pad is available free at Microsoft's Website. The latest version of ActiveX Control Pad also supports the use of Design-time ActiveX controls. We use ActiveX Control Pad in the first few chapters.

FrontPage 97

While ActiveX Control Pad is a simple HTML editor, *FrontPage 97* is a full-blown HTML editor that provides exceptional WYSIWYG capabilities. The FrontPage editor supports frames, and nearly all of the new HTML 3.2 tags. It supports embedding of ActiveX controls, Java applets, VBScript, and JavaScript.

The FrontPage editor is just part of the package. FrontPage 97 is also a complete Website development and management tool. Website creation and management is handled through the FrontPage Explorer. The Explorer helps you manage the organization of your site. It provides tools that will verify each link in your site, apply changes to every page in your site, and so on. Figure 2.4 shows an Explorer view of a midsized Website.

One of the neat features of FrontPage is its concept of WebBots. A *WebBot* provides built-in Web page capabilities that would normally require

Figure 2.4
The FrontPage 97
Explorer.

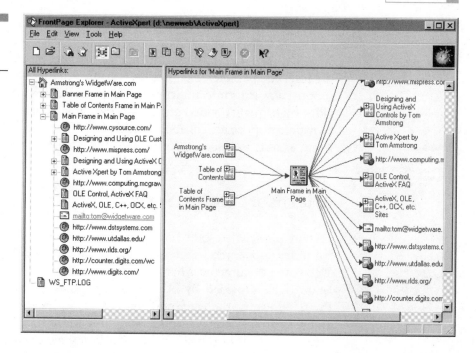

you to write CGI scripts on the server. For example, one is a "Table of Contents" WebBot. By building a Web page that incorporates the TOC WebBot, FrontPage will automatically generate a TOC-type list of every other page within your site. Other useful WebBots include a Timestamp and Search Bot. Certain WebBots require that the server have the FrontPage Server Extensions installed. Microsoft provides FrontPage Server Extensions for most major Web server platforms.

Visual InterDev

FrontPage 97 is a good tool for creating and managing a Website, but *Visual InterDev* is a full-blown Website development tool. In fact, it may belong under the "Development Tools" section; but as I've said, the lines between the products blur. Visual InterDev uses the capabilities of Internet Information Server (IIS). It supports Active Script Pages, Active Data Objects, Web Design-time controls, and so on. Visual InterDev is also closely integrated with Microsoft's other Visual Development tools, such as Visual C++, Visual Basic, and Visual J++.

NetMeeting

NetMeeting is a groupware, information-sharing product that is an add-on for Internet Explorer. *NetMeeting* is conferencing software that provides support for real-time multimedia-based collaboration. NetMeeting provides high quality video and audio over low-bandwidth connections. It provides support for collaboration through the use of a common whiteboard as well as other groupware-type capabilities.

Microsoft Index Server

Version 3.0 of Microsoft's IIS product includes the Microsoft Index Server. An index and search server provides high-speed indexing and querying of Web-based documents. Microsoft's Index Server provides capabilities similar to those provided by other search engines available on the Web (e.g., Excite). However, the Microsoft *Index Server* is designed more for indexing and searching Websites that are being hosted by IIS—not every document on the Web. One of the neat features of Index Server is that it can index (and therefore search) Microsoft Office documents. This feature makes it a good search engine for corporate intranets that use Microsoft's Office products.

Microsoft NetShow

Microsoft's *NetShow* is a multimedia delivery package for Web servers running IIS. NetShow contains two primary features. The first is NetShow On-Demand, which provides streaming audio and video to Web-based clients. The second is NetShow Live, which provides multicasting of audio over a corporate intranet or LAN environment.

Microsoft Merchant Server

Microsoft's *Merchant Server* provides a turnkey merchandising environment for retail-style Websites. It contains a feature called the Shopping Cart that makes it easy for clients to purchase items through the Web. Merchant Server provides secure payment technology and other security options. If you're looking to set up a retail-oriented site, take a look at this.

As with most Microsoft Web server products, however, it requires Windows NT and IIS.

Microsoft Proxy Server

A proxy server is a gateway to the Internet and the Web. *Proxy servers* are typically used in corporate LAN environments to provide LAN users direct access to the Web. Using a proxy server, each user no longer needs a dial-out line to an ISP. Instead, access is provided through the LAN environment. One feature of a proxy server is that individual client machines can run non-Internet protocols to access the Internet. As we discussed in the last chapter, the Internet (and, thus, the Web) uses the TCP/IP protocol. However, using the proxy server, client workstations can still use their native protocol (maybe Novel's IPX/SPX) to access the Web.

Another feature provided by a proxy server is local LAN caching. In corporate environments, many local users may access the same resources on the larger commercial Web. A proxy server can cache often referenced Website pages locally on the proxy server. This speeds up access to these Websites. Proxy servers also provide tight control over what Websites a user might visit. Since all Web access proceeds through the proxy server, the server administrator can block access to certain sites or certain areas of the Web. This, of course, makes sure that we don't spend all day at our most favorite, non-work-related sites.

Microsoft Commercial Internet System

Microsoft's *Commercial Internet System* is a suite of related Web services. The CIS is targeted to Internet Server Providers (ISPs), Web publishers, and corporations committed to creating a compelling Web presence. The suite contains News, Chat, Mail, and Merchant services, and a number of others. Table 2.1 lists some of the services that are part of the CIS.

Basically, the Commercial Internet System provides everything you need to build just about anything in the Internet and Web environment using Microsoft, Windows-based products. The stuff here was provided almost exclusively by UNIX servers before Microsoft implemented CIS for Windows NT Server.

TABLE 2.1

Commercial
Internet System
Components

Product	Description
News Server	A news server to host electronic discussions. The Internet newsgroups are an example of this technology.
Content Replication System	A service to replicate Web-based content across Websites.
Conference Server	Provides the Internet Chat and Internet Locator servers to support real time chat rooms and the ability to locate users on the Web.
Personalization System	Provides software to help personalize a Website so that each visitor has his or her own "profile."
Membership System	A membership system that maintains user accounts, authorizations, and billing system events.
Merchant Server	Retail Website services. See previous discussion.
Information Retrieval Server	Supports full-text searches across distributed Websites.
Commercial Internet Mail Server	Provides a complete, Internet-standards-based mail server.
Internet Address Book Server	Provides white pages—like services for commercial Internet.

Office 97

Microsoft's new Office 97 product contains several new features that support Web environments. Each Office product (e.g., Word, Excel) now supports native HTML-based input and output. You no longer need the Internet Assistance products added on to Office 95.

Office 97 applications also support the new Active Documents standard so that you can access Office documents directly within Internet Explorer. Office application also supports direct embedding of Web hyperlinks. Basically, Office 97 gives you a look at where all of Microsoft's applications are heading—directly to the Web. All of Microsoft's products, including its operating systems, will be deeply integrated with Web technologies.

WEB RESOURCES:

URL	Description
http://www.microsoft.com/intdev	ActiveX Control Pad information.
http://www.microsoft.com/frontpage	FrontPage 97 information.
http://www.microsoft.com/vinterdev/	Visual InterDev information.
http://www.microsoft.com/netmeeting	NetMeeting information.
http://www.microsoft.com/netshow	NetShow information.
http://www.ms-normandy.com/	Microsoft Commercial Internet System information.
http://www.microsoft.com/proxy/	Microsoft's proxy server information.
http://www.microsoft.com/merchant/	Merchant Server information.
http://www.microsoft.com/office	Office 97 information.

Summary

By now, you should realize that Microsoft is very serious about the Web, both the commercial Internet and corporate intranets. Microsoft has embraced the Internet and its related technologies and is moving aggressively to adapt and extend its existing Windows-based technologies, tools, and products. By doing so, Microsoft is taking an evolutionary approach to Web-based development by building on its existing technologies, tools, and products.

Microsoft's focus is centered around what it calls its *Active Platform*. The Active Platform is composed of three primary parts: *ActiveX, Active Desktop,* and the *Active Server.*

ActiveX is based on Microsoft's proven Component Object Model technology (COM). COM is a system-level service that supports the creation of software components. ActiveX describes those core technologies that have been turned over to The Open Group for standardization. The other Active Platform technologies are based heavily on ActiveX.

The Active Desktop incorporates all of Microsoft's client-side technologies, which includes ActiveX controls, the ActiveX SDK, Internet Explorer, Active Documents, and Active Scripting. Additional functionality is provided by the Win32 Internet functions contained in WININET.DLL.

The Active Server is comprised mostly of technologies used by Microsoft's Web Server, the Internet Information Server. IIS provides basic Web services such as an efficient HTTP engine, and also provides a number of features that are specific to IIS. Server-side scripting using VBScript and JScript makes it easy to develop server applications that generate dynamic HTML-based pages. The Internet Services API (ISAPI) provides CGI-like capabilities on the server, but does so in a way that is very efficient on Windows-based platforms. The Active Data Object (ADO) programming model provides database-independent access to external data sources that can be incorporated into Web-based applications.

Microsoft has adapted its complete development tool line to take advantage of these new ActiveX-based technologies. Visual C++, the MFC libraries, the Active Template Library, Visual Basic, and Visual J++ all make it easy to develop Web-based applications.

Microsoft also provides a number of HTML-based editor and Website management products. ActiveX Control Pad, FrontPage 97, and Visual InterDev provide varying levels of HTML-based document creation and management capabilities. A number of other Web-based products are also available from Microsoft.

3

HTML and Cascading Style Sheets

In this chapter we cover the primary language of the Web environment: HTML. Sure, there are several books that cover HTML, but I think one chapter is enough to get a good handle on what it is and what it can do. It is our aim to build several Web pages as we learn basic HTML techniques. Along the way, we also discuss ActiveX and HTML as well as Cascading Style Sheets (CSS). Cascading style sheets make it easier to design Web pages using normal page layout techniques. They also allow you to quickly customize all of the pages on your Website at once. After we understand how to build static Web pages with HTML, we move on to JavaScript and VBScript in the next chapter. These scripting languages give us several additional capabilities within our Web pages.

NOTE: *All of the examples are on the CD-ROM as a small Website. If you don't feel like typing, just start up your favorite browser and follow along.*

HTML—The Language of the Web

HTML, or *Hypertext Markup Language,* is *the* language in the Web environment. The development of HTML language along with a standard protocol (HTTP) to transport HTML documents is the primary reason for the tremendous growth of the Web. HTML provides a way to describe documents in a platform-independent way and the Web, via the Internet, provides an inexpensive way of publishing them to the world.

NOTE: *Even though HTML is the language of the Web, it is also quickly becoming an important language of Windows development. Microsoft is using HTML (and CSS) throughout its ActiveX strategy. If you have any doubt, open up any new Microsoft development tool (e.g., Visual InterDev, Visual C++ 5.0), bring up the InfoViewer help system and right-click in the window. Guess what? You're in Internet Explorer. Click* **View Source** *and you'll see a bunch of HTML and style-sheet syntax.*

What Was Old Is New Again

Writing documents with HTML is very similar to what we did back in the 1980s when using DOS-based word processors. The graphic limitations of DOS, and the fact that most machines were equipped with monochrome monitors made it impossible to develop true WYSIWYG editing software.

Anyway, when using an editor back then, you had to embed in the document special characters that indicated a particular text attribute. For text that you wanted to be **bold,** you would place the "begin-bold" tag before the text and the "end-bold" attribute after the text. The monitor wouldn't necessarily display the text as bold, you just had to imagine it, or print the document to ensure that the text was actually bold. Various "attribute" keys or keywords were used to signify particular text characteristics.

Editing this way killed a lot of trees. During those days, when creating a complex document, I would make a few changes and then print the document to see how it looked; then, go back to make a few adjustments to the document and print it again to see how it looked. Thankfully, with the increased power of personal computers, we now have WYSIWYG editors that really do show how your document will look *before* you print it.

Well, with HTML, we're back to the old way of doing things: Make a change to the HTML document, load it up in two or three browsers to see how it looks, edit the document again, and so on. However, it is getting better. Today, programs like Microsoft's FrontPage 97 allow you to create Web pages without having to know all of the details of HTML. However, because HTML is still evolving, in many cases you have to hand-edit, or "tweak," the file in order to add functionality that current HTML editors do not support. Plus, HTML has become *the* rich data type in Windows environments. It is important to understand how HTML works and what it can do.

Why HTML?

The Internet, where HTML was born, is a very large collection of disparate computers. IBM mainframes, DEC VAXes, Sun Workstations, Macintoshes, Intel PCs, and many others, are all hooked together to create the Internet. In such an environment, good standards and least-common-denominator solutions are the norm. HTML documents are standard ASCII text files. Such documents are inherently multiplatform. They use an old standard that nearly all current operating systems understand.

The World Wide Web Consortium and HTML

HTML is "owned" by the World Wide Web Consortium, also known as the W3C. The *W3C* was formed in 1994 to develop and promote common standards for use on the World Wide Web. It is a multinational consortium hosted by the Massachusetts Institute of Technology Laboratory for Computer Science in the United States; the Institut National de Recherche en Informatique et en Automatique [INRIA] in Europe; and the Keio University Shonan Fujisawa Campus in Asia. The work of the consortium is funded by commercial members such as Sun, IBM, and Microsoft.

The consortium was initially established in collaboration with the European Laboratory for Particle Physics (also know as CERN), where the creator of the Web, Tim Berners-Lee, worked. Tim is currently the Director of the W3C. The W3C controls the draft, review, and final specifications of HTML. The W3C also maintains a number of other standards related to the Web.

HTML Version 2.0

HTML version 2.0 is based on IETF RFC 1866. All of the major browsers support the features specified in version 2.0. *HTML 2.0* was the first version that provided the majority of the functionality available in HTML today. However, version 2.0 did not have several important features, such as tables, and browser makers added their own enhancements to the standard to make the Web environment more effective.

HTML Version 3.0

The HTML version 3.0 draft was originally released in March of 1995. It was a major upgrade to the 2.0 version, and included support for tables, text flow around figures, and additional support for mathematical expressions. Many new features were added to existing tags, and various, often used extensions were added to the specification as well.

HTML version 3.0 proved to be too major a change that tried to be all things to all people. In September of 1995, version 3.0 was allowed to expire *before* it became a ratified standard. It was then superseded by HTML version 3.2.

HTML Version 3.2

HTML version 3.2 was introduced in draft form shortly after the version 3.0 draft was allowed to expire. Version 3.2 took a less ambitious approach than version 3.0 by addressing only the widely used extensions to the version 2.0 specification. Most of these additions had already been implemented in the field and the WC3 needed only to clarify the use of the most popular elements. The primary new functional areas added by version 3.2 are: Tables, support for applets and browser-side scripting, text flow around images, and support for superscripts and subscripts.

HTML version 3.2 became a W3C Recommendation on January 14, 1997, and is currently supported by the two major browsers: Netscape's Navigator and Microsoft's Internet Explorer. HTML version 3.2 is the primary focus of this chapter.

HTML Version 4.0?

The W3C is currently working on the next version of HTML. Code named *Cougar*, this version of HTML will include several new enhancements. Microsoft is trying to influence the standard with its new dynamic HTML (code-named *Trident*) technology. At the same time, Netscape is pushing its own additions to HTML, which are different from those being proposed by Microsoft.

Microsoft's dynamic HTML technology is part of Internet Explorer version 4.0. It provides an object model for HTML, thus allowing more control over the pages within the browser. Dynamic HTML also allows the user to modify the text while browsing the page. The modified page can then be written back to the server. Netscape's additions include absolute positioning of text and images within documents, which is currently a major deficiency in HTML. It also allows layering or overlapping of images and text. The W3C will probably merge the best of these enhancements in HTML version 4.0.

HTML Extensions

Web-based technology is advancing at an alarming rate. Browser vendors are releasing products as fast as they can develop them. Businesses and individuals realize how important the Web is, and how it is changing the way we do business and interact with each other. This massive shift in mindset is creating tremendous pressure on software development and support techniques. Software vendors are moving as fast as they can to add features, hoping to make their technology the one that will become the de facto standard.

This frenetic pace of software development has caused many pundits to speculate that the software life cycle is extremely compressed with regards to Web-based software. Vendors such as Microsoft and Netscape release a new version of their browser every few months. The standards bodies, who have a six-month comment period on proposed standard changes and additions, can't incorporate vendor changes fast enough.

For this reason, most vendors will extend the HTML language by adding additional tags to support features that they feel are necessary to increase the usability of their products. Because the HTML language is growing larger and larger, and the fact that vendors augment the standard well before it is actually finalized, the W3C is changing the way HTML standards are handled. In the future, the standard will be broken up into pieces called *extensions*. This will allow continued enhancement of Web standards, but on a smaller, more specific scale.

There are currently three important standards based on this new technique: The Object, Layout, and Style Sheet standards. All three are important enough to warrant individual discussion.

W3C Object Specification

The HTML specification allows the insertion of images, via the IMG element, into Web documents. However, as the Web pages become more like software applications instead of static documents, there are needs for other data types. Examples include multimedia images, Java applets, ActiveX controls, and so on.

To provide broad support for user-defined media, the W3C is currently working on a draft specification for inserting software objects within HTML documents. This specification focuses on using the new OBJECT tag to provide this support. The OBJECT element will supersede the use of Netscape's EMBED element and Sun's Java-based APPLET element, and will provide a vendor-neutral way of specifying Java applets, ActiveX controls, and so on. Internet Explorer fully supports the OBJECT tag, and we discuss and use it throughout the book.

NOTE: *As of April 15, 1997, the Object specification was still in draft form.*

W3C Style Sheet Specification

Style sheets provide Web-page designers with considerable more control over how a page looks by allowing them to define styles. A *style* defines the font, point size, color, indents, and so on for a specific page or a number of pages. Basic HTML provides only limited control over these aspects of a page.

The HTML 3.2 specification does not describe the implementation of style sheets. Instead, they are addressed in a related specification. Internet Explorer supports the use of style sheets with the STYLE element, and we also cover this later in the chapter.

NOTE: *The Cascading Style Sheet Specification became a W3C recommendation on December 16, 1996.*

W3C Layout Specification

The HTML language lacks an ability to describe overlapping elements. In other words, you cannot place text on top of text and you cannot place images on top of images. The style sheet specification overcomes some of these limitations as it allows overlapping text, but it does not provide complete control over all of the elements of a page. The *Frame-based Layout* specification provides complete two-dimensional control over the elements of a page. Microsoft provides an ActiveX control that implements the layout specification. We cover this ActiveX control in Chapter 5.

NOTE: *The Frame-based layout specification is still in draft form.*

WEB RESOURCES:

URL	Description
http://www.w3.org/	The World Wide Web Consortium's site.
http://www.w3.org/pub/WWW/Style/	W3C style sheet resources.

http://www.w3.org/pub/WWW/TR/ WD-object	W3C OBJECT tag draft.
http://www.w3.org/pub/WWW/TR/ WD-forms.html	W3C HTML forms working draft.
http://www.w3.org/pub/WWW/TR/ WD-script.html	W3C client-side scripting work draft.
http://www.w3.org/pub/WWW/TR/	A list of current W3C drafts and recommendations.
http://www.w3.org/pub/WWW/TR/ REC-html32.html	The specification for HTML version 3.2.
http://www.w3.org/pub/WWW/TR/ REC-CSS1-961217.html	The specification for cascading style sheets.
http://www.w3.org/pub/WWW/TR/ WD-layout.html	W3C draft for frame-based layout using style sheets.
http://www.ncsa.uiuc.edu/General/ Internet/WWW/HTMLPrimer.html	Good primer on HTML.
http://www.wdvl.com/Authoring/ HTML/	Lots of good HTML resources.
http://spock.fcs.uga.edu/cs/ web_seminar/	A good tutorial on building HTML-based pages.

Uniform Resource Locators

As we've discussed in Chapter 1, the Web is a very large collection of networked machines. Each of these machines contains a number of resources that are made available to users in the Web environment. Users typically access these resources through their Web browsers. In such an environment, it is important that each Web resource have a unique address. The Web provides a standard for addressing resources called a Uniform Resource Locator or URL.

A *URL* specifies the exact location of a resource within the Web environment. It is composed of four parts: The method of accessing the resource, the address of the machine that contains the resource, the resource location on the machine (a filename), and finally any parameters that should be passed to the resource. Here are some typical URLs:

```
http://www.WidgetWare.com/default.htm
mailto:tom@widgetware.com
news://msnews.microsoft.news
```

The URL's four component parts are divided like this:

```
method://Web.Node.Address:port/Node-Path-To-Resource?Parameters
```

Access Method

The first part of the URL is the access method, which specifies the particular protocol required to access the indicated resource. There are a number of supported protocols, and you can add your own if you like. There are a number of standard, well-known access methods. These are shown in Table 3.1.

Internet Node Address

The second part of the URL is the actual Internet Protocol (IP) address. Typically this will be a readable name such as www.microsoft.com, but it could also be the straight IP numeric address. You can also specify the IP port number by appending a colon and the port number. Port 80 is the standard HTTP port and this is the default if one is not specified. Here are some examples:

TABLE 3.1

URL Access Methods

Access Method	Description
http: Hypertext Transfer Protocol	The most commonly used URL protocol. Specifies a resource that understands the HTTP protocol.
mailto: email@address	Invokes any local email client with the specified address as the recipient.
ftp: File Transfer Protocol	Downloads the file specified by the URL using FTP.
file: Local Filename	Opens the specified local file in the browser.
news: News Server	Launches the news server application and goes to the news group specified.

```
//www.sky.net:80
//198.42.244
```

Local File Path

Following the node address is an optional pathname on the server. One common usage in the HTTP protocol is to specify the local user name preceded by a tilde (~). This will typically point directly to the user's home directory, and any path is relative to this directory. Of course, this local path is relative to the one provided by the HTTP software on the server and in many cases will not reflect the actual physical path to the resource. Here are some examples:

```
/~toma/faq.htm
/~toma/public/documents/
```

If a specific file is not specified, the Web server will provide the default. On most UNIX-based machines the default filename is INDEX .HTML. On Windows NT it is usually DEFAULT.HTM. However, the default filename can be changed by the administrator.

Parameters

Parameters can be specified as the fourth part of the URL. Parameters and their delimiters are defined by the specified access method. For the HTTP protocol, the pound sign (#) signifies a bookmark or NAME reference within an HTML document. Other access methods will define their own parameter delimiters. The first example following specifies an HTML bookmark, and the second example shows specifying the word "diazo" as a parameter to the WEBSTER program.

```
http://www.sky.net/~toma/faqgen.htm#DesignMode
http://gs213.sp.cs.cmu.edu/prog/webster?diazo
```

HTML Editors and Other Tools

As we go through this chapter learning HTML, there are several ways that you can follow along. You can just read and comprehend the example

HTML; you can type in the examples using a simple editor, such as Windows Notepad; or you can use a full-featured HTML editor such as Microsoft's FrontPage 97.

As we've already discussed, an HTML document is pure ASCII text, and for a long time, the only way to build HTML-based documents was to use a simple ASCII text editor. This was primarily because the HTML standards were evolving so quickly that tool vendors could not produce advanced editing software fast enough. When they released an editor, it was already outdated. If it didn't contain support for the latest and greatest HTML tags, it couldn't be used effectively.

However, building a whole Website with Notepad requires you to have a deep understanding of HTML (as well as masochistic tendencies). Since you're coding direct HTML, it's easy to make mistakes as you enter the appropriate tags, text, and images, but you do have complete control over the resulting Web page.

Today, the HTML standards have settled down, and there are several good WYSIWIG-type HTML editors. These editors allow you to build Web pages with virtually no knowledge of HTML. However, it's just like everything else. Everything is fine until you run into that one problem that you can't figure out or you need to do something with a new element that the editor doesn't support. I recommend that you use something akin to Notepad for the examples in this chapter. They aren't that complex, and you'll probably learn more anyway.

A Simple Example

To get acclimated to building a Web document, let's quickly develop a simple Web page. Start up Notepad and type in the following:

```
<HTML>
<HEAD>
<TITLE>My First Web Page</TITLE>
</HEAD>
<BODY>
<H1>Here is some text.</H1>
</BODY>
</HTML>
```

Save the file as SIMPLE.HTM and start up Internet Explorer. Once Internet Explorer is started, enter the path to your SIMPLE.HTM file in Internet Explorer's **Address:** area and press **Enter.** Your first Web

Figure 3.1
Our first Web page.

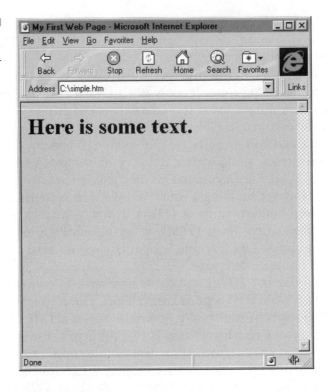

page will display in Internet Explorer. It should look something like Figure 3.1.

Designing WidgetWare.com

Throughout this book, we use the WidgetWare.com Website for some of our examples. As we move through the chapters, we progressively convert the site from where it began, as a simple set of static HTML-only pages, to a site that uses most of Microsoft's client-side ActiveX technologies. To give you an idea of where we are starting, take a look at Figure 3.2.

The initial version of WidgetWare.com consisted of a main page that used only basic HTML elements. However, it is very effective at what it was designed to do: deliver developer-type information. At the top of every page is a hyperlink menu that allows the user to navigate from page to page within the site. Each document then has a series of graphics and paragraphs as well as links to other sites. In this chapter, we cover the main

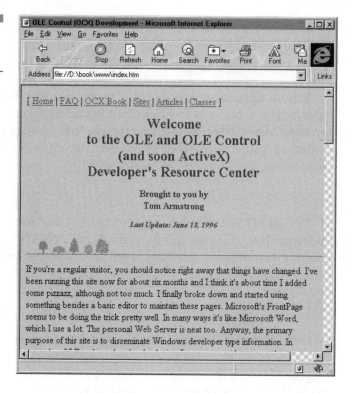

Figure 3.2
Initial WidgetWare
.com main page.

page to use three frames. In later chapters, we add ActiveX controls, JavaScript, VBScript, and Java applets.

HTML Basics

There are a large number of books on the HTML language. As I mentioned earlier, the purpose of this chapter is to provide you with a crash course in HTML and introduce you to some of the features of the new HTML 3.2 specification as well as some of the features of Internet Explorer. There are whole books written on HTML, but my goal is to condense it down to one chapter that doesn't insult your intelligence.

Elements and Tags

The HTML language is defined as a number of *elements* that specify the format of the "page" being described. Each element affects the data (e.g., some text or an image) that follows it. For example, the following HTML code specifies that the text should be displayed in **bold** type.

```
<B>This text is bold.</B>
```

B is an element of the HTML language, and **<B>** is known as a *tag*, specifically a begin tag. An element is enclosed within less-than (<) and greater-than (>) symbols to create the tag. **</B>** is an end tag. An end tag is indicated with a slash (/) before the element name. The begin- and end-tag pairs make it easy to nest elements like this:

```
<B>This is bold and <I>this is italicized.</I></B>
```

Not all HTML elements support nesting, but most do. Not all HTML elements have end tags, but most do. Not all HTML elements require the end tag, but most do. Basically, there are always exceptions.

Attributes

HTML elements can also have attributes. *Attributes* modify a specific behavior of an element. For example, the simple **P** element specifies the beginning of a paragraph of text. The **P** element has one attribute: ALIGN. The ALIGN attribute allows you to indicate how the paragraph should be aligned, either LEFT (the default), CENTER, or RIGHT.

```
<P ALIGN = CENTER>This sentence is centered.</P>
<P ALIGN = RIGHT>This sentence is aligned right.</P>
```

Comments

You can add comments to your HTML documents by surrounding them with the HTML comment element (!--). Although the comment indicator isn't easy to type nor is it intuitive, it does allow you to add comments. Also, as we see later, the comment element allows you to "hide" elements not supported in older browsers. The HTML 2.0 COMMENT element can also be used, but most HTML developers use the newer one. Here's an example of each comment element:

```
<!-- This starts the comment.
     Finally, this ends the comment -->
<COMMENT>
     Comments can also be embedded using
     the HTML 2.0 COMMENT element
</COMMENT>
```

Colors

Several HTML elements support the COLOR attribute. The value of the COLOR attribute can be specified in two different ways, either as a red, green, blue mix (RGB), or hex values, or you can use explicit color names such as red, green, blue, and so on. Here are some examples using the COLOR attribute. (See Table 3.2.)

```
<body bgcolor="blue">
<h4><font color="#0000FF" size="2">
Last update: June 18, 1996</font></h4>
<TABLE bgcolor="Ivory">
```

TABLE 3.2

HTML Color Types

Method	Description	Example
RGB value	A red-green-blue value indicated as a triplet of 2-digit hex values. For example, pure red is coded as FF0000 and pure blue as 0000FF. Internet Explorer also allows you to specify the triplet in the form RGB(xx,xx,xx).	Color = "#FF0F00" Color = "FF00FF" Color = RGB(CC,CC,CC) Color = RGB(00,FF,00)
Color name	Both Internet Explorer and Navigator support 16 different colors by name. These include: aqua, black, blue, fuchsia, gray, green, lime, maroon, navy, olive, purple, red, silver, teal, white, and yellow. These names are part of the HTML 3.2 standard and will be supported by other browsers as well.	Color = red Color = silver

NOTE: *Actually, both Internet Explorer and the latest version Netscape Navigator support an additional 124 colors that were originally part of the Cascading Style Sheets specification. Here they are in alphabetical order, the original 16 VGA colors plus the additional 124 X11-based colors:*

AliceBlue, AntiqueWhite, Aqua, Aquamarine, Azure, Beige, Bisque, Black, BlanchedAlmond, Blue, BlueViolet, Brown, BurlyWood, CadetBlue, Chartreuse, Chocolate, Coral, CornFlowerBlue, Cornsilk, Crimson, Cyan, DarkBlue, DarkCyan, DarkGoldenrod, DarkGray, DarkGreen, DarkKhaki, DarkMagenta, DarkOliveGreen, DarkOrange, DarkOrchid, DarkRed, DarkSalmon, DarkSeaGreen, DarkSlateBlue, DarkSlateGray, DarkTurquoise, DarkViolet, DeepPink, DeepSkyBlue, DimGray, DodgerBlue, FireBrick, FloralWhite, ForestGreen, Fuchsia, Gainsboro, GhostWhite, Gold, Goldenrod, Gray, Green, GreenYellow, Honeydew, HotPink, IndianRed, Indigo, Ivory, Khaki, Lavender, LavenderBlush, LawnGreen, LemonChiffon, LightBlue, LightCoral, LightCyan, LightGoldenrodYellow, LightGray, LightGreen, LightPink, LightSalmon, LightSeaGreen, LightSkyBlue, LightSlateGray,

LightSteelBlue, Light Yellow, Lime, LimeGreen, Linen, Magenta, Maroon, MediumAquamarine, MediumBlue, MediumOrchid, MediumPurple, MediumSeaGreen, MediumSlateBlue, MediumSpringGreen, MediumTurquoise, MediumVioletRed, MidnightBlue, MintCream, MistyRose, Moccasin, NavajoWhite, Navy, OldLace, Olive, OliveDrab, Orange, OrangeRed, Orchid, PaleGoldenrod, PaleGreen, PaleTurquoise, PaleVioletRed, PapayaWhip, PeachPuff, Peru, Pink, Plum, PowderBlue, Purple, Red, RosyBrown, RoyalBlue, SaddleBrown, Salmon, SandyBrown, SeaGreen, Seashell, Sienna, Silver, SkyBlue, SlateBlue, SlateGray, Snow, SpringGreen, SteelBlue, Tan, Teal, Thistle, Tomato, Turquoise, Violet, Wheat, White, WhiteSmoke, Yellow, and YellowGreen

Anchors

The anchor (**A**) element is what makes HTML powerful. It provides the hyperlinking capability that the Web is known for. *Hyperlinks*, in a programmatic sense, are just GO TOs. They specify a direct link to another Web page anywhere that a URL can specify.

The anchor element has several attributes, the most important of which is HREF. *HREF* specifies a hyperlink to another HTML page or other Web resource. One click from the user and off you go. The HREF attributes specifies the location of the jump with a URL. Here are some examples:

```
<A HREF = "http:\\www.cnn.com">Click here to go to CNN</A>
<A HREF = "next.htm">Next Page</A>
<A HREF = "email.htm"><IMG SRC = "mailbox.gif"></A>
```

Most browsers highlight, underline, or in some way indicate that the text or graphic is a hyperlink to some other document. In Internet Explorer, text is underlined, and images show that they are hyperlinks by drawing a border around the image. However, this occurs only if the page designer specifies a nonzero border size for the image.

The second most important anchor attribute is NAME. The *NAME* attribute allows you to indicate a specific, "named" position within an HTML document. This can be within the current document or one halfway around the world. This is similar to the concept of a bookmark in most editors such as Microsoft Word.

```
<!-- The top of a document specified with a named anchor -->
<A NAME = "Top"></A>
...
<!-- This points to a named anchor -->
<A HREF = "#Top">Back to top</A>
```

```
<!-- HREF to a named anchor in another document -->
<A HREF = "faq.htm#Top">Back to main page</A>
```

There are other important anchor attributes, but these two are the primary ones that we plan to use, at least initially. Later, when we discuss HTML frames we encounter the TARGET attribute.

Minimal Page Requirements

An HTML document should always contain a small number of common tags. These tags tell the browser various global items, such as the HTML version of the document, whether the document contains HTML text, and the document title. Table 3.3 shows the basic HTML elements and the code below shows a minimal HTML document.

```
<!DOCTYPE HTML PUBLIC "-//W3C//DTD HTML 3.2//EN">
<HTML>
<HEAD>
<TITLE>A Minimal Web Page</TITLE>
</HEAD>
<BODY>
</BODY>
</HTML>
```

An HTML document contains two major sections: the header and the body. The header section, which is enclosed within the HEAD tags, describes the document's global characteristics. The information contained in the header will not be rendered within the browser's client area.

TABLE 3.3

Basic HTML Elements—In typical document order

Element	Description
!DOCTYPE	The first element of an HTML document. It specifies the version of the document. It is required with HTML version 3.2.
HTML	The HTML element begins the HTML portion of the document. This tells the browser to begin interpreting the following text as HTML.
HEAD	Specifies the heading area of the document. The TITLE is placed here along with any of these other header-specific elements: ISINDEX, BASE, STYLE, SCRIPT, META, and LINK.
TITLE	The title of the document. This is a required element and is contained within the bounds of the HEAD element. Most browsers display this text in the title bar.
BODY	The BODY element demarcates the body of the document. The majority of the HTML elements are used here.

The body section contains the actual text and images that are ultimately displayed.

Header Elements

The header section describes the document's global characteristics. A number of elements can be used only within the HEAD begin and end tags. These are known as HEAD elements. Each one is subsequently described.

BASE

By default the browser uses the URL specified to load the document as the full, absolute URL of the document. Then, when loading links within the document, the browser will attach the absolute URL to any relative URLs to locate the links. However, the BASE element can be used to explicitly state the absolute URL.

```
<!-- BOOK.HTM -->
...
<BASE HREF="http://www.WidgetWare.com/book.htm">
```

By using the BASE element, your documents can be moved freely because relative link references will maintain their validity. In the previous example, if I now move BOOK.HTM to a different directory, my internal, relative links will still work, because the browser will use the BASE URL instead of the new location of the page.

ISINDEX

The ISINDEX element is used in conjunction with a server-side CGI-style script to facilitate searching. ISINDEX is not used much today and isn't relevant to our discussion in this chapter.

LINK

The LINK element specifies a URL that establishes a relationship between documents. This element found little use in version 2.0 of HTML, but has now been updated with additional attributes that support HTML-based style sheets. We discuss this in more detail in the style sheet section.

META

The META element provides high-level information to the browser, search engines, and other interested applications. The META tag provides several useful features, many of which can be browser-specific. The META element attributes are described in Table 3.4.

You can use the META element to specify user-defined information. For example, FrontPage inserts this META tag in each of the documents it produces. The NAME and CONTENT attributes are used as comments to describe the application that generated the document.

```
<META NAME="GENERATOR" CONTENT="Microsoft FrontPage 2.0">
```

Since the information contained within the META element is user-defined, you can do whatever you want. Certain server applications index the pages of a site by scanning for META elements containing index information. The author of each page places a META element with index keywords, say, for example:

```
<META NAME="Keywods" CONTENT="ActiveX, OLE, COM, MFC, Windows">
```

The HTTP-EQUIV attribute is used, among other things, to do something called *client-pull*. The HTTP-EQUIV attribute is used to specify information that would normally come from the server application via the HTTP protocol. By specifying "Refresh," Internet Explorer will *pull* either the current or specified page from the server. For example, the following code will automatically reload the page every 10 seconds.

TABLE 3.4	**Attribute**	**Description**
META Element Attributes	HTTP-EQUIV	Provides information to the browser as if it was retrieved from the server.
	NAME	A user-defined string.
	CONTENT	A user-defined string. Most browsers have specific options for this attribute when used with HTTP-EQUIV.
	URL	A URL. Typically used with the "Refresh" option of HTTP-EQUIV.

```
<META HTTP-EQUIV="Refresh" CONTENT="10">
```

The page continually loads every 10 seconds, forever. If, instead, we specify a URL of another page, it will be loaded instead. So, when you move your Website from one server to another you can do something on this order:

```
<!DOCTYPE HTML PUBLIC "-//IETF//DTD HTML//EN">
<html>
<head>
<meta http-equiv="Refresh"
     content="3; URL=http://www.WidgetWare.com/">
<title>We've Moved</title>
</head>
<h2 align="center">We've Moved</h2>
<h2 align="center">
The ActiveX Developer's Web site has moved.
Please update your links with our new address.
</h2>
<a href="http://www.widgetware.com/">
<p align="center">http://www.WidgetWare.com/"</p>
</a>
</body>
</html>
```

This page states that the site has moved, and then uses the "Refresh" option to wait three seconds before taking users to the new site by loading the page specified in the URL attribute. The syntax is a little tricky on this one. Notice that the URL attribute is embedded within the CONTENT attribute. The address of the new location is also a hyperlink. This allows visitors to jump immediately to the new site with a mouse click, if they don't want to wait three seconds.

SCRIPT

One of the most powerful new features of HTML is the concept of scripting. *Scripting* allows a Web-page developer to embed programmable logic within a page. This new facility turns an HTML-based page into an dynamic document. The page is no longer merely a static display of formatted data. With scripting, a whole new world is opened to the developer. We cover scripting in more detail in later chapters. Our purpose here is to introduce you to the topic and explain the scripting-specific elements provided in HTML.

HTML 3.2 added the SCRIPT element to support the incorporation of scripts within HTML-based pages. The SCRIPT element has several attributes that we discuss in the next chapter. The primary one is LAN-GUAGE, which specifies the specific scripting language being used. Intenet Explorer supports both JScript (Microsoft's imple-mentation of Netscape's JavaScript) and VBScript. Here's an example of a simple page with some VBScript contained in the SCRIPT element.

```
<html>
<head>
<TITLE>Our First Script</TITLE>
<SCRIPT LANGUAGE="VBScript">
  <!--
    document.write "<CENTER>"
    document.write "<H2>" & "Here's some information about your browser" & "</H2>"
    document.write "Name: " & Window.Navigator.AppName & "<BR>"
    document.write "Version: " & Window.Navigator.AppVersion & "<BR>"
    document.write "Code name: " & Window.Navigator.AppCodeName & "<BR>"
    document.write "User agent: " & Window.Navigator.UserAgent
    document.write "</CENTER>"
    document.close
  -->
</SCRIPT>
</head>
<body>
</body>
</html>
```

Several things are going on here. First, within the HEAD element we've added some VBScript code with the SCRIPT element. The actual script code is surrounded by the comment element so that older browsers that do not support HTML version 3.2 will not try to interpret it. You should also notice that there isn't any data within the body of the page, but when you load this page into Internet Explorer, you see something resembling Figure 3.3.

When the page is loaded the script code is executed. The script code then dynamically generates HTML-based data and passes it to the browser's parsing engine. While doing so it gathers run-time-specific information about the browser in which it is running. This data is then displayed. We discuss the specifics of what the document.write command is in the next chapter. Right now, I just wanted to demonstrated how scripting can generate dynamic Web pages.

The data in Fig. 3.3 was generated as the page was loaded. Once you have actual code that can execute within a Web page, it's also nice to have user-written objects to use. HTML 3.2 also allows the embedding of user-written objects via the OBJECT and APPLET tags. We discuss these in a moment.

Figure 3.3
Our first script-based
page.

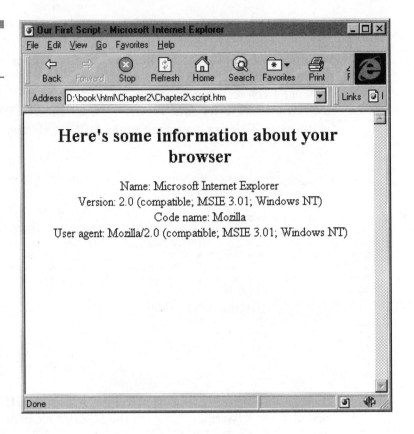

STYLE

The STYLE element contains the new style sheet attributes. *Style sheets* give you a tremendous amount of control over how your text and images are displayed. Style sheets are a recent addition to the HTML specification and provide fine, typesetting-like detail for your pages. We discuss this in more detail later in the chapter.

TITLE

The TITLE element is simply the title of the document. This is the only required HEAD element. Both the begin and end tags are required. Most browsers display this text in the title bar (see Fig. 3.3). The document title is also used as the name of your page in a browser's "favorites" list. You should pick a concise title for each of your pages.

 # The Body Element

The HEAD element describes the document's high-level characteristics. The second major part of an HTML document is contained in the BODY element. The images and text that are displayed in the browser are maintained here. The majority of HTML elements are used within the BODY section of a document.

The BODY element has several attributes, which are listed in Table 3.5. Most of these attributes provide default values for the page, but can be overridden by other elements within the body of the document. Here's an example of a document that uses a JPEG image for a background, uses white as the color for visited links, and red for nonvisited links. Also, the left and top margins are set to one pixel.

```
<body
  background="blusky.jpg"
  link="#FF0000" vlink="#FFFFFF"
  topmargin="1" leftmargin="1" >
```

The majority of the elements discussed in the rest of this chapter are used within the BODY section. In other words, they will be *contained* within the begin body (<BODY>) and end body (</BODY>) tags.

TABLE 3.5

BODY Element
Attributes

Attribute	Effect
ALINK = *color*	Specifies the color to display for the active hyperlink.
BACKGROUND = *url*	A URL that specifies a background image for the page.
BGCOLOR = *color*	Specifies the background color of the page.
BGPROPERTIES = FIXED	Specifies that the background image should be fixed. This provides a watermark effect.
ID = *value*	An identifier for the element within the document.
LEFTMARGIN = *n*	Specifies the left margin in pixels. If zero, the margin will be on the left edge of the window.
LINK = *color*	Specifies the color of hyperlinks that have not been visited.
STYLE = *css properties*	Style sheet information.
TEXT = *color*	Specifies the color of text within the document.
TOPMARGIN = *n*	Specifies the top margin in pixels. If zero, the margin will be the very top of the browser (or frame) window.
VLINK = *color*	Specifies the color to display for hyperlinks that have already been visited.

Paragraphs and Line Breaks

The Web is primarily a publishing medium—although it's quickly becoming an application development medium as well. What would publishing be without the paragraph? The most often used element in HTML is the paragraph (<P>) element. It is used to separate paragraphs of text. The paragraph has but one attribute, ALIGN, which allows you to LEFT, RIGHT, or CENTER justify your text. The default is the typical LEFT alignment. Following is a simple document with three paragraphs.

```
<p>Paragraph one. This paragraph is left justified using the
ALIGN=LEFT attribute of the paragraph element. To make the
paragraph a bit longer, I added this line.</p>

<p align="center">Paragraph two. This paragraph is centered
within the window using the ALIGN=CENTER attribute of the paragraph
element. To make the paragraph a bit longer, I added this line.</p>

<p align="right">Paragraph three. This paragraph is right
justified using the ALIGN=RIGHT attribute of the paragraph element.
To make the paragraph a bit longer, I added this line.</p>
```

The important thing to note from the preceding example is that the blank lines between the paragraphs do absolutely nothing to the final format of the document. Also, the line breaks within the paragraphs do nothing as well. The text within the paragraph tags is formatted for display by the browser. Line breaks are determined by the size of the browser window. This should be apparent by examining Fig. 3.4.

If you do need to break your paragraph lines at a specific point, you can use the line break <BR> element to provide an explicit line break. The line break element uses only the begin tag <BR>; an end tag does not make sense. Here's an example based on the previous one.

```
<p>Paragraph one.<br>
This paragraph is left justified using the ALIGN=LEFT attribute
of the paragraph element.<br>
To make the paragraph a bit longer, I added this line. </p>

<p align="center">Paragraph two.<br>
This paragraph is centered within the window using the ALIGN=CENTER
attribute of the paragraph element.<br>
To make the paragraph a bit longer, I added this line. </p>

<p align="right">Paragraph three.<br>
This paragraph is right justified using the ALIGN=RIGHT attribute
of the paragraph element.<br>
To make the paragraph a bit longer, I added this line. </p>
```

Figure 3.4
Paragraphs in
Internet Explorer.

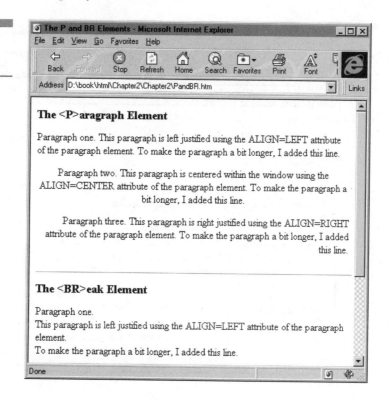

Figure 3.4
Paragraphs in
Internet Explorer.

With the explicit line breaks inserted, the browser now displays something that resembles Fig. 3.5.

Lists

The list elements provide simple bulleted, numbered, and indented lists. There are five basic list types: bulleted, ordered, definition, menu, and directory. Menu and directory lists are very similar to the ordered list, so I'm only going to cover the first three list types.

Bulleted lists are created with the UL (unordered list) and LI (line item) elements. Here's a simple bulleted list:

```
<ul>
  <li>Bullet Item 1</li>
  <li>Bullet Item 2</li>
  <li>Bullet Item 3</li>
  <li>Bullet Item 4</li>
</ul>
```

Figure 3.5
Paragraphs and line
breaks.

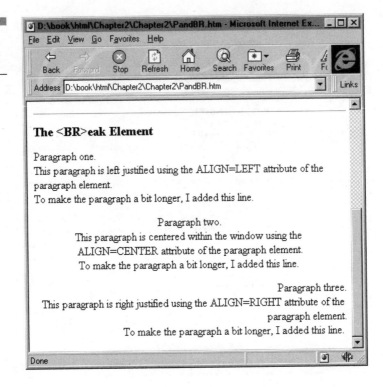

An *ordered list* begins with the OL element. Five "order" types are supported via the TYPE attribute: large and small letters, large and small Roman numerals, and decimal numbers. Here's a simple ordered list that uses the numbered type. It also demonstrates the START attribute, which allows you to begin the list with an arbitrary number or letter.

```
<ol type=1 start=10>
  <li>Item Number 1</li>
  <li>Item Number 2</li>
  <li>Item Number 3</li>
</ol>
```

The *definition list* can be used to present text in a typical term-definition format. The list begins with the DL element. Terms are identified with the DT (definition term) element and the corresponding definition is indicated with the DD element. Here's an example:

```
<dl>
  <dt>ActiveX
```

Figure 3.6
The list elements in
action.

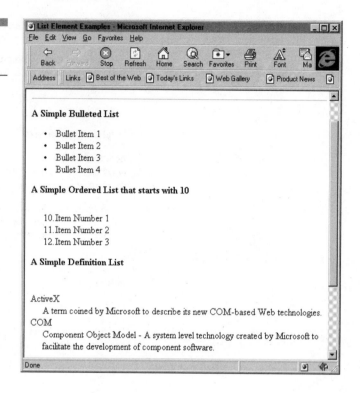

```
<dd>A term coined by Microsoft to describe its new COM-based
    Web technologies.
<dt>COM
<dd>Component Object Model - A system level technology
    created by Microsoft to facilitate the development of
    component software.
</dl>
```

Figure 3.6 shows the three lists that we developed previously in Internet Explorer.

Character Formatting

Basic HTML provides a number of elements to affect the basic formatting of text (see Table 3.6). The heading elements (H1 through H6) provide six levels of heading style formats, which basically change the point size

TABLE 3.6

Character Formatting Elements

Element	Tag	Effect
Paragraph	P	Indicates the begin and end of a paragraph. Text between the tags is word-wrapped by the browser.
Line break	BR	Explicitly breaks a line.
No line break	NOBR	Disallows breaking of a line.
Section division	DIV	Acts as a container for a series of elements. For example, it allows you to establish ALIGN-ment for a series of paragraphs.
Heading	H1 through H6	Heading styles. H1 uses the largest font and H6 uses the smallest font. The H elements produce bold text.
Bold	B or STRONG	Emphasizes the text, usually bold.
Italics	I or EM	Italicizes the text.
Underline	U	Underlines the text
Indented quotes	BLOCKQUOTE	Indents both the left and right margins of the enclosed text.
Superscript or Subscript	SUB and SUP	Superscripts or subscripts the text.
Smaller or bigger font	SMALL or BIG	SMALL makes the font one size smaller than the current font size and BIG makes the font one size larger. These tags behave just like the <FONT SIZE = –1> and <FONT SIZE = +1> elements.
Fixed-space text plus no processing of HTML tags	PLAINTEXT	This element is useful for displaying HTML code. The text is displayed in a fixed-space font and all the HTML code between the tags is not processed.
Fixed-space text	CODE PRE	CODE uses a fixed-spaced font. This is good for programming language text.
Default font	BASEFONT	Specifies the default font face, size, and color.
font	FONT	Specifies a specific font face, size, and color for a section of text.

of the font. Heading one (H1) is the largest font, and heading six (H6) is the smallest.

Specifying Font Characteristics

Internet Explorer implements and enhances several Netscape extensions related to character fonts. The BASEFONT element allows the setting of the default font face, size, and color. The face is the name of a specific font such as "Arial" or "Courier New." It can be any font on the local machine displaying the page. The font size is an integer from one through seven, where seven is the largest font size. The font color is a standard HTML color. Multiple font faces can be specified and the first one found on the machine will be used.

The FONT element provides a way to specify a font for a particular piece of text. It supports the same attributes as the BASEFONT element: FACE, SIZE, and COLOR. The SIZE attribute can be specified relative to the BASEFONT. To increase the size of a font relative to the BASE-FONT size, you can use this syntax <FONT SIZE = +1>. This, of course, increases the font size by one. Decreasing the font size this way works as well.

Here are some examples.

```
<BASEFONT FACE="Courier New" SIZE = 3 COLOR = Blue>
This text is displayed in the Courier New font and the color of
this text is blue.<BR>


<BASEFONT FACE = "Arial" SIZE = 3 COLOR = Red>
This text is displayed in the Arial font and the color of this text
is red.<BR>


<FONT SIZE = +1>The font size was increased to four<BR>
<FONT SIZE = +1>It's still four because we've specified it relative
                to the BASEFONT<BR>
<FONT SIZE = 5>Now the font size is five.<BR>


<FONT FACE = "Times New Roman" COLOR = Black>
We've now changed the font to &quotTimes New Roman&quot"<BR>
<FONT SIZE = -1>
It will stay Times New Roman until it is reset by another BASEFONT
or FONT element.<BR>
```

Figure 3.7 shows how these examples display in the browser.

Figure 3.7
Character formatting.

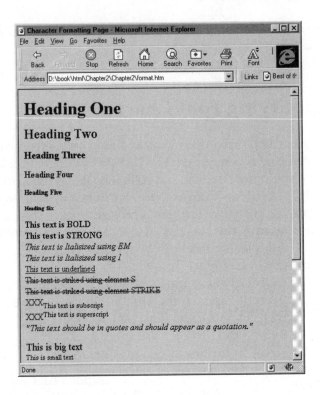

Special Characters

HTML provides special character mnemonics for foreign characters and other nontypical characters. Table 3.7 shows the most commonly used characters, their numeric value, and any shorthand mnemonic. A special character is specified using the HTML escape character, the ampersand (&) followed by a numeric character code or a mnemonic. Here are some examples

```
&#169      <!-- The copyright symbol -->
       <!-- A non-breaking space using the mnemonic -->
&lt        <!-- The less than character -->
&quot      <!-- A double quote -->
```

In cases where you need to use a character that is part of HTML, such as the less-than character (<), you should use the mnemonic character. We use this syntax for specifying special characters later when working with cascading style sheets. By using different Windows fonts, we can use special characters to provide very efficient graphics for our pages.

TABLE 3.7

Commonly Used
Special Characters

Character	Mnemonic	Value
Copyright	&copy	&#169
Nonbreaking space		
Registered trademark	&reg	&#174
Less than	&lt	&#60
Greater than	&gt	&#62
Quotation mark	&quot	&#34
Ampersand	&amp	&#38

Images

The old phrase, "a picture is worth a thousand words," is definitely true in the Web environment. Graphics brighten up a Web page and can make the page more intuitive and easy to use. The trouble is, a graphic download takes as long as or longer than downloading a thousand (text) words. So, for a fast Website, you want your graphics files as small as possible.

Graphics, or images, are specified in HTML with the image (IMG) element. The image element has several attributes. The ALIGN attribute determines how text will flow around the image or how text is justified. Table 3.8 lists the IMG element attributes.

The ALT tag provides a string of text that will be shown if the image itself is not displayed. If the user has turned off display of images at the browser level or if the image file cannot be found, the text specified in the ALT tag is displayed instead. Also, Internet Explorer will pop up a "tool tip" with the text from the ALT attribute if the cursor is positioned over the image.

Internet Explorer has five extension attributes for the IMG element. The CONTROLS, DYNSRC, LOOP, and START attributes provide embedded support for video clips and VRML worlds. The USEMAP attribute is used to specify a client-side image map.

Image Maps

Image maps allow you to build graphic images that hyperlink to various URLs depending on where the user clicks within the image. There are two

TABLE 3.8

IMG Tag Attributes

Attribute	Options and Effect
ALIGN = *align-type*	Specifies how surrounding text will align with the image. TOP—Text is aligned with the top of the image. MIDDLE—Text is aligned with the middle of the image. CENTER—Text is aligned with the center of the image. BOTTOM—Text is aligned with the bottom of the image. LEFT—The image is left justified with any text flowing around it. RIGHT—The image is right justified with any text flowing around it.
ALT = *text*	Alternate text to display if the image is not loaded. Also provides the text for Internet Explorer's "tool tips." It is important to provide text for this tag. Some users browse the Web with their browsers set to "Do not load images." By specifying alternate text, they can still navigate your site.
BORDER = *n*	The size of the border surrounding the image. The border is displayed only if the image is a hyperlink.
CONTROLS	Shows a set of video clip controls. Used with the DYNSRC attribute.
DYNSRC = *url*	Specifies the URL of a video clip (.AVI) or VRML world to display. This attribute is used with the START and LOOP attributes.
HEIGHT = *n* WIDTH = *n*	The height and width of the image. If this is provided, the browser will typically draw an empty rectangle prior to loading the image. If these extents are different from the actual size of the image, the image is stretched or compressed to fit within the specified boundaries.
HSPACE = *n* VSPACE = *n*	Specifies the surrounding margins for the image.
ID = *name*	Specifies a unique name for the image within the document. Useful for scripting as it provides a handle for scripting objects.
ISMAP = *image*	Specifies that the image is a server-side image map. A click on the image send the coordinates to the server.
LOOP = *n*	How many times to loop through the dynamic image specified with the DYNSRC attribute.
SRC = *url*	Specifies the URL of the image. Multiple image types are supported by Internet Explorer: GIF, JPG, and BMP.
START = *value*	Specifies when the video clip or VRML world specified by the DYNSRC attribute should begin playing. The two options are: FILEOPEN—Start when the document is loaded. MOUSEOVER—Start with the cursor moves over the image.
USEMAP = *url*	Specifies the image for a client-side image map. Use with the MAP element.

types of image maps, server-side, and client-side. Server-side maps are specified with the ISMAP attribute and client-side maps use the USEMAP attribute.

Server-side maps require that you write some server-side CGI code, so we focus on client-side maps here. The first step in implementing a client-side image map is to create an image that can be divided up into sections. Next, you use the MAP and AREA elements to partition the image into smaller areas that will trigger a link to another page. Here's a simple example from the CD-ROM, the output of which code is displayed in Figure 3.8:

```
<HTML>
<HEAD>
<TITLE>Client-Side Image Map</TITLE>
</HEAD>
<BODY>
<MAP NAME="MAP">
    <AREA shape="RECT" COORDS="0, 0, 125, 50" HREF="red.htm" ALT="Red">
    <AREA shape="RECT" COORDS="0, 50, 125, 100" HREF="blue.htm" ALT="Blue">
```

Figure 3.8
A client-side image map.

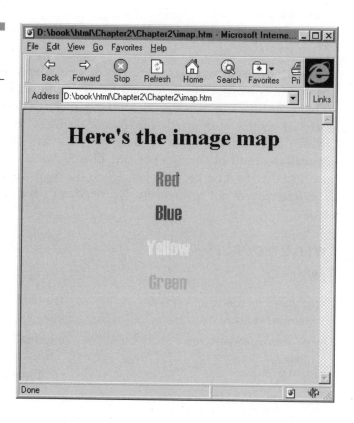

```
        <AREA shape="RECT" COORDS="0, 100, 125, 150" HREF="yellow.htm" ALT="Yellow">
        <AREA shape="RECT" COORDS="0, 150, 125, 200" HREF="green.htm" ALT="Green">
</MAP>
<H1><CENTER>Here's the image map</H1>
<IMG SRC="colormap.gif"
  USEMAP="#MAP">
</CENTER>
</BODY>
</HTML>
```

The USEMAP attribute of the IMG element specifies the name of a MAP block. The MAP element specifies, via the AREA element, the exact coordinates of the "hot" regions of the image. The SHAPE attribute supports rectangles, circles, and arbitrary polygons. Our example divides the 125 × 200 pixel image into four rectangular sections. The COORD attribute expects the coordinates in x1, y1, x2, y2 format.

Clicking in the "Blue" area loads BLUE.HTM, and so on. By specifying the ALT attribute of the AREA element, client-side image maps will also work in browsers that do not support images or have image display disabled.

Animated GIFs

The GIF image format has proved to be very adaptable to the Web environment. Initially GIFs were used for efficient, static images on a page. Then someone dug through the GIF89a specification and realized that the GIF format supported transparency and interlacing of the image (which allows progressive rendering). Well, the GIF89a specification also allows multiple images per file. This makes it easy to implemented animated GIFs. The browser just loops through the images within the file and you've got animation! No need for Java or an ActiveX control.

WEB RESOURCES:

URL	Description
http://www.reiworld.com/royalef/ gifanim.htm	The GIF89a specification.
http://www.microsoft.com/ imagecomposer/	Information on Microsoft's Image Composer and GIF Animator products.

Frames

One of the first steps to activate WidgetWare.com was to add frame capability. *Frames* provide a way to break your presentation up into different categories or areas. The most typical use for frames that I've seen is the heading-content-data view, which we use at the WidgetWare site. I'm sure you've seen this. It is an effective way of providing access to the material within your Website. The top frame contains the major content areas of the site, the left frame contains subcategory links for the main categories, and the large frame contains the content pages. Figure 3.9 is a look at the final frames-based page that we build later in this section.

When frames were first introduced, users quickly added this capability to their pages. It was a neat feature and seemed to make sense. However, frames had a problem: They took longer to load and made using the browser's **Back** button confusing. It would take the browser back to the top-level page, not the previous frame-based page. So, frames made a retreat because they were causing too much confusion. But now, thanks

Figure 3.9
WidgetWare.com
with frames.

to better understanding by page developers and enhancements to the browser, they're making a comeback.

NOTE: *However, not everyone appreciates frames. For specific reasons why, you can check out the "I Hate Frames Club" at http://www.wwwvoice.com/framm.html.*

Frames are a way of breaking up a page into different views. Each view is a full HTML-based document. In Fig. 3.9, you are actually looking at four different documents, three of which actually contain displayable content. The document that you don't see is the one that contains the definition or description of this main page. It uses the FRAMESET and FRAME elements.

To make our discussion of frames easier, the example uses five simple Web pages: WHITE.HTM, GREEN.HTM, BLUE.HTM, GREY.HTM, and YELLOW.HTM. I use these documents as the contents of our frames in the next few examples. They are all similar to this:

```
<!DOCTYPE HTML PUBLIC "-//IETF//DTD HTML//EN">
<html>
<head>
<title>Blue Page</title>
</head>
<body BGCOLOR = "blue">
<h1>Blue Blue Blue Blue Blue Blue Blue Blue</h1>
<h1>Blue Blue Blue Blue Blue Blue Blue Blue</h1>
<h1>Blue Blue Blue Blue Blue Blue Blue Blue</h1>
<h1>Blue Blue Blue Blue Blue Blue Blue Blue</h1>
<h1>Blue Blue Blue Blue Blue Blue Blue Blue</h1>
<h1>Blue Blue Blue Blue Blue Blue Blue Blue</h1>
<h1>Blue Blue Blue Blue Blue Blue Blue Blue</h1>
<h1>Blue Blue Blue Blue Blue Blue Blue Blue</h1>
</body>
</html>
```

Following is a simple frame definition document. Remember, this page does not contain any content. Its purpose is to describe how the referenced documents are displayed. Figure 3.10 displays the resulting output.

```
<!DOCTYPE HTML PUBLIC "-//IETF//DTD HTML//EN">
<html>
<head>
<title>Frame One</title>
</head>
<frameset rows="50%, 50%">
```

```
            <frame src="blue.htm">
            <frame src="yellow.htm">
</frameset>
</html>
```

The FRAMESET tag starts the definition of frame container. Within the FRAMESET tag you specify your frames using the FRAME tag. The most important FRAME attribute is SRC. SRC provides the URL of the HTML file that will reside within the frame. The FRAMESET tag is a container and so it must be terminated with a /FRAMESET end tag. The FRAME tag however is not, so no ending </FRAME> tag is required.

In our example, we specify a FRAMESET with two rows, where each will consume 50 percent of the available browser space. We then must provide FRAME elements to describe the two frames. Our example provides only the SRC attribute with the appropriate URLs. The outcome is shown in Fig. 3.10. Table 3.9 describes the various FRAMESET attributes.

Let's try something more difficult.

```
<!DOCTYPE HTML PUBLIC "-//IETF//DTD HTML//EN">
<html>
```

Figure 3.10
Our first frame-based page.

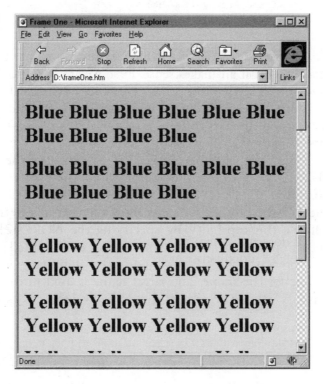

TABLE 3.9

FRAMESET
Attributes

Attribute	Effect
COLS = *column_widths*	Creates a frame with columns. The widths can be specified in pixels, percentages, or relative size.
ROWS = *row_widths*	Creates a frame with rows. The widths can be specified in pixels, percentages, or relative size.
FRAMEBORDER = *1 or 0*	A 3D border is displayed if the value is 1 and a value of 0 indicates no border.
FRAMESPACING = *spacing in pizels*	Indicates additional spacing between any borders.

```
<head>
<title>Frame Example Two</title>
</head>
<frameset rows="50%, 50%">
    <frameset cols = "100, *">
        <frame src="blue.htm">
        <frame src="green.htm">
    </frameset>
    <frame src="yellow.htm">
</frameset>
</html>
```

The nesting of the FRAMESET tags is confusing at first, but with a little thought it all makes sense. First, we are creating a FRAMESET with two rows. The first row contains another FRAMESET, which contains two columns. The first column will start out with an explicit width of 100 pixels, and the next column is relative (*) in size. Finally, the last row is by itself. Figure 3.11 shows what it looks like.

Notice the scroll bars in Fig. 3.11. By default, if the information in the HTML document cannot be displayed, the browser will provide scroll bars. You can disable this by setting the SCROLLING attribute to "NO." By default, the browser will also allow the user to size the frames. You can disable this capability by specifying the NORESIZE attribute. Several other options are available with frames; each is listed in Table 3.10.

The frame NAME attribute is also important. It provides a "target" name for the frame. The target name is used in the anchor element to specify where a document should be loaded. Let's look at an example:

```
<!DOCTYPE HTML PUBLIC "-//IETF//DTD HTML//EN">
<html>
<!-- DEFAULT.HTM -->
<head>
```

Figure 3.11
Our Frame Two
example.

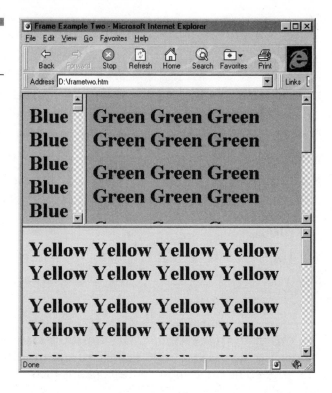

```
<title>Armstrong's WidgetWare.com</title></head>
<frameset rows="40,*">
    <frame src="frbanner.htm" name="banner" scrolling="no"
    frameborder="0">
    <frameset cols="150,*">
        <frame src="frconten.htm" name="contents" frameborder="0">
        <frame src="frmain.htm" name="main" frameborder="0">
    </frameset>
    <noframes>
    <body>
    <p>This web page uses frames, but your browser doesn't
       support them.</p>
    </body>
    </noframes>
</frameset>
</html>
```

This is the main page for WidgetWare.com. When a user specifies a URL
that does not contain a specific document (e.g., http://www.WidgetWare
.com), the server provides a default Web page. On most UNIX servers this is
INDEX.HTML, and on most Windows NT servers it is DEFAULT.HTM.
WidgetWare is hosted on a NT server, so our main frame definition page
we'll name DEFAULT.HTM.

TABLE 3.10

FRAME Attributes

Attribute	Effect
ALIGN = *align-type*	The type of alignment for the frame. One of TOP, CENTER, BOTTOM, LEFT, or RIGHT.
FRAMEBORDER = *1 or 0*	A 3D border is displayed if the value is 1 and a value of 0 indicates no border.
MARGINHEIGHT = *height in pixels*	Height of the frame margin.
MARGINWIDTH = *width in pixels*	Width of the frame margin.
NAME = *name*	The name of the frame. This is used as a TARGET value when loading documents into a specific frame.
NORESIZE	The user cannot resize the frame window.
SCROLLING = *yes or no*	If yes, a scroll-bar is provided for scrolling.
SRC = *url*	The address for the frame. Typically a URL.

In this main page, each FRAME element contains a NAME attribute. The purpose here is to provide a target for any anchors that we use in our other pages. The uppermost frame contains FRBANNER.HTM. Here's a look at it.

```
<!DOCTYPE HTML PUBLIC "-//IETF//DTD HTML//EN">
<html>

<head>
<title>Banner Frame in Main Page</title>
<base target="contents">
</head>
<body>
...
[<a href="frconten.htm" target="contents">Home</a>
|<a href="faq.htm" target="contents">FAQs</a>
|<a href="books.htm" target="contents">Books</a>
|<a href="articles.htm" target="main">Articles</a>
|<a href="bookstore.htm" target="contents">Other Books</a>
...
</body>
</html>
```

All of the anchors in the banner page specify a specific frame target. If the user clicks on the "FAQ" link, the FAQ.HTM page is loaded in the "contents" frame. By giving each of our frames a name, we can now explicitly load documents in those frames from within other documents. This is one of the more powerful features of frames. It simplifies navigation for the user. Our banner page will always stay at the top of the document, and we update the "contents" and "main" frames with any selected content.

TARGET and BASE TARGET

The TARGET attribute in our anchor code above specifies where to load the referenced document when the anchor is selected. Also, notice the TARGET attribute on the BASE element in the header section of the document. This specifies a default target for any anchors in the document. You can specify a frame or "window" name as we've done here, or can specify one of four special targets: _blank, _self, _top, and _parent. These special targets can be used wherever the TARGET attribute is used.

_blank

Specifying a target of _blank opens up a new browser window to display the document. I've not used this one much, but I do notice that some sites will launch a new instance of the browser under certain conditions. This is how they do it.

_self

The _self target loads the specified document in the document window that contained the hyperlink. When working in the main window of a frame, this will be the most often used target. You are basically loading the new link in place of the existing document. This is the typical behavior when browsing links that are part of your site. A hyperlink replaces the content displayed in the main window.

_top

The _top target loads the document into the full browser window. This is different from _blank, which loads a completely new copy of the browser. You would typically use the _top target when linking to documents on sites outside of your own. For example, the WidgetWare site contains

Figure 3.12
Link to an external
page.

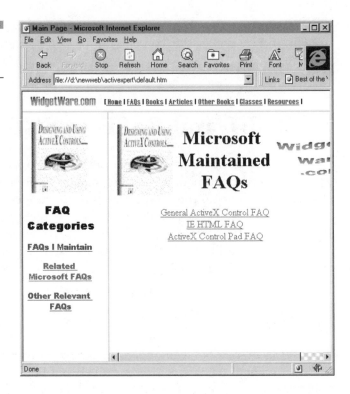

links to FAQs maintained at other sites. Figure 3.12 shows a link to Microsoft's ActiveX Control FAQ. When the user selects this link, we should specify a target of _top. This loads the Microsoft FAQ pages and replaces completely any pages that are part of WidgetWare.com. This is the behavior that users expect.

We could also specify a TARGET of _self, which would create the multiframe view shown in Fig. 3.13. If you do this too many times, there isn't much to see. There are some cases, though, where this might be useful. If you want to keep the user at your site, you might do this. This would normally be the case if you expect the user to actually stay at your site and is referencing the external page briefly. However, do it too much and the user will probably not come back.

_parent

The _parent TARGET loads the document into the parent frame of the current document. In most cases this will behave just like _top.

Figure 3.13
External page with a
TARGET of _self.

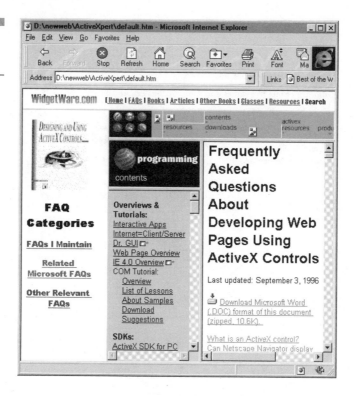

To give you an idea of how all of this works, the examples on the CD-ROM contain the pages shown in Fig. 3.14. It should help you understand how each the TARGET attribute works.

Floating Frames

Internet Explorer also has the ability to create independent frames within HTML documents. Basically this allows you to open a simple browser window anywhere within your HTML document. A browser within a browser. This technique is called a *floating frame*. (See Fig. 3.15.)

A new element, IFRAME, provides the floating frame functionality. Whenever it is encountered by a browser, a frame window is opened up right there. Text will wrap around the frame and parameters are provided to aid in the alignment of the frame, much like the IMG element. The parameters are the same as for the FRAME tag. Here's a quick example of a floating frame:

Figure 3.14
Testing the TARGET
attribute.

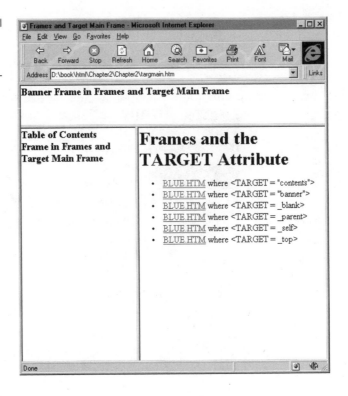

```
<HTML>
<HEAD>
<TITLE>Floating frames</TITLE>
</HEAD>
<BODY>
<CENTER>
<H1>A Floating Frame</H1>
<HR>
<IFRAME NAME="FLOATING"
        HEIGHT="300"
        WIDTH="300"
        SRC="BLUE.HTM">
</IFRAME>
</CENTER>
</BODY>
</HTML>
```

Figure 3.16 displays what you can do using Microsoft's Active Document technology. By specifying a Microsoft Word file as the SRC document, Internet Explorer will load and display the Word document within the floating frame. Of course for this to work, the workstation must already have either Word or the Word Viewer installed locally.

Figure 3.15
A floating frame.

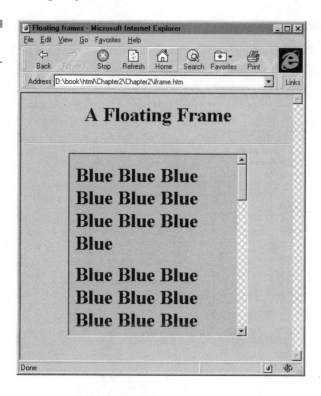

WEB RESOURCES:

URL	*Description*
http://www.customcpu.com/personal/ kparker/webit/frame_tutor/ index.html	A good introduction to frames.

Tables

HTML tables provide the Web-page designer with a powerful new tool. *Tables* allow you to separate your page into sections. Tables are similar to frames, but tables operate within the same HTML-based document. Frames divide independent documents.

If you've used a good word processor such as Microsoft Word, then you've probably used tables. HTML tables are no different, although they do provide several more options that you don't typically get with a word

Figure 3.16
Word document in a
floating frame.

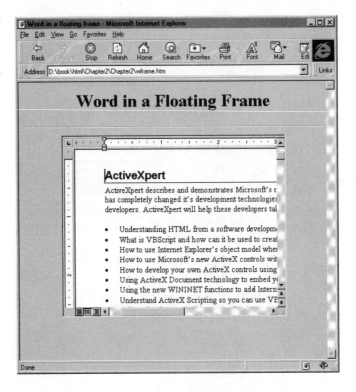

processing package. Tables are created using the TABLE, TR, and TD elements. The begin and end TABLE tags contain the table row (TR) and table detail (TD) elements. In other words, the TR and TD elements don't work outside of the TABLE tag begin-and-end pair. Here's a simple table:

```
<Table
   BGColor = "white"
   Border = 2
   BorderColor = "black">
<TR>
<TD>This is row 1, column 1
<TD>This is row 1, column 2
<TR>
<TD> This is row 2, column 1, though a bit longer
<TD> This is row 2, column 2
```

This is pretty straightforward. We have a table with two columns and two rows that has a white background and a black border. Tables aren't required to have borders, and most sites don't use them. By default the columns are sized to the largest element, the text is left aligned, and is centered vertically within the cell. See Fig. 3.17 for a look at our simple table.

Figure 3.17
HTML tables.

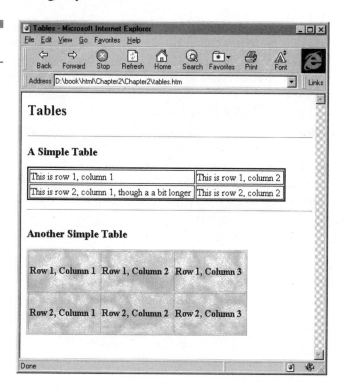

The size of the table matrix is determined by the number of TR and TD tags encountered as the browser parses the TABLE block. Every time a TR tag is encountered, a new row is started; from then on a column is created for every TD tag encountered, until either the TR end tag is encountered or a new row is started. The following specifies a two-row table where each row has three columns. See the second table in Fig. 3.17.

```
<TABLE Border = 1
       Background = "clouds.gif"
       Height = 140>
<TR>
<TD><b>Row 1, Column 1</b>
<TD><b>Row 1, Column 2</b>
<TD><b>Row 1, Column 3</b>
<TR>
<TD><b>Row 2, Column 1</b>
<TD><b>Row 2, Column 2</b>
<TD><b>Row 2, Column 3</b>
</TABLE>
```

Of course, if you specify only two TD tags in one of the rows, everything will work, but if you have borders around your columns, it may look strange. However, if you don't use borders, this isn't a problem. As you can see from the example, you can specify a background image for the table, its height, and so on. Whole chapters have been written on tables; for more details, take a look at the TABLE-based elements and attributes in Tables 3.11 and 3.12.

Tables are used extensively on the Web for page layout design. It provides capabilities that page designers have wanted for a long time. Of course, tables weren't necessarily created for this purpose, but, hey, it works. For example, take a look at Fig. 3.18. You can't tell by looking, but in order to create such a clean, segregated layout, you have to use a bunch of tables. For illustration, the table borders are turned on in Fig. 3.19.

NOTE: *We'll also be using the TABLE element when working with ActiveX controls in later chapters. The TABLE element is the simplest way to align controls in a basic Web page. There are other ways, too, such as using Microsoft's Layout ActiveX control, or using a browser that supports the new HTML Layout specification. As of this writing, however, none do.*

TABLE 3.11

Table Elements

Tag	Description
CAPTION	Specifies a caption for the table. The ALIGN and VALIGN attributes are supported.
TABLE	Specifies a table.
TD	Defines a cell within a table. Supports most of the TABLE attributes plus COLSPAN and ROWSPAN. COLSPAN indicates that the contents of the cell will extend into the space of the adjoining cell(s). ROWSPAN does the same for rows.
TBODY	Used by tables that have headers and footers to specify attributes for groups of rows.
THEAD	Defines a table header. The ALIGN, ID, VALIGN, and STYLE attributes are supported. Supports the ID and STYLE attributes.
TFOOT	Defines a table footer. The ID and STYLE attributes are supported.
TH	Specifies a row or column heading for a table. Most of the TABLE attributes are supported, plus COLSPAN and ROWSPAN.
TR	Creates a table row.

TABLE 3.12

Table Attributes

Name	Description
Align = *value*	The default item alignment, either LEFT, RIGHT, or CENTER. This attribute specifies the wrap behavior of text. LEFT—The default CENTER—The table is centered on the page. RIGHT—The table is right justified with any text placed to the left of the table.
Background = *url*	A URL of either a .GIF, .JPG, or .BMP file to use as the table's background.
Bgcolor = *color*	The default background color for the whole table.
Border = *n*	Specifies the border size of the table. The default is zero pixels.
BorderColor = *color*	Specifies the color of the border.
BorderColorDark = *color* BorderColorLight = *color*	To support 3D, you can specify both the dark and light color of the border.
CellPadding = *n*	The size in pixels of the padding between the contents of each cell in the table.
CellSpacing = *n*	The size in pixels of the padding from the frame to the cells.
Clear = *value*	Specifies how text following the table should be formatted. NO = Text follows the table. This is the default. LEFT = Text is shown on the next left-aligned line. RIGHT = Text is show on the next right-aligned line. ALL = Text flows around the table.
Cols = *n*	The number of columns in the table.
Frame = *value*	Specifies which of part of the border around a table will be displayed. You can use this to create tables that separate only their columns, and so on. Several options are available. The default is BORDER, which displays the table with a border delineating each cell. Others include: ABOVE, BELOW, HSIDES, LHS, RHS, VSIDES, and BOX.
Id = *name*	Specifies a unique identifier for the table.
NoWrap	Don't wrap the contents of the table if it extends beyond the right margin.
Rules = *value*	Specifies how the inner borders are displayed. The FRAMES attribute controls the border surrounding the table whereas the RULES attribute controls the inner borders. Several options are available. NONE—Remove all inner borders. GROUP—Shows horizontal borders between table groups.

TABLE 3.12
(Continued)

Name	Description
	ROWS—Show a border separating only the rows of a table. COLS—Show a border separating only the columns of a table. ALL—Show borders between both rows and columns.
Style = *CSS property*	Specifies the style of the table using CSS properties.
Valign = *value*	Specifies how the table will be aligned vertically. One of TOP, MIDDLE, BOTTOM, or BASELINE.
Width = *n*	The specific width of the table, either in pixels or a percentage.

WEB RESOURCES:

URL	*Description*
http://junior.apk.net/~jbarta/tutor/ tables/index.html	An introduction to tables.
http://www.w3.org/pub/WWW/TR/ WD-tables.html	Description of tables from RFC 1942.

Figure 3.18
Tables used for page layout.

Figure 3.19
Page layout with
tables visible.

Forms

HTML forms provide a very simple way of obtaining input from the user. HTML is primarily a static description language. However, it does provide the concept of data entry via the FORM element. In later chapters we cover JavaScript and VBScript, which provide a more robust way of asking the browser user for input. Here we just briefly cover the concept of HTML forms.

In most cases, browser-side forms require help from the Web server. After the data is accepted from the user (via the browser), it is passed, via HTTP, to the server for processing. This is typically in the form of a CGI script. The server accepts the data and passes any response back to the browser as a new HTML page. Search engines typically make heavy use of this type of processing. The query is entered by the user, it is passed to the server, and the server passes back a dynamically built HTML-based page showing the result of the search.

The FORM tag starts the definition of an HTML form. The FORM element is a container, so all other elements encountered before the ending /FORM tag are part of the form. A form will typically contain a number of INPUT elements. The INPUT element currently provides only the basic GUI controls. A text box, radio button, check box, drop-list style combo box, push buttons, and an image control. Take a look at the following simple form-based page. Also, take a look at Fig. 3.20 to get an idea of what it produces.

```
<HTML>
<HEAD>
<TITLE>Forms Example</TITLE>
</HEAD>
<BODY>
<h3>A Browser Survey</h3>

<FORM action="http://www.WidgetWare.com/Submit_Survey"
      method="POST">
  <p>What is your favorite browser?</p>
  <select name="BROWSER" size="1">
     <option>Netscape Navigator</option>
     <option>Internet Explorer</option>
     <option>Netscape Communicator</option>
  </select>
    <p>What operating environment do you use?</p>
    <input type="radio"
        checked name="WINDOWS 3.X"
        value="V1">Windows 3.1<br>
    <input type="radio"
        name="OS"
        value="WINDOWS 32">
        Windows 95 or Windows NT<br>
    <input type="radio"
        name="OS"
        value="UNIX">
        UNIX<br>
    <input type="radio"
        name="OS"
        value="OS2">
        OS/2<br>
    <input type="radio"
        name="OS"
        value="MAX">
        Macintosh<br>
    <input type="radio"
        name="OS"
        value="OTHER">
        Other</p>
    <input type="submit"
        name="Submit"
        value="Submit">
    <input type="reset"
        name="Reset"
        value="Reset"></p>
</form>
</BODY>
</HTML>
```

Our example is a two question "survey." The form begins with the FORM element that specifies two attributes. The METHOD attribute can be either POST or GET. This describes how the data is passed to the server. The ACTION attribute specifies the location of a program on the server. In our case, it will be a simple script that formats the data, sends an email, and finally returns a page with the words, "Thank you for completing the survey." This will all occur when the user pushes the **Submit** button on the form, but we're getting ahead of ourselves.

The INPUT and SELECT elements are used to add the GUI controls to the form. The INPUT element handles everything except the drop-list-style combo box. It is created with the SELECT element. The different INPUT element control types are created by specifying the TYPE attribute.

In our example, we first use the SELECT element to provide a drop-list of possible browser options. Each possible selection is specified with the OPTION element. We then provide a series of radio buttons, allowing users to select their operating system. Notice that each control is given a name via the NAME attribute along with its corresponding value via the OPTION element or VALUE attribute. When the form is submitted to the server, the data will be passed in "NAME=VALUE" pairs.

The whole form, all of the NAME=VALUE pairs, is submitted to the server when the submit action occurs. The special INPUT TYPE of "Submit" provides a push button for this event. An INPUT TYPE of "Reset" resets the contents of each control on the form to its default value. These are specified in our example as the last two controls within the form. (See Fig. 3.20 and Table 3.13.)

TABLE 3.13

FORM Attributes

Attribute	Description
ACTION = *url*	Specifies a URL that is typically an executable program (e.g., CGI script).
METHOD = *value*	Specifies how the data is passed to the server. Either POST or GET.
OnSubmit = *event*	Specifies a JScript or VBScript procedure to call when the form is submitted.
TARGET = *window*	Specifies where to load the results of the submission of the form. The default is to load the results directly into the window that submitted the form. Other values include: the name of a specific window, _blank, _parent, _self, and _top

Figure 3.20
The FORM element in
action.

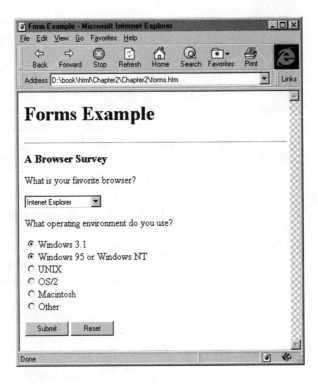

WEB RESOURCES:

URL	*Description*
http://agora.leeds.ac.uk/nik/Cgi/start.html	A good CGI tutorial.
http://www.yahoo.com/Computers/World_Wide_Web/CGI_Common_Gateway_Interface/	CGI resources from Yahoo.
http://junior.apk.net/~jbarta/tutor/forms/index.html	A good forms tutorial.

The Object Element

The HTML 3.2 OBJECT element enables the embedding of images, Java applets, documents, and ActiveX controls with HTML-based pages. We use the OBJECT element throughout the book, first to embed ActiveX controls and later to embed Java applets. Table 3.14 details the attributes available with the OBJECT element. We review the details in Chapter 5.

TABLE 3.14	Element	Description
Object Attributes	ALIGN = *type*	Specifies the alignment of the object. One of BASELINE, CENTER, LEFT, MIDDLE, RIGHT, TEXTBOTTOM, TEXTMIDDLE, TEXTTOP. The behavior is similar to the IMG element's ALIGN attribute.
	BORDER = *integer*	If the object is a hyperlink, this specifies the width of the outlining border.
	CLASSID = *url*	Specifies the ID of the object. ActiveX controls use the form: "CLSID:128-bit-class-identifier."
	CODEBASE = *url*	A URL that specifies where the object resides. This allows the downloading of the component to the local machine.
	CODETYPE = *type*	Specifies the media type.
	DATA = *url*	Describes data for the object. The format of the data is dependent of the object itself. This object uses this attribute to find object-specific data.
	DECLARE	Declares the object but does not actually instantiate it.
	HEIGHT = *integer*	The suggested height of the object. This allows the browser to draw an outline of where the object will display when loaded.
	HSPACE = *integer*	Indicates the amount of horizontal space that should be added to the object between any text to the object's left or right.
	NAME = *name*	The name of the object.
	SHAPES	Indicates shaped hyperlinks are supported.
	STANDBY = *text*	Provides text to display while the object is loading.
	TABINDEX = *n*	Sets the tabbing order index.
	TITLE = *text*	Sets the title of the form.
	TYPE = *type*	The Internet media type.
	USEMAP = *url*	The URL of an image map to use with the object.
	VSPACE = *integer*	Indicates the amount of vertical space that should be added to the object between any text on the top or bottom of the object.
	WIDTH = *integer*	The suggested width of the object. This allows the browser to draw an outline of where the object will display when loaded.

The MARQUEE Element

The MARQUEE element provides a simple mechanism to scroll text horizontally within your Web page. It is limited, however, as it can only scroll basic text. A more powerful marquee mechanism is provided by Microsoft's Marquee ActiveX control, which we cover in Chapter 5. Table 3.15 lists the MARQUEE element attributes. Here are some examples of using the MARQUEE element:

```
<p><marquee>
The MARQUEE element scrolls simple text.
</marquee></p>

<p><font size="30" color="tomato" face="Comic Sans MS">
<marquee bgcolor="ivory">
```

TABLE 3.15

MARQUEE Element Attributes

Name	Description
ALIGN = *align-type*	Specifies how surrounding text will align with the marquee. TOP—Text is aligned with the top of the image. CENTER—Text is aligned with the center of the image. BOTTOM—Text is aligned with the bottom of the image. LEFT—The image is left justified with any text flowing around it. RIGHT—The image is right justified with any text flowing around it.
BEHAVIOR = *value*	How the text will scroll. One of these values: SCROLL—The text will start on one side and scroll across and off the screen. This is the default. SLIDE—The text will scroll in from off the screen and will then stop and remain. ALTERNATE—The text will scroll in and then alternate back and forth across the screen.
BGCOLOR = *color*	The background color for the marquee.
DIRECTION = *value*	In which direction should the text initially scroll. Either LEFT or RIGHT.
HEIGHT = *n* WIDTH = *n*	The height and width of the marquee. This can be specified as pixels or a percentage of the screen.
HSPACE = *n*	Specifies the horizontal margin for the marquee.
VSPACE = *n*	Specifies the vertical margin for the marquee.
LOOP = *n*	Specifies how many the times the marquee should loop through its behavior.
SCROLLAMOUNT = *n*	How many pixels the marquee should scroll with each successive drawing.
SCROLLDELAY = *n*	How many milliseconds should elapse between each successive drawing.

```
You can however, change the bgcolor and characteristics of the font.
</marquee></font>

<p><marquee align="middle" behavior="slide" bgcolor="red">
This marquee aligns in the 'middle' and slides,
which means it stops when it reaches the left margin.
</marquee></p>

<p><font size="20" color="darkorchid" face="Arial">
<marquee bgcolor="wheat" direction="right">
Scrolling using DIRECTION=RIGHT, the color 'wheat' is quite pink.
</marquee></font></p>
```

Cascading Style Sheets

Style sheets are a major addition to the HTML language. They provide the Web developer with nearly total control over the placement, font, color, and size of text within a Web page. We achieved some of this by using tables, but style sheets make designing the page less of a "trial-and-error" exercise.

Style sheets enable the page designer to separate the "display" of information from the actual content. For example, you can set up the text of a page, and then modify its "style" independently. Another way to describe a style sheet is that it is a template. In Microsoft Word you can define a "template" that defines the font, size, and other attributes of a block of text within a Word document. By using such a standard, user-defined template, all of your documents will look similar.

As I'm writing this book, I have several "styles" that I use, all of which are part of a Word template. One style for chapter headings, three different paragraph headings, and miscellaneous ones for source code, notes, and figures. If I want to change the point size on the source code examples, all I have to do is change the source code "style" and the change is reflected throughout the document.

You get the idea. Style sheets are the same thing. They provide a way to specify the look of all documents that include the defined styles, and by tweaking a style attribute you can affect the look of an entire document. In a moment, we set up a style sheet that mimics a Microsoft Word template, but first let's go over the basics.

The CSS Standard

This section is based on the December 17, 1996, Cascading Style Sheet Level 1 W3C Recommendation. Internet Explorer implements the majority of the style sheet features described in this specification. At the time of this writing, Netscape's browsers do not support Cascading Style Sheets; instead, they are pursuing another JavaScript-based standard, called appropriately JavaScript Style Sheets. Our focus will be on the support provided by Internet Explorer. Eventually, both Netscape's and Microsoft's implementations will come together, and they will be based on the W3C's recommendation.

NOTE: *Netscape is working on its own implementation of style sheets call JavaScript-Based Style Sheets or JSSS for short. Netscape's specification indicates that it will fully support the CSS standard, so adding style sheet support with CSS should work with the two major browsers. For more information, here's the URL to the JSSS specification: http://developer.netscape.com/library/documentation/jsstyles.htm.*

Style Basics

Style sheets allow you to modify the attributes of a specific HTML element. Here's a simple example:

```
H1 { color: red }
```

That single line redefines the behavior of the H1 element. It sets the color of the text within any H1 tag to red. Just like that, you can affect the text in every H1 block within a page. The **color:** parameter is known as a *property* and **red** is the *value* of the property. Here's a more complex H1 style:

```
H1 { font: 16pt "Arial";
     font-weight: bold;
     margin-left: 0.25in;
     color: black }
```

Here we're setting the font, its weight, the margin, and color of the text. There are around 35 properties that you can specify when setting the attributes of a particular HTML element, and all elements support the use of style properties (if, of course, the browser supports CSS). Table 3.16 shows the font tag properties defined in the proposed recommendation. Internet Explorer supports the majority of these.

Style sheets can be added to a document in three basic ways: In-line, embedded, or linked.

TABLE 3.16

Font Properties

Property	Description	Values	Examples
font-size	The size of the font	Absolute or relative size. Relative sizes are to the parent	font-size: 14-pt font-size: 2.5 cm font-size: 150%
font-family	A list of desired font families. In most cases only one font should be defined.	The list can contain two types of fonts: A specific font family or a generic family	font-family: "Arial" font-family: 'monospace'
font-weight	The weight of the desired font	A keyword indicating the desired font weight. One of extra-light, light, demi-light, medium, demi-bold, bold, extra-bold, bolder, lighter	font-weight: bold font-weight: light
font-style	A special font style	A keyword indicating the desired style: normal, italic, small caps, oblique	font-style: normal font-style: italic small caps
font-variant	Varies the font to produce either normal or small caps text	Normal or small caps	font-variant: small caps
font	Specifies the major elements of a font. All within one property	The font-weight, font-style, font-size, line-height, font-family. Certain rules apply	font: bold 12-pt "Arial" font: sans-serif

In-line styles are used to affect a small portion of a document. The STYLE tag is specified within the tag itself (like an attribute). In-line specification is applicable only to the tag where it is specified. Here's a quick example:

```
<P STYLE = "font 24pt Arial">
  This Text is 24 point
<P>
This text probably isn't.
```

The in-line technique can be used to override global styles. If you want to affect a larger block of text, you can use the SPAN tag. It establishes a style over a series of tags until the end SPAN tag is found.

```
<SPAN STYLE = "color: red">
<P>
This text is Red.
<UL>
<LI STYLE = "color: green"> This Line is Green.
<LI> This line should be Red.
</UL>
</SPAN>
```

In-line styles are useful for those instances where you need to affect a small amount of text. A better method for managing your documents is to use either an embedded or linked block of styles. This makes it much easier to make global changes to all of your documents. The STYLE tag can be used at the top of the document to specify global styles for a specific page like this:

```
<STYLE TYPE="text/css">
<!--
    H1   { font: 20pt "Garamond";
           font-weight: bold;
           margin-left: 0.25in;
           color: red }
    H2   { font: 14pt "Arial";
           font-weight: bold;
           margin-left: 0.50in;
           color: blue }
    H3   { font: 12pt "Arial";
           font-weight: bold;
           margin-left: 0.75in;
           color: brown }
    PRE { font: 9pt"Courier New";
           font-weight: normal;
           margin-left: 0.75in;
           color: black }
    P    { font: 11pt "New Times Roman";
           margin-top: -0.25in;
           margin-bottom:0.0in;
           margin-left: 0.5in;
           margin-right: 0.5in
           font-weight: normal;
           line-height: 14pt;
           text-indent: 0.25in;
           color: black }
-->
</STYLE>
```

This is an example of an embedded style sheet. It must be embedded in each document that you want to affect with this style. Another option, for those styles that should affect several documents, is to "link" to a style sheet. The syntax for a link uses the LINK element that we discussed at the beginning of the chapter. In our previous example, you would place the text of the style definition into a file on the server, say STYLES.CSS, and you would then add this to the header section of each dependent document.

```
<LINK REL=STYLESHEET TYPE="text/css" SRC="http://www.yoursite.com/styles.css">
```

As the page is loaded, the browser will also load the styles specified in the LINK element. So, with one small change to STYLES.CSS, your whole site changes.

The STYLE tag has one parameter, TYPE, that specifies the specific MIME type used by CSS. This is always "**text/css**." The previous embedded style block sets up a style sheet that provides a Web content developer with a Microsoft Word-type template. The resulting output is very similar to what I see in Word as I'm working on this chapter. Figure 3.21 shows how a page using this style block looks in Internet Explorer.

Figure 3.21 is nice if you want to present text in the normal, book-oriented way, but this is just the beginning. Style sheets let you do just about anything. Using negative margins, you can overlap text, offset text just a little to create text shadows, you name it. The best place to see what CSS can do is to visit some of the sites on the Web that make use of the technology. Figures 3.22 and 3.23 show two examples from Microsoft's CSS area.

Figure 3.21
Our embedded style sheet in Internet Explorer.

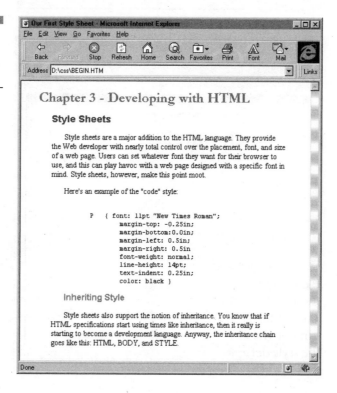

Figure 3.22
Cascading Style
Sheets in action.

Figure 3.23
The Veranda
TrueType font.

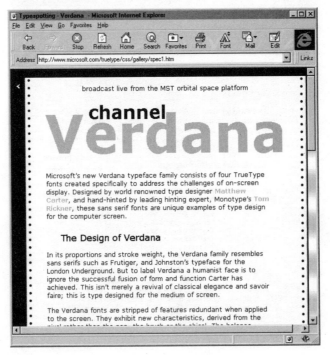

Figure 3.23 shows another feature of Internet Explorer: installable Web fonts. Microsoft makes a number of TrueType fonts available for free at their Website. Fonts are available for both Windows and Macintosh machines. Using CSS, you can quickly change the whole look of your Website. Add this statement to the header section of one of your Web pages.

```
<STYLE TYPE="text/css">
<BODY {font-family: "Comic Sans MS" }
</STYLE>
```

We added these statements *after* our other style statements in our Word-like template document from above. Figure 3.24 shows what it looks like now—quite a change for three lines of HTML code.

Why *Cascading* Style Sheets?

A good question, and we've just demonstrated the answer. Style sheet element properties are cumulative. In other words, they "cascade" as new def-

Figure 3.24

The Comic San MS font.

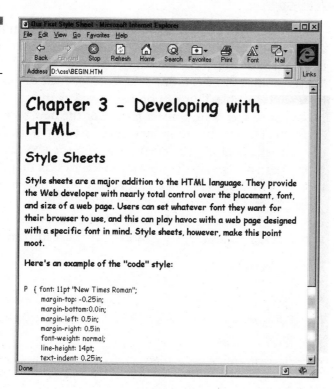

initions are encountered. This allows you to specify a basic set of styles, and then change them slightly in each page by changing only those styles that are different. Of course, at times there will be conflicts in priority of the specified elements. The CSS1 recommendation provides a specific "cascading order." See the specification for more details.

Pseudo Elements

There are certain items in publishing that are somewhat special. These attributes apply to the typography of a document, and are special in that they do not apply to the whole block of text. The CSS1 recommendation specifies two such items: the first line and first letter of a block of text. These two items are called pseudo elements, because there are no HTML elements that specify them. It is up to the browser implementation to support these two pseudo elements. Here's how they are used:

```
<STYLE TYPE="text/css">
P:first-line { font-size: 150% }
P:first-letter { font-size: 300% }
</STYLE>
```

This specifies that the first line of each paragraph will use a larger font, and that the first letter of the paragraph will use an even bigger font—just as we're used to seeing in print.

Cascading Style Sheets deserve a book of their own, and there will soon be several available. This section has served as an introduction to the technology. Style sheets are a major feature of the new browsers that will make designing and maintaining sites more efficient. What follows are the rest of the element property definitions from the CSS recommendation. The properties are separated into four categories: Font properties, which we looked at in Table 3.16; color and background properties are presented in Table 3.17; text properties are shown in Table 3.18; and finally, the CSS block properties are detailed in Table 3.19. These tables provide a quick reference to the many things that style sheets can affect in your Web pages.

WEB RESOURCES:

URL	Description
http://www.w3.org/pub/WWW/Style/css/	Cascading style sheet resources at W3C.
http://www.microsoft.com/truetype/	Free fonts, utilities, and information on CSS.

TABLE 3.17

Color and
Background
Properties

Property	Description	Values	Examples
color	Sets the color of the element.	A named color like red, blue, green, or an RGB triplet. The colors map to standard Windows VGA colors. There are 16.	color: navy color: maroon color: RGB(0,0,255)
background-color	Sets the background color of the element.	Either transparent or a single color.	background-color: transparent background-color: white
background-image	Sets the background image.	A URL.	background-image: url(blue.gif)
background-repeat	Determines how many times the background image will repeat.	A keyword: one of repeat, repeat-x, repeat-y, or no-repeat.	background-repeat: no-repeat background-repeat: repeat-1
background-attachment	If an image is specified should it remain fixed or scroll.	A keyword of either scroll or fixed.	background-attachment: scroll
background-position	If an image is specified, this determines its initial position.	A percentage, explicit length, or one of several keywords.	background-position: right
background	Shorthand way to specify multiple background values.	The value type indicates which background value is being set.	background: red fixed

Testing Your Pages

The HTML specification stipulates that browsers should ignore tags that they don't recognize. This facility allows browser developers to add functionality and basically enhance the HTML language without "breaking" other browsers. This also makes it easier to enhance the HTML language through the standards process (e.g., HTML version 4.0) without breaking any existing pages.

TABLE 3.18

Text Properties

Property	Description	Values	Examples
word-spacing	The spacing between words.	Normal or a specific length	word-spacing: normal word-spacing: 0.25 in
letter-spacing	The spacing between letters.	Normal or a specific length	letter-spacing: normal letter-spacing: 0.25 in
text-decoration	Text decorations such as underline, italics, and so on.	Keywords: none, underline, overline, line-through, blink	text-decoration: underline
vertical-align	Affects the vertical positioning of the element.	Keywords: baseline, sub, super, top, text-top, bottom, text-bottom, or a percentage	vertical-align: baseline
text-transform	Transforms the text of the element to the specified type.	Keywords: capitalize, uppercase, lowercase	H1 { text-transform: capitalize }
text-align	How text is aligned within the element.	Keywords: left, right, center, justify	text-align: right
text-indent	Specified the indent before the first line of text.	A length or a percentage	H1 { text-indent: 1 in }
line-height	The height between two adjacent lines.	The height in number, length, or percentage, or the keyword: normal	font-height: 1.2 font-height: 2 cm

However, this can make testing your pages difficult. If you misspell a tag or attribute you won't get any indication from the browser except that your page won't look right. Just remember this when testing your pages. If something doesn't work as you expect it to, carefully check the spelling and placement of the tags.

There are line-type syntax checkers for HTML pages that can help in several ways. They can test conformance with existing HTML standards, thus ensuring that your pages are viewable in the major browsers, and they can help with debugging your pages. They will report misspelled tags and the like. There are several available for free.

TABLE 3.19

Box Properties

Property	Description	Values	Examples
margin-left margin-right margin-top margin-bottom	Sets one or all of the extents of the element "box."	Either a length, percentage, or the keyword: auto.	H2 { margin-top: 0.5 in } P { margin-left: 1 cm }
margin	Shorthand for the margin properties.		
padding-left padding-right padding-top padding-bottom	Sets one of the padding extents of an element.	Either a length, percentage, or the keyword: auto.	H2 { padding-top: 0.5 m } P { padding-left: 1 cm }
padding	Shorthand for the margin properties.		
border-top-width border-right-width border-left-width border-bottom-width	Sets the width of an element border.	Either an explicit length or one of these keywords: thin, medium, or thick.	H1 { border-top-width: thick }
border-width	Shorthand for all of the border-width properties.		
border-color	The color of the elements border. Each of the four sides can be specified.	A valid color value.	P { border-color: red, blue, white, green }
border-style	Sets the style of the elements border. The style of each side can be specified.	One of: none, dashed, solid, double, groove, ridge, inset, or outset.	{ border-style: solid none }
border-right border-left border-top border-bottom	Shorthand to specify the width, style, and color of an element's border.		H3 { border-top: thick ridge blue }
border	Shorthand to specify the default width, style, and color for an element's border.		H3 { border: solid red }
float	Specifies how an element should	One of: left, right, or none.	IMG { float: left }

TABLE 3.19
(Continued)

Property	Description	Values	Examples
	display when sur-rounded by text. In other words, which sides should allow "float."		
clear	Specifies which sides of an element will not accept other "floating" elements.	One of left, right, none, or both.	IMG { clear: both }
width height	Specifies how the element should respond to scaling.	One of: a length, a percentage, or the keyword auto.	IMG { width: 100px }

WEB RESOURCES:

URL	Description
http://www.cre.canon.co.uk/~neilb/weblink/	WebLink information.
http://www.webtechs.com/html-val-svc/	WebTech's HTML validator.
http://ugweb.cs.ualberta.ca/~gerald/validate/	Another validator.
http://uts.cc.utexas.edu/~churchh/htmlchek.html	HTML Check information.

Summary

HTML is the primary language of the Web environment. It has evolved rapidly within the last few years as the Web environment has grown. HTML is "owned" by the World Wide Web Consortium, also know as the W3C. The W3C is headed by the inventor of the Web, Tim Berners-Lee. HTML version 3.2 is currently the most widely implemented version of HTML. It supports several new features that move Web page development from a word processing exercise to one that requires some programming knowledge to use all of its capabilities.

HTML is basically a page-description language. Through the use of HTML elements and attributes, text and images are described. A browser then interprets an HTML-based document and formats it for display on the user's machine. An element and its attributes describe how a particular piece of data (text or an image) is displayed. An element typically consists of beginning and ending tags. A tag is delimited with the less-than and greater-than characters. A simple example is the **bold** tag: <B>.

An HTML document consists of two sections: The header and the body. The header, which is surrounded by the begin header <HEAD> and end header </HEAD> tags, consists of elements that describe the content of the document. The body of an HTML document contains the data that will ultimately be displayed by the browser. The majority of HTML's elements affect text and image display.

Graphical images are an important aspect of HTML. The IMG element allows the embedding of images. The IMG element has a number of attributes that affect the alignment and display of images. Image maps provide a nontextual technique to navigate through a Website and are created with the MAP and AREA elements. Frames provide a way to break your site's presentation up into different categories or areas. Frames are typically used to provide more effective presentation and navigation through a Website. The HTML TABLE element also provides the Web-page designer with a tool to segregate a page's content. Frames, however, divide independent HTML documents, whereas tables operate on text and images.

Web pages have typically been static in that they display only information and do not accept input from the user. HTML Forms allow user input through the FORM and INPUT elements. A user can enter information which is submitted to a server-side script, thereby providing rudimentary interaction. A better mechanism for client-side interaction is provided by the new SCRIPT element. Scripting allows a Web-page developer to embed programmable logic within a page. This new facility turns an HTML-based page into an truly dynamic document. Scripting, however, is limited, unless it is used with programmable entities such as ActiveX controls and Java applets. The new OBJECT element supports the embedding of these application-level objects.

The HTML language continues to grow as vendors enhance the standards well before they are actually finalized. For this reason, the W3C has broken up the HTML standard into pieces called extensions. One of the more recent extensions pertains to Cascading Style Sheets. Style sheets are a major addition to the HTML language because they provide the Web developer with nearly total control over the placement, font, color, and size of text within a Web page. Style sheets can be added to a document in three basics ways: In-line, embedded, or linked. Style sheets are said to "cascade" because their effect is cumulative.

CHAPTER

JavaScript, VBScript, and the Object Model for Scripting

In the same way that components revolutionized Windows program development, components are revolutionizing the development of Web-sites for intranets as well as the Internet. Microsoft has devoted a lot of time and effort to ensure that the knowledge attained by existing Windows developers will not be wasted when moving over to Web-based development. Microsoft's languages and tools, such as Visual Basic, have been adapted to work in the Web environment.

In this chapter we explore the process of developing a Web page that uses HTML scripting to tie together HTML forms and controls. There is a dearth of information and a lot to learn on the way. First, we discuss the basics of embedding script in an HTML document. We then take a detailed look at JavaScript and VBScript, the two scripting languages available, their similarities, their differences, and where each is best suited. Once we're familiar with the scripting languages, we take a look at the Object Model for Scripting. This is a set of objects exposed by browsers that support scripting, allowing the script writer to easily interact with the browser, its documents, forms, and other characteristics. Then, with all of that under our belts, we can start to write some scripts to manipulate HTML Form objects and ActiveX controls.

We use both Internet Explorer and the ActiveX Control Pad extensively in this chapter. Currently, Internet Explorer is the only browser that supports VBScript, so you will definitely need it for the VBScript examples. The ActiveX Control Pad is a simple HTML-based tool that makes creation of script-based Web pages easier.

ActiveX Control Pad

ActiveX Control Pad is a simple HTML-based editor that provides a Script Wizard for adding scripts to your Web pages, the ability to insert ActiveX controls, and a new entity called an HTML Layout. We use the first two capabilities in this chapter and discuss HTML Layouts in Chapter 5. To get started in this chapter, start up ActiveX Control Pad. You should see something that resembles Fig. 4.1.

ActiveX Control Pad provides us with an initial blank HTML document. We discussed these basic elements in the last chapter. To get a feel for how we plan to develop the sample in this chapter, save the initial document as EXAMPLE1.HTM by selecting **Save As ...** from the **File** menu. Then without closing the document or shutting down ActiveX Control Pad, start up or switch to Internet Explorer and enter the full path and

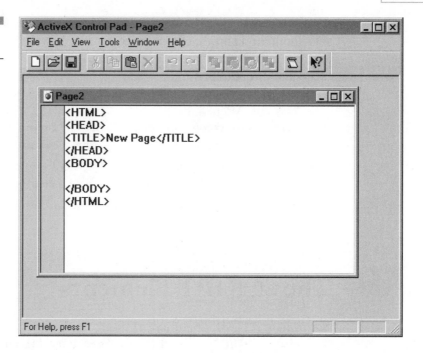

file name of this example (e.g., C:\CHAP4\EXAMPLE1.HTM) in the address field and hit Enter. Internet Explorer will load the page and the title bar should reflect the name in the title block.

Admittedly, our basic page is still pretty bland, so switch back to ActiveX Control Pad and let's make a few changes to the document. Change the TITLE block so that it looks like this:

```
<TITLE>My Scripting Example Page</TITLE>
```

Let's also make the page background white, the text color black, and add some text to the body of the document:

```
<BODY BGCOLOR="WHITE" TEXT="BLACK">
Hello World!
</BODY>
```

Once again save the file in ActiveX Control Pad. Then switch to Internet Explorer and click the Refresh button; this will reload our page. And…Voila! Our page is starting to look like something now. In the BODY block we added color to our page by setting the attributes of BGCOLOR and TEXT for background color and text color respectively. Most element blocks in HTML have attributes associated with them. We discussed basic HTML elements in the last chapter. However, we didn't focus much on those elements used by scripting. Let's do that first.

WEB RESOURCES:

URL	Description
http://www.microsoft.com/workshop/author/cpad/cpad.htm	ActiveX Control Pad overview and download page.
http://www.microsoft.com/ie	Internet Explorer page. Download your free copy here.
http://www.microsoft.com/workshop/author/cpad/tutorial.htm	ActiveX Control Pad tutorial.

The SCRIPT Element

Script in an HTML document typically resides within an element block. This element is aptly named SCRIPT (see Table 4.1). The definition of the script block is:

```
<SCRIPT [LANGUAGE=scripting language]
    [SRC=filename]
    [TYPE=MIME type]
    [FOR=object]
    [EVENT=event]>
</SCRIPT>
```

TABLE 4.1

Script Element
Attributes

Attribute	Description
LANGUAGE = *value*	Declares the scripting language used to parse and interpret the script. Either JavaScript or VBScript.
SRC = *filename*	Notifies the browser to load an external file that contains the script code. The scripts will be included just as if they had been included within the script block.
TYPE = *MIME type*	The MIME type for the script notation.
FOR = *object*	Used with the EVENT attribute to specify an object on which the event should operate.
EVENT = *event*	Used with the FOR attribute, EVENT specifies the event that must occur in the object for the script to execute.

All of the attributes of the script block are optional; however, the LAN-GUAGE attribute will commonly be declared just as a precaution so that the script will not be interpreted incorrectly. If not specified, the default for the LANGUAGE attribute is JavaScript. Once the LANGUAGE attribute has been specified in a SCRIPT block, all following SCRIPT blocks will be interpreted using that scripting language, until otherwise specified. For readability and clarity, it is easier just to specify the language for every script used, then there can be no confusion either by the page designer or the script interpreter.

The SRC attribute can be useful. Suppose over time you develop a script or scripts that you find yourself using in every page you create. Instead of importing the text for the script(s) into every page, you could create a file that contains the code for the script. That file could then be imported dynamically using the SRC attribute. This has two benefits. The first is that you don't have to modify several pages if you find that you made an error in one of the common scripts. The second is that as you add new functionally or scripts to the file, they are automatically included in all of your pages that import the script file.

The TYPE attribute will be defined only if you want to invoke a custom script interpreter to execute the script.

The FOR and EVENT attributes are used in combination to define an event that must occur in order for a script to execute. The most common use of these attributes is to execute a script when the page has been fully loaded. We discuss these two attributes in detail when we discuss the Object Model for Scripting later in this chapter.

Using the example from the previous section, add the following script within the BODY block of the document:

```
...
<BODY BGCOLOR="WHITE" TEXT="BLACK">
Hello World!
<SCRIPT LANGUAGE="JavaScript">
<!--
document.write( "This text written by JavaScript!" )
-->
</SCRIPT>
</BODY>
...
```

As you can see, our script will be interpreted as JavaScript as defined by the LANGUAGE attribute at the start of the script block. This example uses the Object Model for Scripting to write some text dynamically to our page.

Save your work in ActiveX Control Pad and refresh the page in Internet Explorer to see how it looks now. Once the page is loaded, you should have a white background, black text, and the text should read:

```
Hello World! This text written by JavaScript!
```

Of course, this script is not very useful. We could have accomplished the same task just by adding the text directly to the text in the body. But is does show how to define a script block within HTML. Before we continue it would be useful to learn more about the structure and syntax of the scripting languages. Since JavaScript is the default language of the SCRIPT block and is recognized by both Internet Explorer and Netscape's Navigator, we cover it first.

JavaScript a.k.a. JScript

As you can probably guess from the name, JavaScript is based on Sun's Java Language. However, it was not developed by Sun, but by Netscape. JavaScript is not Java! It is a compact, object-based language that attempts to use a structure and syntax similar to Java. Table 4.2 compares the two languages.

Although a de facto standard for Web page scripting, JavaScript was initially specified and implemented by Netscape (under the name LiveWire). Microsoft, on the other hand, had to reverse engineer their own version of JavaScript (called JScript), because it wasn't an open standard.

TABLE 4.2

Comparison of Java and JavaScript

JavaScript	Java
Interpreted and executed by the browser	Compiled on the server, downloaded by the browser, then executed by the Java Virtual Machine
Object-based, uses built-in predefined language, and browser-based classes. Classes can be created, but cannot inherit functionality from other classes.	Truly object-oriented, able to define classes and inherit from them.
Variables do not need to be declared and are loosely typed.	All variables must be declared and are strongly typed.
Cannot access client hard drive directly.	Cannot access client hard drive directly without being digitally signed.

JScript supports the current JavaScript language specification as defined by Netscape; however, Microsoft has begun to define its own extensions to the language. So just as each has attempted to define and control HTML, they are also vying for control of the JavaScript language. However, you can still write scripts that both browsers will execute by using the subset of the language that both support. This is what makes JavaScript an ideal scripting language for Internet Web pages.

However, if you are creating pages for an intranet (where you have more control over the client workstation), you may want to take advantage of one flavor or the other, and if Internet Explorer is your company's browser of choice, you might even look at using VBScript, which we cover later in this chapter.

NOTE: *In December, 1996, Netscape turned over the JavaScript language to a standards body in Europe. The European Computer Manufacturers Association (ECMA) is now responsible for developing a standard specification for the JavaScript language that all tool vendors can use. This should help a great deal in the area of script compatibility between browsers and other tools. JavaScript is a Netscape trademark so the eventual name may change.*

WEB RESOURCES:

URL	Description
http://www.microsoft.com/jscript	JScript Information.
http://www.microsoft.com/vbscript	VBScript Information.
http://www.ecmanews.ecma.ch/	ECMA information. Look under the TC-39 project.

If you are familiar with the syntax of Java or C++, you'll feel right at home with JavaScript. Since you can obtain the full language specifications for both JavaScript and JScript via the Internet, here we just cover the subset of JavaScript that is supported by both Navigator and Internet Explorer. This will give you enough confidence to investigate it in detail yourself.

Data Types and Values

Unlike Java or C++, JavaScript is a loosely typed language. No formal type declarations are given to variables. However, a variable can store any of five internal types of data. Those types, a brief description, and example values can be seen in Table 4.3.

The value stored in a variable is automatically converted by the interpreter when necessary. A number can be printed as a string, and a string can be evaluated as an integer without having to cast or convert it. An example of automatic type conversion would be:

```
x = 5 + "6" // the value of x will be number 11
x = "5" + "6" // the value of x will be the string "56"
```

In the first expression, the addition operator was determined to be a numeric addition because there was at least one numeric value in the

TABLE 4.3	Data Type	Description and Example Values
JavaScript Data Types	Numeric	There is no distinction between integer and decimals in JavaScript.
		Examples of numeric values are: 56 5.6 −5.6
	Logical	Like a Boolean in a formal language. The values are either true or false.
		Valid logical values are: true false
	String	A string is zero or more characters enclosed in double (") or single (') quotes. A string must be delimited by quotes of the same type.
		Example strings are: "Hello World!" 'Hello World!' "\"ActiveXpert\"\nIs an excellent book!"
		A string can contain special characters that represent nonprintable ASCII values.
		Special string characters are: \n indicates a new line character \r indicates a carriage return \t indicates a tab character \b indicates a backspace \f indicates a form feed \" indicates a double quote within the double quoted string
	Null	A special value, meaning that a variable has no assigned value.
	Object	As with any object-based language, an object is a container for values and functions that operate on said data.

expression. Therefore, the interpreter converted the string "6" to a number which was then added to the number 5 to produce the numeric value 11. In the second expression, the addition operator was determined to be a string concatenation operator because both operands were strings. The string "6" was appended to the string "5" producing the string "56".

Declarations

With JavaScript, variables do not have to be declared. When a variable is encounter for the first time, its type is determined by context and it is added to the interpreter's list of variables.

Names of variables in JavaScript must start with a letter (A—Z or a—z) or the underscore character ("_"). The rest of the variable name can be any combination of digits (0—9), and letters (A—Z and a—z). Here are examples of some legal variable names:

```
x
_temp3
LongVariableName
```

NOTE: *Like Java and C++, JavaScript is a case-sensitive language. The variable "abc" is not the same as the variable "ABC."*

The use of a variable is controlled by its scope. There are two scopes a variable can have in JavaScript: global or local. A variable that has global scope can be accessed by any script or function within the document. A variable with local scope can be used only by the script or function in which it is defined. By default all variables are global.

To declare a global variable you simply assign a variable a value. No explicit statement needs to be made to make it global to other SCRIPT blocks or functions. To declare a local variable, the var keyword precedes the variable name on its first use. Let's look at an example of some variable declarations:

```
gValue = 100      // declare a global variable
var lValue        // formally declare a local variable; value will
                  // be assigned later
var lValue = 10   // declare a local variable with a value or ten
```

Operators

JavaScript contains operators and syntax similar to Java or C++. The list of operators in descending order of precedence is shown in Table 4.4.

Objects

As an object-based language, JavaScript allows you to apply object-oriented techniques to your script writing by providing three built-in objects and

TABLE 4.4

JavaScript Operators with Precedence

Type	Operators
call, member	() []
negation/increment	! ~ – ++ ––
multiply/divide	* / %
addition/subtraction	+ –
bitwise shift	<< >> >>>
relational	< <= > >=
equality	== !=
bitwise-and	&
bitwise-xor	^
bitwise-or	|
logical-and	&&
logical-or	||
conditional	?:
assignment	= += –= *= /= %= <<= >>= >>>= &= ^= |=
comma	,

by allowing you to define and create your own. An *object* is one of the internal data types recognized by JavaScript. It is derived from a particular class that can contain properties, methods, and events. An object's properties, methods, and events are accessed using the following syntax:

ObjectName.Property

ObjectName.Method(...)

<SCRIPT LANGUAGE="JavaScript" FOR="*ObjectName*" EVENT="
Event(...)">

Properties are data members (or variables) contained within an object. The properties of an object can by set or read using the following syntax:

// set a property

ObjectName.Property = *value*

// get a property

value = *ObjectName.Property*

Methods are functions contained within an object. Methods typically take some action on the properties within an object, and can give feedback to the caller by returning data. A method would be called as follows:

...

value = *ObjectName.Method*()

if (*value* == true)

{

...

}

...

Events are notifications that an object makes public, and are called when something within that object triggers the event to fire. The JavaScript language provides no mechanism to define an event for a class created by the script writer. Instead, events are defined by components contained within the page, such as HTML form components, Java applets, ActiveX controls, or from the browser itself. When an event occurs, the script writer can tie a script to that event. One example of an event is the onLoad event fired by the browser after a page has been loaded:

```
<SCRIPT LANGUAGE="JavaScript" FOR="window" EVENT="onLoad()">
<!--
window.status = "Document has been loaded!" // update the status bar
-->
</SCRIPT>
```

Built-In Classes and Objects

There are three groups of objects available within JavaScript: objects provided by the JavaScript language; objects provided by the Object Model for Scripting (through the browser); and objects created by the script writer. Objects provided by the Object Model for Scripting can differ based on the browser used to view the page. We discuss the Object Model for Scripting and Internet Explorer in the following section. The JavaScript language itself, however, does provide us with three built-in classes: a string class, a math class, and a date class.

The String Class

Strings in JavaScript are objects (i.e., instances) of the string class. By default, variables that contain a string and even string literals themselves have several properties and methods that can be applied to them. The string object allows you to obtain the length of the string, parse the string, and format the string in HTML.

Table 4.5 contains a list of the properties and methods of the string class as well as a few examples of manipulating and formatting strings. For more detailed documentation of the string class, see the JavaScript language reference.

Several of the methods defined by the string class will format the string in HTML. To create a large, red, bold string, and display it on the page, you can do the following:

```
...
document.write( "ActiveX controls rule!".fontcolor("RED").fontsize(7).bold() )
...
```

The JavaScript interpreter treats the string "ActiveX controls rule!" as a string object. By using methods to set the color, size the font, and make it bold, we don't have to worry about the HTML elements and attributes that make that happen. JavaScript does it for us.

There are also methods of the string class that allow us to parse a string:

```
...
strWhole = "ActiveX controls rule!"
nIndex = strWhole.indexOf( " " ) // find index of the first space character
strSub = strWhole.substring( nIndex, strWhole.length ) // pull out "controls rule!"
document.write( strSub.toUpperCase() ) // display "controls rule!" in upper case
...
```

TABLE 4.5

Properties and
Methods of the
JavaScript String
Class

Properties	Description
length	Contains the length of the string.
Methods	
anchor(nameAttribute)	Makes the string an anchor.
big()	Same as the HTML <BIG> element.
blink()	The text should blink.
bold()	Bold the text.
charAt(index)	Return the character at the index specified.
fixed()	Uses a fixed font, such as Courier.
fontcolor(color)	The color of the font.
fontsize(size)	The size of the font.
indexOf(searchValue, [fromIndex])	Returns the numeric position of the substring.
lastIndexOf(searchValue, [fromIndex])	Returns the numeric position of the last occurrence of the substring.
link(hrefAttribute)	Specifies that the string is a link.
small()	Makes the text smaller.
strike()	Creates a string with strikethrough characters.
substring(nIndex, length)	Returns the specified substring.

By assigning a string value to `strWhole` the interpreter created a string object for us. Using the `indexOf` method, we find the first occurrence of a space in strWhole. We then use the substring method to retrieve the characters of `strWhole` from just after the first space to the end of the string. Lastly, taking advantage of the fact that `strSub` is also a string object, we use the `toUpperCase` method to display the string "controls rule!" in upper case.

NOTE: *Strings in JavaScript, like Java or C++, are indexed starting at zero.*

The Math Class

The second built-in class in JavaScript is the Math class. Unlike the string class, the Math class does not require a variable or a literal to operate. It is a static class, automatically instantiated by the interpreter and globally available. You access properties and methods of the Math class like this:

Math.*property*

Math.*method*(...)

The Math class offers a number of math constants as read-only properties. Also, some common mathematical functions are available as methods of the Math class. Table 4.6 lists the properties and methods exposed by the Math class.

Math statements often will be grouped together in a calculation. As you can imagine, it can be tedious to type the term "Math." in front of every property and method. JavaScript has a built in keyword, `with`, that can alleviate the tedium. For example the statements:

TABLE 4.6	**Properties**	**Methods**
Properties and Methods of the JavaScript Math Class	E	abs(number)
	LN2	acos(number)
	LN10	asin(number)
	LOG2E	atan(number)
	LOG10E	ceil(number)
	PI	cos(number)
	SQRT1_2	exp(number)
	SQRT2	floor(number)
		log(number)
		max(number1, number2)
		min(number1, number2)
		pow(base, exponent)
		random()
		round(number)
		sin(number)
		sqrt(number)
		tan(number)

```
...
x = Math.PI * Math.pow( 5, 2 )
y = Math.sin( 45 )
z = Math.random()
a = x+y+z
...
```

can be written shorthand as:

```
...
with( Math )
{
  x = PI * pow( 5, 2 )
  y = sin( 45 )
  z = random()
  a = x+y+z
}
...
```

In this case, any property or method that does not specifically state the object to use will use the Math object.

The Date Class

The last built-in class in JavaScript is the Date class. It is different from the String or Math class in that its creation has to be explicit. There are three ways to create a Date object. The first creates a date object that contains today's date and time:

```
// creates today's date and time
dateObj = new Date()
```

The second creates a date object containing a specific date specified by a string parameter:

```
dateObj = new Date("[weekday,] month day, year [hours][:minutes][:seconds][GMT+hhmm]")
```

The third creates a date object containing a specific date specified by numeric date parameters with the numeric time parameters optional. If one of the time parameters is not specified, the value for that parameter will be set to zero:

```
dateObj = new Date(year, month, day [, hours][, minutes][, seconds ])
```

JavaScript handles dates very similar to the way Java handles dates. In fact, both share many of the same methods as shown in Table 4.7. Internally both store dates as the number of milliseconds since the base date

TABLE 4.7

Properties and
Methods of the
JavaScript Date
Object

Properties	Methods
None	getDate() getDay() getHours() getMinutes() getMonth() setDate(dayValue) setHours(hoursValue) setMinutes(minutesValue) setMonth(monthValue) setSeconds(secondsValue) getSeconds() getTime() getTimezoneOffset() getYear() parse(dateString) setTime(timeValue) setYear(yearValue) toGMTString() toLocaleString() UTC(year, month, day [, hours] [, minutes] [,seconds])

of January 1, 1970, 00:00:00. Attempting to create a date prior to 1970 will produce unexpected and undocumented results.

All date constructors and methods that accept the date as a string accept the IETF standard date syntax of:

```
"[weekday,] month day, year [hours][:minutes][:seconds][GMT+hhmm]"
```

All date constructors and methods that accept the date as numbers accept the following values as valid:

■ Any year >= 1970

■ The month between 0–11

■ The day between 1–31

■ Hours between 0–23

■ Minutes between 0–59

■ Seconds between 0–59

As stated earlier, a date object must be created using the new statement. However, there are two static methods supplied by the Date object. Like the Math class, these two methods are globally available and must be preceded by the text "Date."

Date.UTC(year, month, day [, hrs] [, min] [, sec])

Date.parse(dateString)

Both static methods return the number of seconds that have occurred since the base date. Both default to GMT; however, with `Date.parse` you can specify an offset from GMT within the date string.

JavaScript provides the String, Math, and Date classes by default, but it also gives script writers the ability to write their own.

JavaScript Functions

A *function* in JavaScript is a named group of statements that perform a task. The definition of a function is as follows:

function *function-name*([arg 1] [, arg 2] [,...])

{

...

[return [*value*]]

}

A function begins with the function keyword followed by the name of the function. Any arguments necessary for the function are contained in parenthesis following the function name. No data types are given to the parameters because JavaScript performs any necessary data-type conversions. JavaScript statements executed by the function are enclosed in curly braces { }.

Functions can also return values. Return types specifications are not required as JavaScript will convert the value to the correct type:

```
function Add( value1, value2 )
{
  return value1 + value2
}
```

A function can accept more parameters than it is formally declared to accept by accessing the arguments as an array. The function keyword used to declare a function is actually declaring a variable that is an object. One of the properties of the function is its arguments. Let's look at an example of a function that accepts a variable number of strings and calls another function named `DisplayParagraph`:

```
<SCRIPT LANGUAGE="JavaScript">
<!--
DisplayStrings( "JavaScript", "is the scripting language", "we are studying" )
```

```
function DisplayStrings( strList )
{
  for( var 1Count = 0; 1Count < DisplayStrings.arguments.length; 1Count++ )
  {
   DisplayParagraph( DisplayStrings.arguments[1Count] )
  }
}

function DisplayParagraph( strLine )
{
  var strTemp = "<P>" + strLine + "</P>"
  document.write( strTemp )
}
-->
</SCRIPT>
```

Via the declaration of the function, `DisplayStrings` has become an object that has a property called "arguments." We can find out how many arguments there are by accessing the length property of the arguments property. Then it's just a simple matter of looping through the arguments, accessing the arguments property as an array to obtain each string passed in and calling the additional `DisplayParagraph` function. The preceding example will produce output on our Web page that looks like:

```
JavaScript
is the scripting language
we are studying
```

JavaScript has three rules of scope for functions. There is scope within a single SCRIPT block, within multiple SCRIPT blocks, and for functions called by events.

You may have noticed in the previous example that the call to `DisplayStrings` was made before the function had been declared; likewise for the call to `DisplayParagraph` in the `DisplayStrings` function. Function order and scope within a single SCRIPT block is not important. The JavaScript interpreter parses the SCRIPT block first, setting up the function and variable tables before any script is executed. This allows function declarations and calls to those functions to occur in any order within the same SCRIPT block.

If we were to place each function in its own SCRIPT block and the call to `DisplayStrings` in yet another SCRIPT block, we would have to order the blocks as follows:

```
<SCRIPT LANGUAGE="JavaScript">
<!--
function DisplayParagraph( strLine )
{
  var strTemp = "<P>" + strLine + "</P>"
  document.write( strTemp )
}
```

```
-->
</SCRIPT>

<SCRIPT LANGUAGE="JavaScript">
<!--
function DisplayStrings( strList )
{
  for( var 1Count = 0; 1Count < DisplayStrings.arguments.length; 1Count++ )
  {
   DisplayParagraph( DisplayStrings.arguments[1Count] )
  }
}
-->
</SCRIPT>

<SCRIPT LANGUAGE="JavaScript">
<!--
DisplayStrings( "JavaScript", "is the scripting language", "we are studying" )
-->
</SCRIPT>
```

When functions occur within multiple script blocks, JavaScript requires forward declaration of those functions. Once declared, a function is global to any SCRIPT block that follows the declaration.

The scope of scripts linked to events is different still:

```
<SCRIPT LANGUAGE="JavaScript" FOR="window" event="onLoad()">
<!--
DisplayStrings( "JavaScript", "is the scripting language", "we are studying" )
-->
</SCRIPT>

<SCRIPT LANGUAGE="JavaScript">
<!--
function DisplayStrings( strList )
{
  for( var 1Count = 0; 1Count < DisplayStrings.arguments.length; 1Count++ )
  {
   DisplayParagraph( DisplayStrings.arguments[1Count] )
  }
}
-->
</SCRIPT>

<SCRIPT LANGUAGE="JavaScript">
<!--
function DisplayParagraph( strLine )
{
  var strTemp = "<P>" + strLine + "</P>"
  document.write( strTemp )
}
-->
</SCRIPT>
```

In this example, the functions are not forward declared, but this doesn't present a problem because all SCRIPT blocks are interpreted before any events on the page are fired. Therefore, all the functions were added to the function table before the call to `DisplayStrings` could be made by the window's `onLoad` event.

Built-In Functions

JavaScript provides three built-in functions:

eval(*string*)

parseInt(*string, [radix]*)

parseFloat(*string*)

The `eval` function takes, as a parameter, a string that represents a JavaScript expression, statement, or series of statements separated by semi-colons. Expressions are evaluated, and statements will be performed just as if they had occurred within SCRIPT blocks within the HTML document. The string can even contain variable and object references. The `eval` function is like having your own personal scripting engine available after the page has been initially parsed. For example, if you had a text area and a button on a page, JavaScript statements and expressions could be entered into the text area. When the button is pressed, an `onClick` event would fire that would query the text area, and perform the JavaScript entered. Not necessarily a practical example, but it does show the power of the `eval` function. We take a look at an example of using the `eval` function in a moment.

The `parseInt` and `parseFloat` functions are used to explicitly convert a string representation of a number into its numeric value. Why would you need these functions if the JavaScript interpreter automatically converts data types from strings to numbers? These two functions are useful when validating form fields. By passing a string from an entry field into the `parseInt` or `parseFloat` function, you can validate that a field contains an integer or floating point number before submitting the form.

Functions as Classes

Previously we talked about the String, Math, and Date classes provided by JavaScript. Well, functions give the script writer a method for defining new classes. As we saw earlier via the argument list, a function is simply an object. All we have to do is extend the definition of that object by adding properties and methods.

Let's create a class to hold contact information. Initially our class will have properties to hold a name, company, and title. First, let's create the class and its properties:

```
<SCRIPT LANGUAGE="JavaScript">
<!--
// define the Contact class and constructor
function Contact( name, company, title )
{
  this.name = name
  this.company = company
  this.title = title
}
-->
</SCRIPT>
```

As in Java or C++, the keyword "this" refers to a specific instance of the class `Contact`. The properties of the class are created dynamically just like JavaScript variables. Simply assigning a value to a property name triggers the JavaScript interpreter to create that property. Let's add a second SCRIPT block to create an object called `myContact`:

```
<SCRIPT LANAGUE="JavaScript">
<!--
myContact = new Contact( "Jim Crespino", "WidgetWare", "CEO" )
-->
</SCRIPT>
```

This creates the object `myContact` from the `Contact` class and assigns the property values. A contact isn't much good without an address, so let's create an address class and add an address property and parameter to our contact class:

```
...
// define the Address class and constructor
function Address( street1, street2, city, state, zip )
{
  this.street1 = street1
  this.street2 = street2
  this.city = city
  this.state = state
  this.zip = zip
}

// define the Contact class and constructor
function Contact( name, company, title, address )
{
  //...
  // Address class as a property of Contact
  this.address = address
}
...
```

Again we use the new statement to create the objects. First we create an object called clientAddress from our Address class and then use that object in the constructor of the Contact class:

```
. . .
clientAddress = new Address( "1010 Wilshire", "3rd floor", "Boston", "MA", "02134" )
myContact = new Contact( "Jim Crespino", "WidgetWare", "CEO", clientAddress )
. . .
```

About the only thing that we have left to do is add a method to each of our classes to display the data in the objects on our page:

```
. . .
// define a function to display strings as paragraphs
function DisplayParagraph( strLine )
{
document.write( "<P>" + strLine + "</P>" )
}

// display the information from the Address class
function DisplayAddress()
{
  DisplayParagraph( this.street1 )
  DisplayParagraph( this.street2 )
  DisplayParagraph( this.city + " " + this.state + " " + this.zip )
}

// define the Address class and constructor
function Address( street1, street2, city, state, zip )
{
    . . .
    // link the Display method to DisplayAddress
    this.Display = DisplayAddress
}

// display the information from the Contact class
function DisplayContact()
{
  DisplayParagraph( this.name )
  DisplayParagraph( this.company )
  DisplayParagraph( this.title )

// call the Display method of the address object
this.address.Display()
}

// define the Contact class and constructor
function Contact( name, company, title, address )
{
    . . .
    // link the Display method to DisplayContact
    this.Display = DisplayContact
}
. . .
```

This time around, we created two functions, one to display address information and another to display contact information. Those functions become methods within the classes by creating a method name—in our case Display—and assigning it the function name. Notice that the parentheses are not included when we assign the function name to the method name. We are not calling the functions at this time; instead we are treating the functions as the objects that they are, and just doing an assignment of one object to another. Also, the functions `DisplayContact` and `DisplayAddress` are still globally visible outside the class definition, but an error will occur if called directly, because the reference to "this" within each of those classes will be invalid.

The only thing left to do is call the Display method of our `myContact` object. That will display the contact information that in turn calls the Display method of the address object to display the address information:

```
...
myContact = new Contact( "Jim Crespino", "WidgetWare", "CEO", clientAddress )
myContact.Display()
...
```

The output from our example should produce:

```
Jim Crespino
WidgetWare
CEO
1010 Wilshire
3rd floor
Boston MA 02134
```

Statements

JavaScript contains statements and syntax similar to Java or C++. Since that is the case, we will do little more than list the statements as presented in Table 4.8.

Internet Explorer and the Object Model for Scripting

JavaScript is a very powerful scripting language; however, it lacks some of the basic functionality that programmers take for granted, such as input

TABLE 4.8

JavaScript
Language
Statements

Statement	Description and Syntax

if...else	Conditionally executes statements depending on a condition.
	
	 if (*condition*)
	 {
	 statement1...
	 }
	 [else
	 {
	 statement2...
	 }]

for	Executes a group of statements while the specified expression is true.
	
	 for (*initialization; expression; increment*)
	 {
	 statements...
	 }

while	Executes a group of statements while the specified condition is true.
	
	 while (*expression*)
	 {
	 statements...
	 }

break	Exits from the current loop. Used in for, while, and for...in loops. Break
continue	Stops the execution of the current iteration of the loop and continues with the next. Used in for, while, and for...in loops. Continue
return	Returns control from a function to the caller, optionally returning a value. return [*expression*]
for...in	Executes a group of statements for each element in an array. for (*variable* in [*object* | *array*]) *statements*...
new	Creates a new class object. new *ClassConstructor*
this	Refers to an instance of a class object. this.{*ObjectProperty*	*ObjectMethod()*}

with	Sets the default object for a group of statements.
	
	 with (*object*)
	 {
	 statements...
	 }

	Statement	Description and Syntax
TABLE 4.8 (Continued)	function	Declares a function.

		Function *function-name*([*arg 1*] [, *arg 2*] [,...])
		{
		...
		[return [*value*]]
		}

	var	Declares a local variable.
		var *VariableName* [=*value*]
	//	Single comment line.
		[*statement*] // *Comment*
	/*...*/	Multiple comment lines.
		/* *Comments...* */

The * denotes an array of objects.

and output. JavaScript natively has no means of displaying information, receiving user input, or reading from or writing to files on the client system. That functionality is provided by objects within the Object Model for Scripting. Web browsers that support scripting must support the Object Model for Scripting. Both Internet Explorer and Netscape's Navigator support the Object Model for Scripting.

The *browser* is the means by which users view and interact with Web pages. The Object Model for Scripting provides objects to JavaScript that can be used to write information dynamically to the page. We've seen some demonstrations of this in some of the examples in previous sections. Events that occur on the page through interaction with the user are also provided by objects within the Object Model for Scripting. That gives the script writer the ability to tie scripts to events to make Web pages interactive.

The Object Model for Scripting is actually a hierarchy of objects. The root object is the Window. In turn, it contains the other objects as properties. By having access to the window object, you can access all other objects in the Object Model. A graphical representation of the object hierarchy is shown in Fig. 4.2. We take a brief look at each of the objects in the Object Model.

Figure 4.2
Internet Explorer
Object Model.

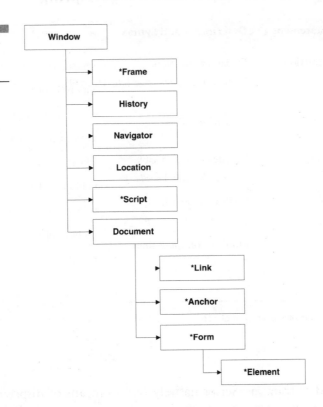

The Window Object

The *window object* is a representation of the browser's window. As Fig. 4.2 shows, each window contains a number of other objects. Each window has an array of frame objects where each frame is itself a window object. The window object contains a history object that exposes various items of history information. The navigator object contains information about the hosting browser. Other objects that are part of the window object are Location, Script, and the Document. We cover each of these in the following sections. To start off, Table 4.9 details each Window object property, method, and event.

The properties, methods, and events of the window object allow a script to determine and, to some extent, control its environment.

It is automatically instantiated by the interpreter, so it is available to all scripts within an HTML document. In JavaScript, properties and methods of objects are referenced using the Object.{Property|Method()} syntax. With the window object, it is as if an implied "with" block has been

TABLE 4.9

Properties, Methods, and Events of the Window Object

Properties	Description
defaultStatus	The default status text for the status bar.
document	The document object of the current window.
frameName	Accesses a specific frame by its name.
frames[]	The frames array of the current window.
history	The history object of the current window.
location	The location object of the current window.
name	The name of the current window.
navigator	The navigator object of the current window.
opener	The Window object of the window that opened the current window.
parent	The Window object of the parent.
self	The Window object of the current window.
status	The status text.
top	The Window object of the topmost window.

Methods	Description
alert(string)	Displays a message box.
clearTimeout(timerID)	Clears the timer.
close()	Closes the window.
confirm(string)	Displays a message with an **OK** and **Cancel** button.
navigate(urlString)	Navigate to the specified URL.
open(urlString, targetString, attributeString)	Opens a new window.
prompt(promptString [, defaultString])	Prompts the user for input.
setTimeout(exprString, milliseconds [, scriptLanguage])	Sets a timer to call a specified function after user-defined interval.

Events	Description
onLoad	Fired after the HTML has been parsed.
onUnload	Fired when the window is unloaded.

applied to all SCRIPT blocks. Typically you would access a property of the window object using:

```
window.alert( "hello" )
```

But the following is also valid:

```
alert( "hello")
```

The Window object is automatically applied to the alert method by the interpreter. This is the only object in the Object Model that works this way. All other objects must be explicitly referenced.

There are several properties and methods of the Window object that you should become familiar with. The first is the alert method. This method takes a string as a parameter and displays that string in a modal message box over the browser's window. This would typically be used to make the user aware of some information, but it is also an excellent debugging tool. You can use the alert method to display variable information at various points in your script. Not pretty, but functional! (Actually, there is a debugger available now for debugging scripts in Internet Explorer, and we discuss it at the end of this chapter.)

Another important feature of the window object is the onLoad and onUnload events—by tying scripts to these events, you can initialize and un-initialize your scripts. An example would be:

```
<SCRIPT LANGUAGE="Javascript" FOR="window" EVENT="onLoad()">
<!--
   gColor = "Red" // create and initialize a global variable
-->
</SCRIPT]

<SCRIPT LANGUAGE="Javascript" FOR="window" EVENT="onUnload()">
<!--
   // Save state by writing a cookie
   document.cookie = gColor
-->
</SCRIPT>
```

The onLoad event is fired after the page has been fully loaded by the browser. Each page in each frame will receive an onLoad event after that page has been loaded.

NOTE: *A "cookie" (in Web terms anyway) is a string value that can be saved on the browser's local machine. It is one way for certain aspects of a Web page to persist, at least with JavaScript. For example, on your site's main page, you might allow a user to specify*

the background and foreground colors that they would like to use when viewing the pages on your site. As part of the selection process, you would save their default colors as cookies. Then when the user visited your site again, some JavaScript code would retrieve the color values from their local machine's cookie cache and set the colors. Basically, cookies allow you to store and retrieve a small amount of user-specific data.

The last two features that we need to be familiar with are the frame array property and top property. These two are often used in conjunction. The *frames property* is actually an array of window objects that represent frames within the document. The elements of the array can be accessed by name or by index. The name comes from the NAME attribute specified in the definition of the frame. Let's assume we have an HTML document that defines three frames—Moe, Larry, and Curly. Those frames can either be accessed as:

```
window.Moe
window.Larry
window.Curly
```

or as:

```
window.frame[0]   // Moe
window.frame[1]   // Larry
window.frame[2]   // Curly
```

As stated earlier, each element of the frame array is itself a window object. Each of these items would have a document object, a name property, and so forth. This is especially useful if you need to call a script or access a form in another frame.

It is likely that the HTML document that your scripts are defined in will not be the document that defines the frames for the window. If that is the case, and you need to access another frame, you will have to use the top property of your window to get to the window that defines the frames. Assume you are writing a script in the document that will be loaded into the Moe frame, and you need to get to a form in the Larry frame. To get to Larry from Moe you would use:

```
Top.Larry....
```

"Top" refers to the document that defines the frames. "Larry" refers to the window created by the <FRAME> tag with the NAME attribute of "Larry". With the window object of that frame, we have access to all of the other objects contained within the window object, such as forms, scripts, links, and the like.

The window lets us do a lot, but we will likely be interested in the contents of the document, which is represented by the document object.

The Document Object

The *document object* is a representation of the HTML document currently loaded in the browser. Its properties and methods are listed in Table 4.10.

Properties	Description
aLinkColor	The color of the active links in the document.
anchors[]	An array of anchor objects.
bgColor	The document's background color.
cookie	Any cookie associated with the document.
fgColor	The foreground color of the document.
forms[]	An array of forms within the document.
lastModified	The date the document was last modified.
links[]	An array of links within the document.
linkColor	The color of links in the document.
location	The location object.
referrer	The URL of the referring document.
title	The document's title.
vLinkColor	The visited link color.

Methods	Description
clear()	Closes the document stream and flushes it to the screen.
close()	Closes the document stream and updates the screen.
open()	Opens the document to allow streamed output.
write(string)	Writes the string into the document.
writeln(string)	Writes the string into the document and appends a new line.

The document objects allows us to write dynamically to the page as it is loading, and to access all of the forms, links, and anchors within the document.

As you've already seen in a number of our examples the document object exposes a write method to allow the script writer to dynamically create text on the page. You simply call `document.write` and pass as a parameter the string that you wish to display.

The forms, links, and anchors are stored in properties by the same name. The forms, links, and anchors properties are arrays of form, link, and anchor objects.

The forms array is similar to the frames array in that it can be accessed either by name or by index. Again the name comes from the NAME attribute set in the form definition. In the next section, we create a form to represent a calculator. In that example, we access the form and the elements in the form by name.

The Form Object

The *form object* represents an HTML form. The forms property of the document object is a list of form objects (see Table 4.11). The forms can be accessed using either a zero-based index into an array or directly using the name specified in the NAME attribute of the form.

TABLE 4.11

Properties and Methods of the Form Object

Properties	Description
action	Sets the action to perform when the form is submitted.
elements[]	An array of elements on the form.
encoding	The encoding of the form. This maps to the ENCTYPE attribute of the FORM element.
method	Determines how the form should be sent to the server.
target	The target window that will display the result of the submission.

Methods	Description
submit()	Submit the form.

Events	Description
onSubmit	Fired when the form is submitted.

The two most important features of the Form object are the element property and the `submit` method.

The *element property* contains an array of element objects. The elements in the array refer to the buttons, text areas, and so forth, that are contained in the form. This array can also be accessed either by name or by index. Again, the name used to access an element comes from the NAME attribute set in the <INPUT> tag for that element.

Assume for a moment that we have a Web page that contains a single form in which the NAME attribute is set to "Feedback". Within the form there are two elements, a text area and a submit button with NAME attributes of "Comments" and "Submit", respectively. To access the two elements from within a script in the document, you would use the following commands:

```
document.Feedback.Comments
document.Feedback.Submit
```

or

```
// access the Comment element on the Feedback form
document.form(0) .element(0)

// access the Submit element on the Feedback form
document.form(0) .element(1)
```

Obviously, using the names to a form and its elements is easier and much more readable.

The submit button is a common element on a form. It provides a way for the data of a form to be sent to a server for processing. One of the most common uses of scripts is to validate the fields of a form before sending them off to a server. This provides two benefits: The server doesn't process bogus data, and users don't have to wait for a response that tells them something was entered incorrectly. By tying a script to the `onClick` event of a submit button, you can validate the form and then call the submit() method of the form if everything is correct.

Using the Feedback form again, you would use the following script to validate the comments that have actually been entered before sending the comments off to the server to be stored:

```
<SCRIPT LANGUAGE="JavaScript" FOR="window.document.Feedback.Submit" EVENT="onClick">
<!--
if ( document.Feedback.Comments <> "" )
{
  // Submit the form if comments exist
  document.Feedback.submit()
```

```
}
else
{
  // Tell the user they must enter comments first
  alert( "Please enter comments before choosing Submit!" )
}
-->
</SCRIPT>
```

The Element Object

The *element object* represents an HTML form element. A form element is defined in HTML using the <INPUT> tag. See Table 4.12.

The element object has properties, methods, and events that allow you to interact with any type of HTML form element. However, only certain properties, methods, and events are valid for certain form elements. For example, an error will occur if you use the select method on a button element, because it is not a selection list.

Events of the element object will be fired when an action occurs within a form element. The onBlur event notifies that an element is losing focus. The onChange event notifies that the value of a text field has changed. The onClick event notifies that a button, radio button, or check box has been clicked. The onFocus event notifies that an element has received focus. And the onSelect event notifies that an item has been selected from a selection list.

The methods of the element object allow a script to make an event occur. The blur method moves focus to the next element in the tab order. The click method performs a mouse click on a button, radio button, or check box. The focus method places focus on a particular element. And the select method selects an item from a list.

The properties of the element object allow you to determine the state of a form element. You can retrieve the value of a text area, see if a check box is checked, or get the selected index from a selection list.

The most common usage of these properties, methods, and events is in the validation of forms. There are two types of validation that can be done to forms. There is field-level validation and there is form-level validation. If you performed field-level validation of a script you would capture the onBlur event of a required field, validate it in the script, and if an invalid entry had been made then you would place focus back on the field. With form-level validation, the user would fill out all of the fields of a form and then click a button when the form is complete. By capturing the button-

TABLE 4.12

Properties and
Methods of the
Element Object

Properties	Description
checked	The checked state of a element.
defaultChecked	The default state of the element.
defaultValue	The default value of the element.
form	The parent form object.
length	The number of options in the element.
name	The name of the element.
options	Retrieves the options attributes for the element.
selectedIndex	Determines which option is selected in the element.
value	The value of the element.

Methods	Description
blur()	Clears the focus.
click()	Clicks the element.
focus()	Sets focus to the element.
select()	Selects the contents of the element.

Events	Description
onBlur	Fired when the element loses focus.
onChange	Fired when the element changes.
onClick	Fired when the element is clicked.
onFocus	Fired when the element gains focus.
onSelect	Fired when the element's contents are selected.

click event, you can spin through the required fields, validate them, and if one is wrong, notify the user and place focus back on that field.

The Link Object

The *link object* represents a link within an HTML document. A link is defined in HTML using the <A> tag with the HREF attribute set. See Table 4.13.

TABLE 4.13

Properties and
Methods of the
Link Object

Properties	Description
hash	Hash portion of the URL.
host	Host portion of the URL.
hostname	Hostname portion of the URL.
href	Href portion of the URL.
pathname	Pathname portion of the URL.
port	Port portion of the URL.
protocol	Protocol portion of the URL.
search	Search portion of the URL.
target	

Events	Description
onClick	Fired when the link is clicked.
onMouseMove	Fired when the mouse moves over the link.
onMouseOver	

The links property of the document object contains a list of link objects. All links within an HTML document are contained within the list and are accessed using a zero-based index.

All properties within the link object are read only. All properties return a part of the URL for the link set by the HREF attribute of the <A> tag, except for the target property that returns the value of the TARGET attribute (see Table 4.14).

The link object also defines three events that can occur within an link tag. The following example creates a link on the page and updates the windows status line with a teaser for the link:

```
<A HREF="http://www.widgetware.com" onMouseOver="Teaser()">WidgetWare</A>
<SCRIPT LANGUAGE="JavaScript">
<!--
function Teaser()
{
  windows.status = "Visit widgetware to view the ActiveX" FAQs
}
-->
</SCRIPT>
```

TABLE 4.14

Example Link
Property Values

Property	Example URL	Returns
hash	http://www.widgetware.com#user	#user
host	http://www.widgetware.com:80	www.widgetware.com:80
hostname	http://www.widgetware.com:80	www.widgetware.com
href		the entire URL
pathname	http://www.widgetware.com/activex	activex
port	http://www.widgetware.com:80	80
protocol	http://www.widgetware.com	http:
search	http://www.widgetware.com?faq	?faq

The Anchor Object

The *anchor object* represents an anchor within an HTML document. An anchor is defined in HTML with the <A> tag (see Table 4.15).

The anchors property of the document object contains a list of anchor objects. All anchors within an HTML document are contained within the list and are accessed using a zero-based index.

Using the name property, you can get or set the name of any anchor.

The Frame Object

The frame list is accessed through the window.frames property.

The Navigator Object

The *navigator object* provides information about the browser itself, such as the name of the browser and its version. (See Table 4.17.)

TABLE 4.15

Properties and
Methods of the
Anchor Object

Properties	Description
name	The name of the anchor.

TABLE 4.16	**Properties**	**Description**
Properties and Methods of the Frame Object	length	The length of the frames object.
	name	The name of the frame.
	parent	The parent window of the frame.
	self	The frame object itself.
	window	The window object of the frame.

	Methods	**Description**
	clearTimeout(timeID)	Clear a previously set timer.
	setTimeout(exprString, milliseconds [, scriptLanguage])	Set a timer to call a function after a specified interval.

If you are authoring Web pages for multiple browsers, it may be necessary to check which browser is being used to view your page. You can determine which browser is being used with the following script:

```
<SCRIPT LANGUAGE="JavaScript">
<!--
var strName = navigator.appName
if ( strName == "Microsoft Internet Explorer" )
{
  alert( "browser is Microsoft Internet Explorer" )
}
else
{
  alert( "browser is Netscape Navigator" )
}
-->
</SCRIPT>
```

TABLE 4.17	**Properties**	**Description**
Properties of the Navigator Object	appCodeName	The code name of the browser.
	appName	The application name of the browser.
	appVersion	The version of the browser.
	userAgent	The user agent name of the browser.

The History Object

The *history object* represents the history list of the browser. (See Table 4.18.)

The history list is accessed via the history property of the window object. Unlike most of the other lists within the Object Model for Scripting, the history property does not give you access to the elements of the list; instead, it exposes methods that allow the list to be traversed.

The length property is read only and returns the number of items contained in the browser's history list. In Internet Explorer this property is not supported and currently returns zero.

While the individual URLs contained in the history list cannot be accessed directly, you can force the browser to navigate to either a specific history URL using the go method:

```
// navigate to the first item in the history list
window.history.go( 0 )
```

or relative to the current URL using the back or forward method:

```
// navigate back two pages
window.history.back( 2 )

// navigate forward one page
window.history.forward( 1 )
```

The Location Object

The *location object* represents the current URL. The properties of the location object can be read and set. Setting any of the properties will alter the current URL and automatically triggers the browser to navigate to the

TABLE 4.18

Properties and Methods of the History Object

Properties	Description
length	The number of history items.

Methods	Description
back(relativeIndex)	Go back in the history list.
forward(relativeIndex)	Go forward in the history list.
go(absoluteIndex)	Go to a specific location in the history list.

new URL. The location object properties contain pieces of the actual URL. Table 4.13 (shown earlier in the link object section) describes what each property describes.

The JavaScript Calculator

Now that we have a general understanding of the JavaScript language and the Object Model of Internet Explorer, let's apply some of that knowledge through an example. In this section, we aim to build a calculator. The example includes HTML frames, tables, form fields, JavaScript, ActiveX controls, and the Scripting Object Model.

To start, we need to create three fairly basic HTML documents. You need to start up ActiveX Control Pad. Remember it always creates a basic HTML document for us, so we just need to modify it a little. First, remove the BODY block; we do not need it in this document. Where the body was, we will add our HTML to define the frames:

```
<HTML>
<HEAD>
<TITLE>Tally Calculator</TITLE>
</HEAD>
<FRAMESET COLS="60%,40%">
<FRAME NAME="CalcFrame" SRC=jscalc.htm>
<FRAME NAME="TallyFrame" SRC=jstally.htm>
</FRAMSET>
</HTML>
```

The FRAMESET block defines the number of frames and how they will be divided. Two vertical frames with a 60/40 percent split will work for our calculator. Within the FRAMESET block, we set the attributes for the two frames that we have. We give each frame a name as well as the source document that is loaded into the frame. The full document is shown in ActiveX Control Pad in Fig. 4.3.

After verifying that your document is equivalent to Figure 4.3, choose **File/Save As...** and give your file the name JSCALCFR.HTM.

We now need to create the two pages that will be loaded into the frames. We start with the document that contains the calculator. In ActiveX Control Pad, choose **File/New HTML** to start a new document. We start out simple just to be sure that our frames our working. Just add the following lines within the BODY block:

```
<HTML>
<HEAD>
```

Figure 4.3
JSCALCFR.HTM in
ActiveX Control Pad.

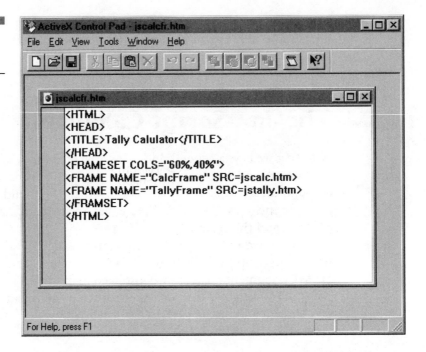

```
<TITLE>Tally Calculator</TITLE>
</HEAD>
<BODY>
<H1 ALIGN=CENTER>Calculator</H1>
<HR ALIGN=CENTER WIDTH=100%>
</BODY>
</HTML>
```

The H1 block creates a heading and places the text "Calculator" in a nice large font. The HR tag creates a horizontal line that will soon separate the calculator from the heading. Figure 4.4 shows how it should all look in ActiveX Control Pad. Now let's save this file by choosing **File/Save As...** and give it the name JSCALC.HTM.

The last document we need to create contains a tally sheet for our calculator. Once again in ActiveX Control Pad choose **File/New** HTML to start a new document. Add the following lines within the BODY block:

```
<HTML>
<HEAD>
<TITLE>Tally</TITLE>
</HEAD>
<BODY>
<H1 ALIGN=LEFT>Tally</H1>
```

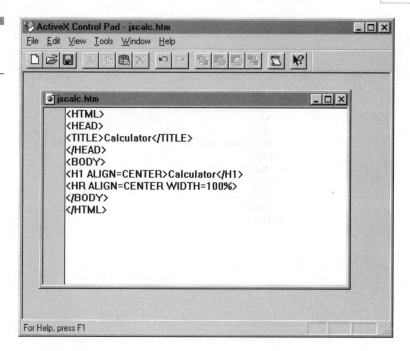

Figure 4.4
JSCALC.HTM in
ActiveX Control Pad.

```
<HR ALIGN=LEFT WIDTH=50%>
<BODY>
</HTML>
```

This time our heading will be the text "Tally" in a nice large font, and again we have a horizontal line that separates the heading from the tally sheet. To save this document, choose **File/Save As...** and give it the name JSTALLY.HTM.

Now let's see how it all looks in Internet Explorer. You might want to leave ActiveX Control Pad running because we switch back and forth between these two programs a lot during the development of our example.

Start Internet Explorer. You do not need to be connected to the Internet. If Internet Explorer attempts to load a home page from the Internet, just choose the STOP button. In the Address field, enter the directory that you have been saving your work to and the file name JSCALCFR.HTM. Internet Explorer should load create our frames and our calculator and tally documents should load into the frames. You should get something that looks like Fig. 4.5.

It's not much, but it's a start. Next, let's get the content of our pages defined. We start with the calculator itself.

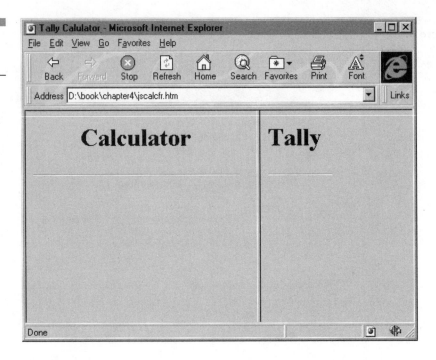

HTML Forms and the Input Element

In ActiveX Control Pad, make JSCALC.HTM the active window. Our calculator is nothing more that an elaborate HTML form. The form is going to contain a 5 × 5 table. The cells of the table each contain a text field to use for the calculator's display as well as buttons for the numbers and operators. The code for the FORM block starts right after the definition of our horizontal line <HR> tag:

```
...
<HR ALIGN=CENTER WIDTH=100%>
```

```
<FORM ACTION="" NAME="Calculator">

<TABLE ALIGN=CENTER COLS=5 BORDER=2 CELLPADDING=1 CELLSPACING=5>

<TR>
<TD COLSPAN=5 ALIGN=CENTER><INPUT TYPE=Text SIZE=50 NAME="Display" WIDTH=100%></TD>
</TR>

<TR>
<TD><INPUT TYPE=Button VALUE="7" NAME="btnSeven"></TD>
```

```
<TD><INPUT TYPE=Button VALUE="8" NAME="btnEight"></TD>
<TD><INPUT TYPE=Button VALUE="9" NAME="btnNine"></TD>
<TD><INPUT TYPE=Button VALUE="/" NAME="btnDivide"></TD>
<TD><INPUT TYPE=Button VALUE="%" NAME="btnPercent"></TD>
</TR>

<TR>
<TD><INPUT TYPE=Button VALUE="4" NAME="btnFour"></TD>
<TD><INPUT TYPE=Button VALUE="5" NAME="btnFive"></TD>
<TD><INPUT TYPE=Button VALUE="6" NAME="btnSix"></TD>
<TD><INPUT TYPE=Button VALUE="*" NAME="btnMultiply"></TD>
<TD><INPUT TYPE=Button VALUE="CE" NAME="btnClearEntry"></TD>
</TR>

<TR>
<TD><INPUT TYPE=Button VALUE="1" NAME="btnOne"></TD>
<TD><INPUT TYPE=Button VALUE="2" NAME="btnTwo"></TD>
<TD><INPUT TYPE=Button VALUE="3" NAME="btnThree"></TD>
<TD><INPUT TYPE=Button VALUE="-" NAME="btnMinus"></TD>
<TD><INPUT TYPE=Button VALUE="C" NAME="btnClear"></TD>
</TR>

<TR>
<TD><INPUT TYPE=Button VALUE="+/-" NAME="btnPlusMinus"></TD>
<TD><INPUT TYPE=Button VALUE="0" NAME="btnZero"></TD>
<TD><INPUT TYPE=Button VALUE="." NAME="btnDecimal"></TD>
<TD><INPUT TYPE=Button VALUE="+" NAME="btnPlus"></TD>
<TD><INPUT TYPE=Button VALUE="=" NAME="btnEquals"></TD>
</TR>

</TABLE>
</FORM>
```

Each button is created using the HTML INPUT element. As we discussed in Chapter 3, the HTML standard specifies a number of simple controls that can be used to get input from the user. In our calculator example, we are using a number of "BUTTON" controls and one ":TEXT" control. Later in our example, we also use an ActiveX control.

Save JSCALC.HTM, and refresh Internet Explorer to take a look at our calculator. It should look like Fig. 4.6.

It sure does look good, but you won't be impressed for long as nothing happens when you press the buttons. We need to add some script to our document that executes when the buttons are pressed. So far we've used straight HTML elements to create our calculator, we now need to add some programmatic actions with scripting.

The buttons can be grouped together to produce seven logical events. A button being pressed can represent either a number, an operation, a clear, a clear entry, a plus/minus, a decimal, or a percent. We make a function for each of these events.

Figure 4.6
Our Calculator form.

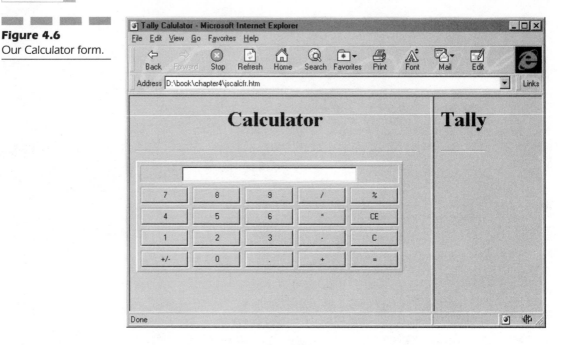

ActiveX Control Pad's Script Wizard

Switch to ActiveX Control Pad and make JSCALC.HTM the active window. We are using script wizard to help us, so before we begin to write our script, let's check our script options. Choose **Tools/Options/Script...**, and make sure that both **Code View** and **JavaScript** are selected, and then choose **OK**. Now, choose **Tools/Script Wizard...** to start the script wizard. To create a function in script wizard, right click in the **Insert Actions** list view and choose New Procedure from the pop-up menu. Script Wizard presents you with a default function called `Procedure1`. Change the procedure name and parameters from "Procedure1()" to "Number(Num)". See Fig. 4.7.

For Script Wizard to recognize the function, you will need to enter a body for each function. At this time, we just want to create stub functions, so just enter a space (" ") in the body. We need to create the 7 functions shown in Table 4.19 using the same steps outlined above.

After you have defined all 7 functions, choose OK in Script Wizard. Script Wizard inserts a SCRIPT block into your document that should look like this:

```
<SCRIPT LANGUAGE="JavaScript">
<!--
```

Figure 4.7
Adding a JavaScript
procedure with
ActiveX Control Pad.

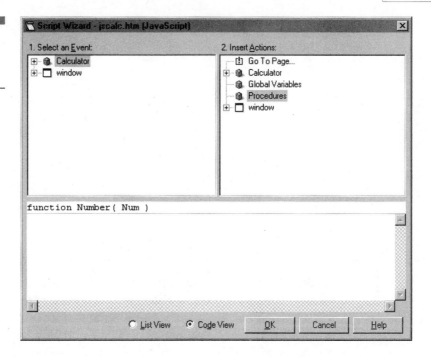

```
function Number( Num )
{

}
function Operation( Op )
{

}
function Decimal()
{
```

TABLE 4.19

Our Calculator
Functions

Function	Description
Number(Num)	Called when the user presses a numeric key.
Operator(Op)	Called when an operator (+, −, *, etc.) button is pressed.
Clear(fButtonPress)	Clears the calculator's display and accumulator.
ClearEntry( )	Clears the calculator's display.
PlusMinus( )	Appends a decimal to the number in the display.
Decimal( )	Toggles the displayed number from positive to negative.
Percent( )	Converts the displayed number into a percentage.

```
}
function PlusMinus()
{


}
function Percent()
{


}
function ClearEntry()
{


}
function Clear(bButtonPress)
{


}
-->
</SCRIPT>
```

Before we code the functions, we need to create some variables to hold various values for the calculator. We need a numeric variable to hold the accumulated value of the calculations, and since our calculator will work in postfix notation, we are always one operator behind, so we need a string variable to hold the last operator. We also need a Boolean variable to indicate that an operator has been pressed and that the next number button pressed should start a new number in the display. Each of these variables is used by all of the functions, so let's make them global.

There is one more variable that we define, which is just a variable of convenience. Within each function, we need access to the calculator's display fairly often. Instead of typing "window.document.Calculator.Display" every time that we might need it, we create an object variable to access the display.

Adding Global Variables with ActiveX Control Pad

To create our four global variables, let's return to Script Wizard. Just as you did to create your procedures, you need to right click in the Insert Action list view; but this time, however, choose New Global Variable. Enter the name Accumulator into the entry field and choose OK. You also need to create the following three variables using the procedure previously outlined: NewNumberNeeded, LastOperator, and Display. After you have entered all four variable names, exit Script Wizard by choosing OK. Script Wizard adds the variables to the top of our script:

```
<SCRIPT LANGUAGE="JavaScript">
<!--
var Accumulator
var NewNumberNeeded
var LastOperator
var Display
...
```

Script Wizard has no mechanism to initialize variables, and in our case that is all right because we use our `Clear` and `ClearEntry` functions to initialize our variables. When the page loads, we call the `Clear` function just as if a user had pressed the button. This sets the variables to their default values and then we are ready to start calculating.

To add the necessary script to our functions, let's return to Script Wizard. From the Insert Action list view, expand the Procedures node. You should see our seven functions. Right click on the ClearEntry function and choose Edit. Script Wizard places `ClearEntry` into the editor. Add the following statements to the body of the function:

```
// create a shortcut
Display = window.document.Calculator.Display
// set the value in the display to zero
Display.value = "0"
// any number button pressed will start a new number
NewNumberNeeded = true
```

NOTE: *Throughout the script example we use the Display shortcut to get and set the value in display. The reason we didn't go one more level down and create a variable named Value and assign it the value of window.document.Calculator.Display.value is that Value would be a string that contains a copy of the value in the display. Getting and setting Value would not change the display in the calculator. By creating a variable called Display and assigning it window.document.Calculator.Display, we are creating an object variable that represents the text field, from which we can get and set the value, thus changing the display of the calculator.*

Now, edit the `Clear` function and add the following statements to its body:

```
// clear the accumulated calculation
Accumulator = 0
// clear any pending operations
LastOperator = ""
// clear the display
ClearEntry()
```

The `Clear` function clears the accumulator and last operator variables, and calls the `ClearEntry` function to clear the display. That takes care of the initialization functions, now we need to call them when the page gets loaded. From the Select an Event list view, expand the Window node and select onLoad. Script Wizard creates a SCRIPT block to be executed on the onLoad event. For the body of this script, just call the Clear function with a parameter of false. The false parameter informs the Clear function that it was called by a script and not a button press. The body of the onLoad event should look like this:

```
// Initialize the calculator
Clear( false )
```

Let's save our work, and see what we have. Choose OK in Script Wizard to save our script and then from ActiveX Control Pad save JSCALC.HTM. Switch to Internet Explorer and refresh JSCALCFR.HTM. Did our script work? If the display has a value of zero in it, then it did. However, the buttons still do nothing.

When a number button gets pressed, we call the Number function, passing it the value of the actual button that was pressed. The Number function should take the value that is passed and either display the new number or add the value of the button as a digit to the existing display. To create the script for the Number function, switch back to ActiveX Control Pad, and start Script Wizard. In the Insert Action list view, expand the Procedures node, right click on the Number function and choose Edit. Enter the following script for the body of the function:

```
// Is it a new number?
if ( NewNumberNeeded )
{
  // Set the display to the number
  Display.value = Num
  // addition numbers are digits
  NewNumberNeeded = false
}
else
{
  // It's not a new number, but is the current number a zero
  if ( Display.value == "0" )
  {
  // Set the display to the number
  Display.value = Num
  }
  else
  {
  // Add the number as a digit to the current display
  Display.value += Num
  }
}
```

With the Number function defined, we can now assign the form buttons to call the Number function when they are clicked. This is easy to do in Script Wizard. In the Select an Event list view, expand the Calculator node. Find btnZero and expand it. Select the onClick event. In the body of the `onClick` event we call the `Number` function with the string value of "0":

```
Number( "0" )
```

We need to do this for the nine other number buttons as well. So find each number button in the Select an Event window and define its `onClick` event to call the `Number` function and pass in the value of the button as a string, such as: Number("1"), Number("2"), and so on.

While we're here, we should go ahead and define the Clear and Clear-Entry buttons as well. The body of the `btnClear onClick` event should contain:

```
Clear( true )
```

And the body of the `btnClearEntry onClick` event should contain:

```
ClearEntry()
```

We've now coded enough of the functions and events that our calculator should do something. Save JSCALC.HTM. Switch to Internet Explorer and refresh JSCALCFR.HTM. Go ahead and start clicking buttons. The number buttons should add digits to the display, and the **C** and **CE** buttons should set the display back to zero. Before we code the operator buttons, let's define the three stray buttons: +/−, ., and %.

Switch back to ActiveX Control Pad and start Script Wizard. In the Insert Action list view, expand the Procedures node, right click on the `PlusMinus` function, and choose Edit. This function just toggles the value in the display between positive and negative. We can easily accomplish this by multiplying the value in the display by −1. The body of the `PlusMinus` function should contain:

```
// The display must contain a value entered by a user
// This prevents a user from clicking plus/minus
// after an operator has been pressed, but before
// a new number has been entered
if ( !NewNumberNeeded )
  Display.value *= -1
```

The code for the `Percent` function is almost identical. The body of the `Percent` function should contain:

```
// The display must contain a value entered by a user
// This prevents a user from clicking plus/minus
// after an operator has been pressed, but before
```

```
// a new number has been entered
if ( !NewNumberNeeded )
  Display.value /= 100
```

The Decimal function simply adds a decimal point to the end of the number in the display. However, there are a few rules we need to follow. Like a number button, the decimal button should begin a new number after an operator has been pressed, and the number cannot already contain a decimal point.

```
// if no numbers have been entered yet, place
// a zero with a decimal following in the display
if ( NewNumberNeeded )
{
  Display.value = "0."
  NewNumberNeeded = false
}
else
{
  // if there is a number in the display already
  // make sure is doesn't have a decimal point
  if ( Display.value.indexOf(".") == -1 )
  {
  NewNumberNeeded = false
  Display.value += "."
  }
}
```

The only thing left is to call the functions when the buttons are pressed. From the Select an Event list view, expand the Calculator node. Locate the three buttons, btnPlusMinus, btnPercent, and btnDecimal, and have them call their respective functions, PlusMinus, Percent, and Decimal.

Once again, let's give it a try. Choose OK in Script Wizard and save JSCALC.HTM in ActiveX Control Pad. Switch to Internet Explorer and refresh JSCALCFR.HTM. Enter a number into the display and click the +/- button a few times—the value should toggle positive and negative. Click the percent button a few times—the decimal should move left two digit each time. Clear the display and enter a decimal value. All that's left is to code the Operator function and tie it to the appropriate buttons.

With the Operator function, we make use of one of JavaScript's unique features: the built-in function, eval. Typically in a function like Operator you would expect to find some kind of conditional statement that would determine the operator passed in and perform that arithmetic function. Thanks to JavaScript's eval function, all we need to do is assemble a string representing the arithmetic expression and call the eval function to evaluate the expression. Once the expression has been evaluated, we place the result in the calculator's display.

Switch back to ActiveX Control Pad and start Script Wizard. In the Insert Action list view, expand the Procedures node, right click on Operator and choose Edit. The code for the Operator function is:

```
// If a number has been entered in the display
// then perform the pending operation
if ( !NewNumberNeeded )
{
  if ( ( LastOperator != "" ) &&
    ( "+-/*".indexOf( LastOperator ) ) > -1 )
  {
  var strEval = Accumulator + LastOperator + Display.value
  Accumulator = eval( strEval )
  }
  else
  {
  Accumulator = Display.value
  }

  Display.value = Accumulator
  LastOperator = Op
  NewNumberNeeded = true
}
```

Now, we need each of the operator buttons, +, −, *, /, and =, to call the `Operator` function while passing the string value of the operation. From the Select an Event list view, expand the Calculator node. Find the buttons: `btnPlus`, `btnMinus`, `btnMultiply`, `btnDivide`, and `btnEqual`. For the `onClick` event of each button call the Operator function, such as `Operator("+")`, `Operator("-")`, and so on.

We are now ready to give our calculator a final try. Choose **OK** in Script Wizard and save JSCALC.HTM, switch to Internet Explorer and refresh JSCALCFR.HTM. The entire calculator should work.

If you look at the entire HTML document in ActiveX Control Pad, it didn't really take too much code to create our calculator. We could easily put this out on a Web page and let the world use our calculator. However, we're not done. We still have to add the tally sheet to our Web page. For that we use an ActiveX control that is included with Internet Explorer.

Adding an ActiveX Control

Switch back to ActiveX Control Pad. We should still have JSCALC.HTM loaded. Leave it loaded because we still need to have some addition script to support our tally page. We also need to open our tally sheet page, so choose File/Open and open JSTALLY.HTM.

We already have a heading and a horizontal line on our page. We are going to add an ActiveX control listbox to our page under the horizontal line. The control will display a "tally" of all the calculations performed.

In ActiveX Control Pad move the cursor to the line following the <HR> tag, at the front of the </BODY> line. To insert an ActiveX control with ActiveX Control Pad choose Edit/Insert ActiveX Control. ActiveX Control Pad will display a dialog with a list of ActiveX controls (see Fig. 4.8). Choose the control named Microsoft Forms 2.0 Listbox from the list and click **OK**.

ActiveX Control Pad then displays the control as well as its properties (see Fig. 4.9). We need to change a few of the control's properties. In the properties dialog, find the Height property and select it. Unlike with Visual Basic, you cannot change the value in the list box. Instead ActiveX Control Pad displays the property's value in an entry field at the top of the dialog. In that entry field at the top of the dialog enter "240" and click Apply.

Now, we have only to insert the control into our HTML document. To do this, just close the window that displays the Listbox control. This will insert an <OBJECT> block into our HTML document that describes our ActiveX control (see Fig. 4.10). We discussed the OBJECT element and its

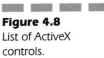

Figure 4.8
List of ActiveX
controls.

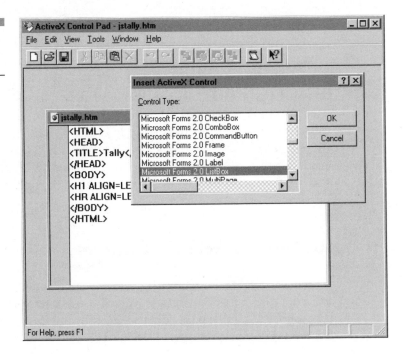

Figure 4.9
Properties of the
Listbox control.

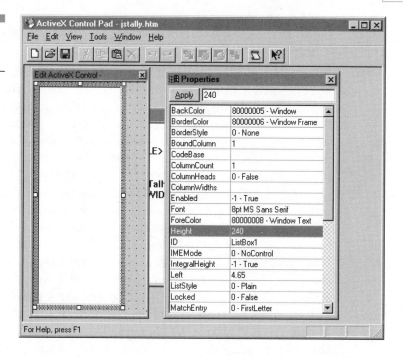

Figure 4.10
HTML for the inserted
control.

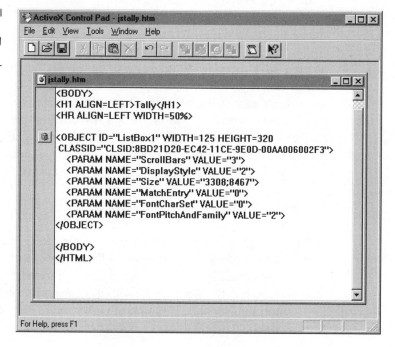

attributes in Chapter 3. We go over each attribute in detail in Chapter 5. For now, we can ignore the attributes added by ActiveX Control Pad.

You might notice that the height of our Listbox is displayed as 400 instead of the 240 that we entered in the properties for the control. Don't worry; ActiveX Control Pad recalculates the height and width properties so that they will display properly in the browser. Speaking of the width, we need to change that property and the ID property. To change the properties of the control, just click on the icon in the margin to the left of the <OBJECT> tag. ActiveX Control Pad will display the Listbox and its properties again. Change the Width property to 110 and the ID property to lbxTally. Again, close the Edit ActiveX Control window to update the <OBJECT> tag. Let's see what it looks like in Internet Explorer.

In ActiveX Control Pad choose File/Save to save JSTALLY.HTM. Switch to Internet Explorer and choose refresh for the JSCALCFR.HTM page. Now, you should have a calculator on the left of the page, and a tally sheet on the right. However, we will still have to add script to both JSCALC.HTM and JSTALLY.HTM to make that tally sheet functional.

In ActiveX Control Pad, we will work on JSTALLY.HTM first. We need to add a function that writes a line to our list box. The function adds lines to the end of the list and starts removing lines at the front of the list after twenty lines are inserted into the list box.

In Script Wizard, right click in the Insert Action list view and choose New Procedure from the pop up menu. Our function is going to add a string to the list box, so we need to accept that string as a parameter. Change Procedure1 to AddToTally(str). We will use the AddItem method of the Listbox control to add our str parameter to the list box. Find lbxTally in the Insert Action list view and expand it. Double click on the AddItem method. Script Wizard adds the AddItem method call to the body of our function. Add Item takes two parameters: the item to add and an index. We won't pass an index; that will cause the list box to add the line to the end of the list. We will pass the str parameter pass to AddToTally as the item to add to the list box. The statement should look like:

```
lbxTally.AddItem( str )
```

Now, we need to add code to remove lines from the top of the list box if the list box contains more than 20 lines. To determine how many lines the list box contains we use the ListCount property of the ListBox control. We also use the RemoveItem method to remove items from the list box. Following the AddItem line in the body of our function, type "if (", then from the Insert Action list view, double click on the ListCount property. This will add the `ListCount` property to our if statement. Then finish typing the statement. The entire line should look like:

```
if ( lbxTally.ListCount == 20 )
```

On the next line, indent a few spaces then in the Insert Action list view, double click on the RemoveItem method. The `RemoveItem` method takes an index parameter that tells what item to delete. In our example, we need to delete the first item in the list, item 0. The entire function should look like:

```
lbxTally.AddItem( str )
if (lbxTally.ListCount==20)
  lbxTally.RemoveItem(0)
```

That's all we have to do for this script. Choose OK from Script Wizard to save our script. The choose File/Save in ActiveX Control Pad to save JSTALLY.HTM. Next, we need to add code to JSCALC.HTM to call the `AddToTally` function when performing an operation in our calculator. So, switch to the JSCALC.HTM window in ActiveX Control Pad and start Script Wizard again. The code that we add is within the Operator() function, so from the Insert Action list view, expand Procedures, right click on Operator, and select Edit from the pop-up menu.

At the top of the function, we call the `AddToTally` function to log the current display and operator. We also add some statements to the end of the function so that a press of the equal button generates the display of the answer in the tally sheet. The lines added to the `Operator` function look like:

```
function Operator( Op )
{
  // If a number has been entered in the display
  // then perform the pending operation
  if ( !NewNumberNeeded )
  {
    // Show the display and operator in the tally sheet
    top.TallyFrame.AddToTally( Display.value + " " + Op )

if ( ( LastOperator != "" ) &&
     ( "+-/*".indexOf( LastOperator ) ) > -1 )
  {
    var strEval = Accumulator + LastOperator + Display.value
    Accumulator = eval( strEval )
  }
  else
  {
    Accumulator = Display.value
  }
```

```
   Display.value = Accumulator
   LastOperator = Op
   NewNumberNeeded = true
}
```

```
// On an equal operation display the total and a separator line
if ( Op == "=" )
{
   top.TallyFrame.AddToTally( Accumulator )
   top.TallyFrame.AddToTally( "----------" )
}
```

Notice that calling `AddToTally` required some help from the browser object model. `AddToTally` does not exist within the scope of the JSCALC.HTM document. We have to tell the script engine explicitly where the `AddToTally` function is defined. Using the top property of the window object, we direct the script engine to JSCALCFR.HTM. Then we direct the script engine to the document that resides within TallyFrame. That document is JSTALLY.HTM where the AddToTally function is defined. It's a roundabout way of getting there, but it's not all that different from dynamically loading a DLL and calling a function in "C".

If we had to reference `top.TallyFrame.AddToTally` a lot within our script, we could have defined a shortcut to `top.TallyFrame` just as we did with our `Display` variable. But as it goes, we need to call `AddToTally` only one more time.

We need to tally the fact that the Clear button was pressed. So the following code should be added to the clear function:

```
function Clear( fButtonPress )
{
   ...
   // Only tally on button press, not initialize
   if ( fButtonPress )
   top.TallyFrame.AddToTally( "C" )
}
```

When we initially coded the `Clear` function, we defined a parameter called `fButtonPress`, which used to define whether the `Clear` function was being called from a function or from the `onLoad` event. We make use of this fact so that we put a "C" in the tally only when the Clear button is pressed, and not when the calculator is being initialized.

This completes the coding of our calculator example, so let's give it a try. Choose OK from Script Wizard and File/Save in ActiveX Control Pad. Switch to Internet Explorer and refresh the JSCALCFR.HTM page. Now, when you perform operations in the calculator, they should be tallied in the list box of the Tally page. Sample output is shown in Fig. 4.11.

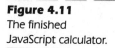

Figure 4.11
The finished
JavaScript calculator.

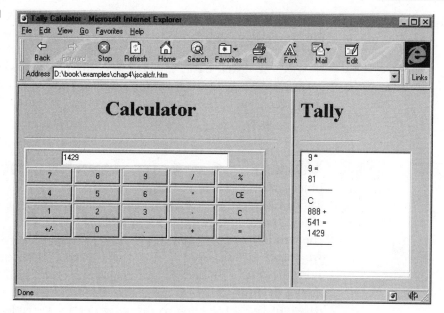

This is a fairly simple calculator and tally sheet. You can continue to enhance it to support memory functions and any other calculator functions that you would like.

NOTE: *If your calculator doesn't function correctly after following the preceding steps, skip ahead to the end of this chapter and read the section on Internet Explorer's Script Debugger. It makes debugging scripts much easier.*

Scripting Take Two: VBScript

JavaScript has been around forever in Internet time, and has become the de facto standard for adding client-side logic to Web pages primarily because it can be used by most browsers. But as in every other Internet technology, there is competition in the scripting world coming from Microsoft in the form of VBScript.

VBScript is a stripped-down version of Visual Basic for Applications, the scripting/macro language used by Microsoft's Office Suite of applications. Since Microsoft already had a scripting language and interpreter, and most Windows programmers are at least familiar with Visual Basic, it wasn't much of a leap for them to add the functionality to Internet

Explorer. However, Internet Explorer is the key. It is currently the only browser that recognizes VBScript. Since that is the case, you may be asking yourself how VBScript even has a chance against JavaScript? Since it is based on Visual Basic, VBScript is easily picked up by Visual Basic programmers. There is no need for them to learn a new language to script their Web pages.

VBScript versus JavaScript

Syntactically, these two languages are very different. JavaScript uses a syntax that should be familiar to most Java and C++ programmers. VBScript uses the syntax of Visual Basic. They also offer a different set of built-in functions and objects. But that is where the differences end.

Functionally, these two languages are quite similar. Both languages offer the ability to create procedural code. They are both loosely typed, doing away with having to formally declare variable types. Neither language can access the client's system directly. Both languages rely heavily on the browser's object model. And both can interact with ActiveX controls and Java Applets.

The reasons you would use one language over the other are: (1) familiarity with the language; (2) potential support provided by your target browsers; (3) one language provides a specific piece of functionality that you need, and the other one does not.

A good example of difference in functionality is the calculator example that we just developed. In our next example, we develop the calculator in VBScript, and you can see that JavaScript has an advantage over VBScript. JavaScript's built-in function `eval` makes our `Operator` function easier to write. Outside of that, both examples perform equally.

Before we discuss our calculator example written in VBScript, let's take some time to familiarize ourselves with the features of VBScript.

Features of VBScript

This section is not going to be a lesson in Visual Basic programming. There are already a number of excellent references out there if you need to learn Visual Basic. Instead, we aim to touch on some of the more important aspects of the language.

Data Types

VBScript contains only one data type, the variant. Variant variables can contain Booleans, numbers, strings, and objects, which are called *subtypes*. The interpreter determines the subtype of the variant by the value assigned and allows operations on the variable based on its subtype.

There are a number of built-in functions that allow you to determine the subtype of a variable and to convert it to another subtype. Table 4.20 shows a list of those functions and a brief description of each.

Declarations

Just like Visual Basic, VBScript allows the use of variables without a declaration. However, to control the scope of a variable, you must declare it properly. VBScript uses the Dim keyword to declare a variable. Scope is determined by placement of the declaration. The format of the Dim statement and its scope rules are:

Dim variablename[(subscripts)]

> Variables declared with Dim outside of a procedure are available to all procedures in any SCRIPT block within the document.

> Variables declared with Dim inside of a procedure are available only within that procedure.

Note that the Dim statements make no provision in their syntax for the assignment of a value. That is because all executable code in VBScript must be contained within a procedure, and assignments are executable statements. Therefore to initialize global variables in VBScript, you have to define a procedure and link it to the window's *onLoad* event.

Procedures can take the form of subroutines or functions. *Subroutines* are typically statements grouped to perform a specific task. *Functions* are similar to subroutines except that they can return a value to the caller and are usually called from within another subroutine or function.

To declare a subroutine or function, you must use the following syntax:

Sub *subname [([ByVal | ByRef] arglist)]*

  [statements...]

  [Exit Sub]

Function Name	Description
TABLE 4.20 VBScript Data Types VarType(*variable name*)	The VarType function takes a variable as a parameter and returns the subtype of that variable. The following constants are returned to signify the subtype: VbEmpty : not initialize vbNull : no valid data vbBoolean : a boolean vbByte : a Byte vbInteger : an integer vbLong : a long integer vbCurrency : currency vbSingle : a single precision floating point number vbDouble : a double precision floating point number vbDate : a date vbString : a string vbObject : an object vbError : an error
TypeName(*variable name*)	This function is similar to TypeName except that it returns a string representing the type: "Empty" : not initialized "Null" : no valid data "Boolean" : a Boolean "Byte" : a byte "Integer" : an integer "Long" : a long integer "Currency" : a currency "Single" : a single precision floating point "Double" : a double precision floating point "Date" : a date or time "String" : a string "Object" : a automation object "Error" : an error
IsArray(*variable name*) IsDate(*variable name*) IsEmpty(*variable name*) IsNull(*variable name*) IsNumeric(*variable name*) IsObject(*variable name*)	These functions return a Boolean indicating whether a variable is of a specific type.
Cbool(*variable name*) Cbyte(*variable name*) Ccur(*variable name*) Cdate(*variable name*) CDbl(*variable name*) Cint(*variable name*) CLng(*variable name*) CSng(*variable name*) CStr(*variable name*)	These functions convert the value of a variant to a specific type.

[statements…]

End Sub

Function *funcname [([ByVal | ByRef] arglist)]*

[statements…]

[funcname = expression]

[Exit Function]

[statements…]

[funcname = expression]

End Function

The scope of procedures in VBScript is simple. All subroutines and functions are visible throughout the entire document.

To examine the difference between global and local variable and get familiar with subroutines, let's take a look at an example HTML document:

```
<HTML>
<HEAD>
<SCRIPT LANGUAGE="VBScript">
<!--
  REM Declare all global variables here
  'Cannot make an initial assignment on declaration
  Dim intGlobalVar
-->
</SCRIPT>
<SCRIPT LANGUAGE="VBScript" FOR="window" EVENT="onLoad">
<!--
  REM Initialize all global variables here
  'VBScript is not case sensitive, this is our global variable
  INTGLOBALVAR = 5
-->
</SCRIPT>
</HEAD>
<BODY>
<INPUT TYPE="button" VALUE="Click Me" LANGUAGE="VBScript"
 ONCLICK="DoIt">
<SCRIPT LANGUAGE="VBScript">
<!--
Sub DoIt
  Dim strLocalVar 'Declare a local variable
  strLocalVar = "Hello" 'Assign our local variable a value
  MsgBox( "Value of intGlobalVar is " + CStr( intGlobalVar ) )
  MsgBox( "Value of strLocalVar is " + strLocalVar )
End Sub
-->
</SCRIPT>
</BODY>
</HTML>
```

This simple example demonstrates a number of things about the VBScript language. Our first SCRIPT block occurs in the HEAD block. It is an in-line script (performed as the page is parsed) and declares our global variable `intGlobalVar`. It is a common convention to declare global variables before any scripts that will access those variables, and the HEAD block is perfect for such a task.

The second SCRIPT block is a little more interesting. The first thing you might notice is that our variable name is all uppercase. This illustrates that VBScript is *not* case sensitive. INTGLOBALVAR and `intGlobalVar` are the same variable to the VBScript interpreter. Second, the assignment is executable code that is not contained within a procedure. If all executable code in VBScript must be contained within a subroutine or a function, then why doesn't this generate an error? When a script is tied to an event, the VBScript interpreter automatically generates a subroutine for that event and all statements within that script are interpreted within the scope of that procedure.

There is an INPUT statement in our document that will create a button by which the `onClick` event calls a VBScript subroutine called `DoIt`. That subroutine is defined in the next SCRIPT block.

The `DoIt` subroutine contains a declaration for a local variable named `LocalVar` and the following line assigns it a string value. `LocalVar` is only visible inside of the `DoIt` subroutine. Then we pop up to alert boxes to display the value of our two variables. In the first alert call we have to convert `intGlobalVar` from an integer to a string so that it can be displayed.

That brings us to an important point. Variant is the only variable type in VBScript, but there are several subtypes that can be contained within a variant. You can tell the subtype of a variable by using the `VarType` or `TypeName` functions, but that is costly in execution time. The easiest way is by naming conventions. Notice our variables are called `intoGlobalVar` and `strLocalVar`. The prefix `int` and `str` give the script writer a idea of the subtype of the variable. In naming variables, Microsoft recommends using the following prefixes, as shown in Table 4.21.

Operators

VBScript and Visual Basic use the same operators. The list of operators in order or precedence is shown in Table 4.22.

Arrays

You can declare two types of arrays in VBScript: fixed-length and dynamic. The syntax for declaring the arrays is:

TABLE 4.21

VBScript Hungarian Notation

Subtype	Hungarian Prefix
Boolean	bln
Byte	byt
Date(Time)	dtm
Double	dbl
Error	err
Integer	int
Long	lng
Object	obj
Single	sng
String	str

Dim *ArrayName*(*ArrayLength*) ' Declare a fixed-length array

Dim *ArrayName*() ' Declare a dynamic array

Both types of arrays begin indexing their elements at index zero. That means that the first element is at index 0, the second element is at index 1, and so forth. Since that is the case, there are always length – 1 elements in an array. If the length of an array is 5, the indexes of the elements are 0, 1, 2, 3, and 4.

TABLE 4.22

VBScript Operators and Precedence

Type	Operators
function call/array subscript	()
exponentiation	^
negation	–
multiplication/division	* /
integer division	\
modulo arithmetic	Mod
addition/subtraction	+ –
string concatenation	&
comparison	= <> < <= > >= Is
logical	Not And Or Xor Eqv Imp &

As the name implies, a fixed-length array cannot be changed at run time. The maximum number of elements that can be stored is based on its declaration in the script.

A dynamic array on the other hand is not given a length at declaration time. This lets the interpreter know that the length of the array will change at run time. It is up to the script writer to ensure that there is always enough room in the array to hold the elements to be stored. The `Redim` statement in VBScript allows the script writer to dynamically change the length of a dynamic array. The syntax of the `Redim` statement is:

Redim [Preserve] *ArrayName(ArrayLength)*

Say, for example, you wanted an array to contain the links on a page, but you don't know how many links are contained within the page at the time you write the script. The following code snippet would do the trick:

```
Dim LinksOnPage()  'Declared in the header


...


Redim LinksOnPage( document.links.length )
For x = 1 to document.links.length
  LinksOnPage(x - 1) = document.links(x) .href
Next
```

In this example, the `LinksOnPage` array is declared as a dynamic array. Possibly on the window object's on-load event our script redeclares the array to hold the number of links on the page. We then spin through the links storing the `href` in our `LinksOnPage` array.

When the `Redim` statement is executed, any data that may have existed in the `LinksOnPage` array would have been lost. If there had been data in the `LinksOnPage` array, and we wanted to keep that data in place, but add to it, we would have used the Preserve option of the `Redim` statement.

Objects

Objects in VBScript take on a different meaning that they do in Visual Basic. The `CreateObject` and `GetObject` functions of Visual Basic have been removed, so there is no way to (directly) create an ActiveX automation server in VBScript. You can, however, create an object that refers to an ActiveX Control embedded within the document, or to an HTML form control, just as we did with the display in our JavaScript calculator example.

Object variables in VBScript must be declared using the Dim statement:

Dim *Object Variable*

Once an object variable has been declared, you assign it a value using the Set statement:

Set *Object Variable* = *Value*

After you have set the object variable, you can access properties and methods of the object just as if you had made full reference to the object:

```
Dim objDisplay
Set objDisplay = window.document.Calculator.Display
'Equivalent to typing window.document.Calculator.Display.value =
"0"
objDisplay.Value = "0"
```

Statements

VBScript uses a subset of Visual Basic statements. The list of those statements, a brief description, and the syntax used are presented in Table 4.23.

The Calculator Example in VBScript

We are going to revisit the calculator that we wrote earlier using JavaScript by rewriting it using VBScript. We still have three HTML documents. The first defines the frames for the window; the second contains the VBScript-based calculator; and the third contains the tally sheet. We will leave the tally sheet as it is to demonstrate how to call a JavaScript function from VBScript.

Instead of going through the tedious procedure of creating the example again, step by step, we're just going to discuss how the examples are different. You're now quite familiar with ActiveX Control Pad, so here we just discuss the syntactic and functional differences between the languages.

To start off, here's the source for VBCALCFR.HTM. After creating it, save it in the same directory as our JavaScript example.

```
<HTML>
<HEAD>
```

TABLE 4.23

VBScript
Statements

Statement	Description and Syntax
Call	Transfer script control to a Sub or Function. Call *procedure [arg 1, arg 2,...]*
Dim	Declares variables and storage space for arrays. Dim *varname* [(*length*)]

Do...Loop	Repeats a group of statements while or until a condition is true.
	Do [{While | Until} *condition*]
	   [*statements*]
	   [Exit Do]
	   [*statements*]
	Loop
	Or:
	Do
	   [*statements*]
	   [Exit Do]
	   [*statements*]
	Loop [{While | Until} *condition*]

Erase	Reinitializes the elements in a fixed-length array, or deallocates storage for a dynamic array. Erase *arrayname*
Exit	Returns control from a procedure or a loop block. Exit Do Exit For Exit Function Exit Sub

For...Next	Repeat a group of statements a specific number of times.
	For counter = *start* To *end* [Step *step*]
	   [*statements*]
	   [Exit For]
	   [*statements*]
	Next

Function	Declares a group of statements as a function.
	Function *funcname* [([ByVal \ ByRef] *arglist*)]
	   [*statements...*]
	   [*funcname* = *expression*]
	   [Exit Function]
	   [*statements...*]
	   [*funcname* = *expression*]
	End Function

	Statement	Description and Syntax
TABLE 4.23 (Continued)	If ... Then ... Else	Conditionally executes statements based on the condition expression.

		If *condition1* Then
		   [*statements...*]
		 [ElseIf *condition2* Then
		   [*statements...*]]
		 [Else
		   [*statements...*]]
		 End If

	On Error	Allows program execution to continue in the event of an error.
		On Error Resume Next
	Randomize	Initialize the random number generator.
		Randomize *[seednumber]*
	ReDim	Used to allocate or reallocate storage for a dynamic array.
		ReDim [Preserve] *arrayname(arraylength)*
	Rem	Used to add comments to script code.
		Rem *comment*
	Select Case	Conditionally executes statements based on the condition expression.

		Select Case *expression*
		   [Case *expressionvalue1*
		     [*statements*]]...
		   [Case Else *expressionvalue2*
		     [*statements*]]
		 End Select

	Set	Assigns an object reference to an object variable.
		Set *objectvar* = {*object*	Nothing}
	Sub	Declares a group of statements as a subroutine.

		Sub *subname [([ByVal \ ByRef] arglist)]*
		   [*statements...*]
		   [Exit Sub]
		   [*statements...*]
		 End Sub

	While ... Wend	Repeats a group of statements while a condition is true.
		While *condition* [*statements]*· Wend

```
<TITLE>Tally Calculator</TITLE>
</HEAD>
<FRAMESET COLS="60%,40%">
<FRAME NAME="CalcFrame" SRC=vbcalc.htm>
<FRAME NAME="TallyFrame" SRC=jstally.htm>
</FRAMSET>
</HTML>
```

The only change to VBCALCFR.HTM (from JSCALCFR.HTM) is the name of the document loaded into the CalcFrame frame. In the case of our VBScript calculator, we load a new file called VBCALC.HTM, which we discuss shortly.

If you use ActiveX Control Pad to create VBCALC.HTM, you need to set the default scripting language to VBScript. To do this, choose **Tools/Options/Script....** This will display the Script Options dialog. Select the Visual Basic Scripting Edition radio button and choose OK. From that point on, all the scripts that you create will be created in VBScript.

NOTE: *You cannot copy JSCALC.HTM to VBCALC.HTM and modify the script code in ActiveX Control Pad. Even though it is legal to mix script languages within an HTML document, ActiveX Control Pad doesn't currently support it. (Notepad does though!)*

As stated earlier, we are not creating VBCALC.HTM step by step, but the listing follows and we take a look at the pieces as they differ from JSCALC.HTM.

```
<HTML>
<HEAD>
<SCRIPT LANGUAGE="VBScript">
<!--
dim Accumulator
dim NewNumberNeeded
dim LastOperator
dim Display
-->
</SCRIPT>
<SCRIPT LANGUAGE="VBScript">
<!--
Sub window_onLoad()
   Clear false
end sub

Sub Number( Num )
    'Is it a new number?
    if NewNumberNeeded = true then
       Display.value = Num 'Set the display to the number
       NewNumberNeeded = false 'addition numbers are digits
    else
```

```
            'Its not a new number, but is the current number a zero
            if Display.value = "0" then
                Display.value = Num 'Set the display to the number
            else
                'Add the number as a digit to the current display
                Display.value = Display.value + Num
            end if
end if
end sub


Sub Operator( Op )
'If a number has been entered in the display
'then perform the pending operation
if NewNumberNeeded = false then
    'Show the display and operator in the tally sheet
    top.TallyFrame.AddToTally( Display.value + " " + Op )

    select case LastOperator
        case "+"
        Accumulator = CDbl( Accumulator ) + CDbl( Display.value )
        case "-"
        Accumulator = CDbl( Accumulator ) - CDbl( Display.value )
        case "*"
        Accumulator = CDbl( Accumulator ) * CDbl( Display.value )
        case "/"
        Accumulator = CDbl( Accumulator ) / CDbl( Display.value )
        case else
        Accumulator = Display.value
    end select
    Display.value = Accumulator
    LastOperator = Op
    NewNumberNeeded = true

    'On an equal operation display the total and a separator line
    if Op = "=" then
        top.TallyFrame.AddToTally( Accumulator )
        top.TallyFrame.AddToTally( "----------" )
    end if
end if
end sub


Sub ClearEntry()
    set Display = window.document.Calculator.Display
    Display.value = "0" 'set the value in the display to zero
    NewNumberNeeded = true 'any number button pressed will start a new number
end sub


Sub Clear( fButtonPress )
    Accumulator = 0 'clear the accumulated calculation
    LastOperator = "" 'clear any pending operations
    ClearEntry 'clear the display
    ' Only tally on button press, not initialize
    if fButtonPress then
    top.TallyFrame.AddToTally( "C" )
    end if
end sub
```

```
Sub Decimal()
   'if no numbers have been entered yet, place
   'a zero with a decimal following in the display
   if NewNumberNeeded = true then
      Display.value = "0."
      NewNumberNeeded = false
   else
      'if there is a number in the display already
      'make sure is doesn't have a decimal point
      if InStr( Display.value, "." ) = 0 then
      NewNumberNeeded = false
      Display.value = Display.value + "."
      end if
   end if
end sub


Sub Percent()
   'The display must contain a value entered by a user
   'This prevents a user from clicking plus/minus
   'after an operator has been pressed, but before
   'a new number has been entered
   if NewNumberNeeded = false then
      Display.value = Display.value / 100
   end if
end sub


Sub PlusMinus()
   'The display must contain a value entered by a user
   'This prevents a user from clicking plus/minus
   'after an operator has been pressed, but before
   'a new number has been entered
   if NewNumberNeeded = false then
      Display.value = Display.value * -1
   end if
end sub
-->
</SCRIPT>


<TITLE>Calculator</TITLE>
</HEAD>
<BODY>
<H1 ALIGN=CENTER>Calculator</H1>
<HR ALIGN=CENTER WIDTH=100%>
    <FORM ACTION="" NAME="Calculator">
<TABLE ALIGN=CENTER COLS=5 BORDER=2 CELLPADDING=1 CELLSPACING=1>
<TR>
<TD COLSPAN=5 ALIGN=CENTER>
        <INPUT TYPE=Text SIZE=50 NAME="Display" WIDTH=100%>
</TD>
</TR>


<TR>
<TD>
        <INPUT LANGUAGE="VBScript" TYPE=Button VALUE="7" ONCLICK="Number &quot;7&quot;"
        NAME="btnSeven">
</TD>
<TD>
```

```
        <INPUT LANGUAGE="VBScript" TYPE=Button VALUE="8" ONCLICK="Number &quot;8&quot;"
        NAME="btnEight">
</TD>
<TD>
        <INPUT LANGUAGE="VBScript" TYPE=Button VALUE="9" ONCLICK="Number &quot;9&quot;"
        NAME="btnNine">
</TD>
<TD>
        <INPUT LANGUAGE="VBScript" TYPE=Button VALUE="/" ONCLICK="Operator
&quot;/&quot;"
        NAME="btnDivide">
</TD>
<TD>
        <INPUT LANGUAGE="VBScript" TYPE=Button VALUE="%" ONCLICK="Percent"
NAME="btnPercent">
</TD>
</TR>


<TR>
<TD>
        <INPUT LANGUAGE="VBScript" TYPE=Button VALUE="4" ONCLICK="Number &quot;4&quot;"
        NAME="btnFour">
</TD>
<TD>
        <INPUT LANGUAGE="VBScript" TYPE=Button VALUE="5" ONCLICK="Number &quot;5&quot;"
        NAME="btnFive">
</TD>
<TD>
        <INPUT LANGUAGE="VBScript" TYPE=Button VALUE="6" ONCLICK="Number &quot;6&quot;"
        NAME="btnSix">
</TD>
<TD>
        <INPUT LANGUAGE="VBScript" TYPE=Button VALUE="*" ONCLICK="Operator
&quot;*&quot;"
        NAME="btnMultiply">
</TD>
<TD>
        <INPUT LANGUAGE="VBScript" TYPE=Button VALUE="CE" ONCLICK="ClearEntry"
        NAME="btnClearEntry">
</TD>
</TR>


<TR>
<TD>
        <INPUT LANGUAGE="VBScript" TYPE=Button VALUE="1" ONCLICK="Number &quot;1&quot;"
        NAME="btnOne">
</TD>
<TD>
        <INPUT LANGUAGE="VBScript" TYPE=Button VALUE="2" ONCLICK="Number &quot;2&quot;"
        NAME="btnTwo">
</TD>
<TD>
        <INPUT LANGUAGE="VBScript" TYPE=Button VALUE="3" ONCLICK="Number &quot;3&quot;"
        NAME="btnThree">
</TD>
<TD>
        <INPUT LANGUAGE="VBScript" TYPE=Button VALUE="-" ONCLICK="Operator &quot;-
&quot;"
```

```
                NAME="btnMinus">
</TD>
<TD>

        <INPUT LANGUAGE="VBScript" TYPE=Button VALUE="C" ONCLICK="Clear true"
         NAME="btnClear">
</TD>
</TR>


<TR>
<TD>

        <INPUT LANGUAGE="VBScript" TYPE=Button VALUE=+/-" ONCLICK="PlusMinus"
         NAME="btnPlusMinus">
</TD>
<TD>

        <INPUT LANGUAGE="VBScript" TYPE=Button VALUE="0" ONCLICK="Number &quot;0&quot;"
         NAME="btnZero">
</TD>
<TD>

        <INPUT LANGUAGE="VBScript" TYPE=Button VALUE="." ONCLICK="Decimal"
NAME="btnDecimal">
</TD>
<TD>

        <INPUT LANGUAGE="VBScript" TYPE=Button VALUE="+" ONCLICK="Operator
&quot;+&quot;"
        NAME="btnPlus">
</TD>
<TD>

        <INPUT LANGUAGE="VBScript" TYPE=Button VALUE="=" ONCLICK="Operator
&quot;=&quot;"
        NAME="btnEquals">
</TD>
</TR>
</TABLE>
</FORM>
</BODY>
</HTML>
```

VBScript ties scripts to events differently than JavaScript. In VBScript a subroutine is created and given a name of Object_Event(), where "Object" is the name of the object within the Object Model for Scripting hierarchy, and "Event" is the specific standard or custom event. Also notice that the false parameter passed to the `Clear` subroutine (not function) is not surrounded by parentheses.

```
...
<SCRIPT LANGUAGE="VBScript">
<!--
Sub window_onLoad()
  Clear false
end sub
-->
</SCRIPT>
...
```

At the beginning of our calculator script, we declare the same four global variables using the `Dim` statement.

```
...
<SCRIPT LANGUAGE="VBScript">
<!--
dim Accumulator
dim NewNumberNeeded
dim LastOperator
dim Display
...
```

The `Number` subroutine doesn't change much except for the syntax of the if statement and comments.

```
...
Sub Number( Num )
  'Is it a new number?
  if NewNumberNeeded = true then
    'Set the display to the number
    Display.value = Num
    'addition numbers are digits
    NewNumberNeeded = false
  else
    'Its not a new number, but is the current number a zero
    if Display.value = "0" then
      'Set the display to the number
      Display.value = Num
    else
      'Add the number as a digit to the display
      Display.value = Display.value + Num
    end if
  end if
end sub
...
```

The internals of the `Operator` subroutine are quite a bit different from before. In JavaScript, we were able to assemble a string that represented our expression and pass it to the `eval` function. VBScript doesn't have a comparable function. Instead, we set up a `Select Case` to conditionally execute based on the `LastOperator` variable. The `Operator` subroutine is also where we call the JavaScript function `AddToTally`.

```
...
Sub Operator( Op )
  'If a number has been entered in the display
  'then perform the pending operation
  if NewNumberNeeded = false then
    'Show the display and operator in the tally sheet
    top.TallyFrame.AddToTally( Display.value + " " + Op )

select case LastOperator
    case "+"
      Accumulator = CDbl( Accumulator ) + CDbl( Display.value )
    case "-"
      Accumulator = CDbl( Accumulator ) - CDbl( Display.value )
    case "*"
      Accumulator = CDbl( Accumulator ) * CDbl( Display.value )
    case "/"
```

```
      Accumulator = CDbl( Accumulator ) / CDbl( Display.value )
    case else
      Accumulator = Display.value
  end select

  Display.value = Accumulator
  LastOperator = Op
  NewNumberNeeded = true

  'On an equal operation display the total and a separator line
  if Op = "=" then
    top.TallyFrame.AddToTally( Accumulator )
    top.TallyFrame.AddToTally( "----------" )
  end if
 end if
end sub
...
```

The `ClearEntry` subroutine sets the value of the `Display` object variable. Notice the use of the Set statement because we are setting the reference to an object. From that point on, accessing the variable is the same as accessing window.document.Calculator.Display.

```
...
Sub ClearEntry()
  set Display = window.document.Calculator.Display
  'Set the value in the display to zero
  Display.value = "0"
  'Any number button pressed will start a new number
  NewNumberNeeded = true
end sub
...
```

The Clear function differs little except for syntax changes.

```
...
Sub Clear( fButtonPress )
  Accumulator = 0      'clear the accumulated calculation
  LastOperator = ""    'clear any pending operations
  ClearEntry           'clear the display

  ' Only tally on button press, not initialize
  if fButtonPress then
    top.TallyFrame.AddToTally( "C" )
  end if
end sub
...
```

The thing to notice about the `Decimal` function is the use of the `InStr` function. Strings are not objects in VBScript. You cannot call the `indexOf` method of a string. Instead, the `InStr` function returns the index of a character in a string.

```
...
Sub Decimal()
  'if no numbers have been entered yet, place
  'a zero with a decimal following in the display
  if NewNumberNeeded = true then
    Display.value = "0."
    NewNumberNeeded = false
  else
    'if there is a number in the display already
    'make sure is doesn't have a decimal point
    if InStr( Display.value, "." ) = 0 then
      NewNumberNeeded = false
      Display.value = Display.value + "."
    end if
  end if
end sub
...
```

The `Percent` and `PlusMinus` subroutines differ only by syntax.

```
...
Sub Percent()
  'The display must contain a value entered by a user
  'This prevents a user from clicking plus/minus
  'after an operator has been pressed, but before
  'a new number has been entered
  if NewNumberNeeded = false then
    Display.value = Display.value / 100
  end if
end sub

Sub PlusMinus()
  'The display must contain a value entered by a user
  'This prevents a user from clicking plus/minus
  'after an operator has been pressed, but before
  'a new number has been entered
  if NewNumberNeeded = false then
    Display.value = Display.value * -1
  end if
end sub
-->
</SCRIPT>

<TITLE>Calculator</TITLE>
</HEAD>

<BODY>
<H1 ALIGN=CENTER>Calculator</H1>
<HR ALIGN=CENTER WIDTH=100%>
<FORM ACTION="" NAME="Calculator">
<TABLE ALIGN=CENTER COLS=5 BORDER=2 CELLPADDING=1 CELLSPACING=1>
<TR>
<TD COLSPAN=5 ALIGN=CENTER>
<INPUT TYPE=Text SIZE=50 NAME="Display" WIDTH=100%>
</TD>
</TR>
```

```
<TR>
<TD>
...
```

The LANGUAGE attribute of each form element is set to VBScript so that the script engine knows how to format the procedure call when the event occurs.

```
...
<INPUT LANGUAGE="VBScript" TYPE=Button VALUE="7" ONCLICK="Number &quot;7&quot;"
NAME="btnSeven">
</TD>
<TD>
<INPUT LANGUAGE="VBScript" TYPE=Button VALUE="8" ONCLICK="Number &quot;8&quot;"
NAME="btnEight">
</TD>
<TD>
<INPUT LANGUAGE="VBScript" TYPE=Button VALUE="9" ONCLICK="Number &quot;9&quot;"
NAME="btnNine">
</TD>
<TD>
<INPUT LANGUAGE="VBScript" TYPE=Button VALUE="/" ONCLICK="Operator &quot;/&quot;"
NAME="btnDivide">
</TD>
<TD>
<INPUT LANGUAGE="VBScript" TYPE=Button VALUE="%" ONCLICK="Percent" NAME="btnPercent">
</TD>
</TR>

<TR>
<TD>
<INPUT LANGUAGE="VBScript" TYPE=Button VALUE="4" ONCLICK="Number &quot;4&quot;"
NAME="btnFour">
</TD>
<TD>
<INPUT LANGUAGE="VBScript" TYPE=Button VALUE="5" ONCLICK="Number &quot;5&quot;"
NAME="btnFive">
</TD>
<TD>
<INPUT LANGUAGE="VBScript" TYPE=Button VALUE="6" ONCLICK="Number &quot;6&quot;"
NAME="btnSix">
</TD>
<TD>
<INPUT LANGUAGE="VBScript" TYPE=Button VALUE="*" ONCLICK="Operator &quot;*&quot;"
NAME="btnMultiply">
</TD>
<TD>
<INPUT LANGUAGE="VBScript" TYPE=Button VALUE="CE" ONCLICK="ClearEntry"
NAME="btnClearEntry">
</TD>
</TR>

<TR>
<TD>
<INPUT LANGUAGE="VBScript" TYPE=Button VALUE="1" ONCLICK="Number &quot;1&quot;"
NAME="btnOne">
</TD>
<TD>
```

```
<INPUT LANGUAGE="VBScript" TYPE=Button VALUE="2" ONCLICK="Number &quot;2&quot;"
NAME="btnTwo">
</TD>
<TD>
<INPUT LANGUAGE="VBScript" TYPE=Button VALUE="3" ONCLICK="Number &quot;3&quot;"
NAME="btnThree">
</TD>
<TD>
<INPUT LANGUAGE="VBScript" TYPE=Button VALUE="-" ONCLICK="Operator &quot;-&quot;"
NAME="btnMinus">
</TD>
<TD>
<INPUT LANGUAGE="VBScript" TYPE=Button VALUE="C" ONCLICK="Clear true" NAME="btnClear">
</TD>
</TR>


<TR>
<TD>
<INPUT LANGUAGE="VBScript" TYPE=Button VALUE="+/-" ONCLICK="PlusMinus"
NAME="btnPlusMinus">
</TD>
<TD>
<INPUT LANGUAGE="VBScript" TYPE=Button VALUE="0" ONCLICK="Number &quot;0&quot;"
NAME="btnZero">
</TD>
<TD>
<INPUT LANGUAGE="VBScript" TYPE=Button VALUE="." ONCLICK="Decimal" NAME="btnDecimal">
</TD>
<TD>
<INPUT LANGUAGE="VBScript" TYPE=Button VALUE="+" ONCLICK="Operator &quot;+&quot;"
NAME="btnPlus">
</TD>
<TD>
<INPUT LANGUAGE="VBScript" TYPE=Button VALUE="=" ONCLICK="Operator &quot;=&quot;"
NAME="btnEquals">
</TD>
</TR>
</TABLE>
</FORM>
</BODY>
</HTML>
```

As you can see, most of the changes to the VBScript calculator are syntax changes. The rest of the changes, as in the `Operator` function, are just the result of functionality differences between the two languages. But whether you load JSCALCFR.HTM or VBCALCFR.HTM, both calculators should operate identically, and the visitor to the page will be none the wiser.

Revisiting WidgetWare.com

Scripting gives the Web developer a powerful new tool when creating documents. Scripting—whether JavaScript or VBScript—provides a way to add logic to a Web page. It also provides ways to do things that are cumbersome using straight HTML.

Updating Multiple Frames

The WidgetWare site uses the familiar three-frame approach that we described in Chapter 3 and depicted in Fig. 4.12. One of the problems with this approach is that in many cases you need to update the contents of more than one frame when the user selects a link. For example, it would be nice if a click on our "Home" anchor would update both of the other two frames. Using HTML, you can specify only one target in the anchor element. Something like this:

```
<a
   href="frconten.htm"
   target="contents">
Home
</a>
```

Using our three-frame approach, we sometimes need to update two frames when an anchor is clicked. Thanks to scripting and the object model we can now do this:

```
<a LANGUAGE="JavaScript"
   href="frconten.htm"
   target="contents"
   onClick="parent.frames[2].location.href='frmain.htm'">
Home
</a>
```

Here we've used the ability to embed script code directly within an anchor. If you need to do more, such as update a number of frames, you can use a separate script block and tie it to the anchor using the NAME attribute. Something like this:

```
<A HREF = "" Name="GoHome">Home</a>
<SCRIPT LANGUAGE ="VBScript">
<!--
SUB GoHome_OnClick()
  parent.frames[1].location.href='frcontent.htm'
  parent.frames[2].location.href='frmain.htm'
END SUB
-->
</SCRIPT>
```

This is just one example. There are hundreds of scripts freely available on the Web. The following table gives you some links to start with. You can also visit WidgetWare.com for others.

Figure 4.12
Three-frame page.

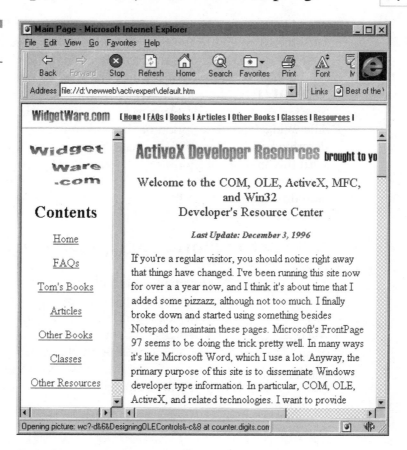

Figure 4.12
Three-frame page.

WEB RESOURCES:

URL	Description
http://www.sapien.net/demo/javascript/	Lots of good JavaScript examples.
http://www.infohiway.com/javascript/ indexf.htm	Over 100 JavaScript examples.
http://intergalactinet.com/www/ javascript/	You guessed it, more JavaScript stuff.

Debugging Scripts

One of the more difficult aspects of developing scripts that run in a browser is debugging the script as you write it. There are several reasons for this. First, to maintain backward compatibility, browsers ignore tags that they don't understand. So, if you mistype the SCRIPT tag or the LANGUAGE attribute, the browser will simply ignore it. Second, most of the tools today don't provide a syntax check of your script code as you type it in. You have to wait until the browser executes it before you find out if you used the correct syntax in your code. And finally, when the browser runs into a problem parsing and executing the script, you get only a very basic description of the problem.

These aspects combine to make writing and testing a script a bit tedious. You write or modify your script, load the page up in the browser, and "exercise" the script. If there is a problem, you typically get something like that shown in Fig. 4.13

Internet Explorer's Script Debugger

To help in the development and deployment of browser-based scripts, Microsoft has released an add-on product for Internet Explorer called the Script Debugger. Internet Explorer's Script Debugger provides everything you could ask for in a debugger. It debugs scripts written in either VBScript or JavaScript, allows you to set breakpoints, has a debug window in which you can view the contents of script variables, shows the call stack, and provides syntax-coloring of your script code.

Figure 4.13
Runtime script error
in Internet Explorer.

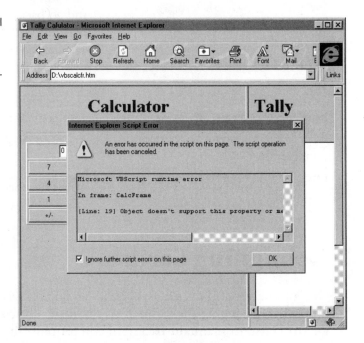

After downloading and installing the Script Debugger, a simple right mouse click in Internet Explorer and selection of **View Source** launches the debugger. Also, if Internet Explorer encounters an error like that displayed in Fig. 4.13, after clicking the **OK** button, the debugger launches automatically.

For example, say I have mistyped a line in our VBScript-based calculator example, something like the following misspelling of "Value" in the Number procedure:

```
Sub Number( Num )
   'Is it a new number?
   if NewNumberNeeded = true then
      document.Calculator.Display.Valeu = Num 'Set the display to the number
      NewNumberNeeded = false      'addition numbers are digits
   else
      ...
   end if
end sub
```

When I first try to use the calculator I get a script error just like that shown in Fig. 4.13. However, after clicking **OK,** the debugger will pop up as shown in Fig. 4.14.

The cursor is placed on the offending line so that you can quickly determine the problem. Our calculator uses frames and so the debugger's **Project Explorer** shows all of the documents that are currently loaded by the browser. To get a better idea of what's going on, you can set a break point on a given line (with the F9 key), and go back to the browser. Once the line is executed again, the debugger will pop up on the break point. At this point, you can examine the call stack or use the **Immediate** window to examine the contents of your variables, and so on. You can also step through your script code just as you do using most of Microsoft's development tools. Figure 4.15 shows the Script Debugger in action.

Web RESOURCES:

URL	Description
http://www.microsoft.com/vbscript	Download the Script Debugger for Internet Explorer.

Summary

JavaScript and VBScript are the two major scripting languages in the Web environment. Scripting allows you to add programmatic actions to

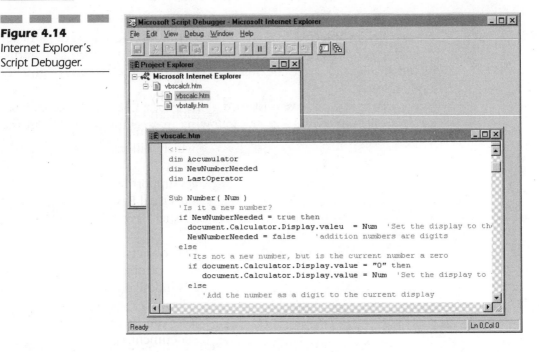

Figure 4.14
Internet Explorer's
Script Debugger.

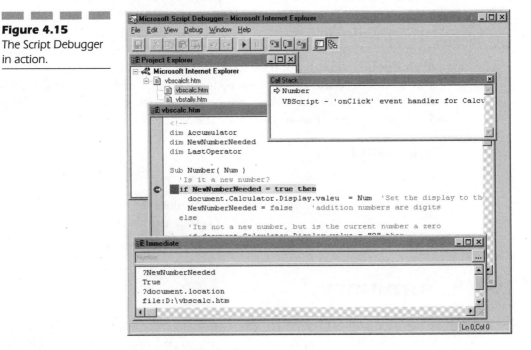

Figure 4.15
The Script Debugger
in action.

Web pages. The script executes on the client machine within the browser. The two major browsers, Netscape Navigator and Communicator and Microsoft's Internet Explorer support scripting. Scripting is added to HTML-based pages via the SCRIPT element.

Although the JavaScript language was initially developed by Netscape, Microsoft has implemented its own version and called it JScript. The JavaScript language has been handed over to a standards body and eventually the language will be standardized, which will make script development easier.

VBScript is one of two scripting languages support by Internet Explorer. VBScript is a subset of both Visual Basic and Visual Basic for Applications. It allows developers that are familiar with Visual Basic to quickly transfer their skills to the Web environment.

The Object Model for Scripting is a set of "objects" that script-enabled browsers support. The OMS exposes a number of objects through a standard hierarchy. The top-level object is the Window object. The Window object provides access to things such as the browser's status bar and other user-interface objects. All other OMS objects can be access through the window object. Other objects include the document, frames, history, and forms objects. Access to these objects allows a script developer to do things that cannot be done with static HTML.

5

Using ActiveX Controls

As we discussed briefly in Chapter 2, ActiveX controls are at the center of Microsoft's Web strategy. Initially ActiveX controls were called OLE controls, and were conceived in early 1994 as a replacement for 16-bit Visual Basic custom controls (also known as VBXs). Visual Basic custom controls used a proprietary architecture and were difficult to implement in other, non–Visual Basic environments. Microsoft designed the new control architecture by enhancing the existing OLE standard. It also made the specification public so that other tool vendors could incorporate OLE controls into their tools. Before the surge in Web popularity, ActiveX controls were also at the center of the component-based software revolution, which has now received a big push by the shift to Web-based development.

Component-based software is a model of software development that uses hardware-style techniques in the creation of software modules. Complex electronic hardware is created using small, standardized integrated computer chips. The chips are inexpensive, provide well-documented and well-defined functionality, and can be used effectively without understanding the internal workings of the chip.

Software components are similar. They strive to completely encapsulate the details of their implementation and expose highly functional, easy-to-use interfaces for software developers. A component-based application is then created by assembling a number of these highly functional software components, just as in the electronic hardware industry. Visual Basic made component-based software a reality in 1991 with its VBX architecture. It continues today with ActiveX controls.

ActiveX controls are small software components that can provide a wide range of software services. They are backed by a well-defined, published standard. ActiveX controls are built upon Microsoft's Component Object Model (COM) and can be plugged in to Visual Basic, Visual C++, Delphi 3, and Visual J++ applications. (Actually, nearly all Windows-based development tools support the use of ActiveX controls.) ActiveX controls can also be embedded directly within HTML-based Web pages. This allows a Web page developer to add significant new functionality to previously static Web pages.

An ActiveX control provides functionality to Web pages in the same way that Java applets do. However, because an ActiveX control gives the developer complete access to the Win32 API, it can provide a tremendous amount of functionality. Anything that you can do with a normal Windows application, you can also do with an ActiveX control. This cannot be said for a typical Java applet, primarily because a Java applet has restricted access to the local machine. ActiveX controls expose their functionality using a technology called Automation.

Automation

Automation is an important, application-level technology based on Microsoft's Component Object Model (COM). (We discuss COM in detail in the next chapter.) Automation is one of the more powerful features provided by the OLE/ActiveX specification. Automation provides a mechanism whereby software modules written by different vendors in different languages can interoperate, something software developers have been needing for a long time.

Automation is the key technology used in most of Microsoft's development tools. For example, every object and class in Visual Basic is an Automation object. Also, most of Microsoft's applications, such as Microsoft Word, Excel, and PowerPoint, expose all of their functionality through Automation. This allows other developers to use these applications as components of their applications.

One of the key features of Automation is its cross-language support. By exposing the functionality of a software module using Automation, it can be accessed using languages such as C++, Delphi's Object Pascal, Visual Basic, JavaScript, and so on. ActiveX controls use Automation exclusively to expose their functionality. They do so using three distinct techniques: properties, methods, and events.

Control (Automation) Properties

Most ActiveX controls have properties. A *property* describes some characteristic of the control. For example, most controls will have color and font properties. By modifying the *BackColor* property of a control, you are affecting a characteristic of the control. Each instance of a control has its own set of characteristics or properties. If you place three Label controls on a Web page, you can set the *BackColor* of each control independently.

A property is typically implemented as a data member of a C++ class. This member variable maintains the state of a specific characteristic of the control. Here's a snippet of code that might implement the *BackColor* and *Caption* property for a control:

```
class Control {
private:
   OLE_COLOR m_BackColor;
   CString   m_strCaption;
   ...
```

```
public:
    OLE_COLOR   GetBackColor();
    void        SetBackColor( OLE_COLOR clr );
    CString     GetCaption();
    void        SetCaption( CString& str );
    ...
};
```

One of the most powerful features of properties, at least from an ActiveX control perspective, is that they can be persistent. When designing a Web page or other application that uses ActiveX controls, you can set the properties to a specific value during the design process. The container application can then persist (or save) these values. Later, when the control is instantiated and displayed, the property values are the same as when you initially designed the application.

This may sound simple, but in reality it is a fairly complex process. Remember, each control is its own, independent component. A specific property value, such as "Red," cannot be saved with the control itself, it must be maintained external to the control. The container application provides this persistence. We talk about this in more detail in Chapter 7, but it will be important when we discuss the OBJECT element in a moment.

NOTE: *A property is accessed a bit differently depending on the language that you are using. Visual Basic hides the fact that a property is accessed through C++ methods. For example, to manipulate the* Caption *property you would do this:*

```
' Set the caption
objControl.Caption = "Delete"
' Retrieve the caption
str = strControl.Caption
```

Visual Basic's syntax hides the fact that access to the property actually proceeds through the accessor methods. Using C++, however, you would use methods to modify and query the property value.

Control (Automation) Methods

Most controls also provide functionality through methods. Whereas control properties typically affect a characteristic of a control, its methods affect and provide distinct behavior. Automation methods are basically the same as C++ methods. They perform some function on the object instance, typically modifying the internal state of the object. Say, for example, we were developing a control that provided simple email services.

It would probably have `Send` and `Receive` methods. The C++ declaration might look something like this:

```
class MailControl {
...
    int        Send();
    int        Receive();
};
```

The C++ comparison holds when discussing instances of controls as each control acts just like an instance of a C++ class (and most often actually is one). By setting a property or calling a method within a control, you are affecting that specific instance of the control.

Control Events

Controls also provide an external communication mechanism called an *event*. Events are generated internally by a control and are then communicated back to the container. The container can then do whatever it wants to. Typically, the container will provide a scripting language, such as Visual Basic, to allow the control user to tie specific code to each control event.

A good example is the `Click` event generated by a button control. When a user clicks on a button control it *fires* its `Click` event. If users of the control need to perform some action on the event, they would add their own code to execute when the event occurs.

The C/C++ comparison here would be the concept of a callback function. A callback function takes as a parameter a pointer to a function that you write. As the callback function executes, it "calls back" into your function with specific information. This is exactly what an event is doing. If we care to, we can add code to the `Click` event that will execute as the control "calls back" to the user. Events provide an out-of-band (asynchronous) signaling mechanism that is useful in event-driven environments such as Windows. This will become clearer as we work through the examples in this chapter as well as those in Chapters 6 and 7.

Control Containers

ActiveX controls must be *hosted* within an ActiveX control container. In other words, they cannot provide their functionality without the services of the container application. An ActiveX container provides several services for a control. It provides a *control site* where the control resides and also provides an execution environment where the control user can set properties, call methods, and act on events generated by the control.

As described earlier, most development tools today provided ActiveX control container support. A Visual Basic form is an example of a good ActiveX control container, so is any Visual C++ window object, or a Delphi 3 or C++ Builder form.

Container Modalities

ActiveX control containers have two basic modes of operation: Design-time and run-time. At design-time, the container instantiates a control and allows the user to manipulate the control's properties. The developer (or control user) will set certain characteristics of the control, such as its size, font, background color, and so on. The actual functionality of the control isn't available in this mode. For example, a timer control will allow its *Interval* property to be set at design-time, but the functionality of the timer control, a periodic set of events, is available only at run-time. At run-time, the control is instantiated, any persistent properties are applied, and the control's functionality is used. In our timer example, the control would start firing events at the specified interval.

Most containers used in development tools such as Visual Basic, Delphi, and so on, function in both modes. During application development, the control is manipulated in design-mode. Later, when the application is executed the control's run-time functionality is used. Some containers, however, operate only in one of the two potential container modes. Internet Explorer, for example, is a run-time only container. ActiveX Control Pad, on the other hand, manipulates controls only in the design phase. We visit container modalities again in Chapter 7.

Internet Explorer

As alluded to previously, Internet Explorer is an ActiveX control container. In this chapter, we use these services to embed several ActiveX controls within Internet Explorer to build interactive Web pages. By using ActiveX controls within Internet Explorer, a tremendous amount of functionality can be added to the existing Web environment. ActiveX controls make

Internet Explorer a rich application development tool. Applications previously written using Visual Basic can now be written to work completely within the confines of the new universal client, the browser.

Basic Internet Explorer—Provided Controls

As we've already discussed, Internet Explorer is a wonderful ActiveX control container. In fact, it ships with several useful controls that you can use both in your applications and on your Web pages. Actually, Internet Explorer is itself a very powerful ActiveX control. Later in this chapter, we use the Internet Explorer control to build our own browser.

Internet Explorer provides those controls listed in Table 5.1. These controls are installed on each machine that installs Internet Explorer and the

TABLE 5.1

Internet
Explorer–Provided
Controls

Control	Description
Web Browser control*	Provides the majority of Internet Explorer's functionality. A full-function Web browser that supports everything that Internet Explorer does.
Timer control*	A nonvisual control that provides periodic events. Useful for performing functions at timed intervals.
Marquee control*	A marquee-style control that will scroll an HTML-based Web document within its frame.
Active Movie control	Displays video, sound, and synchronized video with sound.
HTML Layout control	This control allows the embedding of other ActiveX controls and provides two-dimensional layout capabilities. We discuss this in more detail later.
Microsoft Forms 2.0 controls	ActiveX Control Pad comes with a number of simple controls, such as a label, text box, combo box, list box, and so on—a total of 11 controls.
ActiveX Image control	Displays images encoded in a variety of formats: Windows metafile, JPEG, .GIF, and .BMP.
ActiveX Hotspot control	Allows you to add a transparent area that will fire an event when the mouse moves over it.

*Installed with basic, Internet Explorer—only install.

ActiveX Control Pad. Those marked with an asterisk are installed with the basic, Internet Explorer—only install. Additional Microsoft provided controls are available for free at Microsoft's Website. Some of these are listed in Table 5.2.

WEB RESOURCES:

URL	Description
http://www.microsoft.com/activex/controls/	Microsoft's ActiveX control gallery. Hundreds of ActiveX controls are demonstrated here, including several of Microsoft's controls.

Adding Controls to Your Web Pages with ActiveX Control Pad

To demonstrate what you can do with ActiveX controls, the next few sections use several controls to enhance some of the Web pages at WidgetWare.com. In Chapter 4 we used ActiveX Control Pad to learn about JavaScript and VBScript. We also used it once to add a simple ActiveX control to the "Tally Sheet" page of our calculator. We again use ActiveX Control Pad in this chapter to demonstrate adding controls and VBScript to Web pages.

Where Is the Control?

One of the most important aspects to understand when using ActiveX controls on your Web pages is how they work on the user's machine.

TABLE 5.2

Other Microsoft Controls

Control	Description
Label control	Displays text at different angles, colors, and so on.
Popup Menu control	Provides a pop-up menu within a Web page.
Menu control	Allows you to place a menu button on a Web page. This is useful for drop-down navigation.

When initially designing your pages with ActiveX Control Pad, the control's housing (the *CONTROL.OCX* file) must reside on your local machine. Later, after you have moved the page to your Web server, how does the user's browser get a copy of the control?

Component Download

Browser's that support the embedding of ActiveX controls must also support a new Microsoft technology called *Component Download*. Component Download is based on COM and provides automatic download, verification, and registration of ActiveX components. In other words, the component's object code is copied from a Web server to the local machine.

After the component (typically an OCX or DLL file) is copied locally, the Component Download service ensures the validity of the component, and, depending on the security level of the browser, will register it on the local machine. Once registered, the functionality of the component can be used within the browser. It's not always as simple as described here, because most controls require other files to execute, and this requires specific packaging of the component and these files.

Security is also an issue. Downloading untrusted executable code in the Internet environment isn't a good idea. Microsoft also has a technology, *Authenticode*, that ensures the validity of downloaded components. We discuss this in a moment.

The Object Element

Controls are supported in HTML through the OBJECT element. It allows the embedding of images, documents, Java applets, and ActiveX controls. Here's an example of the OBJECT element for the Timer control that we use in a moment.

```
<OBJECT ID="Timer" WIDTH=39 HEIGHT=39
  CLASSID="CLSID:59CCB4A0-727D-11CF-AC36-00AA00A47DD2"
  CODEBASE="http://activex.microsoft.com/controls/iexplorer/ietimer.ocx"
>
    <PARAM NAME="_ExtentX" VALUE="1032">
    <PARAM NAME="_ExtentY" VALUE="1032">
    <PARAM NAME="Interval" VALUE="5000">
</OBJECT>
```

The OBJECT element has several important attributes. The ID attribute is used to specify a name for the embedded object. This name can then be used to uniquely identify the control when adding VBScript code to the page. The WIDTH and HEIGHT attributes, of course, specify the extents of the object. There are a number of attributes that apply to the OBJECT element. These are listed in Table 5.3. We're not going to cover all of them, just the ones needed to understand how ActiveX controls are supported in HTML-based documents.

TABLE 5.3

Object Element Attributes

Element	Description
ALIGN = *type*	Specifies the alignment of the object. One of BASELINE, CENTER, LEFT, MIDDLE, RIGHT, TEXTBOTTOM, TEXTMIDDLE, TEXTTOP. Their behavior is similar to the IMG element's ALIGN attribute.
BORDER = *integer*	If the object is a hyperlink, this specifies the width of the outlining border.
CLASSID = *url*	Specifies the ID of the object. ActiveX controls use the form: "CLSID:128-bit-class-identifier."
CODEBASE = *url*	A URL that specifies where the object resides. This allows the downloading of the component to the local machine.
DATA = *url*	Describes data for the object. The format of the data is dependent of the object itself. This object uses this attribute to find object specific data.
DECLARE	Declares the object but does not actually instantiate it.
HEIGHT = *integer*	The suggested height of the object. This allows the browser to draw an outline of where the object will display when loaded.
HSPACE = *integer*	Indicates the amount of horizontal space that should added to the object between any text to the object's left or right.
NAME = *name*	The name of the object.
SHAPES	Indicates shaped hyperlinks are supported.
STANDBY = *text*	Provides text to display while the object is loading.
TYPE = *type*	The Internet media type.
USEMAP = *url*	The URL of an image map to use with the object.
VSPACE = *integer*	Indicates the amount of vertical space that should be added to the object between any text on the top or bottom of the object.
WIDTH = *integer*	The suggested width of the object. This allows the browser to draw an outline of where the object will display when loaded.

The CLASSID attribute

The CLASSID attribute is a very important one. As the page is being loaded by the container (e.g., Internet Explorer) the CLASSID is used to locate the control's executable (typically a DLL) on the local machine. COM objects, such as ActiveX controls, are uniquely identified with a 128-bit Globally Unique Identifier (GUID). All COM objects have their own GUID. A CLASSID is just a specific type of GUID. The container uses the Windows registry to map the provided CLASSID to a specific DLL, and the container loads the DLL and executes it. We discuss this process in more detail in Chapter 6, when we discuss Microsoft's Component Object Model.

The CODEBASE attribute

As we've discussed, an ActiveX control may not reside on the machine that is browsing your Web page, and the control must reside on the local machine in order for it to display and for any script to access its functionality. If the control is not installed, the CODEBASE attribute specifies the location for the browser to retrieve the executable.

If the control needs to be installed, the Component Download service is used to download and install the control. It does so by navigating through the specified URL. There are several ways that a control can be packaged for download installation on the local machine. In our previous example, we are specifying the actual .OCX file that needs to be installed. The other option is to package up several dependent files into a Windows cabinet (.CAB) file.

The PARAM element

The PARAM element is valid only within the OBJECT element. Its purpose is to store the property values of the embedded object. The NAME attribute provides the property name and the VALUE attribute provides any value. The TYPE attribute, which isn't shown in our example, indicates the specific Internet media type for the given property. There is also a VARTYPE attribute that is used to specify the specific type of value that is provided.

The data specified via the PARAM element is used by the container to set the property values of the specific control instance. After the control is downloaded, installed, and created, based on the CLASSID and CODE-BASE attributes, the container will read the values from the PARAM element and pass them to the control. In this way, our Timer control will start out with its **Interval** property initialized to 5000.

In our previous example, there are three PARAM tags—one for each property that we have set for the Timer control. As you will soon see, the Timer control actually has more than three properties, but we need to persist only those values that are different from the defaults. Properties that begin with an underscore (e.g., _ExtentY) are internal control properties that it uses for its own purposes.

The Timer Control

The Timer control is shipped with Internet Explorer and will reside on all remote machines that are using Internet Explorer. The Timer control is simple and provides us with a good place to begin. We use the Timer con-

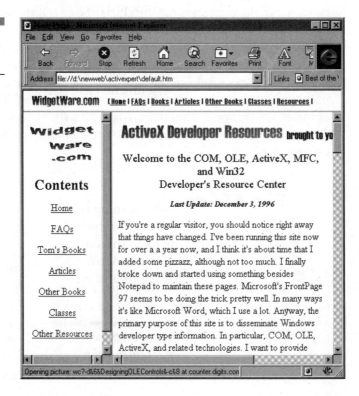

Figure 5.1
WidgetWare.com's Main Page.

trol to periodically change the .GIF image displayed on WidgetWare's main page. Figure 5.1 shows the three-frame main page of WidgetWare .com.

At the top of the lower-left page we currently have a wavy GIF image with the WidgetWare name. What we would like to do is use the Timer control to alternate the images displayed in that area. The first step is to add a Timer control to our page.

Most ActiveX controls will provide some sort of visual representation. However, the Timer control does not, so we can insert the control wherever we want to within our HTML document. To demonstrate how we will add alternating images to WidgetWare's content frame here, we're going to create a new document and practice there. Start ActiveX Control Pad and perform the following:

- Open a new HTML document and set the TITLE to "Time and Image Control Example."

- Using **Edit/Insert ActiveX Control** insert the Internet Explorer Timer control into the document. Set the **Interval** property to 5000 and the **ID** property to "Timer." This is shown in Fig. 5.2.

- Close the Timer control window. This will add HTML code to support the control.

- Save the new document with the name TIMER.HTM.

When you closed the ActiveX control window, ActiveX Control Pad added several lines to your document. Here they are:

```
<OBJECT ID="Timer" WIDTH=39 HEIGHT=39
 CLASSID="CLSID:59CCB4A0-727D-11CF-AC36-00AA00A47DD2">
    <PARAM NAME="_ExtentX" VALUE="1032">
    <PARAM NAME="_ExtentY" VALUE="1032">
    <PARAM NAME="Interval" VALUE="5000">
</OBJECT>
```

We've already discussed the meaning of these elements and attributes. However, as you can see, ActiveX Control Pad did not provide us with a default CODEBASE. We have to do this ourselves either by directly editing the document or setting it in the ActiveX control property dialog. The Timer control properties, methods, and events are listed in Table 5.4.

NOTE: *How do you determine what to put in the CODEBASE attribute? Good question. If you've written the control then it's up to you to provide the location and correct packaging for the control. We discuss this in Chapter 7. However, if you're just using a*

Figure 5.2
Inserting the Timer
Control with ActiveX
Control Pad.

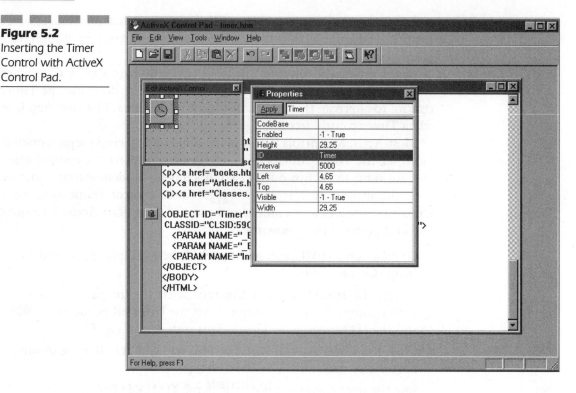

Property	Description
Enabled	Boolean—Enables or disables the timer.
Interval	Long—Sets the interval of the timer, in milliseconds. By setting the value to a negative value or zero, the timer is disabled.

Method	Description
AboutBox	Displays the control's about box.

Event	Description
Timer	Fired periodically depending on the enabled state of the timer and the interval.

TABLE 5.4

Timer Control
Properties,
Methods, and
Events

control provided by someone else, say Microsoft, they will typically provide a .CAB file with the latest version of the control and any dependent files.

Our purpose in adding the control to our document was that we wanted to perform some periodic action. We've set the control's interval to five seconds. However, to actually do something when the timer fires, we have to add some script in the Timer's `Timer` event, something like this:

```
<SCRIPT LANGUAGE="VBScript">
<!--
Sub Timer_Timer()
    ' We need to do something here
end sub
-->
```

Event code is handled by adding a VBScript procedure with a name of the form:

Sub *ControlIDName_EventName()*

'Code goes here

End Sub

Okay, we have a way to do something periodically, but what is it that we wanted to do? We wanted to alternate a series of images within our page. The best way to do this, at least without writing our own control or Java applet, is to use another ActiveX control—the Image control. We need to add that to our page.

The Image Control

Microsoft's Image control is provided with a complete install of Internet Explorer. It provides image support in a way very similar to the HTML IMG element. It progressively renders various image types, such as a Windows metafile, .GIF, JPEG, and Windows bitmap (.BMP) formats. We need to use this control because the HTML IMG element does not allow dynamic modification of the image that is displayed.

Add the Image control to your document. Add it at the top, right after the BODY tag. Set up the properties as indicated in Table 5.5, where Image control properties, methods, and events are listed.

- Set the AutoSize property to TRUE.
- Set the BackColor to white.

TABLE 5.5

Image Control
Properties,
Methods, and
Events

Property	Description
AutoSize	Boolean—If true the control resizes to match the size of the specified image.
BackColor	Long—Specifies the background color of the control.
BackStyle	Long—Specifies whether the control should act transparent or opaque. Options are: 0—Transparent 1—Opaque
BorderColor	Long—Specifies the border color of the control.
BorderStyle	Long—Specifies whether the control should display a border. Options are: 0—None 1—Single line
Enabled	Boolean—Indicates if the control is currently enabled.
PictureAlignment	Long—Specifies the alignment for the image. Options are: 0—The top-left corner. 1—The top-right corner. 2—The center. 3—The bottom-left corner. 4—The bottom-right corner.
PicturePath	URL—Specifies the location of the image to display within the control. Several image formats are supported.
PictureSizeMode	Long—Specifies how the control should behave when sizing the image. Options are: 0—Crops any part of the picture that is larger than the HTML Layout or HTML page. 1—Stretches the picture to fill the HTML Layout or HTML page. This setting distorts the picture in either the horizontal or vertical direction. 3—Enlarges the picture, but does not distort the picture in either the horizontal or vertical direction.
PictureTiling	Boolean—A value of true causes the control to tile the image across the entire area of the control.
SpecialEffect	Long—Specifies a special effect for the control's border. Options are: 0—Object appears flat, distinguished from the surrounding form by a border, a change of color, or both. The default. 1—Object has a highlight on the top and left and a shadow on the bottom and right. 2—Object has a shadow on the top and left and a highlight on the bottom and right. The control and its border appear to be carved into the form that contains them.

Property	Description
TABLE 5.5 (Continued)	3—Border appears to be carved around the edge of the control. Not valid for check boxes or option buttons. 6—Object has a ridge on the bottom and right and appears flat on the top and left.

Method	Description
Move	Moves the control within the HTML page.
ZOrder	Specifies the z-order of the control. Options are: 0—Places the control at the front of the z-order. The control appears on top of other controls. The default. 1—Places the control at the back of the z-order. The control appears underneath other controls.

Event	Description
MouseDown	Fired when the mouse is pressed or released
MouseUp	
MouseMove	Fired as the mouse is moved over the area of the control.

- Set the PictureSize mode to Zoom (3).

- Set the PicturePath property to "widgetware.gif" or any other image that you have access to.

The widgetware.gif is included on the CD-ROM.

After inserting the control and setting the properties, your document should resemble the following code. The shaded lines are ones that you should add to the document as well. They provide just enough content to simulate the "contents" pane of a multiframe page.

```
<HTML>
<HEAD>
<TITLE>Image and Timer Control Example</TITLE>
</HEAD>
<BODY BGCOLOR=white>
<SCRIPT LANGUAGE="VBScript">
<!-+ra-
Sub Timer_Timer()
    'We need to do something here
end sub
-->
</SCRIPT>
<CENTER>
```

```
<OBJECT ID="Image" WIDTH=111 HEIGHT=132
 CLASSID="CLSID:D4A97620-8E8F-11CF-93CD-00AA00C08FDF">
    <PARAM NAME="PicturePath" VALUE="widgetware.gif">
    <PARAM NAME="AutoSize" VALUE="-1">
    <PARAM NAME="BackColor" VALUE="16777215">
    <PARAM NAME="BorderStyle" VALUE="0">
    <PARAM NAME="SizeMode" VALUE="3">
    <PARAM NAME="Size" VALUE="2928;3493">
    <PARAM NAME="PictureAlignment" VALUE="0">
    <PARAM NAME="VariousPropertyBits" VALUE="19">
</OBJECT>
```

```
<H3>Contents</H3>
<p><a href="..\chap3\chapter3.htm">Chapter 3 Examples</a></p>
<p><a href="..\chap4\chapter4.htm">Chapter 4 Examples</a></p>
<p><a href="..\chap5\chapter5.htm">Chapter 5 Examples</a></p>
<p><a href="..\chap6\chapter6.htm">Chapter 6 Examples</a></p>
<p><a href="..\chap7\chapter7.htm">Chapter 7 Examples</a></p>
<p><a href="..\chap8\chapter8.htm">Chapter 8 Examples</a></p>
<p><a href="..\chap9\chapter9.htm">Chapter 9 Examples</a></p>
```

```
<OBJECT ID="Timer" WIDTH=39 HEIGHT=39
  CLASSID="CLSID:59CCB4A0-727D-11CF-AC36-00AA00A47DD2">
    <PARAM NAME="_ExtentX" VALUE="1032">
    <PARAM NAME="_ExtentY" VALUE="1032">
    <PARAM NAME="Interval" VALUE="5000">
</OBJECT>
</BODY>
</HTML>
```

After making all of these changes, save the document and load it up in your favorite browser. You should get something like Fig. 5.3.

We now have all of the pieces we need to alternate an image on our page. All that is left is to add some VBScript code to do the work. You can use the Script Wizard in ActiveX Control Pad or you can just type in the code directly as we go through it.

```
<SCRIPT LANGUAGE="VBScript">
<!--
dim ImageIndex

Sub window_onLoad()
   ImageIndex = 0
end sub
-->
</SCRIPT>
```

Our strategy is to maintain a global variable that contains an index of the current image. The previous code declares a global variable, ImageIndex, and assigns it to zero in the OnLoad event for the document. Variables declared outside of any procedure are global to the document.

```
<SCRIPT LANGUAGE="VBScript">
<!--
```

Figure 5.3
Our New Page in
Internet Explorer.

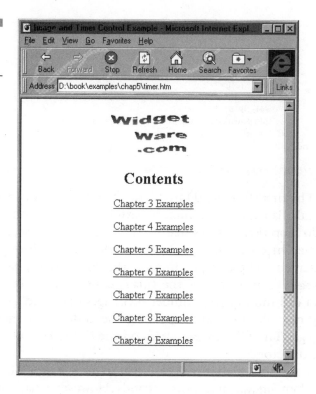

```
Sub Timer_Timer()
   ChangeImage()
end sub
-->
</SCRIPT>
```

Every time the Timer control fires its `Timer` event we will call `ChangeImage`, which will display a different image in the Image control. The `ChangeImage` procedure does all of the work. Here it is:

```
<SCRIPT LANGUAGE="VBScript">
<!--
Sub ChangeImage()
   Dim NewIndex

   ' Get a new image index and make sure it isn't
   ' the same image that is currently displayed
   NewIndex = ImageIndex
   Do While( NewIndex = ImageIndex )
      NewIndex = Int(5 * Rnd)
   Loop
   ImageIndex = NewIndex
   ' Set the PicturePath property to the new image
   Select Case ImageIndex
      Case 0
```

```
        Image.PicturePath = "widgetware.gif"
     Case 1
        Image.PicturePath = "d2small.gif"
     Case 2
        Image.PicturePath = "d1small.gif"
     Case 3
        Image.PicturePath = "activex.gif"
     Case 4
        Image.PicturePath = "xsmall.gif"
   end Select
end sub
-->
</SCRIPT>
```

The first thing we do in ChangeImage is use VBScript's Rnd function to calculate a random integer between zero and four inclusive. We have a do loop that ensures that we don't randomly select the current index value. Once we calculate the new index we fall through a VBScript case statement. There, depending on the index value, we update the PicturePath property of the Image control with the URL to an image. You can modify the number of images displayed by adding or removing case elements and updating the code that generates the random integer. The .GIF images are all on the CD-ROM in the Chapter 5 example directory.

The result of all this work is that we now have a Web page that displays random images every five seconds. However, what happens if the user isn't using a browser that supports ActiveX controls?

NOTE: *When adding script to your pages with ActiveX Control Pad the script will be placed throughout your document. When you're satisfied with the functionality of your page, you should go back through it and place all of your script within one SCRIPT block. This will save download and parse time.*

Browsers That Don't Support ActiveX Controls

Currently, not all browsers support the use of ActiveX controls. There are several reasons for this, the most prominent one being that ActiveX controls are very machine specific. It's difficult to write a control that will work on a Macintosh, UNIX workstation, and all of the flavors of Windows. For this reason, you need to develop your pages so that they will display properly when viewed in non-ActiveX browsers.

NOTE: *Of course, if you're working in a more controlled environment such as an intranet, where you can specify the client platform, this isn't as much of an issue.*

There are several strategies that you can use. First, you could use the JavaScript code to identify the hosting browser and load a browser specific document based on the user's browser type. You could do something like this:

```
<HTML>
<HEAD>
<TITLE>Browser Test Page</TITLE>
</HEAD>
<BODY>
<Script Language = "JavaScript">
<!--
    if ( navigator.userAgent.indexOf( "MSIE" ) != -1)
       window.open( "msie.htm", target="_self" )
    else if ( navigator.userAgent.indexOf( "Mozilla" ) != -1)
       window.open( "nsnav.htm", target="_self" )
-->
</Script>

<h1>If you got here, you are running something besides IE or Navigator</h1>
</BODY>
</HTML>
```

This makes management of your pages more difficult because you will at least double the number of pages that you must maintain. In some cases, however, it may be required. Another solution is to use the same HTML document, but provide similar capabilities to those browsers that do not support ActiveX controls. In our previous example, altering the images is nice, but it doesn't add a lot of functionality to our page, so displaying a single image in noncontrol browsers is an acceptable solution. By adding one new tag to the OBJECT element that embeds our image control we can display an image where the Image control would normally reside.

```
<OBJECT ID="Image" WIDTH=111 HEIGHT=132
 CLASSID="CLSID:D4A97620-8E8F-11CF-93CD-00AA00C08FDF">
    <PARAM NAME="PicturePath" VALUE="widgetware.gif">
    <PARAM NAME="AutoSize" VALUE="-1">
    <PARAM NAME="BackColor" VALUE="16777215">
    <PARAM NAME="BorderStyle" VALUE="0">
    <PARAM NAME="SizeMode" VALUE="3">
    <PARAM NAME="Size" VALUE="2928;3493">
    <PARAM NAME="PictureAlignment" VALUE="0">
    <PARAM NAME="VariousPropertyBits" VALUE="19">
```

```
<IMG SRC="widgetware.gif" WIDTH=111 HEIGHT=132>
</OBJECT>
```

Browsers that don't support ActiveX controls will display the image specified in the IMG tag. This keeps the look of the document the same and the user is none the wiser that anything is different. Another important aspect is that you may need to provide alternate ways of navigating within your Website. We'll keep this in mind as we add additional controls to widgetware.com in the following sections.

The Popup Menu Control

Another ActiveX control that Microsoft makes freely available is the Popup Menu control. As stated earlier, Microsoft and other third-party vendors have several hundred ActiveX controls that you can use on your Web pages as well as in your applications. We're covering only a few of them here to demonstrate various ActiveX control techniques. In Chapters 7 and 8, we build our own controls.

Anyway, the Popup control gives you the ability to pop up a Windows-style menu wherever you need to within your Web page. We're going to use it in our next example to pop up a list of valid URLs within an HTML document. The user will then be able to navigate to the new URL by selecting it from the pop-up menu. A simple example, but it will allow us to use Internet Explorer's Object Model for Scripting.

The CD-ROM contains a series of Web pages that demonstrate the examples in each of the chapters. For our next example, we're going to re-create the main "Chapter 5" examples page. The technique that we demonstrate is also used at widgetware.com, but it's easier to demonstrate with a smaller example. To get us started perform the following:

1. Using ActiveX Control Pad, create a new page.

2. Add a simple heading such as "Chapter 5 Examples," and then add a horizontal rule below the heading (<HR>).

3. Save your new page with the name CHAPTER5.HTM.

To get an idea of where we're going, Fig. 5.4 shows the finished page. The focus of this example is creating the **Quick Navigate** button at the top. When the page is loaded we will use VBScript and Internet Explorer's object model to dynamically create a list of URLs on the page. A button click will then show this list and allow the user to navigate directly.

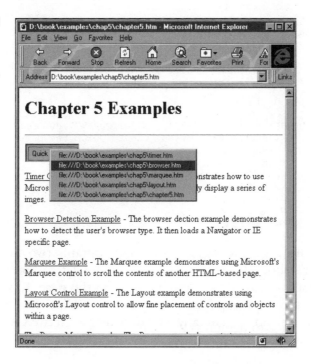

Next, insert an instance of the **Microsoft Popup Menu Control** right after the horizontal rule. The properties, methods, and events of the Popup menu control are shown in Table 5.6. Set the ID of the control to "Popup." We don't need to alter any of the control's other properties, so after inserting the control into your page, close the control window.

The Popup menu control remains hidden until its `Popup` method is called. The control will then pop up and will immediately hide once a menu item is selected or the user clicks the mouse outside of the control. To provide a clue to the user that our page has this pop-up menu capability, let's add a simple command button to our page. Again, using ActiveX Control Pad insert an instance of the **Microsoft Froms 2.0 Command-Button** control. Place it after the Popup control. Set the control's **Caption** property to "Quick Navigate," and the ID of the control to **QuickNavigate** and then close the control window. Your HTML should now look something like this:

```
<HTML>
<HEAD>
<TITLE>Chapter 5 Examples</TITLE>
</HEAD>
<BODY>
<H1>Chapter 5 HTML-based Examples</H1>
```

```
<hr>
OBJECT ID="Popup" WIDTH=1 HEIGHT=1
 CLASSID="CLSID:7823A620-9DD9-11CF-A662-00AA00C066D2">
    <PARAM NAME="_ExtentX" VALUE="26">
    <PARAM NAME="_ExtentY" VALUE="26">
</OBJECT>

<OBJECT ID="QuickNavigate" WIDTH=96 HEIGHT=32
 CLASSID="CLSID:D7053240-CE69-11CD-A777-00DD01143C57">
    <PARAM NAME="Caption" VALUE="Quick Navigate">
    <PARAM NAME="Size" VALUE="2540;847">
    <PARAM NAME="FontCharSet" VALUE="0">
    <PARAM NAME="FontPitchAndFamily" VALUE="2">
    <PARAM NAME="ParagraphAlign" VALUE="3">
</OBJECT>
</BODY>
</HTML>
```

Okay, we now have a page that contains two ActiveX controls and that's about it. Next we need to tie the two controls together using VBScript and add some hyperlinks to the page. To start off, we need to add the following VBScript code to initialize the Popup menu control. You can do it manually, or you can use ActiveX Control Pad's Script Wizard.

TABLE 5.6

Popup Menu Control Properties, Methods, and Events

Property	Type/Description
ItemCount	Long—The number of items in the menu list.
MenuItem	String—A list of the items in the menu list.

Method	Description
AboutBox	Displays the control's about box.
Popup	Pops up the menu control at a given position. If no position information is provided, the control pops up at the current mouse position.
Clear	Clears the items in the menu.
AddItem	Adds an item to the menu.
RemoveItem	Removes an item from the menu.

Event	Description
Click	Fired when a item in the Popup menu is selected. It passes an integer parameter indicating the position in the menu.

```
<SCRIPT LANGUAGE="VBScript">
<!--
Dim LinkArray()
Sub window_onLoad()
   'Make sure our array is large enough
   ReDim LinkArray(document.links.length)

   'Loop through and make a list of URLs in this document
   Dim n
   For n = 0 to document.links.length - 1
      url = document.links(n).href
      Popup.AddItem url, n
      LinkArray(n) = url
   Next
end sub
-->
</SCRIPT>
```

First, we need a global variable to hold the list of URLs that are contained within the page. We DIM a variable outside of any procedure, which makes it global. You should also notice that the variable is not dimmed to a specific size. We're using VBScript's ability to dynamically change the size of an array.

Next, we add some code to the window's onLoad event. As the document is loaded we first dimension our dynamic array to be the exact size that we need, which is the number of hyperlinks on the page. The OMS document object contains an array of hyperlinks contained within the document. We iterate over the array and add each URL to the Popup menu using its AddItem method. We also add the URL to our global array.

You might be asking why do we have to store the URL twice, once in the control, and again in the array? Good question. The Popup menu control does not provide access to the items in the menu, so we have to maintain our own list. We need our own copy because we will navigate to the new URL whenever the URL is selected. Our menu control now has a list of every URL in the document. We now need to do something with it when the user presses the **QuickNavigate** button.

```
Sub QuickNavigate_Click()
   Call PopUp.PopUp
end sub

Sub Popup_Click(item)
   window.top.location = LinkArray( item - 1)
end sub
```

By adding these lines within the SCRIPT block, we're just about finished. When the Click event is triggered, we call the PopUp method of the Popup control. The menu will pop up over the **QuickNavigate** button. If the user selects a URL from the menu, the Popup_Click event will fire. At that point we navigate to the new URL by setting the current window's location property. That's all there is to it. Of course, our page doesn't currently have any hyperlinks on it, so the menu is empty. However, the CHAPTER5.HTM example on the CD-ROM contains hyperlinks for each of the examples in this chapter, something like this:

```
<p><a href="timer.htm">Timer Control Example</a> - The Timer
example demonstrates how to use Microsoft's Timer and Image
controls to periodically display a series of imges. </p>

<p><a href="browser.htm">Browser Detection Example</a> - The
browser dection example demonstrates how to detect the user's
browser type. It then loads a Navigator or IE specific page.</p>

<p><a href="marquee.htm">Marquee Example</a> - The Marquee example
demonstrates using Microsoft's Marquee control to scroll the
contents of another HTML-based page.</p>

<p><a href="layout.htm">Layout Control Example</a> - The Layout
example demonstrates using Microsoft's Layout control to allow fine
placement of controls and objects within a page.</p>

<p><a href="chapter5.htm">The Popup Menu Example</a> - The Popup
example demonstrates using Microsoft's Popup menu and Command
Button controls to "popup" a list of URLs within a page.</p>
```

With these five hyperlinks, the Popup menu looks like that shown in Fig. 5.4. The neat thing is that as additional URLs are added to the page, there is no additional work required. The Popup menu will always be up-to-date because it is populated dynamically.

NOTE: *Don't forget to use Internet Explorer's Script Debugger if you're having difficulties with any of these examples. Developing Web pages with HTML, VBScript, and embedded ActiveX controls is rather difficult, especially if you don't use the debugger. Take a look back at the end of Chapter 4 if necessary.*

The Marquee Control

The Marquee control is one of the neatest "standard equipment" controls that comes with Internet Explorer. In Chapter 3 we took a look at the HTML MARQUEE element, which provides a way to scroll simple text across your Web pages. Microsoft's Marquee control does this and a whole lot more. It allows you to scroll the complete contents of another HTML document. You can scroll multiple HTML documents, tie script code to a left mouse click, and so on. For an idea of what the control can do, its properties, methods, and events are outlined in Table 5.7.

To start our Marquee control example, perform the following:

1. Using ActiveX Control Pad, create a new page.
2. Add a simple title and heading such as "Marquee Example" and then add a horizontal rule below the heading (<HR>).
3. Insert an instance of the Internet Explorer Marquee control after the rule. Size it like the one shown in Fig. 5.5, set the `ScrollDelay` property to "500," the PageFlippingOn property to "1," the `ScrollPixelsX` property to 0, and the `ScrollPixelsY` property to –5. A negative value indicates that the scrolling will proceed from top to bottom.
4. Then, insert two Command Button controls below the Marquee. Name the first button **pbtPause** and set its `Caption` to "Pause," and name the second button **pbtResume** and set its `Caption` to "Resume."
5. Save your new page with the name MARQUEE.HTM.
6. Figure 5.5 shows where we'll be when we're finished.

If you load your new page into the browser, it won't look much like Fig. 5.5. One of the problems you will face when adding controls to a Web page is getting them positioned correctly. The HTML model doesn't (yet) provide much in the way of fine positioning of objects. There is a solution to this problem, and we discuss it in the next example. For now, we will have to use tables to get our button controls to line up properly. The HTML for your page should look something like this:

```
<HTML>
<HEAD>
<TITLE>Marquee Control Example</TITLE>
</HEAD>
<BODY bgcolor="white">
<font face="comic sans MS" color="green">
<h1>Marquee Control Example</h1>
<hr>
<OBJECT ID="Marquee" WIDTH=456 HEIGHT=49
    CLASSID="CLSID:1A4DA620-6217-11CF-BE62-0080C72EDD2D">
        <PARAM NAME="_ExtentX" VALUE="12065">
        <PARAM NAME="_ExtentY" VALUE="1296">
        <PARAM NAME="ScrollPixelsX" VALUE="0">
        <PARAM NAME="ScrollPixelsY" VALUE="-5">
        <PARAM NAME="ScrollDelay" VALUE="500">
        <PARAM NAME="PageFlippingOn" VALUE="1">
        <PARAM NAME="WidthOfPage" VALUE="1000">
</OBJECT>
<TABLE>
<TR>
<TD>
```

TABLE 5.7

Marquee Control
Properties,
Methods, and
Events

Property	Type/Description
ScrollStyleX	The horizontal scrolling style. Either Bounce or Circular.
ScrollStyleY	The vertical scrolling style. Either Bounce or Circular.
ScrollDelay	The time in milliseconds between scrolls of the page. The page image is scrolled by the amount specified via the ScrollPixelsY or ScrollPixelsX properties.
LoopsX	For Circular scrolling this sets the number of times the page is scrolled horizontally. For Bounce scrolling, this specifies the number of bounces. An interval of -1 specifies infinite, and zero indicates a horizontal slide.
LoopsY	For Circular scrolling this sets the number of times the page is scrolled vertically. For Bounce scrolling, this specifies the number of bounces. An interval of -1 specifies infinite, and zero indicates a horizontal slide.
ScrollPixelsX	Number of pixels to move the page horizontally each time Scroll-Delay time passes. The default is 75 pixels.
ScrollPixelsY	Number of pixels to move the page vertically each time ScrollDelay time passes. The default is 0 pixels.
szURL	String—The URL of the HTML page.
DrawImmediate	Boolean—Should the page be progressively rendered. One is true and zero is false. The default is false.
WhiteSpace	The control can append a series of pages. The Whitespace property indicates the amount of white space, in pixels, between the renderings of each page. The default is zero.
PageFlippingOn	Boolean—A value of True indicates that the control will flip between a series of URLs setup using the InsertURL method. A value of False indicates that the pages added through InsertURL will be appended together and rendered as one image.
Zoom	The Marquee control can reduce or enlarge the rendered page by changing the zoom property. It specifies a percentage of the original page size. The default is 100.
WidthOfPage	The width, in pixels, for us when rendering the page. The default is 640. You need to adjust this value if text or images are "cut off" when the page is rendered in the control.

Method	Description
AboutBox	Displays the control's about box.
Pause	Stops any scrolling.

TABLE 5.7
(Continued)

Method	Description
Resume	Resumes scrolling.
InsertURL	Adds a new URL to a list of URLs displayed via the control. This is used when you want to display multiple pages.
DeleteURL	Removes a page from the URL list.
QueryURL	Returns a URL from the list.
QueryURLCount	Returns the number of URLs in the list.

Event	Description
OnStartOfImage	Fired just before a new page is scrolled into the control.
OnEndOfImage	Fired when a page has been completely scrolled.
OnScroll	Fired when the page scrolls.
OnLMouseClick	Fired when the left mouse button is click inside the control's window.

Figure 5.5
Our Marquee
Example.

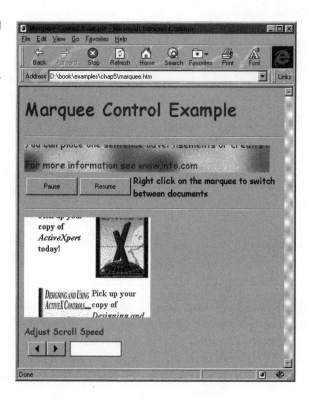

```
<OBJECT ID="pbtPause" WIDTH=96 HEIGHT=32
    CLASSID="CLSID:D7053240-CE69-11CD-A777-00DD01143C57">
        <PARAM NAME="Caption" VALUE="Pause">
        <PARAM NAME="Size" VALUE="2540;846">
        <PARAM NAME="FontCharSet" VALUE="0">
        <PARAM NAME="FontPitchAndFamily" VALUE="2">
        <PARAM NAME="ParagraphAlign" VALUE="3">
</OBJECT>
<TD>
<OBJECT ID="pbtResume" WIDTH=96 HEIGHT=32
    CLASSID="CLSID:D7053240-CE69-11CD-A777-00DD01143C57">
        <PARAM NAME="Caption" VALUE="Resume">
        <PARAM NAME="Size" VALUE="2540;846">
        <PARAM NAME="FontCharSet" VALUE="0">
        <PARAM NAME="FontPitchAndFamily" VALUE="2">
        <PARAM NAME="ParagraphAlign" VALUE="3">
</OBJECT>
<td>Right click on the marquee to switch between documents
</TABLE>
```

Here we have our basic page with three controls. We need to add the shaded lines to set the background color and font, and to help with the layout or placement of the controls on the page. Whenever you run into difficulty getting your objects to place correctly, start using tables. Tables provide a number of options to help with positioning. We're now ready to add some script.

```
<SCRIPT LANGUAGE="VBScript">
<!--
Sub window_onLoad()
    Marquee.insertURL 0, "advert.htm"
    Marquee.insertURL 0, "chapter5.htm"
    Marquee.insertURL 0, "marqcont.htm"
End Sub

Sub pbtResume_Click()
    Marquee.Resume
End Sub

Sub Marquee_OnLMouseClick()
    window.top.location = "chapter5.htm"
End Sub

Sub pbtPause_Click()
    Marquee.Pause
End Sub
-->
</SCRIPT>
```

This should be looking pretty familiar by now. When the form is loaded, we insert three different page URLs into the Marquee control. We have the `PageFlippingOn` property set to TRUE, so the marquee will scroll each page individually. The user must right-click on the marquee to cycle through the different pages. The code for the two command buttons is straightforward, and a left mouse click will jump back to the Chapter 5 examples page.

The Marquee control will scroll the complete contents of the HTML pages that we added via the `InsertURL` method. One use for this control is to scroll "credits" for your page or site. Here's the MARQCONT.HTM file used in the preceding example.

```
<HTML>
<HEAD>
<TITLE>Marquee Content Page</TITLE>
</HEAD>
<BODY bgcolor="white" background="..\images\blusky.jpg" text="red">
<font face ="comic sans MS" size = "4">
<p>
<p>This page is brought to you by widgetware.com
<p>You can place one sentence advertisements or credits here
<p>For more information see www.info.com
<p>What we have here is a scrolling billboard
</BODY>
</HTML>
```

The best way to see this effect is to actually load the page up in Internet Explorer on your machine. The previous page, with its background image and all, is scrolled within the Marquee control's area. Also, as the page is scrolling by, a right mouse click will toggle the next page to display.

To make things a bit more interesting, our page has another Marquee control, and it scrolls the ADVERT.HTM file. Using ActiveX Control Pad create a new file and add the following code. Then save the file as ADVERT.HTM.

```
<HTML>
<HEAD>
<TITLE>Advertisement Page</TITLE>
</HEAD>
<BODY bgcolor="white">
<table cellspacing="15">
<tr>
<td>
<img align="right" src="..\images\xsmall.gif">
<b><font color="blue">Pick up your copy of <i>ActiveXpert</I> today!
<tr>
<td>
<img align="left" src="..\images\d2small.gif">
<b><font color="red">Pick up your copy of <i>Designing and Using ActiveX Controls</I>
today!
</table>
</BODY>
</HTML>
```

Once again we have to use HTML tables to get the images and text to position the way we need them. We're going to scroll this page as an advertisement within our Marquee example page that we started earlier. Using ActiveX Control Pad do the following with the MARQUEE.HTM file.

1. At the end of the OBJECT element for the last Command Button, add a horizontal rule (HR).

2. Insert a second instance of the Marquee control. This time set Page-FlippingOn to 0, the ScrollDelay to 300, the PageWidth to 275, and the szURL value to "ADVERT.HTM." Also, size the control into a relatively small square like that shown in Fig. 5.6.

The Spin Button Control

We're going to allow the user to change the scroll speed of our second Marquee control, and we do this by adding a spin button control to our page. A spin button is part of the regular Windows interface. It allows the user to scroll between numeric values by clicking on one of two directional arrows. Feedback is usually provided by a second label control that

Figure 5.6
Inserting a Second Marquee Control.

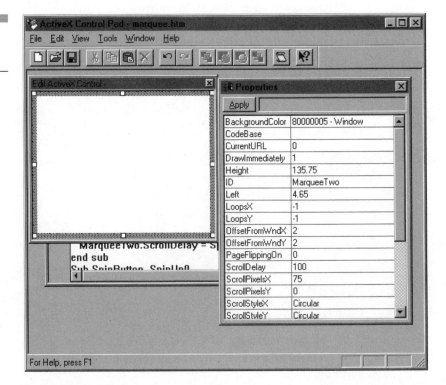

contains the current value maintained by the spin button control. We'll do this as well.

Back in ActiveX Control Pad insert an instance of the Forms 2.0 Spin Button control. The properties, methods, and events are shown in Table 5.8. Set the Max value to 1000, and the initial Value to 300. This corresponds to the value we set our initial `ScrollDelay` to in our Marquee control.

Next, insert an instance of the Forms 2.0 label control following the spin button. We use this to display the current value stored in the spin button control. After inserting the controls, we then need to "wrap" them in a table so they will align correctly, and finally we add some text indicating the purpose of the controls. Here's the resulting HTML. The shaded lines are ones that were added after inserting the controls.

```
. . .
<hr>
<OBJECT ID="MarqueeTwo" WIDTH=236 HEIGHT=181
  CLASSID="CLSID:1A4DA620-6217-11CF-BE62-0080C72EDD2D">
    <PARAM NAME="_ExtentX" VALUE="6244">
    <PARAM NAME="_ExtentY" VALUE="4789">
    <PARAM NAME="ScrollPixelsX" VALUE="0">
    <PARAM NAME="ScrollPixelsY" VALUE="-5">
    <PARAM NAME="ScrollDelay" VALUE="200">
    <PARAM NAME="szURL" VALUE="advert.htm">
```

TABLE 5.8

Spin Button Control Properties, Methods, and Events

Property	Type/Description
Delay	Specifies the period to delay when the user holds down one of the spin buttons.
Min Max	Specifies the minimum and maximum values for the spin button.
Orientation	Specifies if the spin button is arranged horizontally or vertically.
SmallChange	Specifies the amount of change to apply when the user clicks a spin button.
Value	The current value of the spin button.

Method	Description
AboutBox	Displays the control's about box.

Event	Description
Change	Fired when the value property changes.
SpinDown SpinUp	Fired when the specified spin button is clicked.

```
          <PARAM NAME="PageFlippingOn" VALUE="0">
          <PARAM NAME="WidthOfPage" VALUE="275">
</OBJECT>
<p>Adjust Scroll Speed
<table cellspacing="6">
<tr>
<td>
<OBJECT ID="SpinButton" WIDTH=71 HEIGHT=27
    CLASSID="CLSID:79176FB0-B7F2-11CE-97EF-00AA006D2776">
        <PARAM NAME="Size" VALUE="1870;706">
        <PARAM NAME="Max" VALUE="1000">
        <PARAM NAME="Position" VALUE="300">
        <PARAM NAME="SmallChange" VALUE="10">
</OBJECT>
<td>
<OBJECT ID="Label" WIDTH=96 HEIGHT=27
 CLASSID="CLSID:978C9E23-D4B0-11CE-BF2D-00AA003F40D0">
        <PARAM NAME="BackColor" VALUE="16777215">
        <PARAM NAME="Size" VALUE="2540;706">
        <PARAM NAME="BorderStyle" VALUE="1">
        <PARAM NAME="FontName" VALUE="Arial">
        <PARAM NAME="FontEffects" VALUE="1073741825">
        <PARAM NAME="FontHeight" VALUE="240">
        <PARAM NAME="FontCharSet" VALUE="0">
        <PARAM NAME="FontPitchAndFamily" VALUE="2">
        <PARAM NAME="FontWeight" VALUE="700">
</OBJECT>
</table>
</BODY>
</HTML>
```

Microsoft's Layout Control

One of the problems we encountered earlier when working with the examples was getting the controls to position correctly on our pages. In fact, we had to use HTML tables to get our button and label controls to line up. How come? Well, the HTML standard doesn't provide a very robust way of specifying an object's position on the page. Only recently have tables and various IMG alignment attributes been added to the specification to provide at least rudimentary positional placement of images and objects such as ActiveX controls.

To overcome these limitations, Microsoft created its Layout control. The Layout control is based on a new specification that has been submitted to the W3C. The specification describes how to provide exact *x,y* coordinate placement of objects within HTML-based pages. These new capabilities are described as "2-D" layout control, which not only provides exact placement of objects, but also allows them to overlap. This gives the page designer a lot more flexibility when positioning images.

The Layout control is provided with the Internet Explorer install, and is automatically installed if the user chooses the "Full Installation." Along with the installation of the Layout control, the Microsoft Forms 2.0 controls are installed as well.

The Forms 2.0 Controls

Along with the Layout control, Microsoft also provides a number of simple GUI controls that are useful when working with the Layout control. Actually, these controls do not need the Layout control to function, and we've already used several of them in our previous examples. Table 5.9 lists the Forms 2.0 controls shipped with the Layout control install.

To demonstrate the Layout control, let's build another calculator as we did in Chapter 4. However, this time, we'll use all ActiveX controls and VBScript. Because we're using the Layout control, we'll be able to design the control a bit differently, and we'll have more control over the placement of individual controls.

TABLE 5.9

Microsoft's Forms 2.0 ActiveX Controls

Control	Description
Forms 2.0 Label control	A simple label control that displays text. We used this in the Marquee example.
Forms 2.0 Textbox	Used to allow entry of simple text.
Forms 2.0 Combo Box	A drop-down list of text-based options.
Forms 2.0 List Box	A scrollable list of text options.
Forms 2.0 Check Box	A two-state toggle button.
Forms 2.0 Option Button	Also known as a Radio button. Used to select from a group of options.
Forms 2.0 Toggle Button	Like a Radio button. It provides two states.
Forms 2.0 Command Button	A push button. We used this control in several of our previous examples.
Forms 2.0 Tabstrip	A single tab strip. Useful when combined with other tab strips to create the familiar property page type interface.
Forms 2.0 ScrollBar	A Windows scrollbar. Both horizontal and vertical.
Forms 2.0 Spin Button	A bidirectional button. We used this in the Marquee examples.

ActiveX Control Pad has several options specifically for building Web pages using the Layout control. Start up ActiveX Control Pad and create a **New** document. However, this time choose the **New HTML Layout...** option. Instead of creating a simple HTML page, you will get a form-editing dialog like that shown in Fig. 5.7. This is an instance of the Layout control.

NOTE: *If the controls you need aren't displayed on the control palette, just right-click on the palette. This will bring up a list of all of the controls on your machine. From there you can add them to the default control palette.*

The Layout control is actually a full-function ActiveX Control container just like Internet Explorer. It is very much like a Visual Basic form object. You can place controls wherever you want, the controls can overlap and so on, and you ultimately provide functionality by tying the controls together with VBScript.

Figure 5.7
Inserting a New
HTML Layout in
ActiveX Control Pad.

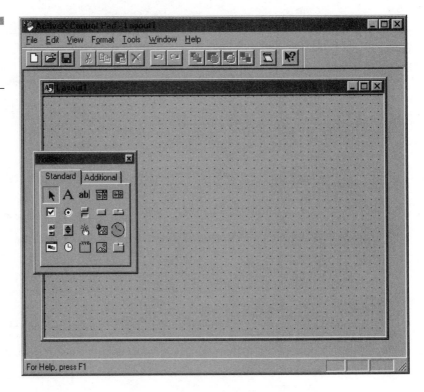

We're not going to go through all of the steps to build the calculator as you should be able to do that by now. Instead take a look at Fig. 5.8, which shows the finished product. There are 20 instances of the Forms 2.0 Command Button, one instance of the Forms 2.0 Text Box, and two instances of the Forms 2.0 Label control.

Two instances of the Label control? Yes, if you look very closely you will see that there is a 3-D look to the text "WidgetWare.com Calculator." By setting the label control's `BackStyle` property to "transparent" you can layer text just like we did using Cascading Style Sheets back in Chapter 3. You cannot do this with straight HTML, and that's what makes the Layout control so useful.

After inserting the 23 control instances and setting their properties, save your layout as CALC.ALX. The source should look something like this:

```
<DIV ID="Layout1" STYLE="LAYOUT:FIXED;WIDTH:148pt;HEIGHT:190pt;">
<OBJECT ID="btnOne"
   CLASSID="CLSID:D7053240-CE69-11CD-A777-00DD01143C57"
   STYLE="TOP:83pt;LEFT:8pt;WIDTH:25pt;HEIGHT:25pt;TABINDEX:0;ZINDEX:0;">
```

Figure 5.8
Our New Calculator.

```
        <PARAM NAME="Caption" VALUE="1">
        <PARAM NAME="Size" VALUE="873;874">
        <PARAM NAME="FontName" VALUE="Comic Sans MS">
        <PARAM NAME="FontEffects" VALUE="1073741825">
        <PARAM NAME="FontHeight" VALUE="240">
        <PARAM NAME="FontCharSet" VALUE="0">
        <PARAM NAME="FontPitchAndFamily" VALUE="2">
        <PARAM NAME="ParagraphAlign" VALUE="3">
        <PARAM NAME="FontWeight" VALUE="700">
</OBJECT>
<OBJECT ID="Label1"
    CLASSID="CLSID:978C9E23-D4B0-11CE-BF2D-00AA003F40D0"
    STYLE="TOP:8pt;LEFT:8pt;WIDTH:149pt;HEIGHT:45pt;ZINDEX:1;">
        <PARAM NAME="ForeColor" VALUE="255">
        <PARAM NAME="VariousPropertyBits" VALUE="8388627">
        <PARAM NAME="Caption" VALUE="WidgetWare.com Calculator">
        <PARAM NAME="Size" VALUE="5239;1587">
        <PARAM NAME="FontName" VALUE="Comic Sans MS">
        <PARAM NAME="FontEffects" VALUE="1073741825">
        <PARAM NAME="FontHeight" VALUE="320">
        <PARAM NAME="FontCharSet" VALUE="0">
        <PARAM NAME="FontPitchAndFamily" VALUE="2">
        <PARAM NAME="FontWeight" VALUE="700">
</OBJECT>
... and so on
```

You won't actually see this source within ActiveX Control Pad; however, when you save the "layout," the preceding information is written to a layout file, usually with an extension of ALX.

ALX Files

We've already mentioned that the Layout control is actually an ActiveX control container. We discuss this more in Chapter 7, but a control container must save the state of its embedded controls in some way. The Layout control does so by writing an .ALX file. The information in the ALX file provides the Layout control everything it needs to re-create itself when embedded within an HTML page. The ALX file cannot be viewed directly within a browser; it can be read and interpreted only by the Layout control. However, it is mostly HTML, and can be edited by hand.

Once the controls are positioned, the next step is to add the VBScript necessary to provide the calculator functionality. This code is very similar to what we did in Chapter 4, with two exceptions. First, we're not using Internet Explorer's object model, and second, we are using all ActiveX controls and not the HTML Form elements. Here's the script code. You can add it by hand to the ALX file or you can use the Script Wizard in ActiveX Control Pad.

```
<SCRIPT LANGUAGE="VBScript">
<!--
dim Accumulator
dim NewNumberNeeded
dim LastOperator


Sub window_onLoad()
    Clear
end sub


Sub ClearEntry()
    'set the value in the display to zero
    txtDisplay.Text = "0"
    'any number button pressed will start a new number
    NewNumberNeeded = true
end sub


Sub Clear()
    Accumulator = 0
    LastOperator = ""
    ClearEntry
end sub


Sub Number( Num )
    'Is it a new number?
    if NewNumberNeeded = true then
        'Set the display to the number
        txtDisplay.Text = Num
        'addition numbers are digits
        NewNumberNeeded = false
    else
        'Its not a new number, but is the current number a zero
        if txtDisplay.Text = "0" then
            txtDisplay.Text = Num
        else
            txtDisplay.Text = txtDisplay.Text + Num
        end if
    end if
end sub


Sub Decimal()
    'if no numbers have been entered yet, place
    'a zero with a decimal following in the display
    if NewNumberNeeded = true then
        txtDisplay.Text = "0."
        NewNumberNeeded = false
    else
        'if there is a number in the display already
        'make sure it doesn't have a decimal point
        if InStr( txtDisplay.Text, ".") = 0 then
            NewNumberNeeded = false
            txtDisplay.Text = txtDisplay.Text + "."
        end if
    end if
end sub
```

```
Sub Percent()
   'The display must contain a value entered by a user
   'This prevents a user from clicking plus/minus
   'after an operator has been pressed, but before
   'a new number has been entered
   if NewNumberNeeded = false then
      txtDisplay.Text = txtDisplay.Text / 100
   end if
end sub


Sub PlusMinus()
   'The display must contain a value entered by a user
   'This prevents a user from clicking plus/minus
   'after an operator has been pressed, but before
   'a new number has been entered
   if NewNumberNeeded = false then
      txtDisplay.Text = txtDisplay.Text * -1
   end if
end sub


Sub btnOne_Click()
   Number "1"
end sub
Sub btnTwo_Click()
   Number "2"
end sub
Sub btnThree_Click()
   Number "3"
end sub
Sub btnFour_Click()
   Number "4"
end sub
Sub btnFive_Click()
   Number "5"
end sub
Sub btnSix_Click()
   Number "6"
end sub
Sub btnSeven_Click()
   Number "7"
end sub
Sub btnEight_Click()
   Number "8"
end sub
Sub btnNine_Click()
   Number "9"
end sub
Sub btnAdd_Click()
   Operator "+"
end sub
Sub btnSubtract_Click()
   Operator "-"
end sub
Sub btnMultiply_Click()
   Operator "*"
end sub
Sub btnDivide_Click()
```

```
      Operator "/"
end sub
Sub btnDecimal_Click()
   Decimal
end sub
Sub btnPlusMinus_Click()
   PlusMinus
end sub
Sub btnEqual_Click()
   Operator "="
end sub
Sub btnClear_Click()
   Clear
end sub
Sub btnClearEntry_Click()
   ClearEntry
end sub


Sub Operator( Op )
   'If a number has been entered in the display
   'then perform the pending operation
   if NewNumberNeeded = false then
      select case LastOperator
         case "+"
            Accumulator = CDbl( Accumulator ) + CDbl( txtDisplay.Text )
         case "-"
            Accumulator = CDbl( Accumulator ) - CDbl( txtDisplay.Text )
         case "*"
            Accumulator = CDbl( Accumulator ) * CDbl( txtDisplay.Text )
         case "/"
            Accumulator = CDbl( Accumulator ) / CDbl( txtDisplay.Text )
         case else
            Accumulator = txtDisplay.Text
      end select

txtDisplay.Text = Accumulator
LastOperator = Op
NewNumberNeeded = true
end if
end sub
-->
</SCRIPT>
```

Adding the Layout Control to a Web Page

One of the neat features of the Layout control is that it provides an efficient way to package functionality for the Web environment. We now have a complete calculator, made up of several ActiveX controls and some VBScript, all encapsulated within one ALX file.

To use our new self-contained, calculator component, use ActiveX Control Pad to create a **New HTML...** page. Then, using the **Edit/**

Insert HTML Layout... insert the CALC.ALX file into the new page. Make the shaded changes shown here, and save the file as LAYOUT.HTM.

```
<HTML>
<HEAD>
<TITLE>Layout Example</TITLE>
</HEAD>
<BODY bgcolor="white">
<center>
<table border="1" >
<tr>
<td>
<OBJECT CLASSID="CLSID:812AE312-8B8E-11CF-93C8-00AA00C08FDF"
    ID="calc_alx" STYLE="LEFT:0;TOP:0">
   <PARAM NAME="ALXPATH" REF VALUE="calc.alx">
</OBJECT>
</table>
</center>
</BODY>
</HTML>
```

We've made the page a bit prettier by centering the calculator and surrounding it with a 3-D table. That's all there is to it. Figure 5.9 shows our finished page.

Figure 5.9
The Layout Control Example.

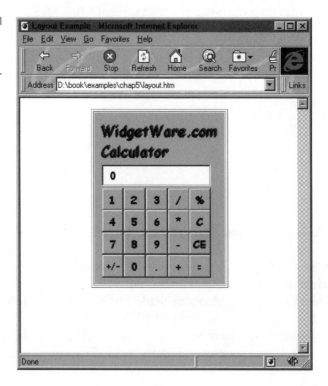

Controls, the Web, and Security

The developer of an ActiveX control has full access to the Win32 API. A control is really just a Windows DLL that is downloaded and installed on the user's machine. Anything a local program can do, a control can do as well. This affords the control developer with the highest possible degree of functionality, but it also creates a potential security problem. Java takes the sandbox approach of not allowing direct access to the local hardware. This helps with security, but it reduces functionality significantly.

To maintain this high level of functionality in ActiveX controls, Microsoft uses the new WinVerifyTrust (*Authenticode*) service to protect local machines from malicious components. Microsoft approaches security in the Web environment like that used in software retail channels. There is no guarantee that the software you buy from a local retailer is benign. There is no guarantee, but there is significant *trust*. When you purchase a software package from a vendor, such as Microsoft, you know where the software came from, and you're confident that it will not harm your machine.

Microsoft has taken the steps to set up such an environment of trust on the Web by providing technologies that ensure the authenticity and integrity of a component. A component is marked with a digital signature based on Microsoft's Authenticode technology. The component's signature is then maintained and verified by a trusted authority.

Digital Signatures

To ensure authenticity and integrity, each component is marked using a public-private key mechanism. This digital signature, which you can view as an complex checksum, is attached to a component. If the component is compromised in any way, the digital signature will become invalid.

Code Signing

To sign your components using Authenticode, so that they can be trusted in the Internet environment, you must register and obtain a certificate from one of the certification authorities such as VeriSign or GTE. After receiving your certificate, you can use the MAKECERT, SIGNCODE, and CHKTRUST utilities provided with the ActiveX SDK to sign your controls. (See Fig. 5.10.)

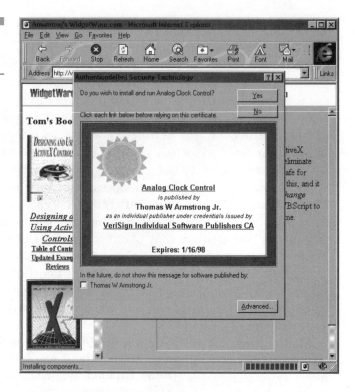

Internet Explorer Security Levels

Internet Explorer will not download components that have not been properly signed. Internet Explorer allows the user to specify the security level. (See Fig. 5.11.) If the security level is set to high, your controls must be signed (if they are not already on the local machine) and they must be safe for scripting and safe for initializing. An ActiveX control must be marked as safe by the developer. We discuss how this is done in Chapter 7. With Internet Explorer's security level set to moderate, the user is asked whether to download and install a particular component. With the safety set to none, components can be downloaded and executed without being signed or marked as safe.

The WebBrowser Control

Internet Explorer is itself primarily just a highly functional ActiveX control. The executable that starts up Internet Explorer 3.0 is IEXPLORE.EXE, which is only about 30K in size. The IEXPLORE executable provides a

Figure 5.11
Internet Explorer
Security Levels.

simple frame for the WebBrowser control. In Internet Explorer 4.0, there is no need for IEXPLORE.EXE because the Windows shell itself can host ActiveX controls. With Internet Explorer 4.0, nearly all of its functionality as well is provided by the WebBrowser control.

Since the WebBrowser control is an ActiveX control, we can access its capabilities within our own applications, just as we do with other ActiveX controls. In this section we aim to build a simple Web browser using Visual C++, MFC, and the WebBrowser control. Once we've done this, our application will support most of the features currently provided by Internet Explorer. We don't have a lot of time to spend on C++ and MFC, but there are several other books on this subject. Instead we focus on using the WebBrowser control to build a browser.

Table 5.10 details the properties, methods, and events exposed by the WebBrowser control. We use several of these in our implementation.

Building the Browser

Start up Visual C++ and perform the following steps to create the initial project.

1. Select **New** and choose a new **MFC AppWizard (exe)** project from the **Projects** tab. Name the project **Browser.** This dialog is shown in Fig. 5.12.

TABLE 5.10

WebBrowser
Control Properties,
Methods, and
Events

Property	Type/Description
Application	IDispatch*—Returns the Automation object of the containing application or that of the WebBrowser object itself.
Busy	Boolean—Returns TRUE if the browser is currently navigating to a new URL.
Container	IDispatch*—The Automation object associated with the browser's container, if any.
Document	IDispatch*—The Automation object for the browser's active document, if any.
Left	Long—Size and extents of the browser control.
Top	
Height	
Width	
LocationName	String—The URL of the current resource.
TopLevelContainer	Boolean—Returns TRUE if the WebBrowser control is the top level container.
Type	String—The type name of the contained document object.

Method	Description
GoBack	Navigates to the previous page, if one has been visited.
GoForward	Navigates to the next page, if one has been visited.
GoHome	Navigates to Internet Explorer's configured start page.
GoSearch	Navigates to Internet Explorer's configured search page.
Navigate	Navigates to a specific, provided URL.
Refresh	Refreshes the current URL.
Refresh2	Refreshes without.
Stop	Stops downloading the page.
AboutBox	Displays the control's about box.

Event	Description
BeforeNavigate	Fired before the browser navigates to a new URL.
FrameBeforeNavigate	

TABLE 5.10
(Continued)

Event	Description
CommandStateChange	Fired when the enabled state of a browser command button changes.
DownloadBegin	Fired when at the start of a URL navigation.
DownloadComplete	Fired when the URL navigation is complete.
FrameNewWindow	Fired when a new browser window is created.
NavigateComplete	Fired upon successful navigation to a new URL.
FrameNavigateComplete	
NewWindow	Fired when a new window is created to display a resource.
ProgressChange	Fired periodically as information is downloaded from a server. Used to indicated the progress of loading a page.
PropertyChange	Fired when a property has changed.
Quite	Fired when the browser is about to exit.
StatusTextChange	Fired when the status bar of the browser is updated.
TitleChange	Fired when the title bar of the browser is updated.

Figure 5.12
Visual C++ New
Project Dialog.

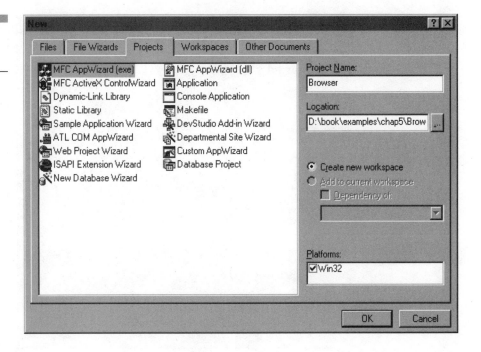

2. In AppWizard Step 1, choose the **Dialog based** application option.

3. In AppWizard Step 2, take the defaults, which should include **About box, 3D Controls,** and **ActiveX controls** support.

4. In AppWizard Step 3, take the defaults of **generate source comments** and **MFC as shared DLL.**

5. ˙ˑ AppWizard Step 4, use the default filenames provided.

6.   ˋal AppWizard dialog is shown in Fig. 5.13. After pressing **OK**
            ˑ dialog, your project will be generated.

The next step is to embed an instance of the WebBrowser control in our dialog. From the **Resource** tab double-click on the IDD_BROWSER_ DIALOG resource. This brings up the dialog editor. The control palette won't have the WebBrowser control on it. We need to select **Project/Add to Project/Components and controls...** to bring up the Component Gallery (see Fig. 5.14). Double-click on the **Registered ActiveX Controls** folder and find the control named "**Microsoft Web Browser Control.**" Insert this control into your project. This will create a Automation wrapper class for the control in the WEBBROWSER.H and .CPP files. It will also add the control to the control palette.

The next step is to build our dialog. In order to make it look somewhat like a real browser, drag and drop an instance of the WebBrowser control

Figure 5.13
AppWizard
Information Dialog.

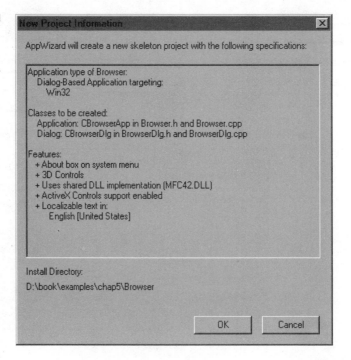

New Project Information   ✕

AppWizard will create a new skeleton project with the following specifications:

Application type of Browser:
    Dialog-Based Application targeting:
        Win32

Classes to be created:
    Application: CBrowserApp in Browser.h and Browser.cpp
    Dialog: CBrowserDlg in BrowserDlg.h and BrowserDlg.cpp

Features:
    + About box on system menu
    + 3D Controls
    + Uses shared DLL implementation (MFC42.DLL)
    + ActiveX Controls support enabled
    + Localizable text in:
        English [United States]

Install Directory:
D:\book\examples\chap5\Browser

                                          OK   Cancel

Figure 5.14
Add the WebBrowser
Control with
Component Gallery.

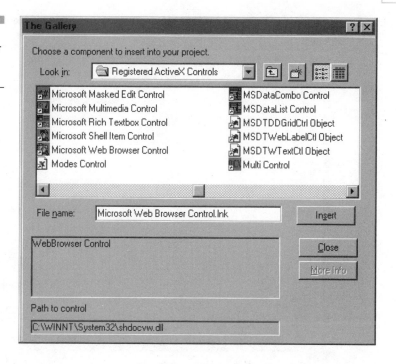

and place it in the center of the dialog. Then remove the **Cancel** button and change the caption of the **OK** button to **Exit.** Then add the controls listed in Table 5.11 to the dialog. Be sure to use the IDs listed. When you're finished, you should have a dialog that looks something like Fig. 5.15.

Trust me, building the dialog is about the toughest part of this project. Once you've got the dialog built, start up Class Wizard, go to the **Member Variables** tab, and add a member variable for each of the listed controls, except for Refresh, Search, and Print buttons. The member names are shown in Table 5.11. When finished, the Class Wizard dialog should look a lot like Fig. 5.16.

NOTE: *Make sure you change the URL EDIT control's styles to include: multi-line and want returns.*

ActiveX Control Wrapper Classes

When you added the WebBrowser control to the Browser project, Component Gallery added an MFC-based class that provides easy access to each of the control's properties and methods. Here's a quick look at the WEBBROWSER.H file.

Figure 5.15
Our Web Browser.

Control Type	Caption	Control ID	Member Name
WebBrowser	none	IDC_BROWSER	m_Browser
Button	Back	IDC_BACK	m_Back
Button	Forward	IDC_FORWARD	m_Forward
Button	Stop	IDC_STOP	m_Stop
Button	Refresh	IDC_REFRESH	NA
Button	Search	IDC_SEARCH	NA
Button	Print	IDC_PRINT	NA
Label	URL:	IDC_STATIC	NA
Edit	none	IDC_URL	m_URL
Label	none	IDC_STATUS	m_Status
Progress	none	IDC_PROGRESS	m_Progress

TABLE 5.11

Controls for Our
Dialog

Figure 5.16
Class Wizard Mapped
Control Members.

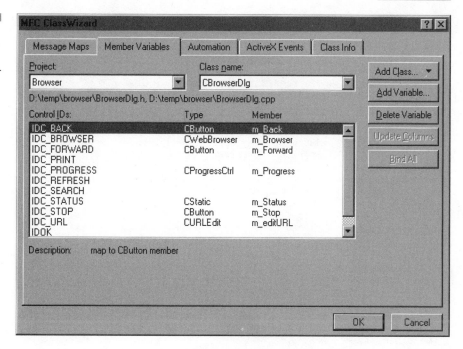

```
#ifndef_WEBBROWSER_H_
#define_WEBBROWSER_H_

/////////////////////
// Machine generated IDispatch wrapper class(es) created by Microsoft Visual C++
// NOTE: Do not modify the contents of this file. If this class is regenerated by
// Microsoft Visual C++, your modifications will be overwritten.
/////////////////////////////

// CWebBrowser wrapper class

class CWebBrowser : public CWnd
{
protected:
   DECLARE_DYNCREATE(CWebBrowser)
public:
   CLSID const& GetClsid()
   {
   static CLSID const clsid =
      { 0xeab22ac3, 0x30c1, 0x11cf, { 0xa7, 0xeb, 0x0, 0x0, 0xc0, 0x5b, 0xae, 0xb } };
      return clsid;
   }
   virtual BOOL Create(LPCTSTR lpszClassName,
               LPCTSTR lpszWindowName, DWORD dwStyle,
               const RECT& rect,
               CWnd* pParentWnd, UINT nID,
               CCreateContext* pContext = NULL)
     { return CreateControl( GetClsid(),
```

```
                            lpszWindowName,
                            dwStyle, rect, pParentWnd, nID);
    }


    BOOL Create(LPCTSTR lpszWindowName, DWORD dwStyle,
            const RECT& rect, CWnd* pParentWnd, UINT nID,
            CFile* pPersist = NULL, BOOL bStorage = FALSE,
            BSTR bstrLicKey = NULL)
    { return CreateControl( GetClsid(),
                    lpszWindowName,
                    dwStyle, rect, pParentWnd, nID,
                    pPersist, bStorage, bstrLicKey);
    }


// Operations
public:
    ...
    void GoBack();
    void GoForward();
    void GoHome();
    void GoSearch();
    void Navigate(LPCTSTR URL, VARIANT* Flags,
                VARIANT* TargetFrameName,
                VARIANT* PostData, VARIANT* Headers);
    void Refresh();
    void Refresh2(VARIANT* Level);
    void Stop();
    LPDISPATCH GetApplication();
    LPDISPATCH GetParent();
    LPDISPATCH GetContainer();
    LPDISPATCH GetDocument();
    BOOL GetTopLevelContainer();
    CString GetType();
    long GetLeft();
    void SetLeft(long nNewValue);
    long GetTop();
    void SetTop(long nNewValue);
    long GetWidth();
    void SetWidth(long nNewValue);
    long GetHeight();
    void SetHeight(long nNewValue);
    CString GetLocationName();
    CString GetLocationURL();
    BOOL GetBusy();
};

#endif // __WEBBROWSER_H__
```

The wrapper class provides us with two ways to dynamically create the WebBrowser control, and as mentioned earlier, we have access to all of the control's properties and methods through our C++ member, m_Browser. We're just about finished writing the browser and we haven't written one line of code yet. Here's where it gets even easier.

When the dialog is initially created, we need to do a few things. A browser's Back and Forward buttons aren't enabled until the user has actually navigated somewhere other than the start page. So we add the following code to `CBrowserDlg::OnInitDialog` in BROWSERDLG.CPP.

```
BOOL CBrowserDlg::OnInitDialog()
{
   CDialog::OnInitDialog();

   ...

   // Set the icon for this dialog. The framework does this automatically
   //  when the application's main window is not a dialog
   SetIcon(m_hIcon, TRUE);
   SetIcon(m_hIcon, FALSE);

   // TODO: Add extra initialization here
   m_Browser.GoHome();
   m_Back.EnableWindow( FALSE );
   m_Forward.EnableWindow( FALSE );

   return TRUE; // return TRUE unless you set the focus to a control
}
```

Next, we add code to handle the Back, Forward, Stop, Search, and Refresh buttons. Before adding the following code, you must first use ClassWizard to add a handler for each button's BN_CLICKED message.

```
void CBrowserDlg::OnBack()
{
   m_Browser.GoBack();
}


void CBrowserDlg::OnForward()
{
   m_Browser.GoForward();

}


void CBrowserDlg::OnStop()
{
   m_Browser.Stop();
}


void CBrowserDlg::OnRefresh()
{
   m_Browser.Refresh();

}


void CBrowserDlg::OnSearch()
{
   m_Browser.GoSearch();

}
```

This is easy enough. When any of these buttons are clicked, all we have to do is call the appropriate method in the WebBrowser control. Looks good. But wait, the Stop button isn't always enabled. It should be enabled only when the browser is actually downloading a page. The Stop button is used to stop this download process, which can get lengthy if the remote machine isn't available. How can we know when to enable or disable the Stop button? Well, we have to handle some of the events that the Web-Browser control fires.

Handling Control Events

In Visual C++, you map a control's events to code using your friend the ClassWizard. Start up ClassWizard and go to the **Message Maps** tab. By selecting the browser control (IDC_BROWSER) in the **Object IDs** listbox, the controls events will be listed in the **Messages** listbox on the right. By clicking the **Add Function...** button, you can add a handler for the specific event. We need to do this for the following events:

- NavigateComplete
- StatusTextChanged
- ProgressChange
- DownloadComplete
- CommandStateChange
- DownloadBegin

The DownloadBegin and DownloadComplete events provided us with an efficient way of handling the enabling and disabling of our browser's Stop button. Here's the code:

```
void CBrowserDlg::OnDownloadBeginBrowser()
{
    m_Stop.EnableWindow( TRUE );
}

void CBrowserDlg::OnDownLoadCompleteBrowser()
{
    m_Stop.EnableWindow( FALSE );
}
```

The Back and Forward buttons must be handled in a similar way. The WebBrowser control fires the CommandStateChange event whenever the state of the Forward or Back buttons changes. The declaration for the event along with the enumerated value that is passed is shown as follows:

```
typedef enum CommandStateChangeConstants {
    CSC_UPDATECOMMANDS = -1,
    CSC_NAVIGATEFORWARD = 1,
    CSC_NAVIGATEBACK = 2
} CommandStateChangeConstants;

void CommandStateChange( CommandStateChangeConstants, VARIANT_BOOL );
```

So, we need to handle enabling or disabling both the Back and Forward button in the CommandStateChange event handler like this:

```
void CBrowserDlg::OnCommandStateChangeBrowser(long Command, BOOL Enable)
{
    switch( Command )
    {
        case CSC_NAVIGATEFORWARD:
            m_Forward.EnableWindow( Enable );
            break;

        case CSC_NAVIGATEBACK:
            m_Back.EnableWindow( Enable );
            break;
    }
}
```

NOTE: *The definitions for the WebBrowser control interfaces are in the EXDISP.H header file that is included with Visual C++ 5.0. You may have to explicitly include this file to get the constant declarations for the CommandStateChange event.*

Next, we need to update our progress indicator. The Internet Explorer object model provides the `ProgressChange` event that notifies the application of the progress of a download operation. The `Progress-Change` event is called periodically as a page or image is being retrieved from a server.

`ProgressChange` passes two parameters. *Progress* contains the amount of total progress that has been achieved and *ProgressMax* contains the maximum amount of progress achievable. So, we can multiply *Progress* by 100 and divide by *ProgressMax* to get the percentage of completion, which, luckily, is exactly what the progress control's `SetPos` method expects. If *Progress* is –1 or *ProgressMax* is zero the download is complete and so we hide the progress control.

```
void CBrowserDlg::OnProgressChangeBrowser(long Progress, long ProgressMax)
{
    if ( Progress == -1 || ProgressMax == 0 )
    {
        m_Progress.ShowWindow( SW_HIDE );
```

```
      return;
   }

m_Progress.ShowWindow( SW_SHOW );
long Percentage = Progress * 100 / ProgressMax;
m_Progress.SetPos( Percentage );
}
```

The other two events finish up the aesthetic detail of our browser. NavigateComplete provides us with a way to update the URL entry field with the more recently visited URL. The StatusTextChange event gives us an opportunity to update the status of our browser. The Web-Browser control fires this event when a user mouses over a hyperlink or when the status of the document download changes, and so on, just like Internet Explorer's status bar. Here's the code:

```
void CBrowserDlg::OnNavigateCompleteBrowser(LPCTSTR URL)
{
    m_editURL.SetWindowText( URL );
}


void CBrowserDlg::OnStatusTextChangeBrowser(LPCTSTR Text)
{
    m_Status.SetWindowText( Text );
}
```

All that is left now is to hook up our **Print** button. However, to understand what's going on here, you need to understand what COM interfaces are as well as the interfaces used by the Active document standard. For now, the following code retrieves the IOleCommandTarget interface from Internet Explorer and calls its print command, which prints the current Web document. After reading Chapters 6 and 7, come back and take a look at this code and it will make a lot more sense.

```
void CBrowserDlg::OnPrint()
{
    IDispatch* pDocument = m_Browser.GetDocument();
    ASSERT( pDocument );

    IOleCommandTarget* pOleCommandTarget = 0;

    pDocument->QueryInterface( IID_IOleCommandTarget,
                               (void**)&pOleCommandTarget );
    ASSERT( pOleCommandTarget );

    pDocument->Release();

    pOleCommandTarget->Exec( NULL,
                             OLECMDID_PRINT,
                             OLECMDEXECOPT_DONTPROMPTUSER,
                             NULL,
```

```
                                          NULL );

        pOleCommandTarget->Release();
}
```

NOTE: *You may need to include DOCOBJ.H to get the declarations for the IOleCommandTarget interface.*

Okay, now build and run the Browser project. You should have a simple browser like that shown in Fig. 5.17.

Wow. Everything looks great. Try out the **Forward, Back,** and **Stop** buttons. Everything should work fine. There is, however, one thing that doesn't yet work. When you enter a URL into the entry field and hit **Enter** nothing happens. To add this capability, we need to trap the WM_KEYDOWN message in the Edit control and call the browser's Navigate method. Here's how we do it.

Start up ClassWizard and, using the **Add Class...** button, add a new class. Call the class **CURLEdit** and derive it from **CEdit.** Before clicking **OK,** you should have a dialog like that shown in Fig. 5.18.

We need to trap the WM_KEYDOWN message so that we can act on the user pressing the Enter key while in the Edit control. Again using ClassWizard trap the WM_KEYDOWN message using the **Message**

Figure 5.17
Our Simple Browser.

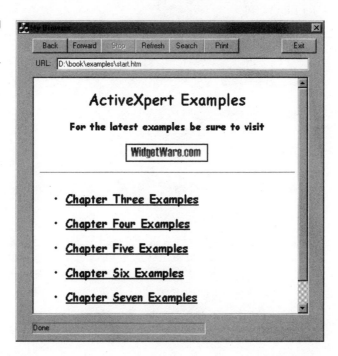

Figure 5.18
Adding the CURLEdit
Class.

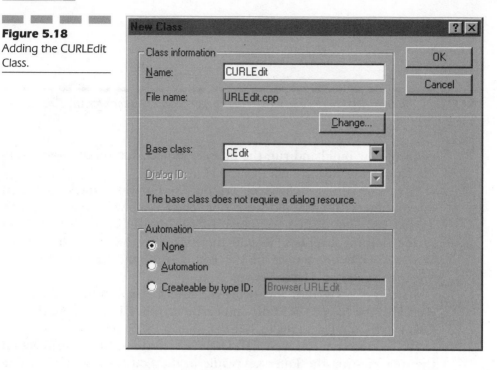

Maps tab. After doing so add the following code to both URLEDIT.H and
URLEDIT.CPP.

```
//URLEdit.h : header file
//

class CBrowserDlg;

class CURLEdit : public CEdit
{
...

// Attributes
protected:
    CBrowserDlg* m_pDlg;

// Operations
public:
    void SetDialog( CBrowserDlg* pDlg );

...

//
// URLEdit.cpp : implementation file
//
```

```
#include "stdafx.h"
#include "Browser.h"
#include "URLEdit.h"
#include "BrowserDlg.h"

...

void CURLEdit::SetDialog( CBrowserDlg* pDlg )
{
   // Maintain a pointer back to the dialog instance
   m_pDlg = pDlg;
}

...

void CURLEdit::OnKeyDown(UINT nChar, UINT nRepCnt, UINT nFlags)
{
    if ( nChar == VK_RETURN )
    {
       CString strURL;
       GetWindowText( strURL );
       m_pDlg->Navigate( strURL );
       return;

    }

    // If not return key, pass it on
    CEdit::OnKeyDown( nChar, nRepCnt, nFlags );
}
```

First we predeclared our `CBrowserDlg` class so we can use it from within our new `CURLEdit` class. We then added a data member and method, `SetDialog`, to maintain a pointer to our dialog class. We use this to call `CBrowserDlg::Navigate` whenever the enter key is pressed. All that is left is to add the appropriate calls to BROWSER DLG.H and CPP.

```
//
// BrowserDlg.h : header file
//
...
class CBrowserDlg : public CDialog
{
...
public:
   void Navigate( CString& strURL );
...
};

//
// BrowserDlg.cpp : implementation file
//

#include "stdafx.h"
#include "Browser.h"
```

```
#include "URLEdit.h"
#include "BrowserDlg.h"
...
BOOL CBrowserDlg::OnInitDialog()
{

...
   // TODO: Add extra initialization here
   m_editURL.SetDialog( this );
   m_Browser.GoHome();
   m_Back.EnableWindow( FALSE );
   m_Forward.EnableWindow( FALSE );

   return TRUE;
}


void CBrowserDlg::Navigate( CString& strURL )
{
   m_Browser.Navigate( strURL, NULL, NULL, NULL, NULL );
}
```

We're finished! You now have your own personal Web browser that you can customize as much as you want. Heck, you can even include it with your applications as long as you follow Internet Explorer's licensing and distribution requirements.

Summary

ActiveX controls are one of the most important elements of Microsoft's new Web development strategy. ActiveX controls provide encapsulation, language-independence, and standard interfaces, all of the characteristics of a good component. Controls expose their functionality through Automation. Automation provides a standard mechanism for independent software modules to interoperate.

An ActiveX control must reside within a control container in order to execute. Example containers include Visual Basic forms, Visual C++ windows and dialogs, Delphi Forms, Internet Explorer, and ActiveX Controls pad. A container can operate in either a design or run-time mode.

Controls are supported in browsers, such as Internet Explorer, through the HTML OBJECT element. The CLSID attribute specifies a unique identifier for the control, CODEBASE specifies where the executable code resides, and any DATA or PARAM tags store the persistent characteristics of the control.

To operate within a container such as Internet Explorer, ActiveX controls must reside on the local machine. The Component Download service provides a container with the ability to download, verify, and install controls from a remote server. To ensure that malicious controls are not downloaded and installed, Internet Explorer requires (with the typical security settings) valid digital signatures on all controls that are downloaded and installed on the local machine.

ActiveX controls can add significant functionality to both browser-based and standard desktop applications. When using control in Web documents, their functionality is harnessed through the use of the browser's scripting language (e.g., VBScript). Internet Explorer itself is one large, highly functional ActiveX control that can be used in your applications.

COM and the Active Template Library

ActiveX covers a broad territory. Microsoft uses ActiveX-based techniques throughout its product line. It is also used heavily by the operating system. In this chapter we take a look at the technology that ActiveX and OLE are based on: Microsoft's Component Object Model (COM). To understand what COM is and how it is used, we plan to develop a simple COM-based component. First we use straight C++ and then move on to the Active Template Library (ATL), which is a template-based, C++ framework for building efficient COM components.

The material in this chapter serves several purposes. First, it introduces the concept of COM. Second, it provides you with a good understanding of what COM is and how it can be used in your applications. And third, it gives an introduction to the technologies that we cover in the chapters to come, all of which are based on COM technologies.

The Component Object Model

Microsoft's Component Object Model is, as the title states, a *model* for designing and building component objects. The model specifies a number of techniques that an implementor can use to provide language-independent, binary standard software modules. Microsoft also provides an *implementation* of COM on all of its Windows platforms. Other platforms, such as Macintosh and UNIX, are supported as well, but not necessarily by Microsoft.

Microsoft's OLE and ActiveX technologies are high-level software services that are built using Microsoft's COM implementation. COM, OLE, and ActiveX are provided with the Windows operating system as a set of COM-based interfaces and a small number of Win32 API calls. As with COM, services such as OLE and ActiveX are also supported on operating systems other than Windows.

NOTE: *Most of Microsoft's ActiveX technologies are being ported to other, non-Windows platforms. Microsoft has turned over specifications and reference implementations of ActiveX to other groups. A new group, called the* Active Group, *is currently working with the Open Group, to make ActiveX an open standard. For more information check out http://www.activex.org.*

A Binary Standard
(or Language Independence)

One important feature of COM is that it provides a binary standard for software components. A binary standard, in a software sense, provides the means by which objects and components, developed with various languages, from disparate vendors, running on heterogeneous platforms, can *interoperate* without any changes to the binary or executable code. This is a major goal of COM and is one that the software development community desperately needs.

Software reuse, which is a primary goal of software development, depends on building modules that can be used in multiple environments. Typically, the software you develop using a specific language, say C++, can be reused effectively only if other component developers work with C++ as well.

For example, if we develop a C++ class for data manipulation, the only way to "reuse" the class is to use it in other applications that are also developed with C++. Only other C++ compilers can understand C++ classes. In fact, because C++ tools do not have a standard way to "mangle" C++ function names, software reuse requires that you use the exact same tool. In other words, to reuse the class, source code must be provided.

Binary reuse allows a developer to create a software component that can be used across languages, tools, and platforms, by distributing only a *binary* component (e.g., DLL or EXE). This is a major boon for software developers. They can choose the best language and tool to develop their components without worrying (as much) about what language or tool another developer might use.

To give you an idea of how C++ objects and COM-based components compare, take a look at Table 6.1. These comparisons may not make perfect

TABLE 6.1	**A C++ Object (Instance of a class)**	**A COM Object**
C++ and COM Objects Compared	Can expose only one public interface. Basically a series of C++ methods.	Will typically expose more than one public interface.
	Language-dependent	Language-independent—COM objects are implemented with and used by various languages.
	No intrinsic version support	Built-in object version support. Location transparency.

sense at this point, but it is important to realize that C++ and COM are two different animals. C++ is a language; COM is a technology.

Location Transparency

Another important COM feature is known as *Location Transparency.* Location transparency basically means that a component user, the client, does not have to know where a particular component is located. The client application uses the same COM services to instantiate and use a component independent of where that component actually resides. The component may reside directly within the client's process space (DLL), it may reside in another process on the same machine (EXE), or it may reside on a machine located hundreds of miles away (a distributed object). COM and *Distributed* COM provide this location transparency. Another term that describes this capability is *Distributed Object Services.* The CORBA standard provides similar capabilities. The important thing to note is that the client interacts with a COM-based component in the exact same way no matter where it resides. The client interface does not change. Location transparency allows developers to build scalable, multitier applications.

OLE and ActiveX

The term OLE has a long history. Back when OLE was first introduced (circa 1991), the term was an acronym for *Object Linking and Embedding.* The primary purpose of OLE, at the time, was to provide object linking and embedding-type support for Windows applications. This *compound document* functionality allowed users to embed Excel spreadsheets directly within Word documents and so on.

Then, with the release of OLE 2.0 (circa 1993), OLE was no longer used as an acronym, but as an umbrella term for several technologies based on the Component Object Model. Many of the new capabilities provided by OLE 2.0 had nothing to do with linking and embedding. A good example of this is OLE Automation (now just called *Automation*), the primary purpose of which is to promote component and application interoperability through language and tool independence and has nothing to do with compound documents.

In April 1996, Microsoft embraced the Web wholeheartedly and in doing so coined the term *ActiveX.* The term ActiveX was used to provide a fresh, new direction in Microsoft's product line. However, the majority of the new ActiveX technologies existed long before April 1996. They were just categorized under a different name: OLE. In general, ActiveX replaced the term *OLE* as the one used to describe the majority of Microsoft's COM-based technologies. With this done, OLE could again be used to describe only those technologies related to compound documents and object linking and embedding.

COM-Based Tools

All of Microsoft's development tools support COM, OLE, and ActiveX to some degree, both from the aspect of developing COM-based components and using them. In this chapter we're going to use straight C++ and later Microsoft's Active Template Library. However, all of the major tools and languages, Visual Basic, C++, and Java, provide good COM-based component support.

C++, Components, and Interfaces

One of the major benefits of developing with object-oriented languages such as C++ and Java is that they provide an effective way of encapsulating software functionality. The object-oriented features of such languages allow encapsulation. An object hides how it is implemented and provides a well-defined, public interface that allows external clients to harness its functionality. COM also provides this capability by defining a standard way of implementing and exposing the interface of a COM-based object.

Following is the C++ class definition for the simple component that we build in this chapter. We start off with a straight C++ class and then convert it into a true COM object. We don't have to build COM objects with C++, but as you will see, COM takes advantage of several C++ techniques.

```
class Math
{
// Here's the interface
public:
    long   Add( long Op1, long Op2 );
    long   Subtract( long Op1, long Op2 );
    long   Multiply( long Op1, long Op2 );
    long   Divide( long Op1, Op2 );

private:
// Implementation
```

```
    string m_strVersion;
    string get_Version();
};

long Math::Add( long Op1, long Op2 )
{
    return Op1 + Op2;
}

long Math::Subtract( long Op1, long Op2 )
{
    return Op1 + Op2;
}

long Math::Multiply( long Op1, long Op2 )
{
    return Op1 * Op2;
}

long Math::Divide( long Op1, long Op2 )
{
    return Op1 / Op2;
}
```

Our class provides basic math operations. You pass in two numbers and the component will either add, subtract, multiply, or divide them and return the result. Our job in this chapter is to turn this class into a COM object that can be used by any language that supports COM-based interfaces. Our first step is to define an interface for our component using an abstract class like this:

```
class IMath
{
public:
    virtual long  Add( long Op1, long Op2 ) = 0;
    virtual long  Subtract( long Op1, long Op2 ) = 0;
    virtual long  Multiply( long Op1, long Op2 ) = 0;
    virtual long  Divide( long Op1, Op2 ) = 0;
};
```

Then we derive from this abstract class and provide the implementation just as we did before:

```
class Math : public IMath
{
public:
    long  Add( long Op1, long Op2 );
    long  Subtract( long Op1, long Op2 );
    long  Multiply( long Op1, long Op2 );
    long  Divide( long Op1, Op2 );
};
```

This is the first step in making our class available to non-C++ users. COM-based technologies, such as OLE and ActiveX, are comprised mostly of interfaces like our earlier `IMath` class. Our new class is abstract, which means it contains at least one pure virtual function, and contains only the public methods of our component class.

This new class is called `IMath` where the "I" indicates that it is an interface declaration. COM uses this nomenclature throughout its implementation. The `IMath` class provides an external interface declaration for our `Math` component. The most important aspect of our new `IMath` class is that it forces the creation of a C++ virtual function table (Vtable) in any derived classes.

The use of virtual functions in a base class is central to the design of COM. The abstract class definition provides a Vtable that contains only the public methods (i.e., the interface) of the class. The `IMath` class contains no data members and no implementation functions. Its only purpose is to force the derived class, `Math`, to implement, virtually, the methods of the component's interface.

COM provides access to its components only through a Vtable pointer and so access to the component's implementation is impossible. Study this example. It is simple and yet contains the core concept of COM: The use of Vtables to provide the interface to a component's functionality. In the end, a COM interface is just a pointer to a pointer to a C++-style Vtable. Figure 6.1 depicts this relationship for our math component.

In our example, there are several concepts that need to be understood. First, all COM-based technologies, such as ActiveX and OLE, contain a number of abstract interface definitions just like our `IMath` class. Ultimately, your job as the developer is to provide an *implementation* for those interfaces. That's one reason why ActiveX is a standard. ActiveX provides the interface declaration and you provide the implementation. So, several

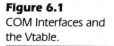

Figure 6.1
COM Interfaces and
the Vtable.

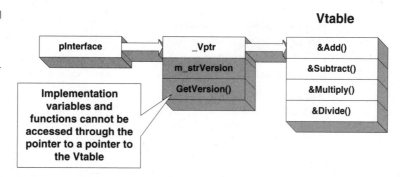

developers can provide different implementations for a standard ActiveX component. This is the concept behind ActiveX controls and all ActiveX technologies. The ActiveX specification defines the abstract classes that you must implement in order to be classified as an ActiveX control.

Second, Microsoft is moving from providing operating system APIs (e.g., the Win32 API) to providing operating system components that expose COM-based interfaces. In this case, you're the user of a component. Instead of making API calls, you obtain an interface for a Windows system component and access its functionality through a COM-based interface. This allows an operating system component's implementation to be replaced without affecting existing applications.

Third, in many cases, you will be both a provider and consumer of COM-based interfaces. ActiveX technologies use COM-based interfaces extensively. Cooperation between ActiveX components is achieved through interfaces. Application startup and negotiation is handled through interfaces that either or both may implement. Basically, COM-based interfaces are everywhere.

Standard COM Interfaces

You now understand that COM contains a bunch of abstract classes that must be implemented. When building a COM-based component, your first job is to implement the one interface that all COM-based components must have: IUnknown. Not only must a component implement IUnknown, but it must provide an implementation of IUnknown for every interface within that component. This is difficult to understand at first, but most COM components expose several interfaces, and remember, an interface is just a pointer to a C++-style interface. We discuss this in more detail shortly.

The IUnknown interface serves two purposes. The first is to provide a standard way for the component user (or client) to ask for a specific interface within a given component. The QueryInterface method provides this capability. The second is to provide a way to manage the component's lifetime externally. The IUnknown interface provides two methods, AddRef and Release, that provide lifetime management of a component instance. Following is the definition of IUnknown.

```
class IUnknown
{
    virtual HRESULT  QueryInterface( REFIID riid, void** ppv ) = 0;
```

```
        virtual ULONG    AddRef() = 0;
        virtual ULONG    Release() = 0;
};
```

As we've discussed, since `IUnknown` is a COM interface declaration, it is an abstract class. It mandates that any deriving class implement the three methods described previously and therefore provides a Vtable with these three methods. Before we go on, we need to stop here and understand that return value from `QueryInterface`, an HRESULT.

HRESULT

Most COM interface methods and API functions return an HRESULT (the exceptions are `AddRef` and `Release`). An HRESULT in Win32 is defined as a `DWORD` (32-bits) that contains information about the result of a function call. The high-order bit indicates the success or failure of the function; the next 15 bits indicate the facility and provide a way to group related return codes; and the lowest 16 bits provide specific information on what occurred. The structure of HRESULT is identical to the status values used by the Win32 API.

COM provides several macros to help in determining the success and failure of a method call. The SUCCEEDED macro evaluates to TRUE if the function call was successful and the FAILED macro evaluates to TRUE if the function failed. Again, these macros aren't specific to COM and ActiveX, but are used throughout the Win32 environment and are defined in WINERROR.H. Return values in Win32 are prefixed with S_ when they indicate success, and E_ to indicate failure.

IUnknown::QueryInterface

The `QueryInterface` method takes a reference to an Interface Identifier (IID), which is a 128-bit unique identifier (specifically a GUID, which we discuss in a moment), and returns a pointer to a specific interface (e.g., `IUnknown`, `IMath`) provided by a COM object. The pointer is returned via the second parameter, which is a pointer to a void pointer.

If we return to our `IMath` example, we now need to make sure our math component implements `IUnknown` on each of its interfaces. Currently, we have only one interface, `IMath`, so we need to do this:

```
class IMath : public IUnknown
{
```

```
public:
    virtual long   Add( long Op1, long Op2 ) = 0;
    virtual long   Subtract( long Op1, long Op2 ) = 0;
    virtual long   Multiply( long Op1, long Op2 ) = 0;
    virtual long   Divide( long Op1, Op2 ) = 0;
};

class Math : public IMath
{
public:
    HRESULT QueryInterface( REFIID riid, void** ppv );
    ULONG   Release();
    ULONG   AddRef();

    long    Add( long Op1, long Op2 );
    long    Subtract( long Op1, long Op2 );
    long    Multiply( long Op1, long Op2 );
    long    Divide( long Op1, Op2 );
};
```

We now have a complete declaration for a COM-based component. If a user needs the services of our math component, he or she will request the IMath interface; since all COM components provide the IUnknown interface, the user can first ask for a pointer to IUnknown, and through IUnknown::QueryInterface can request the IMath interface. By deriving from both IUnknown and IMath we now have to implement seven methods. Three from IUnknown and the four original IMath class methods. Our Vtable now looks like Fig. 6.2.

IUknown::AddRef and IUnknown::Release

Lifetime management of components is handled with the other two methods provided by IUnknown: AddRef and Release. A COM component will typically have several interfaces, where each interface could be connected to multiple external clients. Remember, in our example, our component is really just a C++ class, and what we're discussing is managing the lifetime of a specific C++ class instance. The user will create the instance through some mechanism that we've yet to discuss and will use the capabilities of that instance through its COM-based interfaces. Initially, the instance will be created with the C++ new operator, and we're now trying to determine when the instance can be deleted.

Since an instance of a COM component can have multiple interfaces connected to multiple clients, we need some sort of reference counting capability. Each time a client requests an interface, we increment a counter, and when the client is finished with the interface, we decrement

Vtable

Figure 6.2
Our Math
Component with
IUnknown Added.

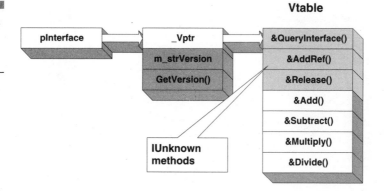

the counter. Eventually, when the outstanding interface reference count goes to zero, our COM component can go away. This is precisely what `IUknown::AddRef` and `IUnknown::Release` do.

So, in our math class example, we will need to maintain an internal reference counter. We'll name it `m_lRef`. When we return an interface, we'll increment the counter, and the client application must then decrement the counter by calling `IUnknown::Release` when finished with the interface.

The component user cannot directly delete our C++ instance; he or she has only a pointer to our C++ Vtable. In reality, the client shouldn't try to delete the object anyway, as there could possibly be other clients accessing the same component object (i.e., C++ instance). Only the component itself, based on its internal reference count, can determine when it can or should be deleted. Following is our math component with the addition of the `IUnknown` implementation.

```cpp
class Math : public IMath
{
public:
    HRESULT QueryInterface( REFIID riid, void** ppv );
    ULONG    Release();
    ULONG    AddRef();

    long     Add( long Op1, long Op2 );
    long     Subtract( long Op1, long Op2 );
    long     Multiply( long Op1, long Op2 );
    long     Divide( long Op1, Op2 );

// Implementation
private:
    // Add a new member variable to keep track of the
    // outstanding interface references to an instantiation
    DWORD m_lRef;
```

```
public:
   Math();
};


Math::Math()
{
   m_lRef = 0;
}


HRESULT Math::QueryInterface( REFIID riid, void** ppv )
{
   switch( riid ) {
      case IID_IUnknown:
      case IID_IMath:
         *ppv = this;

         // We're returning a new interface pointer
         // so call AddRef on the new pointer
         AddRef();
         return( S_OK );
      default:
         return( E_NOINTERFACE );
   }
}


// IUnknown::Release implementation
ULONG Expression::Release()
{
   InterlockedDecrement( &m_lRef );

   // When the reference count reaches zero
   // delete ourselves
   if ( m_lRef == 0 )
   {
      delete this;
      // Can't return m_lRef, it's gone
      return 0;
   }
   else
      return m_lRef;
}


// IUnknown::AddRef implementation
ULONG Expression::AddRef()
{
   InterlockedIncrement( &m_lRef );
   return m_lRef;
}
```

To support the `AddRef` and `Release` functions of `IUnknown` we added a member variable, `m_lRef`, that keeps a count of the current references, or outstanding interface pointers, to our object. The `AddRef` and `Release` functions directly affect a COM interface, but an interface is not an instance of the object itself. This object can have any number of users of its interfaces at a given time, and must maintain an internal count of its active interfaces. When this count reaches zero, it is free to delete itself.

It is important that component users diligently `AddRef` and `Release` the interfaces when appropriate. The `AddRef`, `Release` pair is similar to the `new`, `delete` pair used to manage memory in C++. Whenever a user obtains a new interface pointer or assigns its value to another variable, `AddRef` should be called through the new pointer. You have to be careful though—some COM interface functions return pointers to interfaces, and in these cases, the functions themselves call `AddRef` through the returned pointer. The most obvious example is `QueryInterface`. `QueryInterface` always calls `AddRef` after allocating a new interface, so it isn't necessary to call `AddRef` again.

NOTE: *In our previous example, we use the Win32 API functions InterlockedIncrement and InterlockedDecrement. These provide atomic access to our internal counters and make our component thread safe (at least from a lifetime management perspective).*

Multiple Interfaces

You now understand the concept of a COM interface. One of the powerful features of COM is the fact that each component can, and typically will, expose more than one interface from the same object. Think about it. When you build a C++ class, it has one interface. You encapsulate a component based on its capabilities and provide one public interface for the class user. When building a COM-based component, you must expose multiple interfaces through one C++ instance.

Declaring multiple interfaces within a single C++ class doesn't sound too difficult at first, but it can be rather tricky. Because COM interfaces are really pointers to a C++ style Vtable, a multiple interface class requires multiple Vtables. Another reason that component objects and their interface implementation classes must be closely coupled is for the maintenance of reference counting. When there are multiple interfaces on a COM object, they must all cooperate in the reference counting scheme. There is only one reference count per object, and the interfaces must share it. This coupling is maintained through multiple `IUnknown` interfaces. Remember, each interface has its own implementation of `IUnknown`.

In C++, there are three basic ways to provide multiple interfaces for a COM component: Multiple Inheritance, Interface Implementations, and

C++ class nesting. Of the three methods, we will focus on and use C++ multiple inheritance because that is how the Active Template Library (ATL) implements COM-based interfaces. C++ class nesting is used by the Microsoft Foundation Class Libraries (MFC), which we use in later chapters. For a detailed look at how MFC provides multiple interface support, see my other book: *Designing and Using ActiveX Controls*.

C++ and Multiple Inheritance

In our math component example, we have just one interface, IMath. However, most COM-based components will expose multiple interfaces. Say, for example, that our math component also provided an expression analyzer interface. Here's an example definition:

```
class IExpression : public IUnknown
{
   virtual void SetExpression( string strExpression ) = 0;
   virtual BOOL Validate() = 0;
   virtual BOOL Evaluate() = 0;
};
```

We could then maintain both interfaces in our class by using multiple inheritance like this:

```
class Math : public IMath, public IExpression
{
   // Implementation of the component will include an
   // implementation for each inherited interface
   ...
};
```

The only problem with this approach is that there is a collision with the IUnknown interface, but this isn't a problem because we actually want to "share" the IUnknown implementation. The important point here, though, is that COM components must expose multiple interfaces or, in other words, multiple Vtable pointers. To do this with MI you have to cast a given instance pointer to get the correct Vtable pointer. Here's how the QueryInterface method would look for our previous class.

```
HRESULT Math::QueryInterface( REFIID riid, void** ppv )
{
   switch( riid ) {
     case IID_IUnknown:
     case IID_IMath:
       // MI requires an explicit cast
       *ppv = (IMath*) this;
       break;
```

```
            case IID_IExpression:
               // MI requires an explicit cast
               *ppv = (IExpression*) this;
               break;

         default:
            return( E_NOINTERFACE );
      }

      // We're returning a new interface pointer
      // so call AddRef on the new pointer
      AddRef();
      return( S_OK );
   }
```

The IUnknown interface pointer can be returned through either IMath or IExpression and since they both contain it, we chose IMath arbitrarily. Support for multiple interfaces in an object is one of the most powerful features of COM. We cover this a bit later when discussing the Active Template Library.

Component Housings

So far we've discussed the requirements for a COM-based component. Once a component is designed and implemented with a specific language (C++ in our case), it must then execute within the context of an operating system process. COM-based components are housed either within an executable (EXE), a Windows Dynamic Link Library (DLL), or both. Each housing type has its own characteristics, and the component developer must implement certain functions differently depending on the particular housing.

The term *local server* is used to described a component housing that is an executable. The executable may contain functionality other than providing COM-based components. For example, Microsoft Word is a local server. It provides word processing capabilities for users, but also exposes a number of COM components that other applications can access.

An *in-process server* is a Windows DLL that provides COM-based components. A DLL executes in the context of the calling process, and so the client process has direct memory access to any DLL-based components. This concept becomes important when we discuss COM-based custom interfaces and marshaling.

A *remote server* is a housing that loads and executes on a remote machine. Typically, a remote server will be implemented within an executable; however, this is not a requirement. Components housed only within DLLs can be accessed remotely. COM will provide a *surrogate* process in which the remote DLL can execute.

NOTE: *DCOM-provided in-process surrogate support requires NT 4.0 and Service Pack 2.*

One of COM's benefits is that it provides location transparency for client processes (the user of the component). As we previously described, COM-based services can be implemented in three different configurations: in-process via a DLL on the local machine; across process on the same machine (local server); or on a remote machine via a DLL or executable. The client process, however, requires no knowledge of how the component is implemented or where the service is located. The client creates an instance of a component, and it's up to COM to locate and launch the housing. This makes COM-based components inherently multitier.

There are two primary factors to consider when determining how to implement your components. The first is performance. Because in-process servers execute in the address space of the client process, they provide the best performance. No marshaling of method parameters is required.

Marshaling

Marshaling is the process of transferring function arguments and return values "across" a process or network boundary. This requires copying the values to shared memory so that the other process can access it. Intrinsic types such as `short` and `long` are easy to marshal, but most others, like pointers to structures, are a little more difficult. You can't just make a copy of a pointer because its value (an address) has no meaning in the context of another process. You must copy the whole structure, so the other process can access it.

In-process servers, since they execute directly in the context of the client process, do not require any marshaling (unless you're crossing thread boundaries). In-process servers provide the most efficient way of interacting with COM-based components. Our first component example will be implemented as an in-process server. This way we don't have to worry about providing support for marshaling. If the component is in-process, the client has direct access, through a pointer, to the Vtable of our component interfaces. Figure 6.3 shows how marshaling is handled in local-server and remote-server cases. We talk more about marshaling in the examples later in the chapter.

Class Factories

The component's housing is responsible for providing a standard, language-independent way for a client to instantiate any contained components. COM provides a standard interface, IClassFactory, that all components must provide if they are to be externally created. Following is the definition of IClassFactory. Like all COM interfaces, it must implement IUnknown.

```
class IClassFactory : public IUnknown
{
    virtual HRESULT CreateInstance( LPUNKNOWN pUnk, REFIID riid, void** ppv ) = 0;
    virtual HRESULT LockServer( BOOL fLock ) = 0;
};
```

A class factory is a COM component whose sole purpose is to facilitate the creation of other COM components. Each component housing, either an executable or DLL, must provide a class factory implementation for

Figure 6.3
Cross Process
Marshaling with RPC.

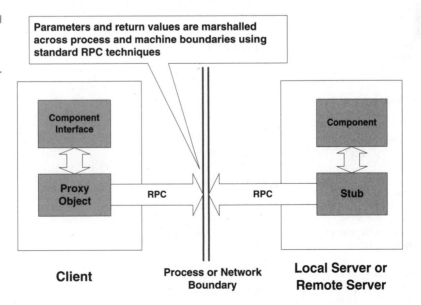

Parameters and return values are marshalled across process and machine boundaries using standard RPC techniques

Component Interface

Proxy Object

RPC

RPC

Component

Stub

Client

Process or Network Boundary

Local Server or Remote Server

each component that can be created externally. The basic `IClassFactory` interface provides just two methods. `CreateInstance` creates an actual instance of the component within the housing, and `LockServer` provides a way for client applications to lock the housing (or server) in memory. By locking the server, the client can ensure that the server will be quickly available. This would typically be done for performance reasons.

Here's a look at the class factory interface for our math component.

```cpp
class MathClassFactory : public IClassFactory
{
protected:
    // Reference count for the ClassFactory instance
    long      m_lRef;

public:
    MathClassFactory();
    ~MathClassFactory();

    // IUnknown implementation
    virtual HRESULT  QueryInterface( REFIID riid, void** ppv );
    virtual ULONG    Release();
    virtual ULONG    AddRef();

    // IClassFactory implementation
    virtual HRESULT CreateInstance( LPUNKNOWN pUnk, REFIID riid, void** ppv );
    virtual HRESULT LockServer( BOOL fLock );
};

HRESULT ExpClassFactory::CreateInstance(LPUNKNOWN pUnk, REFIID riid, void** ppv )
{
    Math*     pMath;
    HRESULT   hr;

    // Initialize the returned pointer to
    // NULL in case there is a problem.
    *ppv = NULL;

    // Create a new instance of Math
    pMath = new Math;

    if ( pMath == 0 )
        return( E_OUTOFMEMORY );

    // Query the requested interface on the
    // new expression instance
    hr = pMath->QueryInterface( riid, ppv );

    if ( FAILED( hr ))
        delete pMath;

    return hr;
}
```

Each component requires a class factory, and the component housing must provide a way for COM to access this class factory. Depending on the housing type, there are two basic techniques. A DLL must export two functions, `Dll-GetClassObject` and `DllCanUnloadNow`, and an executable must register its class factories using the COM API `CoRegisterClassObject`.

We're implementing our math component as an in-process server. Here's the code we need in our exported `DllGetClassObject` function.

```
STDAPI DllGetClassObject( REFCLSID rclsid, REFIID riid, void** ppv )
{
    HRESULT             hr;
    MathClassFactory    *pCF;

    pCF = 0;

    // Make sure the CLSID is for our Expression component
    if ( rclsid != CLSID_Math )
        return( E_FAIL );

    pCF = new MathClassFactory;

    if ( pCF == 0 )
        return( E_OUTOFMEMORY );

    hr = pCF->QueryInterface( riid, ppv );

    // Check for failure of QueryInterface
    if ( FAILED( hr ) )
    {
        delete pCF;
        pCF = 0;
    }

    return hr;
}
```

Remember, the user of our math component will need a pointer to our `IMath` interface. The component user will first create an instance of the component and ask for the `IMath` interface. COM provides basic APIs that allow a user to create instances of COM-based components. The following code demonstrates how a client might access the math component. I've removed error checking and such to make it short and simple.

```
//
// Client.cpp
//
#include "client.h"

#include <initguid.h>
#include "imath.h"
```

```
int main( int argc, char *argv[] )
{
    CoInitialize( NULL );

    IClassFactory* pCF;
    // Get the class factory for the Expression class
    HRESULT hr = CoGetClassObject( CLSID_Math
                        CLSCTX_INPROC,
                        NULL,
                        IID_IClassFactory,
                        (void**) &pCF );

    // using the class factory interface create an instance of the math component
    IUnknown* pUnk;
    hr = pCF->CreateInstance( NULL, IID_IUnknown, (void**) &pUnk );

    // Release the class factory
    pCF->Release();

    IMath* pMath = NULL;
    hr = pUnk->QueryInterface( IID_IMath, (LPVOID*)&pMath );
    pUnk->Release();

    long result;
    result = pMath->Multiply( 100, 8 );
    cout << "100 * 8 is " << result << endl;

    result = pMath->Subtract( 1000, 333 );
    cout << "1000 - 333 is " << result << endl;

    pMath->Release();

    CoUninitialize();

    return 0;
}
```

Before using any COM API functions, the client must first initialize COM with the CoInitialize function. Once COM is initialized the client uses the CoGetClassObject function to retrieve the requested component's class factory interface (specified with the component's CLSID, which we discuss in a moment). Once the client has the class factory, it calls the CreateInstance method to create an actual instance of our math class. Once the instance is created, the client releases the class factory interface.

CreateInstance will return a pointer to the specified interface. In our example, we request an IUnknown interface, and once we have that, we use the QueryInterface method to get a pointer to the component's IMath interface. We could just as easily have requested the IMath interface in our `CreateInstance` call, but I wanted you to see an example of using `QueryInterface` and `Release`.

Once we have a pointer to the `IMath` interface, we use it to perform some basic calculations. After we're finished, we call `Release`, and the component instance is destroyed. You might ask, "How does COM know where our component's housing (the DLL) is located?" The answer is: "In the Registry." COM uses the Windows Registry extensively to store component information.

The Registry

Information that COM and client applications need to locate and instantiate components are stored in the Windows registry. The registry provides nonvolatile storage for component information. Browser applications can determine the number and type of components installed on a system, and so on.

The registry orders information in hierarchical manner, and has several predefined, top-level keys. The one that's most important to us in this chapter is HKEY_CLASSES_ROOT. This section of the registry stores component information.

An important HKEY_CLASSES_ROOT subkey is CLSID (class identifier). It describes every component installed on the system. For example, our math component requires several registry entries before it will work. Here they are:

```
HKEY_CLASSES_ROOT\Math.Component.1 = Chapter 6 Math Component
HKEY_CLASSES_ROOT\Math.Component.1\CurVer = Math.Component.1
HKEY_CLASSES_ROOT\Math.Component.1\CLSID = {A888F560-58E4-11d0-A68A-0000837E3100}

HKEY_CLASSES_ROOT\CLSID\
    {A888F560-58E4-11d0-A68A-0000837E3100} = Chapter 6 Math Component
HKEY_CLASSES_ROOT\CLSID\
    {A888F560-58E4-11d0-A68A-0000837E3100}\ProgID = Math.Component.1
HKEY_CLASSES_ROOT\CLSID\
    {A888F560-58E4-11d0-A68A-0000837E3100}\VersionIndependentProgID = Math.Component
HKEY_CLASSES_ROOT\CLSID\
    {A888F560-58E4-11d0-A68A-0000837E3100}\InprocServer32 = c:\server\server.dll
HKEY_CLASSES_ROOT\CLSID\
    {A888F560-58E4-11d0-A68A-0000837E3100}\NotInsertable
```

The first three lines create a "Programmatic Identifier" for our math component. A component's CLSID is its unique identifier, but it's not very readable nor is it easy to remember. COM provides this concept of a

ProgID to make it easier for us humans to interact with components. We cover this in more detail in the next section. The third line provides a mapping from the ProgID for our control, directly to its corresponding CLSID.

The last set of lines add all of the information necessary for COM to locate our component housing. There's a cross-reference for our ProgID along with component version information. However, the most important entry of all is the **InProcServer32** key. It describes the exact location of a component's housing. Table 6.2 describes each of the keys in more detail.

Component Categories

Basic registry entries provide only limited information about a component. In the early days of COM-based technologies, a few registry entries were all that were needed to specify gross functionality of a component. The absence or existence of a subkey provided a lot of information. Now, however, with the large number of COM-based components installed on a typical machine, a more granular and useful approach to categorizing the capabilities of components is needed.

Microsoft has responded to this need by providing a new mechanism for describing a component's functionality. The new specification, called component categories, provides both system- and user-defined categories for various components. The information is still stored in the Registry, but a new component is provided that makes it easy to add and remove

TABLE 6.2	Entry	Purpose
Important Registry Key Entries	ProgID	Identifies the ProgID string for the COM class. It must contain 39 characters or less, and can contain periods.
	InprocServer32	Contains the path and filename of the 32-bit DLL. It does not have to contain the path, but if it does not, it can be loaded only if it resides within Windows PATH. We discuss the term *in-process* server in a moment. 16-bit versions do not include the "32" extension.
	LocalServer32	Contains the path and filename of the 32-bit EXE. We discuss the term *local server* in a moment.
	CurVer	The ProgID of the latest version of the component class.

entries without any knowledge of the Registry itself. We discuss this in more detail in the next chapter.

OLEVIEW

A good tool for inspecting the registry from a COM perspective is the OLEVIEW utility provided with Visual C++ (and the Platform SDK). It provides several different views of the components on your system as well as a number of other useful capabilities. Figure 6.4 shows OLEVIEW in action.

Globally Unique Identifiers or GUIDs

In distributed object- and component-based environments, unique identification of components is paramount. COM uses a technique described in the Distributed Computing Environment (DCE) standard for Remote

Figure 6.4
OLEVIEW in Action.

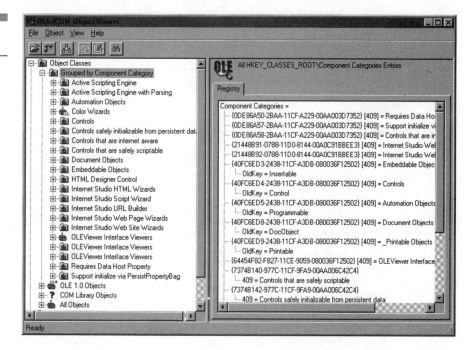

Procedure Calls (RPC). The standard describes something called a Universally Unique Identifier (UUID). The Win32 RPC implementation is based on the OSF RPC standard and so uses this concept extensively.

A UUID is a 128-bit value that is statistically guaranteed to be unique. This is achieved by combining a unique network address (48 bits) with a number of other values. COM's implementation of the UUID is called a *Globally* Unique Identifier (GUID), but is basically identical to a UUID. GUIDs are used by COM to identify component classes (CLSID), interfaces (IID), type libraries, and component categories (CATID), to name a few. Following are the GUIDs used by our math component example:

```
// {A888F560-58E4-11d0-A68A-0000837E3100}
DEFINE_GUID( CLSID_Math,
          0xa888f560, 0x58e4, 0x11d0, 0xa6, 0x8a, 0x0, 0x0, 0x83, 0x7e, 0x31, 0x0) ;
// {A888F561-58E4-11d0-A68A-0000837E3100}
DEFINE_GUID( IID_IMath,
          0xa888f561, 0x58e4, 0x11d0, 0xa6, 0x8a, 0x0, 0x0, 0x83, 0x7e, 0x31, 0x0) ;
```

The DEFINE_GUID macro creates a global constant that can be used throughout your programs, both on the client and server sides. However, you can define the value only once. COM provides a set of macros to make management of this process easy. At the point in your programs where you want to define a GUID structure, you must include INIT-GUID.H before the header file that includes the declarations. Here's how it looks in our first math example.

```
//
// imath.h
//


// {A888F560-58E4-11d0-A68A-0000837E3100}
DEFINE_GUID( CLSID_Math,
          0xa888f560, 0x58e4, 0x11d0, 0xa6, 0x8a, 0x0, 0x0, 0x83, 0x7e, 0x31, 0x0) ;
// {A888F561-58E4-11d0-A68A-0000837E3100}
DEFINE_GUID( IID_IMath,
          0xa888f561, 0x58e4, 0x11d0, 0xa6, 0x8a, 0x0, 0x0, 0x83, 0x7e, 0x31, 0x0) ;

class IMath : public IUnknown
{
public:
    virtual long    Add( long Op1, long Op2 ) = 0;
    virtual long    Subtract( long Op1, long Op2 ) = 0;
    virtual long    Multiply( long Op1, long Op2 ) = 0;
    virtual long    Divide( long Op1, Op2 ) = 0;
};


#include "client.h"

#include <initguid.h>
#include "imath.h"
```

By including INITGUID.H, you change the meaning of the DEFINE_ GUID macro, such that it no longer just declares the GUID's variable, but it defines and initializes it.

In our math example, we need two GUIDs. The CLSID identifies our component, and the IID identifies our custom COM-based interface. There are a number of ways to generate GUIDs for your components. When using Visual C++'s AppWizard, ClassWizard, and ATL Object Wizard, they will be generated automatically for you. You can program- matically generate them with COM's `CoCreateGuid` function. You can also generate them using two programs provided with Visual C++. UUIDGEN is a command line utility that you can use if you need to generate a sequence of GUIDs for your projects. The command line pre- sented here will generate a list of 50 GUIDs and write them to the spec- ified file.

```
c:\msdev\bin\uuidgen -n50 > Project_Guids.txt
```

The other program, GUIDGEN, is graphical and provides several for- matting methods for the created GUIDs. In our case we need the DEFINE_GUID format. By using the **Copy to clipboard** option, you can

Figure 6.5
GUIDGEN Utility.

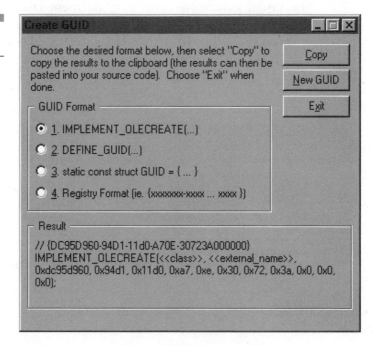

paste the GUID definition directly into your source. Figure 6.5 shows the GUIDGEN program.

The COM API provides several functions for comparing GUIDs, creating GUIDs, and converting GUID types. Some of the more useful ones are shown in Table 6.3.

Programmatic Identifiers

A component is uniquely identified by its CLSID. However, remembering a component's CLSID can be rather difficult. COM provides another mechanism for naming a component, the Programmatic Identifier or ProgID. A ProgID is a simple character string that is associated through the registry to a specific component.

For example, we've chosen a ProgID of "**Math.Component**" for our math component. Using the ProgID it's much easier to specify an understandable component name, as in this Visual Basic code.

```
Dim objMath as Object
Set objMath = CreateObject( "Math.Component" )
objMath.Add( 100, 100 )
Set objMath = Nothing
```

The Visual Basic `CreateObject` statement takes as a parameter the component's ProgID. Internally, the statement uses the COM `CLSIDFromProgID` function to convert the ProgID into the component's actual CLSID. `CreateObject` then uses `CoCreateInstance` to create an instance of the component.

	Function	Purpose
TABLE 6.3		
Useful GUID Helper Functions	`CoCreateGuid( GUID* pGuid)`	Programmatic way of generating one unique GUID.
	`IsEqualGUID( REFGUID, REFGUID)`	Compares two GUIDs.
	`IsEqualIID( REFIID, REFIID)`	Compares two IIDs.
	`IsEqualCLSID( REFCLSID, REFCLSID)`	Compares two CLSIDs.
	`CLSIDFromProgID( LPCOLESTR, LPCLSID)`	Returns the CLSID for the given ProgID.
	`ProgIDFromCLSID( REFCLSID, LPOLESTR*)`	Returns the ProgID from the CLSID.

COM APIs

Microsoft provides a number of Win32 API functions specific to COM, ActiveX, and OLE. There are over a hundred COM-specific calls and we can't cover them all here. However, by studying the major COM API functions, we can garner a good understanding of how COM works. The COM API functions provide the basis of higher-level services such as OLE and ActiveX. You should also remember that COM is basically just a bunch of interface definitions that must be implemented by you, and these API calls just get things started. Table 6.4 shows the API functions that we use in this chapter.

COINITIALIZE AND COINITIALIZEEX. `CoInitialize` initializes the COM libraries and DLLs so that the other APIs can be used. `CoInitialize` takes one parameter, which currently is reserved and should be NULL.

TABLE 6.4

Basic COM Functions

Function	Purpose
`CoInitialize` `CoInitializeEx`	Initialize the COM libraries for use by a process.
`CoUninitialize` (Client and Server)	Release the COM libraries when its services are no longer needed. Not used by in-process servers.
`CoGetClassObject` (Client)	Get an instance of a class factory for a specific COM object.
`CoCreateGUID` (Client and Server)	Creates a new unique GUID.
`CoCreateInstance` (Client) `CoCreateInstanceEx` (Client)	Create an instance of a specific COM object, which may be on a remote machine.
`CoRegisterClass` (EXE Server)	Register the existence of a class factory for a particular COM object.
`DllCanUnloadNow` (in-process Server)	Called periodically by COM to determine if the DLL can be unloaded (i.e., when there are no objects instantiated within the DLL housing). Implemented by in-process servers.
`DllGetClassObject` (in-process Server)	Entry point implemented by in-process servers so that its class factory interfaces can be obtained by client processes.

`CoInitializeEx` was added to support the different COM threading models. Prior to NT 4.0, COM support only the apartment threading model, which is the default. `CoInitializeEx` takes two parameters. The first is reserved and should be NULL, and the second is one of the threading models from the following `COINIT` enumeration:

```
typedef enum tagCOINIT{
   COINIT_APARTMENTTHREADED = 0x2,    // Apartment model
   COINIT_MULTITHREADED     = 0x0,    // OLE calls objects on any thread.
   COINIT_DISABLE_OLE1DDE   = 0x4,    // Don't use DDE for Ole1 support.
   COINIT_SPEED_OVER_MEMORY = 0x8,    // Trade memory for speed.
} COINIT;
```

COUNINITIALIZE. `CoUninitialize` is called to free the use of the COM libraries and DLLs. `CoUninitialize` should be called only if `CoInitialize` has been successfully called previously. Also, every call to `CoInitialize` should be balanced with a corresponding call to `CoUninitialize`.

COREGISTERCLASSOBJECT. `CoRegisterClassObject` is called by a server to register its class factories as available. `CoRegisterClassObject` must be called for every class factory provided by an executable. This should be done as soon as possible before processing the Windows message loop. `CoRegisterClassObject` is used only by executables. In-process servers export the `DllGetClassObject` function to expose its component's class factories. (See Table 6.5.)

COGETCLASSOBJECT. `CoGetClassObject` is used by a COM client to obtain a pointer to the `IClassFactory` interface of the specified component class. The `IClassFactory` pointer can then be used to create multiple instances of the component class.

COM will ensure that the server is either loaded (DLL) or running (EXE). If the component is housed within a DLL, COM will load the DLL and retrieve the requested interface by calling its exported `DllGetClassObject` function. If the component is contained within an executable that is not running, COM will launch the executable, either locally or remote, wait for the server to register its class factories with `CoRegisterClassObject` and will then return the requested interface to the client.

For NT 4.0 and above, the COSERVERINFO parameter is used to allow instantiation on remote systems. The COSERVERINFO structure allows specification of the server name as a UNC name (e.g., "\\twa_nt"), DNS name (e.g., "www.WidgetWare.com"), or straight IP address (e.g., "191.51.33.1").

```
typedef struct _COSERVERINFO
{
```

TABLE 6.5

CoRegister-
ClassObject
Parameters

Parameter	Description
REFCLSID rclsid	The CLSID for the component class being registered.
LPUNKNOWN pUnk	The IUnknown pointer for the component class being registered.
DWORD dwClsContext	The requested context for the executable. This can be one of the following: CLSCTX_INPROC_SERVER CLSCTX_INPROC_HANDLER CLSCTX_LOCAL_SERVER CLSCTX_REMOTE_SERVER
DWORD flags	REGCLS flags specify how multiple instances of the component should be created. One of the following: REGCLS_SINGLEUSE REGCLS_MULTIPLEUSE REGCLS_MULTI_SEPARATE
LPDWORD lpdwRegister	A value returned that must be used when deregistering the class object using the CoRevokeClassObject function.

```
    DWORD dwReserved1;
    LPWSTR pwszName;
    COAUTHINFO *pAuthInfo;
    DWORD dwReserved2;
} COSERVERINFO;
```

In most cases the client should use the shorthand CoCreateInstance function described next. There are two cases when a client application might use CoGetClassObject. First, if the client application intends to create several instances of the component object. In this case, retrieving only one copy of the class factory for the creation of these components will be more efficient. The second case is when the client application requires access to the IClassFactory::LockServer method in order to lock the component housing in memory for some reason, which would typically, again, be performance related. Table 6.6 details the CoGetClassObject parameters.

COCREATEINSTANCE. CoCreateInstance is used by the client application to create an instance of the specified component class. It is a helper function that calls CoGetClassObject to get a class factory for the component and then uses the IClassFactory::CreateInstance method to create the component instance. You should use CoCreateInstance instead of performing the three-step process shown as follows, unless your requirements match those discussed previously.

TABLE 6.6

CoGetClassOb-
ject Parameters

Parameter	Description
REFCLSID rclsid	A reference to the CLSID for the specific component.

DWORD dwClsContext	The requested context for the server housing. This can be one, two, or all of the following:
	    CLSCTX_INPROC_SERVER
	    CLSCTX_INPROC_HANDLER
	    CLSCTX_LOCAL_SERVER
	    CLSCTX_REMOTE_SERVER

COSERVERINFO pServerInfo	Pointer to COSERVERINFO structure.
REFIID riid	A reference to an IID for the specific interface to be returned from the created class object. This will normally be IClassFactory so that the client can create an instance of the required component.
VOID** ppvObj	A void pointer to return the specified interface.

```
// What CoCreateInstance does internally
CoGetClassObject(..., &pCF );
pCF->CreateInstance(..., &pInt );
pCF->Release();
```

CoCreateInstance's parameters are similar to those required by CoGetClassObject. The only difference is that the client using CoCreateInstance will ask for the specific interface on the component (e.g., IDispatch) instead of an IClassFactory pointer.

To support distributed COM, the CoGetClassObject method uses a previously reserved parameter to pass in the COSERVERINFO parameter. However, CoCreateInstance did not have one reserved so a new method, CoCreateInstanceEx, is required. CoCreateInstanceEx is used to create an instance of the COM object on a remote machine. The fourth parameter supports the new COSERVERINFO parameter. The format is the same as described earlier with the CoGetClassObject function.

Also, to improve performance when creating a component instance, the MULTI_QI structure was added to allow the client to QueryInterface for multiple interfaces in one call. The MULTI_QI structure allows you to provide an array of IIDs. This array will be returned with the array of interfaces. The parameters for CoCreateInstance and CoCreateInstanceEx are shown in Tables 6.7 and 6.8.

```
typedef struct _MULTI_QI
{
    const IID*    pIID;
```

TABLE 6.7

CoCreate-
Instance
Parameters

Parameter	Description
REFCLSID rclsid	A reference to the CLSID for the specific component.
IUnknown* pUnkOuter	The controlling outer unknown, when using aggregation.
DWORD dwClsContext	The requested context for the server housing. This can be one, two, or all of the following: CLSCTX_INPROC_SERVER CLSCTX_INPROC_HANDLER CLSCTX_LOCAL_SERVER CLSCTX_REMOTE_SERVER
REFIID riid	A reference to an IID for the specific interface to be returned from the created component object.
VOID** ppvObj	A void pointer to return the specified interface.

```
    IUnknown *    pItf;
    HRESULT       hr;
} MULTI_QI;
```

DLLCANUNLOADNOW. DllCanUnloadNow is implemented by in-process servers. Its purpose is to allow COM to periodically check to determine if the DLL can be unloaded. DllCanUnloadNow takes no

TABLE 6.8

CoCreate-
InstanceEx
Parameters

Parameter	Description
REFCLSID rclsid	A reference to the CLSID for the specific component.
IUnknown* pUnkOuter	The controlling outer unknown, when using aggregation.
DWORD dwClsContext	The requested context for the server housing. This can be one, two, or all of the following: CLSCTX_INPROC_SERVER CLSCTX_INPROC_HANDLER CLSCTX_LOCAL_SERVER CLSCTX_REMOTE_SERVER
COSERVERINFO* pServerInfo	Information about the remove server machine.
ULONG	Number of QueryInterfaces to perform for the MULTI_QI structure.
MULTI_QI	An array of MULTI_QI structures. This makes it more efficient to retrieve a series of interfaces back from the create call.

parameters and returns either S_FALSE indicating that the DLL can not be unloaded, or S_OK, which indicates the DLL can be unloaded.

DLLGETCLASSOBJECT. DllGetClassObject is implemented by in-process servers to expose the class factories for its component objects. When a client application requests a component housed within an in-process server, COM calls the DllGetClassObject entry point within the DLL with the parameters described in Table 6.9.

A Simple COM-based Client and Server

To demonstrate these techniques, we're going to build two COM-based C++ examples. These examples are simple and use straight C++ and COM APIs. We are doing all the work ourselves without any support from a framework such as MFC or the Active Template Library (ATL). The examples are simple but demonstrate the basic concepts used in COM. Later in this chapter, we use Microsoft's new Active Template Library to reimplement the server example.

TABLE 6.9	Parameter	Description
DllGetClassOb-ject Parameters	REFCLSID rclsid	A reference to the CLSID for the specific component.
	DWORD dwClsContext	The requested context for the DLL. This can be one of the following: CLSCTX_INPROC_SERVER CLSCTX_INPROC_HANDLER CLSCTX_LOCAL_SERVER
	LPVOID pvReservered	Reserved. Must be NULL.
	REFIID riid	A reference to an IID for the specific interface to be returned from the created COM object. This will normally be IClassFactory so that the client can create an instance of the requested component.
	VOID" ppvObj	A void pointer to return the specified interface.

Before we begin, there is an important change we need to make to our component's interface. Our initial abstract class definition looks like this:

```
class IMath : public IUnknown
{
public:
    virtual long  Add( long Op1, long Op2 ) = 0;
    virtual long  Subtract( long Op1, long Op2 ) = 0;
    virtual long  Multiply( long Op1, long Op2 ) = 0;
    virtual long  Divide( long Op1, Op2 ) = 0;
};
```

There's one problem with this declaration. COM expects each interface method to return an HRESULT. In our case we're returning the result of the operation. We need to return an HRESULT instead and pass back the result of our operation through a parameter like this:

```
class IMath : public IUnknown
{
public:
    virtual HRESULT  Add( long Op1, long Op2, long* pResult ) = 0;
    virtual HRESULT  Subtract( long Op1, long Op2, long* pResult ) = 0;
    virtual HRESULT  Multiply( long Op1, long Op2, long* pResult ) = 0;
    virtual HRESULT  Divide( long Op1, Op2, long* pResult ) = 0;
};
```

This is a bit disconcerting because returning values from methods reduces the complexity. We now have to deal with a pointer to return the result. Returning an HRESULT from each method is one of the rules of COM. However, there are techniques (the IDL `retval` keyword) available that allow the client application to treat each method as if it actually returns the result and not the HRESULT. We discuss this in our client example later in this chapter.

STDMETHOD and STDMETHODIMP

The COM header files provide several macros for you to use when declaring and implementing COM-based interfaces. To make things simpler, up to this point I've been using straight C++ code in the examples. However, Microsoft recommends using these macros because they insulate the developer from platform differences. The initial macros that we need to understand are STDMETHOD and STDMETHOD_, and STDMETHOD-

IMP and STDMETHODIMP_. Using these macros, here's the new definition of our `IMath` interface.

```
class IMath : public IUnknown
{
public:
    STDMETHOD( Add( long, long, long* ))        PURE;
    STDMETHOD( Subtract( long, long, long* ))   PURE;
    STDMETHOD( Multiply( long, long, long* ))   PURE;
    STDMETHOD( Divide( long, long, long* ))     PURE;
};
```

The actual expansion of STDMETHOD_ depends on the target platform and if you're using C or C++. The expansion for Win32 using C++ is shown as follows:

```
// OBJBASE.H


#define STDMETHODCALLTYPE        _stdcall
...
#define STDMETHOD(method)        virtual HRESULT STDMETHODCALLTYPE method
#define STDMETHOD_(type,method)  virtual type STDMETHODCALLTYPE method
#define PURE                     = 0


#define STDMETHODIMP             HRESULT STDMETHODCALLTYPE
#define STDMETHODIMP_(type)      type STDMETHODCALLTYPE
```

By expanding this macro, our code is very similar to our earlier examples. The only difference is the addition of the return type `_stdcall`. This is a Microsoft specific calling convention, which is used by the Win32 API functions. It specifies that the callee will clean up the stack after the call. PURE is just another way of saying pure virtual (i.e., "=0").

Most COM interface methods will return a standard HRESULT. This is the only difference between STDMETHOD and STDMETHOD_. STDMETHOD always returns an HRESULT, and STDMETHOD_ allows the developer to specify a return type. Here's how STDMETHOD is used in `IClassFactory`.

```
STDMETHOD( LockServer(BOOL fLock) ) PURE;


// Expands to this


virtual HRESULT _stdcall LockServer(BOOL fLock) = 0;
```

You use the STDMETHOD macros to declare your interface methods, both the abstract and class definitions, and the only difference is the PURE qualifier. Here's the code for our deriving class.

```
class Math : public IMath
{
...
public:
    // IUnknown
    STDMETHOD(QueryInterface( REFIID, void** ));
    STDMETHOD_(ULONG, AddRef());
    STDMETHOD_(ULONG, Release());


    // IMath
    STDMETHOD(Add( long, long, long* ));
    STDMETHOD(Subtract( long, long, long* ));
    STDMETHOD(Multiply( long, long, long* ));
    STDMETHOD(Divide( long, long, long* ));
};
```

And finally, when providing the class implementation you use the STDMETHODIMP macros. Here's the actual implementation of our math class.

```
STDMETHODIMP Math::Add( long lOp1, long lOp2, long* pResult )
{
    *pResult = lOp1 + lOp2;
    return S_OK;
}


STDMETHODIMP Math::Subtract( long lOp1, long lOp2, long* pResult )
{
    *pResult = lOp1 - lOp2;
    return S_OK;
}


STDMETHODIMP Math::Multiply( long lOp1, long lOp2, long* pResult )
{
    *pResult = lOp1 * lOp2;
    return S_OK;
}


STDMETHODIMP_(long) Math::Divide( long lOp1, long lOp2, long* pResult )
{
    *pResult = lOp1 / lOp2;
    return S_OK;
}
```

The Server Project

Our server application provides the implementation of our IMath interface and therefore implements and houses our Math component. Throughout this chapter you've seen its definition, so we won't spend much time on it here. To build the example, fire up Visual C++. Then, using AppWizard, create a **Dynamic Link Library** project with a name of **Server.** This will create a simple Visual C++ project with no source files. Figure 6.6 shows the project being created.

Next, we need to declare our abstract component interface and its CLSID and IID. You've seen this before, but here it is all together. Type in the following and save it in a file called IMATH.H.

```
//
// imath.h
//


// {A888F560-58E4-11d0-A68A-0000837E3100}
DEFINE_GUID( CLSID_Math,
          0xa888f560, 0x58e4, 0x11d0, 0xa6, 0x8a, 0x0, 0x0, 0x83, 0x7e, 0x31, 0x0);
// {A888F561-58E4-11d0-A68A-0000837E3100}
DEFINE_GUID( IID_IMath,
          0xa888f561, 0x58e4, 0x11d0, 0xa6, 0x8a, 0x0, 0x0, 0x83, 0x7e, 0x31, 0x0);
```

Figure 6.6
The Visual C++ DLL Project.

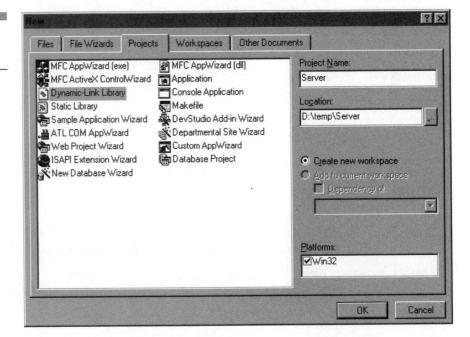

```
class IMath : public IUnknown
{
public:
    STDMETHOD( Add( long, long, long* ))        PURE;
    STDMETHOD( Subtract( long, long, long* ))   PURE;
    STDMETHOD( Multiply( long, long, long* ))   PURE;
    STDMETHOD( Divide( long, long, long* ))     PURE;
};
```

We need to separate our interface definition, CLSID, and IID from the actual implementation so that we can provide just this information to our client program. With only this information, the client program can access our component's functionality. Actually, the client doesn't need the CLSID, as we will access the component through its ProgID, but it doesn't hurt to put it here.

You can either type in the DEFINE_GUID entries as they are here, or you can use the GUIDGEN utility to create your own. Next, we need to declare our component class and a class factory for the component. Create a new file called MATH.H and enter the following code:

```
//
// math.h
//

#include "imath.h"

extern long g_lObjs;
extern long g_lLocks;

class Math : public IMath
{
protected:
    // Reference count
    long          m_lRef;

public:
    Math();
    ~Math();

public:
    // IUnknown
    STDMETHOD(QueryInterface( REFIID, void** ));
    STDMETHOD_(ULONG, AddRef());
    STDMETHOD_(ULONG, Release());

    // IMath
    STDMETHOD(Add( long, long, long* ));
    STDMETHOD(Subtract( long, long, long* ));
    STDMETHOD(Multiply( long, long, long* ));
    STDMETHOD(Divide( long, long, long* ));
};
```

```
class MathClassFactory : public IClassFactory
{
protected:
   long        m_lRef;

public:
   MathClassFactory();
   ~MathClassFactory();

   // IUnknown
   STDMETHOD( QueryInterface(REFIID, void** ));
   STDMETHOD_(ULONG, AddRef());
   STDMETHOD_(ULONG, Release());

   // IClassFactory
   STDMETHOD( CreateInstance(LPUNKNOWN, REFIID, void**));
   STDMETHOD( LockServer(BOOL));
};
```

You've seen most of this code before as well. We derive our math class from our `IMath` interface class, which derives from IUnknown. We then provide declarations for the IUnknown and `IMath` methods. The two global variables keep track of the total number of component instances within the DLL and the number of calls that have been made to `IClass-Factory::LockServer`. Next, we declare a class factory class for our math component. Now it's time to look at the implementation. Create a MATH.CPP file and add the following.

```
//
// Math.cpp
//

#include <windows.h>
#include "math.h"

//
// Math class implementation
//
Math::Math()
{
   m_lRef = 0;

   // Increment the global object count
   InterlockedIncrement( &g_lObjs );
}

// The destructor
Math::~Math()
{
   // Decrement the global object count
   InterlockedDecrement( &g_lObjs );
}
```

In our constructor, we initialize the internal reference counter to zero and increment the global instance count for the DLL. Our destructor then decrements the global count. Next, add the following.

```
STDMETHODIMP Math::QueryInterface( REFIID riid, void** ppv )
{
    *ppv = 0;

    if ( riid == IID_IUnknown || riid == IID_IMath )
        *ppv = this;

    if ( *ppv )
    {
        AddRef();
        return( S_OK );
    }
    return (E_NOINTERFACE);
}


STDMETHODIMP_(ULONG) Math::AddRef()
{
    InterlockedIncrement( &m_lRef );
    return m_lRef;
}


STDMETHODIMP_(ULONG) Math::Release()
{
    if ( InterlockedDecrement( &m_lRef ) == 0 )
    {
        delete this;
        return 0;
    }

    return m_lRef;
}
```

This provides the implementation of our three IUnknown methods. Our component supports only two interfaces: The required IUnknown and our custom IMath. QueryInterface checks to see that the client has requested one that is supported and returns a pointer to a pointer to our component's Vtable. Before it returns, it increments the internal reference count by calling AddRef. The AddRef and Release implementations are just as we discussed earlier.

```
STDMETHODIMP Math::Add( long lOp1, long lOp2, long* pResult )
{
    *pResult = lOp1 + lOp2;
    return S_OK;
}


STDMETHODIMP Math::Subtract( long lOp1, long lOp2, long* pResult )
{
```

```
    *pResult = lOp1 - lOp2;
    return S_OK;
}


STDMETHODIMP Math::Multiply( long lOp1, long lOp2, long* pResult )
{
    *pResult = lOp1 * lOp2;
    return S_OK;
}


STDMETHODIMP_(long) Math::Divide( long lOp1, long lOp2, long* pResult )
{
    *pResult = lOp1 / lOp2;
    return S_OK;
}
```

This is our no-brainer implementation, but at least it doesn't get in the way of our understanding of COM at this point. Next, we have the implementation of our class factory class.

```
MathClassFactory::MathClassFactory()
{
    m_lRef = 0;
}


MathClassFactory::~MathClassFactory()
{
}


STDMETHODIMP MathClassFactory::QueryInterface( REFIID riid, void** ppv )
{
    *ppv = 0;

    if ( riid == IID_IUnknown || riid == IID_IClassFactory )
       *ppv = this;

    if ( *ppv )
    {
       AddRef();
       return S_OK;
    }

    return(E_NOINTERFACE);
}


STDMETHODIMP_(ULONG) MathClassFactory::AddRef()
{
    return InterlockedIncrement( &m_lRef );
}


STDMETHODIMP_(ULONG) MathClassFactory::Release()
{
    if ( InterlockedDecrement( &m_lRef ) == 0 )
```

```
        {
            delete this;
            return 0;
        }


    return m_lRef;
}


STDMETHODIMP MathClassFactory::CreateInstance
        ( LPUNKNOWN pUnkOuter, REFIID riid, void** ppvObj )
{
    Math*       pMath;
    HRESULT     hr;


    *ppvObj = 0;

    pMath = new Math;

    if ( pMath == 0 )
        return( E_OUTOFMEMORY );

    hr = pMath->QueryInterface( riid, ppvObj );

    if ( FAILED( hr ) )
        delete pMath;

    return hr;
}


STDMETHODIMP MathClassFactory::LockServer( BOOL fLock )
{
    if ( fLock )
        InterlockedIncrement( &g_lLocks );
    else
        InterlockedDecrement( &g_lLocks );

    return S_OK;
}
```

Again, we've covered most of this already. The only exception is the actual implementation of the `LockServer` method. Our server housing (the DLL) maintains a count of calls to lock the server. We use this counter in our housing implementation next.

After saving the preceding MATH.CPP file, create a new file and call it SERVER.CPP. It will provide the housing code for our component. IMATH.H, MATH.H, and MATH.CPP comprise our component implementation. We now need housing code to wrap our component. Here it is:

```
//
// server.cpp : Defines the initialization routines for the DLL.
//
```

```
#include <windows.h>

#include <initguid.h>
#include "math.h"

long    g_lObjs = 0;
long    g_lLocks = 0;

STDAPI DllGetClassObject( REFCLSID rclsid, REFIID riid, void** ppv )
{
    HRESULT             hr;
    MathClassFactory    *pCF;

    pCF = 0;

    // Make sure the CLSID is for our Expression component
    if ( rclsid != CLSID_Math )
        return( E_FAIL );

    pCF = new MathClassFactory;

    if ( pCF == 0 )
        return( E_OUTOFMEMORY );

    hr = pCF->QueryInterface( riid, ppv );

    // Check for failure of QueryInterface
    if ( FAILED( hr ) )
    {
        delete pCF;
        pCF = 0;
    }

    return hr;
}

STDAPI DllCanUnloadNow(void)
{
    if ( g_lObjs || g_lLocks )
        return( S_FALSE );
    else
        return( S_OK );
}
```

First, we include INITGUID.H to actually define the GUIDs used by the DLL. Next we define the two global variables that maintain our housing reference counts. Remember, COM requires that a DLL export two functions (actually there are four, but we discuss these in the later examples) to be a true component housing. First, we implement DllGetClassObject. COM calls this entry point on behalf of a component client. We first check to make sure the client is requesting a component that our DLL supports. If we recognize it, we create an instance of our math class factory and call `QueryInterface` on the interface requested by the client. Our math class factory supports only `IUnknown` and `IClassFactory`. If the client, or COM, requests anything else, we return an error.

Thanks to our two global variables, our implementation of `DllCanUnloadNow` is easy. We check to see if there are any outstanding instances of the math component and the number of calls that have been made to `LockServer`. If either is nonzero, the DLL cannot be unloaded.

There is one remaining step. To export our two functions in SERVER.CPP, we need a SERVER.DEF file. Create a file so named and add the following:

```
;
; Server.def : Declares the module parameters for the DLL.
;

LIBRARY        "SERVER"
DESCRIPTION    'SERVER Windows Dynamic Link Library'

EXPORTS
        ; Explicit exports can go here
        DllGetClassObject      PRIVATE
        DllCanUnloadNow        PRIVATE
```

Before building the project, use the **Insert/Files into project…** menu item to insert the MATH.CPP, SERVER.CPP, and SERVER.DEF files into the project, and then build the project. The final step is to register the math component. The CD-ROM contains a SERVER.REG file that looks very similar to this:

```
REGEDIT
HKEY_CLASSES_ROOT\Math.Component.1 = Chapter 6 Math Component
HKEY_CLASSES_ROOT\Math.Component.1\CurVer = Math.Component.1
HKEY_CLASSES_ROOT\Math.Component.1\CLSID = {A888F560-58E4-11d0-A68A-0000837E3100}
HKEY_CLASSES_ROOT\CLSID\{A888F560-58E4-11d0-A68A-0000837E3100} = Chapter 6 Math
Component
HKEY_CLASSES_ROOT\CLSID\{A888F560-58E4-11d0-A68A-0000837E3100}\ProgID = Math.Component.1
HKEY_CLASSES_ROOT\CLSID\{A888F560-58E4-11d0-A68A-0000837E3100}\VersionIndependentProgID
= Math.Component
HKEY_CLASSES_ROOT\CLSID\{A888F560-58E4-11d0-A68A-0000837E3100}\InprocServer32 =
c:\book\chap6\server\debug\server.dll
HKEY_CLASSES_ROOT\CLSID\{A888F560-58E4-11d0-A68A-0000837E3100}\NotInsertable
```

If you used the existing GUIDs in our example, all you have to modify in the SERVER.REG file is the actual location of SERVER.DLL via the **InProcServer32** entry. However, if you generated your own GUIDs, you'll have to update all of the CLSID entries with the new GUID. After you've typed in or updated the SERVER.REG file, merge it into the registry using REGEDIT or by double-clicking on the file in Explorer.

NOTE: *The Registry editor program is REGEDIT.EXE on Windows 95 and REGEDIT32.EXE on Windows NT. You can register .REG files by double-clicking the file icon from File Manager or the Windows Explorer. Since this is managed through a file association, you can also just type* **start server.reg** *from the command line.*

Now that we've built the simple COM-based math component, we need to build a client application access to test its functionality.

The Client Project

Our client application is a simple Win32 console application. Using App-Wizard, create a **Console Application** and name it **Client**. Again, this is just a basic project and AppWizard will supply only the .MAK file. The project characteristics are shown in Fig. 6.7.

Next, create a file called CLIENT.CPP and add the following code:

Figure 6.7
The Client Application
Project Settings.

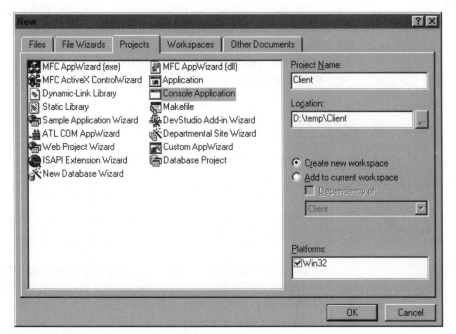

```
//
// client.cpp
//

#include <windows.h>
#include <tchar.h>
#include <iostream.h>

#include <initguid.h>
#include "..\server\imath.h"

int main( int argc, char *argv[] )
{
    cout << "Initializing COM" << endl;
    if ( FAILED( CoInitialize( NULL )))
    {
        cout << "Unable to initialize COM" << endl;
        return -1;
    }

    char* szProgID = "Math.Component.1";
    WCHAR   szWideProgID[128];
    CLSID  clsid;
    long lLen = MultiByteToWideChar( CP_ACP,
                        0,
                        szProgID,
                        strlen( szProgID ),
                        szWideProgID,
                        sizeof( szWideProgID ) );

    szWideProgID[ lLen ] = '\0';
    HRESULT hr = ::CLSIDFromProgID( szWideProgID, &clsid );
    if ( FAILED( hr ))
    {
        cout.setf( ios::hex, ios::basefield );
        cout << "Unable to get CLSID from ProgID. HR = " << hr << endl;
        return -1;
    }

    IClassFactory* pCF;
    // Get the class factory for the Math class
    hr = CoGetClassObject( clsid,
                        CLSCTX_INPROC,
                        NULL,
                        IID_IClassFactory,
                        (void**) &pCF );
    if ( FAILED( hr ))
    {
        cout.setf( ios::hex, ios::basefield );
        cout << "Failed to GetClassObject server instance. HR = " << hr << endl;
        return -1;
    }

    // using the class factory interface create an instance of the
    // component and return the IUnknown interface.
    IUnknown* pUnk;
```

```
hr = pCF->CreateInstance( NULL, IID_IUnknown, (void**) &pUnk );

// Release the class factory
pCF->Release();

if ( FAILED( hr ))
{
    cout.setf( ios::hex, ios::basefield );
    cout << "Failed to create server instance. HR = " << hr << endl;
    return -1;
}

cout << "Instance created" << endl;

IMath* pMath = NULL;
hr = pUnk->QueryInterface( IID_IMath, (LPVOID*)&pMath );
pUnk->Release();
if ( FAILED( hr ))
{
    cout << "QueryInterface() for IMath failed" << endl;
    return -1;
}

long result;
pMath->Multiply( 100, 8, &result );
cout << "100 * 8 is " << result << endl;

pMath->Subtract( 1000, 333, &result );
cout << "1000 - 333 is " << result << endl;

cout << "Releasing instance" << endl;
pMath->Release();

cout << "Shutting down COM" << endl;
CoUninitialize();

return 0;
}
```

We start off by including the IMATH.H header file from the server project. Before doing so, we include INITGUID.H so that the components GUIDs will be defined. In main, we first initialize the COM libraries. Our example uses the component's ProgID to determine the correct CLSID. Before we can call `CLSIDFromProgID`, however, we first have to convert our ANSI ProgID into a Unicode string. All COM, OLE, and ActiveX calls have native Unicode implementations, so all strings must be converted to Unicode before passing them to any COM API functions.

After retrieving the CLSID for the component, we call `CoGetClass-Object` and request a pointer to the class factory interface for the math component. We then create an instance of the math component by calling `CreateInstance`. After we create the instance, we release the class factory interface. `CreateInstance` returns an IUnknown pointer, through which we finally query for `IMath`. Once we have an `IMath` pointer, we use the component's services to do some simple calculations.

When we're finished, we release our IMath interface pointer. We then call `CoUninitialize` before the application terminates.

After entering the code above, insert CLIENT.CPP into the client project and build it. By running the client in debug, you can step into our server code. Take your time and really understand this simple COM-based client-server example. It contains the essence of COM-based development.

Now that we understand the basics of COM, let's take a look at a tool that makes COM-based development at little easier, the Active Template Library.

The Active Template Library

The Active Template Library (ATL) is a framework that helps in the creation of small, COM-based components. The ATL uses the new template-based features of C++ and is provided with source code as part of the Visual C++ development environment. The development environment also includes a number of Visual C++ Wizards that make it easy to get your ATL projects started.

NOTE: *ATL Version 2.0 works with Visual C++ version 4.2b. However it is not included with the product, but can be downloaded from Microsoft's Website at: http://www.microsoft.com/visualc/prodinfo. ATL (version 2.1, which is basically version 2.0 repackaged) is included as part of Visual C++ 5.0.*

Basic ATL Features

The ATL provides support for implementing the core aspects of a COM-based component. Many of the tedious implementation details that we had to deal with in our last example are taken care of by the ATL template classes. Here's a quick list of what the ATL provides. We cover some of these in this chapter and others in Chapter 7.

- An AppWizard to create the initial ATL project.
- An Object Wizard for adding various component types to the project.
- Default support for basic COM functionality such as IUnknown and IClassFactory.
- Custom interface marshaling support.
- Support for basic IDispatch (Automation) and *dual interfaces.*
- Great support for developing lightweight ActiveX controls.

Compared to the Microsoft Foundation Class (MFC) Libraries

The purpose of the ATL is to facilitate the creation of small, COM-based components. The purpose of MFC is to speed development of larger, Windows-based applications. There is some overlap in functionality, though, primarily in the area of OLE and ActiveX support.

For example, you can create ActiveX controls with both the ATL and MFC. By using MFC and the Control Wizard, you can create a fully functional ActiveX control by adding just a few lines of code to the thousands provided by MFC. However, to use the control, you have to distribute the MFC runtime. The main MFC runtime DLL is about one megabyte in size, which can be prohibitive in low-bandwidth environments such as the Web. The ATL also has complete support for ActiveX controls. However, you have to write a lot of the code yourself, and to do so you need a solid understanding of COM and the ActiveX control specification.

This is just one example. In most cases where you're developing a COM-based component that has little or no visual aspect, the ATL is the way to go. If you're developing a Windows-based application with lots of visual functionality, you'll probably want to use MFC. This is just a guideline, though I would recommend that you get some experience with both before making a final decision (i.e., your mileage will vary).

An Example Server

To demonstrate some of the features of the ATL, we now convert our server example from straight C++ to using the ATL. To start off, we use the Visual C++ ATL AppWizard to create the initial project.

The ATL COM AppWizard

The ATL COM AppWizard is a Visual C++ Wizard that steps you through the initial creation of an ATL-based project (Fig. 6.8 and Table 6.10). You will use AppWizard only once per project. After the project is created you will use the ATL Object Wizard to add components to your project. Start up Visual C++ and perform the following steps:

- Select **New...** from the **File** menu.
- From the **Projects Tab** Select an **ATL COM AppWizard** project.
- Select an appropriate directory and name the project "**AutoSvr.**"
- Click **Finish.**

The ATL Object Wizard

The initial project created using the ATL AppWizard provides only basic housing support for your components, and does not actually provide the files needed for building a specific component. To do that, you have to use the new ATL Object Wizard. The Object Wizard is accessed through the Visual C++ **Insert/Add ATL Component...** menu item.

Figure 6.8
Creating the ATL
Project.

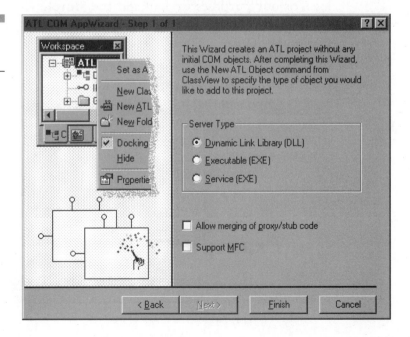

TABLE 6.10

Files Created by the
ATL AppWizard

File	Description
AUTOSVR.CPP	The main project file. This file contains the support functions required by COM to provide a housing for our components.
AUTOSVR.IDL	The IDL file for our project. You will add interface and method definitions here. The MIDL compiler will process this file to create a type library for the project.
AUTOSVR.DEF	Windows definition file. For DLL projects contains the exposed entry points. This file is not created for EXE projects.
AUTOSVR.RC	The resource definition file for the project.
STDAFX.H and STDAFX.CPP	Definitions and includes for the ATL framework.

The main Object Wizard dialog is shown in Fig. 6.9. There are three different categories of objects that you can add to your project: **ATL Controls, ATL Miscellaneous,** and **ATL Objects.** The ATL Controls category provides two basic control types and a **Property Page** object. We discuss these in detail in the next chapter. The ATL Miscellaneous section allows you to create a COM-based object that is a Windows dialog. For our purposes we will add the **Simple Object** type from the **ATL Objects** section. After clicking the **Next** button, you should see a dialog like Fig. 6.9.

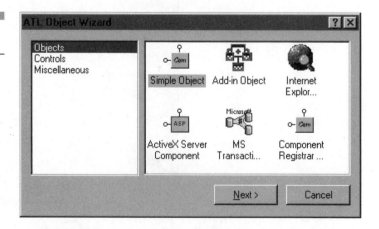

Figure 6.9
ATL Object Wizard.

Figure 6.10
ATL Object Wizard
Names.

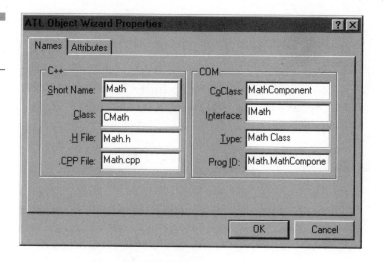

Object Wizard Names

A series of dialogs is presented depending on the object type selected. For a simple COM object, information for two dialogs, Name and Attributes, must be populated. For more complex object types, such as ActiveX con-

TABLE 6.11

Object Wizard
Name Options

Field	Description
Short Name	This entry provides the basis, or prefix, for the rest of the entries on the page. It does not map directly to any particular attribute. As you change this value the entries for the rest of the page change as well.
Class	The name used for the C++ class that implements the object.
.H and .CPP file	The header and implementation files.
CoClass	The name of the COM class. This name will be used by external clients as the "type" of component.
Interface	The name of the interface to create for your object. Our object will initially expose the IMath interface that we've been describing in this Chapter.
Type	The human readable name of the component that will be placed in the registry. This has no programmatic value.
ProgID	This is the programmatic identifier for the component. Clients may use this identifier to location and instantiate our component.

trols, additional information is required. Again, we cover these in more detail when we build an ActiveX control with the ATL in the next chapter.

Figure 6.10 shows the Object Wizard's **Names** dialog with appropriate values for our project. Table 6.11 details the purpose of each option. For our example, we've set the **Short Name** to "Math" and change both the **CoClass** and **ProgID** entries by appending the work "Component."

Object Wizard Attributes

The **Attributes** dialog allows us to specify basic COM support options for our component. Many of the details of each option are beyond the scope of this chapter. We haven't covered things such as COM threading models and the concept of COM aggregation so we take the defaults here. Figure 6.11 shows the attributes dialog and Table 6.12 details each option. After setting each option, click the **OK** button and the source files for our new object will be created.

CComModule

The CComModule class provides basic housing support for COM objects. It is used in both the DLL and EXE implementations. When the ATL AppWizard generated our main project file, AUTOSVR.CPP, it added a

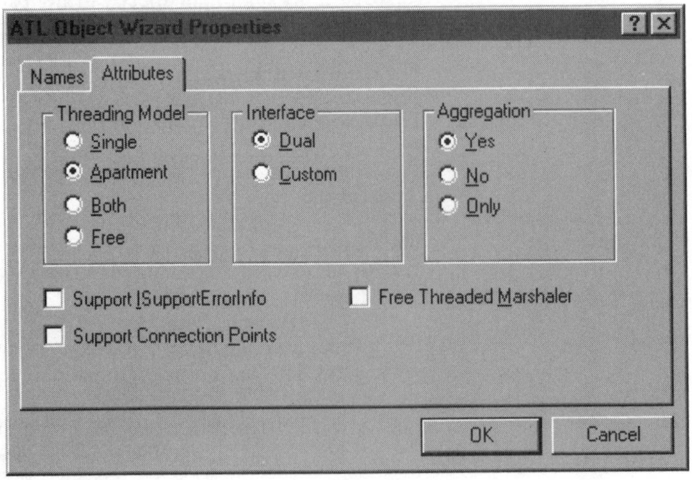

Figure 6.11
ATL Object Wizard Attributes.

	Field	Description
TABLE 6.12 Object Wizard Attribute Options	Threading Model	Several threading models are available for COM-based components: Single—The component uses but one thread. Apartment—Objects reside only within their own thread. Both—Specifies that the component can support both the apartment and free-threading models. Free—The component supports free-threading model.
	Interface	We haven't discussed the concept of a *dual* interface yet, but Microsoft recommends that components support a dual interface if possible. A dual interface implements both a custom interface and the standard Automation IDispatch interface. This gives the client a choice in how it will access the component's functionality.
	Aggregation	Aggregation is a COM technique that allows one component to incorporate, or reuse, the functionality of another component. The internal component must explicitly support this technique by delegating its IUnknown implementation. These options allow a component to decide whether or not to support aggregation.
	Support for ISupportErrorInfo	If you select this option, the Object Wizard will provide a default implementation for the ISupport-ErrorInfo interface. This provides a robust server-to-client error-reporting mechanism.
	Support Connection Points	By selecting this option, the Wizard will provide a default implementation of COM's connection point interfaces. We discuss these in Chapter 7.
	Free-Threaded Marshaler	Free-threaded marshaling provides default marshaling of interface pointers between threads in a single process.

global instance of the CComModule class and named it _Module. Global objects are created as soon as a module is executed and this sets everything in motion in our DLL.

There are a number of support functions implemented in CComModule and most of them provide basic COM support. You can check the ATL documentation for complete details. Here we're only going to cover those methods used in our implementation. Here's the AUTOSVR.CPP from our example:

```cpp
//
// AutoSvr.cpp : Implementation of DLL Exports.
//


#include "stdafx.h"
#include "resource.h"
#include "initguid.h"
#include "AutoSvr.h"


#include "AutoSvr_i.c"
#include "Math.h"


CComModule _Module;


BEGIN_OBJECT_MAP(ObjectMap)
    OBJECT_ENTRY(CLSID_MathComponent, CMath)
END_OBJECT_MAP()


/////////////////////////////////////////////////////////////////////////
// DLL Entry Point

extern "C"
BOOL WINAPI DllMain(HINSTANCE hInstance, DWORD dwReason, LPVOID /*lpReserved*/)
{
    if (dwReason == DLL_PROCESS_ATTACH)
    {
        _Module.Init(ObjectMap, hInstance);
        DisableThreadLibraryCalls(hInstance);
    }
    else if (dwReason == DLL_PROCESS_DETACH)
        _Module.Term();
    return TRUE; // ok
}


/////////////////////////////////////////////////////////////////////////
// Used to determine whether the DLL can be unloaded by OLE


STDAPI DllCanUnloadNow(void)
{
    return (_Module.GetLockCount()==0) ? S_OK : S_FALSE;
}


/////////////////////////////////////////////////////////////////////////
// Returns a class factory to create an object of the requested type

STDAPI DllGetClassObject(REFCLSID rclsid, REFIID riid, LPVOID* ppv)
{
    return _Module.GetClassObject(rclsid, riid, ppv);
}


/////////////////////////////////////////////////////////////////////////
// DllRegisterServer - Adds entries to the system registry
```

```
STDAPI DllRegisterServer(void)
{
    // registers object, typelib and all interfaces in typelib
    return _Module.RegisterServer(TRUE);
}


//////////////////////////////////////////////////////////////////////////
// DllUnregisterServer - Removes entries from the system registry

STDAPI DllUnregisterServer(void)
{
    _Module.UnregisterServer();
    return S_OK;
}
```

First we have the global declaration of our CComModule class. We then have a set of ATL macros that declare the component objects supported by the module. In our case we have only one, the Math component that we added earlier using the ATL Object Wizard. The BEGIN_OBJECT_MAP macro defines the beginning of an array of component object declarations. For each component in our house, there will be a corresponding OBJECT_ENTRY entry. The OBJECT_ENTRY macro contains the information required, the CLSID, and internal class name to create an instance of the component through the exported DllGetClassObject function.

The rest of the file implements the four entry points required by COM for a DLL housing. DllCanUnloadNow uses our global CComModule instance to determine if the DLL can be unloaded. DllGetClassObject, DllRegisterServer, and DllUnRegisterServer, do the same. As you can see, CComModule handles this basic functionality for us.

This is the basic functionality provided by AppWizard when you created the project. We also used the ATL Object Wizard to add our CMath class. This created a MATH.H and MATH.CPP file. The .CPP file starts out looking like this:

```
// Math.cpp : Implementation of CMath
#include "stdafx.h"
#include "AutoSvr.h"
#include "Math.h"


/////////////////////
// CMath
/////////////////////
```

Not much there; we have to add our code here in a moment. There is a bit more though in the header file. Here's what the ATL Object Wizard generated in our MATH.H file.

```
/////////////////////
// CMath
/////////////////////

class ATL_NO_VTABLE CMath :
        public CComObjectRootEx<CComSingleThreadModel>,
        public CComCoClass<CMath, &CLSID_MathComponent>,
        public IDispatchImpl<IMath, &IID_IMath, &LIBID_AUTOSVRLib>
{
public:
    CMath()
    {
    }

DECLARE_REGISTRY_RESOURCEID(IDR_MATH)

BEGIN_COM_MAP(CMath)
    COM_INTERFACE_ENTRY(IMath)
    COM_INTERFACE_ENTRY(IDispatch)
END_COM_MAP()

// IMath
public:
};
```

ATL_NO_VTABLE

Our CMath class is created by inheriting from multiple ATL template classes. Before we go through each one, let's look at some of the macros used in the header declarations. The first one, ATL_NO_VTABLE, actually equates to _declspec(novtable). This directive tells the compiler not to produce a VTable for the class, which basically makes the class's construction and destruction code smaller.

There are a number of restrictions to remember when using the NO_VTABLE option. Basically, you should not call virtual functions or functions that will result in a virtual call in the class constructor or destructor. You can remove the ATL_NO_VTABLE macro from the declaration if you're not sure if your class follows the rules. It's just an attempt to reduce the size of the generated code.

DECLARE_REGISTRY_RESOURCEID

Next, we have the DECLARE_REGISTRY_RESOURCEID macro. This macro expands to a call to the ATL Registry component, called the *Reg-*

istrar. The Registrar provides a simple, data-driven mechanism to update the registry with information about our component. By default, the ATL Object Wizard creates a *ComponentName.RGS* file (in our case MATH.RGS) that contains a script for updating the registry. Here's what it looks like:

```
HKCR
{
    Math.MathComponent.1 = s 'Math Class'
    {
        CLSID = s '{8C30BC11-B8F2-11D0-A756-B04A12000000}'
    }
    Math.MathComponent = s 'Math Class'
    {
        CurVer = s 'Math.MathComponent.1'
    }
    NoRemove CLSID
    {
        ForceRemove {8C30BC11-B8F2-11D0-A756-B04A12000000} = s 'Math Class'
        {
            ProgID = s 'Math.MathComponent.1'
            VersionIndependentProgID = s 'Math.MathComponent'
            ForceRemove 'Programmable'
            InprocServer32 = s '%MODULE%'
            {
                val ThreadingModel = s 'Apartment'
            }
        }
    }
}
```

The script uses a special BNR (Backus-Nauer) syntax for describing each of the component's registry entries. The script is actually stored in the projects resource file. So, the DECLARE_REGISTRY_RESOURCEID expands to this:

```
static HRESULT WINAPI UpdateRegistry(BOOL bRegister)
{
    return _Module.UpdateRegistryFromResource(IDR_MATH, bRegister);
}
```

This method is ultimately called by both the `DllRegisterServer` and `DllUnregisterServer` functions in AUTOSVR.CPP. A full discussion of the ATL Registry component is beyond our scope. However, to modify your component's registry information, you need only directly edit the appropriate .RGS file and rebuild the project. It will be pulled in as a resource and when the component is registered the Registry information will be updated.

The next set of macros are as follows:

NOTE: *COM objects should support self-registration by exposing the standard COM functions:* DllRegisterServer *and* DllUnregisterServer. *In our previous example, we updated the registry with a .REG file; we no longer need to perform this manual process. The ATL Registrar does the work for us and we can use the standard way of registering a DLL-based server:* REGSVR32.EXE SERVER.DLL.

```
BEGIN_COM_MAP(CMath)
    COM_INTERFACE_ENTRY(IMath)
    COM_INTERFACE_ENTRY(IDispatch)
END_COM_MAP()
```

COM_INTERFACE_ENTRY

Each COM object will typically support a number of interfaces. Our math component will support two: IMath and IDispatch. IMath should be familiar to you. It's our custom COM interface for our component. We haven't discussed IDispatch yet, but will discuss it shortly. IDispatch is an important interface because it provides Automation support for our component. (We used Automation back in Chapter 5 when working with ActiveX controls, and we cover it in detail in a moment.)

Anyway, the BEGIN_COM_MAP and END_COM_MAP macros create a table of interfaces that your component exposes through QueryInterface. Each interface is specified using the COM_INTERFACE_ENTRY macro. In the next chapter, when we create an ActiveX control with ATL, this map will contain a large number of interfaces, but our simple example contains just the two shown earlier.

Okay, that covers the macros used in our header file. Now let's look at the class definition itself:

```
class ATL_NO_VTABLE CMath :
      public CComObjectRootEx<CComSingleThreadModel>,
      public CComCoClass<CMath, &CLSID_MathComponent>,
      public IDispatchImpl<IMath, &IID_IMath, &LIBID_AUTOSVRLib>
{
public:
   CMath()
   {
   }

   ...

   // IMath
public:
};
```

CComObjectRootEx

Each class that is a COM object must derive from one of the CComObjectRoot classes. CComObjectRoot manages the reference counting for the component. As you can see from the preceding code snippet, IUnknown support is provided by deriving from CComObjectRootEx.

NOTE: *One of the best sources of information about ATL is the source itself. Template libraries such as ATL provide the complete source for their implementation. You can find the source in the \DevStudio\VC\ATL\Include directory.*

CComCoClass

Our CMath classes also derives from CComCoClass. CComCoClass provides a class factory for our component as well as basic methods to retrieve its CLSID and component-specific error information. When the template expands, you get something like this:

```
class CComCoClass
{
public:
    DECLARE_CLASSFACTORY()
    DECLARE_AGGREGATABLE(T)
    typedef T _CoClass;
    static const CLSID& WINAPI GetObjectCLSID() {return *pclsid;}
    static LPCTSTR WINAPI GetObjectDescription() {return NULL;}
    static HRESULT WINAPI Error(LPCOLESTR lpszDesc,
        const IID& iid = GUID_NULL, HRESULT hRes = 0)
    {
        return AtlReportError(GetObjectCLSID(), lpszDesc, iid, hRes);
    }
...
};
```

The important thing to notice here is that CComCoClass provides our component's class factory through the DECLARE_CLASSFACTORY macro. This macro eventually expands to provide the class with an instance of one of the CComClassFactory classes. The rest of the methods deal mostly with error reporting.

CComClassFactory

Most components built using ATL get their class factory through inclusion of the CComCoClass class. The CComClassFactory provides the two standard class factory methods: `CreateInstance` and `LockServer`. Though a simple implementation, it does save us from implementing all of the class factory code that we did in the last example. Here's a quick look at the class template:

```
class CComClassFactory :
    public IClassFactory,
    public CComObjectRootEx<CComGlobalsThreadModel>
{
public:
    BEGIN_COM_MAP(CComClassFactory)
        COM_INTERFACE_ENTRY(IClassFactory)
    END_COM_MAP()

    // IClassFactory
    STDMETHOD(CreateInstance)(LPUNKNOWN pUnkOuter, REFIID riid, void** ppvObj);
    STDMETHOD(LockServer)(BOOL fLock);
    ...
};
```

Remember, the class factory is itself a COM object and so it derives from `CComObjectRootEx`.

IDispatchImp

The final class in our implementation is `IDispatchImp`. This class provides the default `IDispatch` implementation for our component. Our component contains a dual interface, which is composed of both a custom interface like our previous example, plus a full implementation of the Automation interface: `IDispatch`. `IDispatch` requires the server to implement four methods: `GetIDsOfNames`, `GetTypeInfoCount`, `GetTypeInfo`, and `Invoke`. However, thanks to ATL, we have to do the work to implement only our specific, `IMath`-related methods.

The IDispatch Interface

We discussed and used Automation in Chapter 5. Automation is a standard mechanism that allows language-independent interoperation of software modules. To provide this language-independent option, most COM-based components support Automation as their method of exposing functionality.

Automation is based on COM's `IDispatch` interface. The `IDispatch` interface provides a series of methods that allow a client application to dynamically access functionality within an Automation-based server. Dynamic invocation is slightly different from our earlier COM Vtable interface technique of our math component.

When using a Vtable interface, the client application requires some compile-time knowledge of the component's interface, either through a type library or by including the component's interface declaration at compile time (e.g., IMATH.H). This implements *early binding* of the component's interface.

A component that implements its methods using `IDispatch` instead of a custom interface provides a number of additional capabilities. The interaction between the client and server applications can use *late binding* of the component's interface methods. The client doesn't require compile-time declarations of the server's component interface and so on.

This makes it easy for a server component to change its interface (even at runtime!) without requiring the client application to be recompiled or relinked. Of course, if the interface methods are changed, this should be communicated in some way to the client application so that it can take advantage of the new features.

Another significant feature added by using `IDispatch` is that of standard marshaling. The default COM implementation provided by Windows contains a number of data types that can be used by components that use the `IDispatch` interface. Intrinsic support for these data types makes it easy to build components that work across local and remote process.

Most COM interfaces are like our `IMath` example. They provide a structure that requires a rigid implementation of an abstract class. COM defines the abstract class (interface), but the application developer must provide a unique implementation of that abstract class. `IDispatch` is a little different, because it adds a level of indirection to the Vtable style interfaces that we've studied so far. One term for this new interface type is `dispinterface`, for dispatch interface. That term succinctly describes how `IDispatch` differs from the standard Vtable implementation. The client does not access a component's functionality through the Vtable pointer as we did with `IMath`, instead the client must first "lookup" the function, provide an internal identifier for the desired function, and finally invoke or "dispatch" the function. Examine Fig. 6.12.

As you can see from the illustration, there's more going on here with the `IDispatch` interface. The client still gets a Vtable pointer, but now that Vtable doesn't actually have direct access to the `IMath` methods, the request must first go through `IDispatch::Invoke`. `Invoke` contains a parameter that maps the method call to a specific entry in the dispatch map. This additional level of indirection is what provides for late binding

Figure 6.12
IDispatch Vtable and
Dispatch Table.

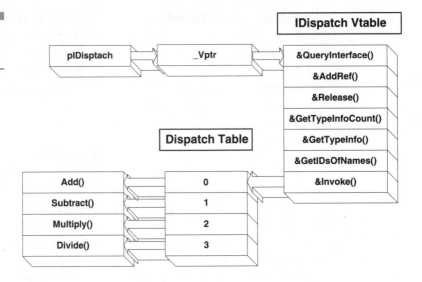

to a component's methods. Table 6.13 describes the four methods of the IDispatch interface.

Dual Interfaces

We now have the pieces we need to understand the concept of a *dual interface*. Dual interfaces are implemented by a server component and provide the client application two different ways to access its functionality. A dual interface combines a Vtable interface (e.g., IMath) with the standard IDispatch interface. This allows the client to choose which interface it wants to use.

Figure 6.13 depicts what our math component would look like with a dual interface. It is a combination of our custom Vtable interface (IMath) and the IDispatch that we implement using ATL. The math methods are exposed directly through our Vtable *and* through IDispatch.

Why should we expose two interfaces that provide basically the same functionality? The primary reason is performance. If the server has an in-process (DLL) implementation, then no marshaling is required. The client can directly bind to the custom interface methods and make very efficient calls. The performance provided using this method is identical to direct C or C++ function bindings.

However, if the client requires late-binding functionality, it can use the IDispatch implementation. This technique is of course slower because more of the work is done at run-time instead of compile-time, but in

TABLE 6.13

IDispatch Methods

Method	Description
Invoke	Invoke provides most of the functionality of the IDispatch interface. It takes eight parameters, the most important of which is the DISPID. The DISPID is mapped to a specific offset within the dispatch table and determines which component class method is invoked.
GetIDsOfNames	GetIDsOfNames provides a facility for the controller to map the textual Automation server property or method name, such as "Multiply," to its numeric DISPID. The DISPID can then be used with the Invoke function to actually access the property or method of the server.
GetTypeInfo	A controller that provides dynamic lookup and calling of Automation methods won't typically have all of the type information necessary to populate the Invoke dispparams structure. An Automation server should call GetTypeInfoCount to determine if the component can provide type information, and if it can, should then call GetTypeInfo to get the type information for the component.
GetTypeInfoCount	GetTypeInfoCount is used by the controller to determine if the component object contains type information that can be provided to the controller. Setting the passed in parameter to one indicates that type information is available and setting the parameter to zero indicates that no type information is available.

Figure 6.13
Math Class with a
Dual Interface.

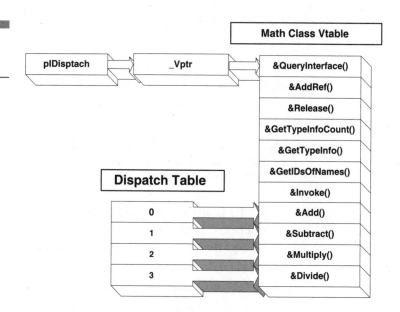

many instances late binding is necessary. We take another look at various client-binding techniques later in the chapter.

NOTE: *Microsoft's Active Scripting technology, which we looked at using in Chapter 4 and will look at implementing Chapter 9, makes heavy use of Automation. In fact, only those components that expose an* IDispatch-*based interface can be used with the client- and server-side scripting languages such as VBScript and JScript.*

Adding Interface Methods

So far we've just discussed the functionality provided by ATL. Now, we add some functionality. The Object Wizard added two new files, MATH.CPP and MATH.H and also made some entries in our component's .IDL file, which we discuss in a moment. First, we need to add our four methods to the new component class.

```
class ATL_NO_VTABLE CMath :
    public CComObjectRootEx<CComSingleThreadModel>,
    public CComCoClass<CMath, &CLSID_MathComponent>,
    public IDispatchImpl<IMath, &IID_IMath, &LIBID_AUTOSVRLib>
{
public:
    CMath()
    {
    }


DECLARE_REGISTRY_RESOURCEID(IDR_MATH)


BEGIN_COM_MAP(CMath)
    COM_INTERFACE_ENTRY(IMath)
    COM_INTERFACE_ENTRY(IDispatch)
END_COM_MAP()


// IMath
public:
    STDMETHOD(Add)( long, long, long* );
    STDMETHOD(Subtract)( long, long, long* );
    STDMETHOD(Multiply)( long, long, long* );
    STDMETHOD(Divide)( long, long, long* );
};
```

This should be familiar; we've just added the declarations for our simple math functions. Here's the actual implementation in MATH.CPP, which is basically the same as our earlier implementation:

```
///////////////////
// CMath
///////////////////
STDMETHODIMP CMath::Add( long op1, long op2, long* pResult )
```

```
{
    *pResult = op1 + op2;
    return S_OK;
}

STDMETHODIMP CMath::Subtract( long op1, long op2, long* pResult )
{
    *pResult = op1 - op2;
    return S_OK;
}

STDMETHODIMP CMath::Multiply( long op1, long op2, long* pResult )
{
    *pResult = op1 * op2;
    return S_OK;
}

STDMETHODIMP CMath::Divide( long op1, long op2, long* pResult )
{
    *pResult = op1 / op2;
    return S_OK;
}
```

Type Information

In our previous math example, any client wanting to use the services of our component would need some a priori knowledge of our component's interface. Information such as what interfaces are supported and what parameters each method takes, and so on, would have to ascertained from our IMATH.H header file. COM provides a more general and programmatic technique of providing this information to potential clients. It's called type information.

A component's type information is created using Microsoft's Interface Definition Language (IDL). When using the ATL, each component housing will have an associated .IDL file that contains type information for every component within the housing. This file is compiled into a binary format—called a type library—using Microsoft's IDL compiler (MIDL.EXE). After compiling the type information, it should be distributed along with the component either within the housing itself or as a separate .TLB file. The **TypeLib** registry entry provides a way for client applications and component browsers to locate a component's type information.

The Interface Definition Language

Microsoft's Interface Definition Language is based on the DCE RPC specification. In general, the IDL is used to describe remote procedure call interfaces, but Microsoft has extended the specification to include support for COM-based interfaces. One purpose of IDL, at least in the context of COM-based components, is to define, in a language-independent way, a component's interface (i.e., its methods and parameters). This definition can then be used by clients of the component. Because IDL is also used to support RPC-like capabilities, it can also produce marshaling code so that the components' interface can be used across process and network boundaries.

NOTE: *Prior to the widespread support of IDL, Microsoft used the Object Description Language (ODL). The ODL language was designed specifically for Automation. Today, the IDL language is used instead. It is more functional than ODL and provides support for the older ODL language.*

The IDL language uses a C-style syntax, so defining a component's interface is very similar to declaring the C++ class. You can define structure types, enumerator types, and so on using IDL. A complete description of IDL is beyond he scope of this chapter, so we'll just cover some the main features that we will use in our example. Following is the AUTOSVR.IDL file. Add the highlighted code to the file.

```
//
// AutoSvr.idl : IDL source for AutoSvr.dll
//

// This file will be processed by the MIDL tool to
// produce the type library (AutoSvr.tlb) and marshalling code.

import "oaidl.idl";
import "ocidl.idl";

    [
        object,
        uuid(8C30BC10-B8F2-11D0-A756-B04A12000000),
        dual,
        helpstring("IMath Interface"),
        pointer_default(unique)
    ]
    interface IMath : IDispatch
    {
        HRESULT Add( [in] long, [in] long, [out, retval] long* pResult );
        HRESULT Subtract( [in] long, [in] long, [out, retval] long* pResult );
        HRESULT Multiply( [in] long, [in] long, [out, retval] long* pResult );
        HRESULT Divide( [in] long, [in] long, [out, retval] long* pResult );
    };

    [
        uuid(8C30BC01-B8F2-11D0-A756-B04A12000000),
```

```
    version(1.0),
    helpstring("AutoSvr 1.0 Type Library")
]
library AUTOSVRLib
{
    importlib("stdole32.tlb");
    importlib("stdole2.tlb");

    [
        uuid(8C30BC11-B8F2-11D0-A756-B04A12000000),
        helpstring("Math Class")
    ]
    coclass MathComponent
    {
        [default] interface IMath;
    };
};
```

The first section defines our IMath dual interface. IDL definitions are preceded with an attribute block. These attributes, enclosed within the brackets ([ ]), provide additional information about the following definition. Our IMath interface definition begins with several attributes:

```
        [
            object,
            uuid(8C30BC10-B8F2-11D0-A756-B04A12000000),
            dual,
            helpstring("IMath Interface"),
            pointer_default(unique)
        ]
```

The object attribute specifies that we're describing a COM-based interface and not an RPC one. Next, the uuid keyword specifies the GUID of our interface. The dual keyword indicates that the interface provides both a custom, Vtable interface as well as the standard Automation interface, IDispatch. The helpstring keyword specifies some text that a object browser might display. The pointer_default attribute sets the default pointer attribute for any pointers defined within the interface. Next, we have the interface definition.

```
interface IMath : IDispatch
{
    HRESULT Add( [in] long, [in] long, [out, retval] long* pResult );
    HRESULT Subtract( [in] long, [in] long, [out, retval] long* pResult );
    HRESULT Multiply( [in] long, [in] long, [out, retval] long* pResult );
    HRESULT Divide( [in] long, [in] long, [out, retval] long* pResult );
};
```

The interface describes the COM-based interface in our component. This matches almost exactly with our C++ class declaration. The major differences are in the listing of the parameters. IDL has several keywords that can be applied to method parameters. The `in` and `out` keywords specify the direction of the parameter. By providing this information, you provide COM with information that will help make the parameter-marshaling process more efficient. The `retval` keyword specifies that the parameter should be treated as the return value for the method. That takes care of the interface definition for our component. The remaining IDL lines pertain to the housing and its contained components.

```
[
    uuid(8C30BC01-B8F2-11D0-A756-B04A12000000),
    version(1.0),
    helpstring("AutoSvr 1.0 Type Library")
]
library AUTOSVRLib
{
    importlib("stdole32.tlb");
    importlib("stdole2.tlb");


    [
        uuid(8C30BC11-B8F2-11D0-A756-B04A12000000),
        helpstring("Math Class")
    ]
    coclass MathComponent
    {
        [default] interface IMath;
    };
};
```

The attribute block describes the type library as a whole. It has a GUID, a version, and a helpstring. The helpstring provides textual information for component browser applications. The library keyword specifies the name of the library and typically encloses all of the definitions for the specific housing. It may interface module, type, and component definitions. In our example, our server just has our one math component, and it is specified using the `coclass` keyword. The `coclass` keyword specifies individual components and the interfaces that they support. Our math component exposes the `IMath` dual interface, which is its default interface. Table 6.14 provides a summary of the basic IDL keywords.

Build the Server

We're now ready to build the server project. Thanks to ATL, we added a small number of lines compared to our previous, straight C++ example. The ATL provided basic housing, reference counting, class factory, and self-registration support, all of which we had to implement ourselves in the previous example.

TABLE 6.14

Basic IDL Keywords

Keyword	Description
object	Begins the definition for COM-based custom interface. The object keyword is followed by several attributes that describe additional interface capabilities.
uuid	The GUID that uniquely defines the given interface, type library, or component class.
dual	Indicates that the interface is dual. A dual interface exposes both a Vtable-based and IDispatch-based interface. All methods in a dual interface must return an HRESULT, but can use the retval keyword to specify a returned value.
helpstring	Specifies a string that can be displayed by tools such as component and interface viewers.
interface	Specifies the actual name of an interface. The name is then used in the coclass section to specify the interfaces supported by a component.
coclass	Describes the interfaces supported by a given COM object. The GUID specifies identifies the component itself.
default	Specifies the default component interface. A component object can have at most two default interfaces, one for the source and one for the sink programmable interfaces.
in/out/retval	For method calls, this indicates the direction of each parameter. The retval keyword describes which parameter should be treated as the return value of the method.

To quickly test our AUTOSVR component, you can start up OLE-VIEW, put it in **Expert Mode,** and open up the **Automation Objects** section. The component will have a name of **Math Class.** Open the math class node, and OLEVIEW will attempt to load the component. If all goes well, you should see the three interfaces that the component supports, as in Fig. 6.14.

Visual Basic as Client

To test our ATL server, we're going to use Visual Basic to build a client application. Visual Basic is a great tool for developing COM-based applications, especially if you use Automation. Automation is Visual Basic's favorite technology. Every object in Visual Basic—be it an ActiveX control, a form, a Visual Basic class—is actually an Automation component.

Figure 6.14
AUTOSVR in
OLEVIEW.

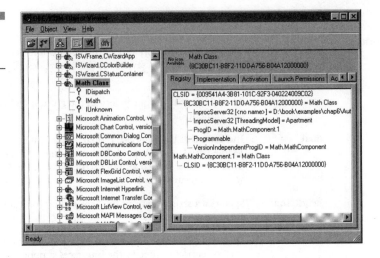

With this popular environment it is very important that your components support Automation.

Not only does Visual Basic provide a great Automation environment, it also supports COM Vtable interfaces. We've already discussed the differences between a Vtable interface and one based on the standard IDispatch; now we get to see the differences in action.

Start up Visual Basic and do the following:

1. Create a new project of type: **Standard EXE**

2. Build a form with three entry fields with the names: **txtOp1, txtOp2,** and **txtResult.**

3. Add three buttons with the names: **cmdDynamic, cmdIDBinding,** and **cmdStatic.**

4. Place three more entry fields to the left of each button. Use a control array with the name **txtTime.**

5. When you're finished, the form should look something like Fig. 6.15.

Our example is going to demonstrate the three types of Automation interface binding supported by Visual Basic: Late, ID, and Early. The different techniques are also described as late, early, and very early in the Visual Basic documentation. When a client application accesses the functionality provided by a component it can choose one of these three techniques. The first two techniques require that the component provide an interface based on IDispatch. The final technique requires that the com-

Figure 6.15
Visual Basic Client
Form.

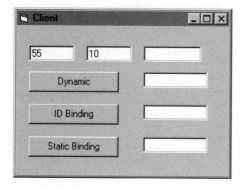

ponent implement a dual interface. Our math component does this, so all three options are available.

Late Binding (or Dynamic Binding)

Late binding is one of the more powerful features of Automation. It allows a client application to determine a component's functionality at run-time. The method names and parameter types are not used during the client development process. Instead the functionality is queried for and called at run-time.

In other words, the client application will query for the DISPID of the method to call and finally called Invoke through the IDispatch interface. Basically everything occurs at run-time. This is most expensive technique and provides no compile-time type checking. All type checking is performed at run-time by the server *as the method is called.* If an incorrect type is passed, a run-time error results.

Because of the run-time aspect of this technique, it is also the slowest technique. However, it is the most flexible because everything is determined at run-time. The server interface can change and the client will not have to be recompiled to take advantage of these changes. To demonstrate late binding, add the following code to your Visual Basic project. Call the code when the **Dynamic** button is clicked.

```
Const ITERATIONS = 40000

Private Sub cmdDynamic_Click()
    ' An example of late binding
    Dim obj As Object
    Dim Start, i As Long
```

```
    Set obj = CreateObject("Math.MathComponent.1")
    Start = Timer
    txtResult = obj.Add(txtOp1, txtOp2)
    For i = 1 To ITERATIONS
        obj.Add txtOp1, txtOp2
    Next
    txtTime(0) = Timer - Start
    Set obj = Nothing
End Sub
```

We first dimension a variable of type `Object`, which is Visual Basic's way of containing an `IDispatch`-based component. We then retrieve an IDispatch pointer by calling `CreateObject` and passing our component's ProgID. The ITERATIONS constant is declared in the **(General)** section outside of any procedure. A `For` loop is used to iteratively call the Add method in our component. There is also some timer logic that displays the time take to perform the iteration. When we're finished, we set our `obj` variable to nothing, which releases the `IDispatch` interface to our component.

This is the most expensive technique for accessing an Automation component's capabilities. However, because Visual Basic dynamically determines how to call the `Add` method, long-term flexibility is achieved.

ID Binding (or Early Binding)

In the previous example, Visual Basic may have to call `IDispatch:`
`:GetIDsOfNames` for each call to our component's `Add` method. Plus, no type checking can be performed because Visual Basic has no knowledge of the component's type information. A second binding technique called ID Binding provides the increased performance and the security of compile-time type checking. Visual Basic has to load the type library of the component in order to apply this technique.

The Visual Basic **References** option will add a type library to your project. You can then treat the reference as a true Visual Basic data type. As your project is compiled, Visual Basic will check the syntax and parameter types against your components type information. Also, Visual Basic will save the DISPIDs for each method and property. This removes the run-time requirement to query for each method and property DISPID. One of the drawbacks of this approach is that a recompile is necessary if the interface to a component changes. Here's our code for the ID binding test.

```
Private Sub cmdIDBinding_Click()
    ' An example of ID (early) binding
    Dim obj As MFCMathComponent
```

```
      Dim Start, i As Long
      Set obj = New MFCMathComponent
      Start = Timer
      txtResult = obj.Add(txtOp1, txtOp2)
      For i = 1 To ITERATIONS
          obj.Add txtOp1, txtOp2
      Next
      txtTime(1) = Timer - Start
End Sub
```

This code references a new class: MFCMathComponent. Visual Basic will use the custom `IMath` interface if it is available in the component. In order to actually time and test ID binding, we created an MFC-based Automation server that mimics the behavior of our AUTOSVR component. MFC-based Automation components do not provide inherent dual interface support. So, by binding to the type library at compile time, Visual Basic will do its best to provide the best performance—it does so by caching the DISPIDs for each method.

Early Binding (or Very Early Binding)

Early binding also requires that the server provide type information. It is the most efficient and is also the least flexible. As always, there is a trade-off. Early binding provides good type checking because the client can use the type information to verify parameters and return types at compile time instead of at run-time. Method binding is directly through the Vtable so there are no DISPIDs or calls to `GetIDsOfNames` or `Invoke` required. If the server is implemented in a DLL, as it is in our case, the speed of early binding is equivalent to a direct DLL-type function call. Here's the Visual Basic code to time very early binding to our `IMath` interface.

```
Private Sub cmdStatic_Click()
    ' An example of late (very early) binding
    Dim obj As New MathComponent
    Dim Start, i As Long
    Start = Timer
    txtResult = obj.Add(txtOp1, txtOp2)
    For i = 1 To ITERATIONS
        obj.Add txtOp1, txtOp2
    Next
    txtTime(2) = Timer - Start
End Sub
```

After keying all of this code, you can now do your own performance testing. Table 6.15 lists our results.

TABLE 6.15

Interface
Performance
Comparison

Binding Method	Time (40,000 iterations)
Dynamic	24.24219
ID (Early)	17.40234
Vtable (Very Early)	10.88672

Summary

Microsoft's Component Object Model (COM) is the basis for technologies such as OLE and ActiveX. COM provides several things that software developers have needed for a long time. COM provides a language-independent, binary standard for software components as well as location transparency. Location transparency is the ability to distribute software modules across processes and machines. OLE and ActiveX are application-level technologies that are built on top of COM.

COM objects are similar to C++ objects in that they encapsulate a module's functionality by exposing a well-defined interface. COM objects are different from C++ instances in one important way: COM objects typically expose more than one interface. COM objects can be implemented in just about any language, but because COM uses the concept of a virtual function table, C++ has implementation advantages.

COM is about interfaces and every COM interface must implement `IUnknown`. `IUnknown` endows each interface with a standard way to locate other interfaces within a component and reference counting, which manages the lifetime of the component. COM objects must reside within an operating system process. On Windows systems, COM objects are implemented within DLLs or executables, which is called the component housing. Each housing must implement the standard COM techniques for exposing a class factory. A class factory is itself a COM component whose only purpose is to create instances of other COM objects.

The Windows Registry is important to the COM environment. It manages several keys that are used by COM as well as client programs. COM makes heavy use of something called a GUID. A GUID is a unique 128-bit number that uniquely identifies interfaces and components. COM is made up of several Win32 APIs and a large number of interface declarations.

The Active Template Library (ATL) is a framework that facilitates the creation of small, COM-based components. The ATL uses the newer template-based features of C++, and is provided with source code as part of the Visual C++ development environment. The ATL COM AppWizard gets your project started by providing a basic housing implementation. The ATL Object Wizard is then used to add specific components. The ATL is comprised of several classes that provide default implementations for the most common COM requirements. The `CComModule` class provides basic housing support through implementations of `DllGetClassObject` and `DllCanUnloadNow`. It also provides support for self-registration through the ATL Registrar component, which makes it easy to update the Windows registry.

Automation is a standard mechanism that allows language-independent interoperation of software modules. To provide this language-independent option, most COM-based components support Automation as their method of exposing functionality. Automation is supported through a standard COM interface: `IDispatch`. The `IDispatch` interface provides a series of methods that allow a client application to dynamically access functionality within a server. A dual interface combines a custom COM interface with `IDispatch`. A COM object describes its interfaces through type information. Type information is created with Microsoft's Interface Definition Language (IDL). An IDL file is compiled using the MIDL compiler to produce a binary type library. The type library is then distributed with the component.

Developing ActiveX Controls with the ATL

In Chapter 5, we discussed using ActiveX controls in Web pages as well as in Windows applications. In this and the next chapter we learn even more about ActiveX controls by developing our own. There are several tools available to facilitate the development of controls: the Microsoft Foundation Classes (MFC), Visual Basic, and the Active Template Libraries. There are several books on developing controls using MFC, so we cover using the ATL in this chapter and then cover developing controls with Visual Basic in Chapter 8.

Developing ActiveX Controls

Back in Chapter 5, we discussed how controls expose their functionality through properties, methods, and events, and that they required the existence of a control *container* to actually provide this functionality. We now need to discuss them in a bit more detail, now that you have Chapter 6 under your belt.

ActiveX controls are COM-based, in-process servers. In other words, they are DLLs that implement a number of standard COM interfaces. Back in Chapter 6, we developed a small COM-based component that was housed in a DLL. Based on the "correct" definition of what an ActiveX control is, the component we developed in Chapter 6 is actually an ActiveX control. However, it won't work in any of today's control containers. Why? Because most containers expect a control to implement a number of interfaces, not just `IUnknown` and the dual interface that we implemented in the Chapter 6 example.

What Language/Tool Should I Use?

For a long time there was only one basic technique for building ActiveX controls: the Microsoft Foundation Class (MFC) Libraries. However, since the beginning of 1997, there have been a number of new tools released by Microsoft that provide support for developing ActiveX controls. Let's take a quick look at the tools available.

C++ and the Microsoft Foundation Class Libraries

The first method and probably still the most effective way of developing ActiveX controls is to use MFC. By writing controls with MFC, you get a well-tested framework that is now in its seventh revision (with Visual C++ 5.0), a large amount of MFC-based documentation and example controls, and a very efficient development environment (AppWizard and Class-Wizard).

Developing controls with MFC requires some knowledge of C++ and the primary reason that we're not using MFC in this chapter is that there are a number of good books that cover control development using MFC (including one of mine: *Designing and Using ActiveX Controls*). The secondary reason is that developing controls with MFC has one drawback. The finished controls are dependent on MFC's run-time DLLs (e.g., MFC42.DLL). To distribute your controls, you also have to distribute a one megabyte DLL, and in the Internet environment this can sometimes be difficult and inefficient.

C++ and the Active Template Library

On February 17, 1997, Microsoft released version 2.0 of the Active Template Library. This version contains full support for the development of ActiveX controls. ATL version 2.1, which was released with Visual C++ 5.0, is functionally identical to version 2.0. The only changes have to do with integration with Visual C++.

The Active Template Library is the future of COM/ActiveX development. There is no doubt about this. Microsoft learned a lot when they built MFC and they're now applying this to their second-generation framework, the ATL. Version 2.0 provides full support for the creation of ActiveX controls. It even supports several features not supported by MFC (e.g., dual interfaces).

One drawback of using the ATL is that there, again, is a dearth of information to help the beginning developer. This book provides a good introduction to ATL, but I'm sure complete books on this new framework will be forthcoming. (Actually, I'm currently writing one. Check widgetware .com for more details.)

Another drawback is that the ATL doesn't do everything that MFC does for you. You don't realize how much is done for you by MFC until you have to do something without it. However, by using the ATL you get a lot more control (because you have to understand it to implement it) over what your controls do. Bottom line: If you want to develop professional-looking, and efficient ActiveX controls, you should use ATL. It provides the most flexibility and is the best COM-based development tool available, at least for C++ developers.

C++ and the ActiveX Control Framework

The ActiveX Control Framework (ACF) is a lightweight version of the MFC libraries and was developed by the Visual Basic group for implementing the controls that ship with Visual Basic. Just like the ATL, it provides a way to develop controls that do not have to carry around the overhead of MFC. The ACF is provided as part of the Platform SDK. You'll find it in the SAMPLES directory. The BASECTL directory that contains the framework (in the FRAMEWRK directory) and several example controls. The framework also enables you to build efficient Automation servers.

The reason the ACF is in the SAMPLES directly is that Microsoft does not support it. This may be a major factor when determining which tool to use. There is no guarantee that Microsoft will upgrade the framework to work with newer control standards and such. And now that ATL is available, which provides similar capabilities, and is supported, I don't expect that they will. One other problem with the ACF is that there is very little information on it. The included README.TXT file is the extent of the documentation and that hasn't been updated for over a year.

The primary benefit of using the ACF is that you can produce very small controls that have no dependencies on MFC's DLLs, and if you're really careful, you can even eliminate any dependency on the C run-time libraries (MSVCRTx0.DLL). A control with no DLL dependencies and a size of around 25K goes a long way in the Web environment. Another benefit of using the ACF is that it can be used by non-Visual C++ compilers such as Borland C++, and so on. The bottom line on the ACF is that you should probably use the ATL. It provides all of the features of the ACF and it is supported by Microsoft. However, it you like to tinker, the ACF is a small, understandable framework that will teach you a lot about implementing ActiveX controls.

Java and Visual J++

ActiveX controls are inherently based on Microsoft's COM. Java, on the other hand, is not. Visual J++ allows you to use ActiveX controls. However, to write a fully functional ActiveX control using it will require a lot of work. Basically, there is not framework like MFC or ATL provided with Visual J++ that would make the process easy. You can, however, develop a JavaBean using Java and use the ActiveX bridge to treat the bean like an ActiveX control.

Visual Basic

With the release of Visual Basic version 5.0, you can now develop highly functional controls with one of the most popular Windows development languages. As you'll see in the next chapter, Visual Basic allows you to do just about everything you can do using either of the other techniques described here. However, just as the MFC-based technique requires that you distribute the MFC run-time with your controls, Visual Basic also has this requirement.

A Short History of ActiveX Controls

ActiveX controls, or OLE controls at the time, were introduced as an OLE-based technology in early 1994 as a replacement for the aging Visual Basic custom control (VBX). The technology was new and there were very few development tools that supported the actual use of OLE controls when developing software. Finally, in late 1995, Visual Basic 4.0 was released. This version finally provided support for building applications based on OLE controls. You could actually develop controls starting with the Visual C++ version 2.0 (circa late 1994). However you could not use them within Visual C++ until Visual C++ version 4.0 was released in late 1995.

The initial version of the OLE control specification, now called the OLE Control '94 specification, required a control to implement a number of COM-based interfaces. Most of these interfaces were part of the compound document specification because controls were really just in-process compound document servers with a couple of new, control-based interfaces.

Then, in early 1996, after more than two years' experience with implementing and using OLE Controls, Microsoft modified the specification significantly and called it the OLE Control '96 specification. (Shortly after this document was released, Microsoft coined ActiveX.) The new specification addresses a number of performance issues inherent with the earlier '94-specification controls. IT also adds significant new features and capabilities for controls and containers.

The OLE Control '94 Specification

The original OLE control architecture was specified as an extension to the existing OLE Compound Document specification. An OLE control had to implement all of the interfaces required by a compound-document-embedded server with in-place activation capabilities. Additionally, OLE controls had to implement several new control-specific interfaces. In all, a control that meets the OLE Control '94 specification would implement more than 15 COM-based interfaces. These are listed in Table 7.1 along with a short description of their purpose.

Implementing a COM-based component, such as an OLE control, that requires 15 interface implementations is a lot of work. Fortunately, MFC provided an implementation for the majority of these interfaces, and so building OLE Controls based on this early specification wasn't too overwhelming.

One of the problems with the OLE Control Specification was that it provided only guidelines as to how a control should implement its interfaces. Also, an application that wanted to behave as an OLE control container (e.g., Visual Basic) had to implement a number of COM-based interfaces. Early on, there were several problems in getting controls to behave similarly in each of the available containers. To help with this situation, Microsoft released a document that described how a container and its controls should interact with each other. Much of this coordination was already specified via the compound-document specification, but there was still a need for a document that would help developers understand the complex relationship between a control and its container. The resulting document was titled *OLE Controls and Container Guidelines* Version 1.1 (circa late 1995). The guideline put forth the minimum requirements that a control or control container must meet. It describes the interfaces that are mandatory and those that are optional.

TABLE 7.1	**Control-side Interface**	**Description**
OLE Control '94 Interfaces	`IOleObject`	The `IOleObject` interface provides the essence of the OLE compound document architecture. Through this interface, the container and server communicate to negotiate the size of the embedded object (the control in our case) as well as getting the MiscStatus bits for the control.
	`IOleInPlaceObject`	A control must implement `IOleInPlaceObject` to support the ability to be activated and deactivated in-place within the container. The interface also provides a method to notify the control when its size changes or is moved within the container.
	`IOleInPlaceActiveObject`	A control must implement `IOleInPlaceActiveObject` to provide support for the use and translation of accelerator keys within the control. Many of `IOleInPlaceActiveObject`'s methods are not required for ActiveX controls.
	`IOleControl`	`IOleControl` is a new interface added to support ActiveX Controls. It provides methods to enhance the interaction with the control's container. `IOleControl` primarily adds functionality so that the control and container can work together when handling keyboard input.
	`IDataObject`	A control implements this interface to provide graphical renderings to the container.
	`IViewObject2`	The `IViewObject2` interface is implemented by controls that provide a visual aspect. `IViewObject2` provides the container with methods to tell the control to render itself within the container's client area.
	`IPersistStream` `IPersistStreamInit` `IPersistStorage`	The persist interfaces are implemented by the control so that they may persist their values within the containers structured storage. A control's properties can persist between instantiations.
	`IProvideClassInfo`	`IProvideClassInfo` is implemented by an ActiveX Control to allow a client application (usually a container) to efficiently obtain the type information for the control. It contains only one method, `GetClassInfo`, that returns an interface pointer that provides access to the control's binary representation of its type library.
	`ISpecifyPropertyPages`	The `ISpecifyPropertyPages` interface provides a way for the container to query the control for its list of property pages. `ISpecifyPropertyPages` has only one method: `GetPages`. The `GetPages` method is called by the container. The container provides a pointer to a CAUUID structure that will return a counted array

TABLE 7.1
(Continued)

Control-side Interface	Description
	of CLSIDs. This enumerates all of the property page CLSIDs used by the control. The container uses these CLSIDs with a COM function, typically `CoCreate-Instance`, to instantiate the page objects.
`IPerPropertyBrowsing`	`IPerPropertyBrowsing` provides a way for the control to provide additional information about its properties.
`IPropertyPage2`	The `IPropertyPage2` interface is implemented by each property page component, and provides the container with methods to get the size, move, create, destroy, active, and deactivate the component's property page windows.
`IConnectionPoint-Container`	This interface is used to provide the container with an outgoing `IDispatch` interface. This enables the control to communicate events to the container.
`IConnectionPoint`	A control can support several *event sets*. For each one, the control must provide an implementation of the `IConnectionPoint` interface.
`IDispatch`	A control's properties and methods are provided through its `IDispatch` interface.

OLE Control '96 Specification

Although OLE controls provided a wonderful new technology that validated the concept of component-based development, they weren't perfect. The large number of interfaces and methods that a control had to implement, coupled with the requirement that most controls create a window when executing, made them somewhat "heavy." Building an application with a large number of OLE controls could be problematic. There were also some functionality holes that needed to be filled. To address these issues, Microsoft released, in early 1996, the OLE Control '96 specification. The changes to the existing control specification are embodied mostly by a series of new interfaces. These interfaces, and the basic functionality they provides is detailed in Table 7.2.

Control and Container Guidelines Version 2.0

Along with the OLE Control '96 specification, Microsoft released a document providing guidelines for control and container developers. By fol-

TABLE 7.2

New OLE Control
'96 Interfaces

Control-side Interface	Description
IPointerInactive	Provides a way for the control to respond to user interaction (mouse moves and clicks) when the controls is not in the active state.
IOleInPlaceSiteEx	Adds flicker-free redrawing methods.
IOleInPlaceSite-Windowless	Provides support for windowless controls.
IQuickActivate	Provides a more efficient way of initially loading and drawing a control.
IViewObjectEx	Adds drawing optimizations, flicker-free drawing, support for nonrectangular and transparent objects, and new control-sizing options.
IPersistPropertyBag	More efficient ways of storing and retrieving text-based control properties. This is a new interface that allows a control to support textual persistence. This provides support for the HTML PARAM element instead of the DATA element.
IProvideClassInfo2	The new IProvideClassInfo2 interface provides an additional method, GetGUID, which returns the GUID specified in the GUIDKIND parameter. This is useful when the container is implementing a control's outgoing, or event, interface.

lowing the guidelines, developers can help make their controls and containers work reliably together. The ActiveX control is becoming ubiquitous within development tools and applications. The large number of controls and containers, with their specialized functionality, makes it imperative for certain guidelines to be followed. By following the guidelines a developer makes the control or container useful within the largest number of development environments. The following items provide an introduction to the guideline document.

- **A COM object** An ActiveX control is just a specialized COM object. The only basic requirements for a control is that it support self-registration and the IUnknown interface. These are the only true requirements of a control. However, such a control could not provide much functionality. The guidelines provide for a control developer to add only those interfaces that the control needs, with the ultimate purpose being to make a control as lightweight as possible.

- **Self-registration** A control must support self-registration by implementing the DllRegisterServer and DllUnregisterServer functions, and must add the appropriate embeddable objects and automation server entries in the registry. A control must also use the component categories API to indicate what services are required to host the control.

- **Interface support**   If a control supports an interface, it must support it at a basic level. The document provides guidelines for each potential ActiveX control and container interface. It describes which methods must be implemented within an interface if that interface is implemented.

- **Persistence support**   If a control needs to provide persistence support, it must implement at least one `IPersist` interface, and should if possible support more than one. This makes it easier for a container to host the control. Support for `IPersistPropertyBag` is highly recommended because most of the major containers provide a "Save as text" capability.

- **Ambient properties**   If a control supports ambient properties, it must respect a certain number of ambient properties exposed by the container. They are `LocalID`, `UserMode`, `UIDead`, `ShowGrabHandles`, `ShowHatching`, and `DisplayAsDefault`.

- **Dual interfaces**   ActiveX controls and containers are strongly encouraged to support dual interfaces. If you recall from Chapter 6, an automation server implements a dual interface by providing both an `IDispatch` interface as well as a custom interface for its methods and properties.

- **Miscellaneous**   ActiveX controls should not use the WS_GROUP or WS_TABSTOP window flags, as this may conflict with the container's use of these flags. A control should honor a container's call to `IOleControl::FreezeEvents`. When events are frozen a container will discard event notifications from the control.

The Control and Containers Guideline document made a significant change in what is actually required for a COM object to *be* an ActiveX control. The first bulleted item mentioned basically states that the only *requirement* for an ActiveX control is that it support self-registration and support `IUnknown`. That's it! This is quite a change from the earlier specification and guidelines that required a control to implement at least 15 interfaces. What the document is saying is that any COM object that provides self-registration *is* an ActiveX control.

What the document is really saying is that a control now has tremendous flexibility in choosing what interfaces it should implement. In most cases, if you want your component to function as an ActiveX control, you will need to implement a number of interfaces. The new 2.0 guidelines have basically put all of the pressure on container developers. Since a control can pick and choose the interfaces it wants to implement, the container must be very careful about what it *assumes* a control can do.

This new definition of what a control is has caused a lot of consternation in the developer community, and as of this writing it hasn't been completely resolved. It's not all that bad—tools such as MFC and the ATL make it easy to implement *full-function* controls that implement the 20 or so interfaces that allow them to work in most containers. However, the guideline document details something called *Control Functional Categories.* This details what functionality a control might provide by describing those interfaces that actually provide the control's functionality. It's a good way to group the interfaces that a control should implement, and that is how we'll go through the next few sections.

ActiveX Control Functional Categories

The Control and Containers Guidelines document specifies a number of functional categories that a control can elect to implement. An ActiveX control is just a COM object that supports those interfaces required to implement any desired functionality. In the next few sections we cover each of these functional categories. At the end of this chapter, we actually implement a full-function ActiveX control, and as we go through each functional category, code fragments from our control example will be presented.

Basic COM Support

An ActiveX control is first and foremost a COM object and therefore, it must provide the most basic COM service: an implementation of the `IUnknown` interface. Of course, to create an instance of a control, the control housing (a DLL in our case) must also have a class factory, which requires the implementation of one of the `IClassFactory` interfaces. As we discussed in the last chapter, the ATL provides support for `IUnknown` and `IClassFactory` through `CComObjectRootEx` and `CComCoClass` classes. This implementation is the same as for any COM object, and we covered this back in Chapter 6.

Self-Registration

A control must also support self-registration. Again, the ATL provides support for self-registration through the default DLL implementation. To support self-registration, the control housing must export the `DllReg-isterServer` and `DllUnregisterServer` entry points. We covered this in Chapter 6. When adding a COM object with the Object Wizard, it creates an ATL Registrar file explicitly for our component. Following is the RGS file for our example control:

```
HKCR
{
    NoteCtl.NoteCtl.1 = s 'NoteCtl Class'
    {
        CLSID = s '{96BF44BF-9BE5-11D0-A71F-2C3690000000}'
    }
    NoteCtl.NoteCtl = s 'NoteCtl Class'
    {
        CurVer = s 'NoteCtl.NoteCtl.1'
    }
    NoRemove CLSID
    {
        ForceRemove {96BF44BF-9BE5-11D0-A71F-2C3690000000} = s 'NoteCtl Class'
        {
          ProgID = s 'NoteCtl.NoteCtl.1'
          VersionIndependentProgID = s 'NoteCtl.NoteCtl'
          ForceRemove 'Programmable'
          InprocServer32 = s '%MODULE%'
          {
              val ThreadingModel = s 'Apartment'
          }
          ForceRemove 'Control'
          ForceRemove 'Programmable'
          ForceRemove 'Insertable'
          ForceRemove 'ToolboxBitmap32' = s '%MODULE%, 1'
          'MiscStatus' = s '0'
           {
             '1' = s '131473'
           }
          'TypeLib' = s '{96BF44B0-9BE5-11D0-A71F-2C3690000000}'
          'Version' = s '1.0'
        }
    }
}
```

Registry Entries

Self-registration is basically the act of adding several keys to the Windows registry. ActiveX controls have a number of special registry entries that control containers (and COM itself) will use when iterating through the registry. Each of the following control entries is a subkey under \HKEY_CLASSES_ROOT\CLSID.

CONTROL. The **Control** entry indicates that the component is an ActiveX Control. This entry allows containers to easily identify the ActiveX Controls available on the system by searching through the registry looking only for CLSIDs with a **Control** subkey.

PROGRAMMABLE. The **Programmable** key specifies that the component supports Automation. Automation is the technology that allows COM-based components to expose their functionality to development tools such as Visual Basic and Delphi. Most ActiveX controls support Automation through an IDispatch or dual interface.

INPROCSERVER32. This entry indicates that the control is a 32-bit in-process server. Or, in other words, that the component is implemented within a DLL housing. The value for this entry is the explicit location of the component.

INSERTABLE. The `Insertable` entry indicates that the component can be embedded within an OLE Document container. This is the entry used by OLE Document containers like Visio, Word, and Excel. OLE Document containers populate the "Insert Object" dialog by spinning through the registry looking for components marked with the `Insertable` key. Controls should add this subkey only if they can provide functionality when embedded within an OLE Document container.

MISCSTATUS. The `MiscStatus` entry specifies options of interest to the control container. These values can be queried before actually embedding the control. The value for this entry is an integer equivalent of a bit mask value comprised of optional OLEMISC flags.

PROGID. The value of the `ProgID` entry is set to the current, version-specific ProgID for the control. This is no different from the entries for our components in earlier chapters.

TOOLBOXBITMAP32. The `ToolboxBitmap32` entry value specifies the filename and resource ID of the bitmap used for the toolbar of the container. Both MFC and the ATL store a control's bitmap within the DLL.

TYPELIB. The `TypeLib` entry value specifies the GUID and actual location of the type library for the component.

VERSION. The value of this subkey indicates the current version of the control.

Component Categories

Early in the days of ActiveX controls the above registry entries were all that were needed to specify the functionality of a control. The **Control** registry key indicated the existence of a control, and the **Insertable** key indicated whether or not the control could function as a simple OLE embedded server. Today, however, the functional capabilities of all COM-based components (especially controls) continues to expand at a rapid rate. A more efficient and useful mechanism of categorizing the capabilities provided by these objects is needed. The control guidelines require that new controls support component categories.

The CATID

Component Categories are identified using a category ID (CATID). A CATID is just another name for the 128-bit GUIDs used throughout COM. Along with the CATID there is a locale ID, specified by a string of hexadecimal digits, and a human-readable string. The known CATIDs are stored in the registry under the **HKEY_CLASSES_ROOT\Component Categories** key. Figure 7.1 shows some of the registry entries under this key.

The older registry entries that were previously used to categorize components are supported for backward compatibility. As you can see from Fig. 7.1, some registry entries have an **OldKey** entry. This provides a way to map the older registry mechanism to the new component categories one. Table 7.3 lists the CATIDs associated with the old registry entries.

Categorizing Your Controls

You categorize a control in two different ways: first by the control's capabilities and second by the capabilities required by its potential container. Two new registry entries are used to communicate this information. The **Implemented Categories** entry lists those category capabilities that your control provides, and the **Required Categories** entry lists those categories that your control requires from a container. These subkeys are added below the CLSID of a control. Here's an example:

Figure 7.1
OLEVIEW and
Component
Categories.

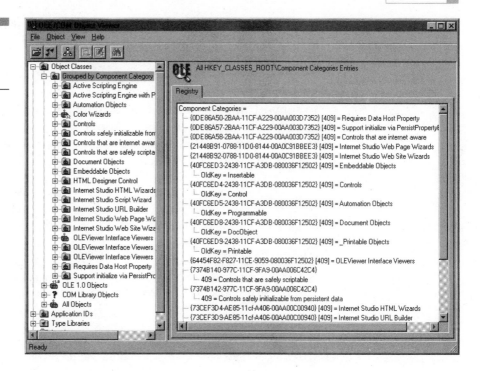

```
HKEY_CLASSES_ROOT\CLSID\{12345678-...}
        ; CATID for "Insertable"
        \Implemented Categories\{40FC6ED3-2438-11cf-A3DB-080036F12502}
        ; CATID for "Control"
        \Implemented Categories\{40FC6ED4-2438-11cf-A3DB-080036F12502}
        ;The CATID for an internet aware control
        \Implemented Categories\{...CATID_InternetAware...}
        ;Our control requires ISimpleFrame support
        \Required Categories\{...CATID_SimpleFrameControl...}
```

TABLE 7.3

Category IDs for
Old Registry Entries

Old Registry Entry	CATID Symbol from COMCAT.H	GUID
Control	CATID_Control	*40FC6ED4-2438-11cf-A3DB-080036F12502*
Insertable	CATID_Insertable	*40FC6ED3-2438-11cf-A3DB-080036F12502*
Programmable	CATID_Programmable	*40FC6ED5-2438-11cf-A3DB-080036F12502*
DocObject	CATID_DocObject	*40FC6ED8-2438-11cf-A3DB-080036F12502*
Printable	CATID_Printable	*40FC6ED9-2438-11cf-A3DB-080036F12502*

Currently, the component categories specification describes a few standard categories. Additional categories will be added as the technologies require them. For example, the ActiveX Scripting model uses two component categories to indicate scripting support within controls. Table 7.4 shows some of the defined categories as of this writing.

To support this new concept of component categories, Microsoft has defined two new COM interfaces: `ICatRegister` and `ICatInformation`. Also, Microsoft has provided a component that implements the Component Categories Manager.

TABLE 7.4

Component
Categories

CATID Symbol from COMCAT.H	Purpose
CATID_PersistsToMoniker, CATID_PersistsToStreamInit, CATID_PersistsToStream, CATID_PersistsToStorage, CATID_PersistsToMemory, CATID_PersistsToFile, CATID_PersistsToPropertyBag	Used by Internet aware controls to indicate which persistence methods they support. These can be used to indicate that a interface is required if the control only supports one persistence method.
CATID_SimpleFrameControl	The control implements or requires the container to provide `ISimpleFrameSite` interface support.
CATID_PropertyNotifyControl	The control supports simple data binding.
CATID_WindowlessObject	The control implements the new windowless feature of the Control '96 specification.
CATID_VBFormat CATID_VBGetControl	The control uses one or both of these Visual Basic specific interfaces.
CATID_VBDataBound	The control supports the advanced data binding interfaces.
CATID_RequiresDataPathHost	The control expects help from the container with its data path properties. The container must support `IBindHost`.
CATID_InternetAware	The control implements or requires some of the Internet-specific functionality, in particular the new persistence mechanisms for Web-based controls. The control also handles large property values with the new data path property type. This includes support for asynchronous downloads.
CATID_SafeForScripting	The control is safe for use within scripting environments.
CATID_SafeForInitializing	The control can safely be initialized.

The Component Categories Manager

To make it somewhat easy to add component category support to your controls, Microsoft provides the Component Categories Manager (CCM). It is a simple in-process server that implements the `ICatRegister` and `ICatInformation` interfaces. Component categories are just defined registry entries, and the CCM provides a simple way to maintaining these entries within the registry. To create an instance of the CCM, you use the COM `CoCreateInstance` API and pass in the defined CCM CLSID: `CLSID_StdComponentCategoriesMgr`. `CoCreateInstance` will return either the `ICatRegister` or `ICatInformation` interface.

ICatRegister

The `ICatRegister` interface provides methods for registering and unregistering a specific components categories. Here's its definition:

```
interface ICatRegister : IUnknown
{
    HRESULT RegisterCategories(
        ULONG cCategories,
        CATEGORYINFO rgCategoryInfo[]);

    HRESULT UnRegisterCategories(
        ULONG cCategories,
        CATID rgcatid[]);

    HRESULT RegisterClassImplCategories(
        REFCLSID rclsid,
        ULONG cCategories,
        CATID rgcatid[]);

    HRESULT UnRegisterClassImplCategories(
        REFCLSID rclsid,
        ULONG cCategories,
        CATID rgcatid[]);

    HRESULT RegisterClassReqCategories(
        REFCLSID rclsid,
        ULONG cCategories,
        CATID rgcatid[]);

    HRESULT UnRegisterClassReqCategories(
        REFCLSID rclsid,
        ULONG cCategories,
        CATID rgcatid[]);
};
```

There are six registration methods, but three are used to reverse the registration process. The unregister methods just do the opposite of the register methods. The `RegisterCategory` method takes the count and an array of `CATEGORYINFO` entries and ensures that they are registered on the system as valid component categories. This means placing them below the **HKEY_CLASSES_ROOT\Component Categories** entry. In most cases the category will already be in the registry, but it doesn't hurt to make sure. Here's the definition of the CATEGORYINFO structure and some simple code that shows using the `RegisterCategory` method.

```
typedef struct tagCATEGORYINFO
{
   CATID catid;
   LCID lcid;
   OLECHAR szDescription[ 128 ];
} CATEGORYINFO;

#include "comcat.h"
HRESULT CreateComponentCategory( CATID catid, WCHAR* catDescription )
{
   ICatRegister* pcr = NULL ;
   HRESULT hr = S_OK ;

   // Create an instance of the category manager.
   hr = CoCreateInstance( CLSID_StdComponentCategoriesMgr,
                          NULL,
                          CLSCTX_INPROC_SERVER,
                          IID_ICatRegister,
                          (void**)&pcr );
   if (FAILED(hr))
      return hr;

   CATEGORYINFO catinfo;
   catinfo.catid = catid;
   // English locale ID in hex
   catinfo.lcid = 0x0409;

   // Make sure the description isn't too big.
   int len = wcslen(catDescription);
   if (len>127)
      len = 127;
   wcsncpy( catinfo.szDescription, catDescription, len );
   catinfo.szDescription[len] = '\0';

   hr = pcr->RegisterCategories( 1, &catinfo );
   pcr->Release();

   return hr;
}
```

This code creates an instance of the Component Category Manager and queries for the `ICatRegister` interface. If everything works, a CATE-

GORYINFO structure is filled out with the component information and the `RegisterCategory` method is called.

To actually add "**Implemented Categories**" registry entries for a specific control, you use the `RegisterClassImplCategories` method. The method takes three parameters: the CLSID of the control, a count of the number of CATIDs, and an array of CATIDs to place under the "**Implemented Categories**" key. Here's some code to mark a control as implementing the "**Control**" category.

```
ICatRegister* pcr = NULL ;
HRESULT hr = S_OK ;

// Create an instance of the category manager.
hr = CoCreateInstance( CLSID_StdComponentCategoriesMgr,
                       NULL,
                       CLSCTX_INPROC_SERVER,
                       IID_ICatRegister,
                       (void**)&pcr );
if (SUCCEEDED(hr))
{
   // Register that we support the "Control" category
   CATID rgcatid[1];
   rgcatid[0] = CATID_Control;
   hr = pcr->RegisterClassImplCategories(clsid, 1, rgcatid);
}

if (pcr != NULL)
   pcr->Release();
```

To add "**Category Required**" entries for a control, you can use the `RegisterClassReqCategories` method. The method takes the same parameters as `RegisterClassImplCategories` and so the code is nearly identical to that shown earlier.

The ATL Registrar Component

The ATL Registrar component allows us to add component categories for our controls without writing any code. To add an entry to the "**Implemented Categories**" or "**Category Required**" keys to the registry for your control, just add the key and value to your control's .RGS file like this:

```
'Implemented Categories'
{
   '{40FC6ED4-2438-11cf-A3DB-080036F12502}'
}
'Implemented Categories'
```

```
{
    '{40FC6ED5-2438-11cf-A3DB-080036F12502}'
}
'Category Required'
{
    '{40FC6ED7-2438-11cf-A3DB-080036F12502}'
}
```

OLE Document Interfaces

The technology that allows an ActiveX control to be embedded within a container has been around a long time. The OLE Document standard (called Compound Documents at the time) was created in 1991 and was the major part of OLE. Actually, OLE at the time was an acronym for *Object Linking and Embedding*. When ActiveX controls came along, the OLE Document standard was enhanced to allow document servers to expose programmatic functionality.

Today, if your control needs to provide a visual representation and basic interaction with the user through mouse clicks and such, it must support the basic OLE Document interfaces. The OLE Document specification contains a number of interfaces that a control should implement if it expects to provide visual functionality. The most important OLE Document interfaces are discussed in the next few sections.

IOleObject and IOleObjectImpl

The IOleObject interface provides basic embedded object support so that the control (i.e., OLE Document server) can communicate with the container. The IOleObject interface contains 21 methods, of which most are easy to implement and only a few are of interest to ActiveX controls. The SetExtent, and GetExtent methods are used to negotiate a control's actual extent or size, and the GetMiscStatus method returns the OLEMISC status bits that we just covered.

The ATL provides a functional implementation of the IOleObject interface through its IOleObjectImpl class. The class provides the basic functionality that most controls will need. Although the interface has 21 methods, only a few are actually needed by a control and so the ATL implements only that subset.

Restricting the Size of a Control

As an example of how you might modify a control's behavior, let's demonstrate overriding one of `IOleObject`'s methods. Certain controls may need to restrict their size or shape. When a control user changes the extents of a control, the container notifies the control of the new size through the `IOleObject::SetExtent` method. The SetExtent method takes as a parameter a SIZEL structure containing the new extents for the control. In order to restrict the size of the control, we just need to override the default `SetExtent` method, check the new extents, and modify them if we need to. Here's how to do it for our forthcoming example control.

```
// NoteCtl.h : Declaration of the CNoteCtl
...
class ATL_NO_VTABLE CNoteCtl :
...
```

```
    STDMETHOD (SetExtent) (DWORD dwDrawAspect, SIZEL *psizel)
    {
        ATLTRACE(_T("SetExtent sizing control to 1000x1000\n"));
        psizel->cx = psizel->cy = 1000;
        return IOleObjectImpl<CNoteCtl>::SetExtent(dwDrawAspect, psizel);
    }
...
};
```

The SIZEL structure provides the extents in OLE's favorite unit: HIMETRIC. In our previous example, we force the control size to always be a square of 1000 HIMETRIC units.

NOTE: *The ATLTRACE macro is similar to MFC's TRACE macro. When a project is compiled and executed in debug mode, ATLTRACE messages are displayed in Developer Studio's debug output window.*

IViewObject[x] and IViewObjectImpl

The second OLE Document interface that is important to a control is actually a set of related interfaces. The IViewObject, IViewObject2, and IViewObjectEx interfaces are all related. Each interface is an extension of the other. The `IViewObject` interfaces provide a way for the container to retrieve a graphical rendering of the control. A control implements this interface and draws its representation onto a device context provided by the container. The initial version of this interface, IViewObject, was part of the original OLE Document specification. Then with the release of the Control '94 specification, one additional method was added, GetExtent, that allowed the container to get a control's extents through this interface instead of IOleObject. Then, as part of the Control '96 specification, IViewObject2 was enhanced to create IViewObjectEx. The new interface includes five new methods that facilitate flicker-free drawing, non-rectangular objects, hit testing, and additional control-sizing options.

The ATL provides an implementation and support for all three of these view interfaces through its IViewObjectImpl class. The most important method of IViewObjectEx is the Draw method. Control containers call this method whenever they need the control to render itself. A number of parameters are passed, most of which deal with how and where to render the control's representation. The ATL provides a simplification of the drawing process and ultimately calls the CCom-Control::Draw method.

IDataObject and IDataObjectImpl

The IDataObject interface is used by compound document servers to provide the container with a method of rendering data to a device other than a device context. ActiveX controls typically use the IOleView[x] interface instead of IDataObject, but it can be implemented if needed.

IOleInPlaceObject

A control must implement the compound document IOleInPlaceObject interface to support the ability to be activated and deactivated in-place within the container. The interface also provides a method to notify the control when its size changes or is moved within the container.

IOleInPlaceActiveObject

A control must implement IOleInPlaceActiveObject to provide support for the use and translation of accelerator keys within the control. Many of IOleInPlaceActiveObject's methods are not needed for ActiveX controls.

Automation (IDispatch) Support

We've described Automation and the implementation of `IDispatch` in pretty good detail at this point. Automation is very important to ActiveX controls as it is their primary way of interacting with the outside world. The guidelines document recommends that controls implement their Automation interfaces using a dual interface, as it provides the most efficient and flexible implementation. Luckily, as we saw in Chapter 6, the ATL makes implementation of dual interfaces easy.

Automation is also used in other areas of ActiveX controls. An ActiveX control container exposes its *ambient* properties though an IDispatch-based interface. Also, control events are implemented with Automation through an additional technique called *Connectable Objects,* which we cover in a moment.

Standard and Stock Properties

The ActiveX Control specifications provide a set of properties that are standard and should be used when implementing a property that provides common functionality. This provides a uniform interface for the control user. Examples of such common properties include *Font* and *Back-Color.* Table 7.5 lists the standard properties currently defined by the standard. You will also encounter the term *stock* property. Tools such as MFC and the ATL, provide default implementations of most standard properties. When they do, they are termed stock properties.

Ambient Properties

ActiveX controls can exist only within the context of a control container. The container provides the environment through which the control provides its functionality. A control, however, can learn a lot about this environment by communicating with the container. The control standard specifies that containers should expose a set of ambient properties. These ambient properties allow the control to query for certain container characteristics. An example of an ambient property is the *UserMode* ambient. As we discussed earlier, a container has two modes of operation: design-time and run-time. A control can determine which mode the container is currently in by checking the user mode ambient property.

Property	Description
Appearance*	Appearance of the control (e.g., 3D)
AutoSize*	If TRUE the control should size to fit within its container.
BackColor*	The Background color of the control.
BorderStyle*	The style of the controls border. A short that currently supports only two values. A 0 indicates no border, and 1 indicates to draw a normal single line border around the control. More styles may be defined in the future.
BorderColor*	The color of the border around the control.
BorderWidth*	The width of the border around the control.
BorderVisible*	Show the border.
DrawMode*	The mode of drawing used by the control.
DrawStyle*	The style of drawing used by the control.
DrawWidth*	The width of the pen used for drawing.
FillColor*	The fill color.
FillStyle*	The style of the fill color.
Font*	The font used for any text in the control.
ForeColor*	The color of any text or graphics within the control.
Enabled*	TRUE indicates that the control can accept input.
hWnd*	The hWnd of the controls window.
TabStop	Should the control participate in the tab stop scheme.
Text* Caption*	A BSTR that indicates the caption or text of the control. Both of these properties are implemented with the same internal methods. Only one of the two may be used.

* Indicates stock implementation provided by ATL.

Ambient properties are provided by the default IDispatch of the container. As a control is loaded into the container, the ambient dispatch is passed to the control. The control saves this pointer and when it needs an ambient property value, it calls through the IDispatch pointer. Each of the ambient properties has a specified DISPID, and so access to the property is easy. Table 7.6 lists the specified ambient properties. There is one

TABLE 7.6

Ambient Properties

Property	Description
BackColor	Background color of the control.
DisplayName	The name of the control as given by the container. This name should be used when the control needs to display information to the user.
Font	The recommended font for the control.
ForeColor	Foreground color for text.
LocaleID	The container's locale identifier.
MessageReflect	If this property is TRUE, the container supports reflecting messages back to the control.
ScaleUnits	A string name for the container's coordinate units (e.g., "twips" or "cm").
TextAlign	Indicates how the control should justify any textual information. 0—Numbers to the right, text to the left 1—Left Justify 2—Center Justify 3—Right Justify 4—Fill Justify
UserMode	Returns TRUE if the container is in run mode, otherwise the container is in design mode.
UIDead	The UIDead property indicates to the control that it should not accept or act on any user input directed to the control. Containers may use this property to indicate to the control that it is in design mode or that it is running, but the developer has interrupted processing during debugging.
ShowGrabHandles	If TRUE the control should show grab handles when UI active.
ShowHatching	If TRUE the control should show diagonal hatch marks around itself when UI Active.
DisplayAsDefault	The container sets this property to TRUE for a button style control when it becomes the default button within the container. This occurs when the user tabs to the specific control or the control is actually the default button on the form, and the focus is on a nonbutton control. The button should indicate that it is the default button by thickening its border.
SupportsMnemonics	If TRUE, the container supports the use of Mnemonics within controls.
AutoClip	If TRUE, the container automatically clips any portion of the control's rectangle that should not be displayed. If FALSE, the control should honor the clipping rectangle passed to it in the IOleInPlaceObject's SetObjectRects method.

caveat though: containers do not have to expose all of these properties. However, most of the good containers do.

ATL and Ambient Properties

The container's ambient properties can be accessed by an ATL-based control through the *GetAmbient* methods provided by the CComControl class. Each method name begins with GetAmbient and is followed by the appropriate ambient name. For example, following is some code from our sample control (that we will add later) that uses several ambient properties.

```
BOOL bUserMode = FALSE;
GetAmbientUserMode( bUserMode );
if ( bUserMode == FALSE )
{
    HFONT hOldFont = 0;
    IFont* pFont = 0;
    if ( SUCCEEDED( GetAmbientFont( &pFont )) && pFont )
    {
        HFONT hFont;
        pFont->get_hFont( &hFont );
        hOldFont = (HFONT) SelectObject( hdc, hFont );

        pFont->Release();
    }

    BSTR bstr;
    if ( SUCCEEDED( GetAmbientDisplayName( bstr )))
    {
        DrawText( hdc,
                  OLE2A( bstr ),
                  -1,
                  &rc,
                  DT_TOP | DT_SINGLELINE );
    }

    if ( hOldFont )
        SelectObject( hdc, hOldFont );
}
```

Standard Control Methods

The ActiveX Control specification recommends two standard control methods that controls should implement if they provide the specific behavior (Table 7.7). The Refresh method causes an immediate redraw of the control and the DoClick method causes the control to fire the standard Click event.

	Method	Description
TABLE 7.7 Standard Control Methods	Refresh	Causes the control to force a redraw.
	DoClick	Fires the standard click event within the control.

Connectable Objects and Control Events

To support events, ActiveX control uses a COM technology called *Connectable Objects*. Connectable objects are Automation-based components that support both incoming and outgoing IDispatch interfaces. For a control to support outgoing events it must implement the IConnectionPointContainer and IConnectionPoint interfaces. The container must also support events, as half of the event functionality will be provided by the container application.

The IConnectionPointContainer interface contains two methods: FindConnectionPoint and EnumConnectionPoints. EnumConnectionPoints provides a way for the container to iterate over all of the connection points within a control. The FindConnectionPoint method requires an interface ID (IID) to identify the specific interface that a container is looking for. Each of these methods provides a way for the container to obtain a pointer to the control's IConnectionPoint interface.

The container uses the IConnectionPoint::Advise method to set up the event connection with the control by passing an implementation of IDispatch that implements (as methods) the control's events. After this interface is set up, the control can "fire" events by calling methods through this IDispatch. It's just like Automation, only in reverse. The container implements the controls events as methods, which allows the control to fire the events by calling methods within the container.

Standard Events

Just as it does with properties and methods, the ActiveX control standard describes a set of standard events that a control can implement. The events are primarily for graphical controls. Each of the standard events is listed in Table 7.8.

Event	Description
Click	Fired by a BUTTONUP event for any mouse button.
DblClick	Fired by BUTTONDBLCLK message for any mouse button.
Error	Fired by the control when an error occurs.
KeyDown	Fired by the WM_SYSKEYDOWN or WM_KEYDOWN message.
KeyPress	Fired by the WM_CHAR message.
KeyUp	Fired by the WM_SYSKEYUP or WM_KEYUP message.
MouseDown	Fired by the BUTTONDOWN event for any mouse button.
MouseMove	Fired by the WM_MOUSEMOVE message.
MouseUp	Fired by the BUTTONUP event for any mouse button.

Property Pages

One of the most important aspects of a control's functionality is its properties. ActiveX controls have the option of providing a series of control-specific property pages. Property pages allow the presentation of control-specific information. The guidelines document recommends that all controls that expose properties also implement property pages. Property pages are typically used during the design phase to provide a rich environment for the control user to manipulate the control. Figure 7.2 shows the property page for the control we build at the end of the chapter.

Each property page is itself a COM object. It is actually a separate component that is instantiated independently by the container application. Certain standard property pages may be provided by the development tool. For example, ATL provides an implementation of three common property pages: fonts, colors, and pictures. However, you will typically implement a specific property page for each of your controls.

Most development tools (e.g., Visual Basic) provide a default property browser window for your control's properties. However, this is not always the case. For this reason you should always provide a complete set of property pages for your control.

During the design process, the control user can modify your control's properties. The container will ask the control for its list of property pages. The container will then instantiate each property page component individually and merge them to form a property sheet. As property values are

Figure 7.2
Our Finished
Control's Property
Page.

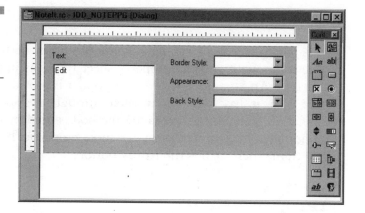

modified the property page communicates directly with the control (through its IDispatch) to update any values. Figure 7.3 shows our complete control's property sheet.

Property pages are supported by three COM interfaces. Let's take a brief look at each.

ISpecifyPropertyPages

A control implements the ISpecifyPropertyPages interface. The container queries through this interface for a list of supported property pages. ISpecifyPropertyPages has but one method, GetPages. The ATL provides the implementation of GetPages in the CComControlBase class.

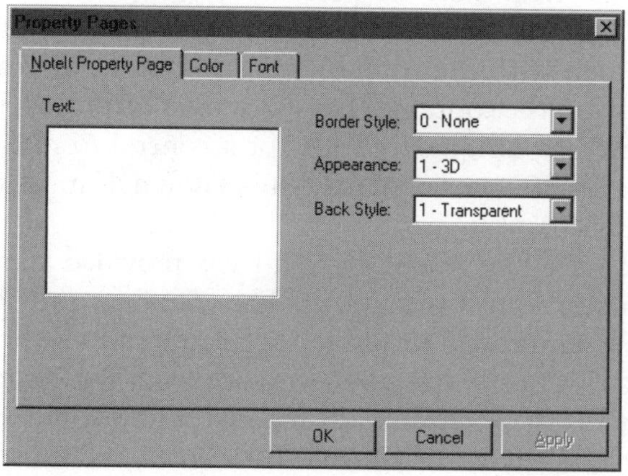

Figure 7.3
Control's Property
Sheet.

`IPropertyPageSite`

`IPropertyPageSite` facilitates communication between the property page component and the property sheet frame as implemented by the container. An `IPropertyPageSite` pointer is provided to each property page after it has been instantiated through `IPropertyPage::Set-PageSite`. The `OnStatusChange` method is used by the property page to indicate to the frame that one or more properties have been modified. The frame then enables the **Apply** button.

`IPropertyPage2`

The `IPropertyPage2` interface is implemented by each property page component, and provides the container with methods to get the size, move, create, destroy, active, and deactivate the component's property page property window. The container creates a frame for each property page and uses these methods to manage the displaying of the property sheet. This allows the property sheet to appear and behave as if driven by one application, when in fact, a property sheet is comprised of individual components housed within a frame window created by the container.

Property Persistence

One of the most important aspects of ActiveX controls is their ability to persist their state. As part of the design process, control users will modify a control's state by manipulating its properties. A control embedded within a container is an instance of that control. Each control within the container has its own set of property values, which make the instance unique. In order for a control to maintain the state of its properties after the container shuts down, it must support some persistence mechanism.

The OLE Document standard has provided support for component persistence since its inception. The container provides the environment whereby embedded servers (e.g., controls) can save and restore their internal states. Controls require assistance from the container because it is in charge of the complete document or development environment. For example, when using a Visual Basic form, the form itself maintains the state of any embedded controls in the .FRM file. The embedded controls have very little knowledge of how the form saves their states.

All this is done through a series of COM interfaces. There are a number of such interfaces as they have evolved over the years. For ActiveX controls, the three most important persistence interfaces are `IPersist-Stream`, `IPersistStreamInit`, and `IPersistPropertyBag`.

`IPersistStream` is part of the OLE Document specification and provides a simple mechanism for a component to persist its state. A stream is a simple file structure, defined by OLE, that provides a stream-oriented structure to the component. The component (a control) implements the `IPersistStream` interface, which contains methods such as `Load` and `Save`. The client application (our container) determines if the component supports persistence by doing a `QueryInterface` for one of the `IPersist` interfaces. In our example, the control would return a pointer to its implementation of `IPersistStream`. The container would then create and open a stream and pass this as a parameter to the `IPersistStream::Load` and `IPersistStream::Save` methods.

The `IPersistStreamInit` interface was added with the ActiveX Control specification and provides a way for the control to initialize its state before it is actually loaded. A new method was added, `InitNew`, to support this capability. By implementing `InitNew` a control can initialize its state (like a constructor) before any persistent information is applied.

A new persistence interface is `IPersistPropertyBag`. It was added as part of the Control '96 specification, which now allows "textual" persistence. `IPersistPropertyBag` and the container-side interface, `IPropertyBag`, provide an efficient method of saving and loading text-based properties. The control implements `IPersistPropertyBag`, through which the container calls `Load` and `Save` and which informs the control to either initialize itself or to save its property values. It does this through the `IPropertyBag::Read` and `IPropertyBag::Write` methods provided by the container. The property bag persistence mechanism is very effective in a Web-based environment where a control's property information may be stored within the actual HTML document.

When using controls in Web environments, support for `IPersist-PropertyBag` allows the control to use the HTML PARAM element. If a control implements `IPersistStreamInit` instead, its properties are persisted using the HTML DATA element, which stores the data in an unfriendly binary format. By default, ATL-generated controls get support for `IPersistStreamInit`. In our example, we add the implementation for `IPersistPropertyBag` so our controls will work effectively in Web environments.

Building an Example Control

Okay, that finishes up our whirlwind coverage of the ActiveX control specifications. Now, to demonstrate what is really required to develop an ActiveX control, we're going to develop one with the ATL. We'll build a basic control that uses most of the control functionality provided by ATL. It's hard to cover everything you can do with the ATL and ActiveX controls in one chapter, but we'll try. By covering the basics of how controls work and how ATL implements the various control interfaces, you should then have a solid foundation on which to develop your own controls. Also, you should visit www.WidgetWare.com and check out the ActiveX Control FAQ area when you encounter problems developing your own controls. There, you'll find answers to over 100 questions on COM, OLE, and ActiveX development.

Starting the Project

We covered creation of a basic ATL project in Chapter 6. An ActiveX control is an in-process server, or DLL. So, to start our initial ActiveX control project, we need to create a simple, DLL-based COM project using the ATL COM AppWizard. (See Fig. 7.4.)

This step creates a skeletal ATL project that provides basic COM in-process support. It exposes the four required DLL entry points: DllGet-

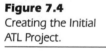

Figure 7.4
Creating the Initial
ATL Project.

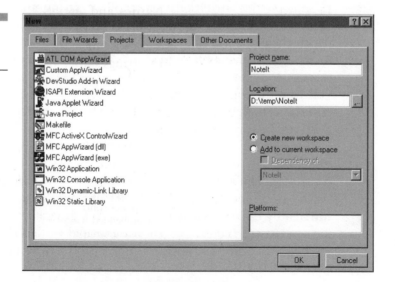

`ClassObject`, `DllCanUnloadNow`, `DllRegisterServer`, and `Dll-UnregisterServer`. The first two are for supporting COM and the last two are for self-registration support.

Next, we need to add a component class that will provide the implementation of our ActiveX control. We do this using the ATL Object Wizard. To start the ATL Object Wizard select **Insert/New ATL Object...** from the Developer Studio menu.

ATL Object Wizard

As we discussed in Chapter 6, the ATL Object Wizard steps you through adding components to basic ATL projects created with the ATL AppWizard. The Object Wizard will add skeletal code for several categories of ATL-based components. Each of these is described in Table 7.9.

We focus on the "Controls" category here in this chapter. After Clicking on the **Controls** category (shown in Fig. 7.5), you are presented with three control-specific objects. Each of these is described in Table 7.10. For our initial project, we're going to create an **ATL Full Control.** Select this option and click the **Next** button.

The Names and Attributes Tabs

The Object Wizard provides a series of four tabbed dialogs for setting the characteristics of our new ActiveX control. We covered the options available on the first two tabs, **Names** and **Attributes,** in Chapter 6. The default settings for these tabs are fine for our control. However, so that the class and filenames are consistent for our example, name the control class **NoteCtl** so you get the name settings shown in Fig. 7.6.

	Type	Description
TABLE 7.9 Object Wizard Categories	Objects	Various COM object types, from simple to complex Microsoft Transaction Server objects.
	Controls	Three component types are provided here. A full ActiveX control, which provides default implementations of all control-related interfaces. An Internet Explorer control, which implements those interfaces required to be embedded within Internet Explorer, and a property page component, which most controls should provide.
	Miscellaneous	Uncategorized COM objects such as a Windows dialog.

Figure 7.5
ATL Object Wizard
Control Types.

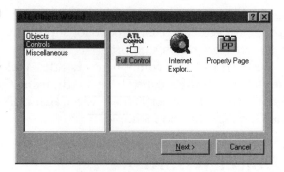

The Miscellaneous Tab

The Miscellaneous tab is used to provide ActiveX control-specific information to the Object Wizard. The various options presented here are used only by ActiveX controls. For our example control, toggle off the **Opaque** view status, but take the default options for the rest. The resulting dialog is shown in Fig. 7.7. The following section describes each of the options on the **Miscellaneous** tab.

View Status and Transparent or Nonrectangular Controls

The **View Status** option indicates whether your control will act as an opaque control or as a transparent control. The OLE Control '96 specification added functionality that makes it easier to develop "transparent" controls. Transparent controls can also be described as "nonrectangular" controls. The gist behind all of this is that the background of the control can be transparent.

For example, Visual Basic has long had a *line* control whose purpose is to draw a simple line. Developing a control that mimics Visual Basic's line

TABLE 7.10

ActiveX Control
Types

Type	Description
Full Control	A control that implements those interfaces that allow it to work in all containers.
Internet Explorer Control	A control project that implements only those interfaces required by Internet Explorer.
Property Page	A property page component.

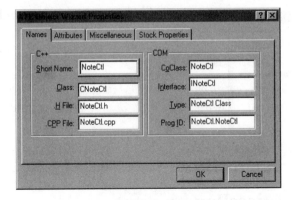

Figure 7.6
Name Settings Tab.

control was rather difficult using the earlier OLE Control '94 specification. Graphical controls based on this specification used a window to render their graphical representation. Windows are rectangular creatures and so a difficulty arises when trying to draw items that do not completely "fill" a rectangle.

Controls based on the new specification do not typically require an actual window to do their work, so the creation of truly nonrectangular controls is much easier. If your control's representation can be drawn in a rectangular space, you should choose the **Opaque** option. By doing so the container can draw the background of your control quickly. It basically just does a `FillRect` call with the background color. On the other hand, if you're developing a control that is transparent or nonrectangular, you should toggle off the **Opaque** option (as we did).

The **Solid Background** option is pertinent only when you choose the **Opaque** option. It indicates that your control definitely has a solid background as opposed to a hatched pattern. This also allows the container to

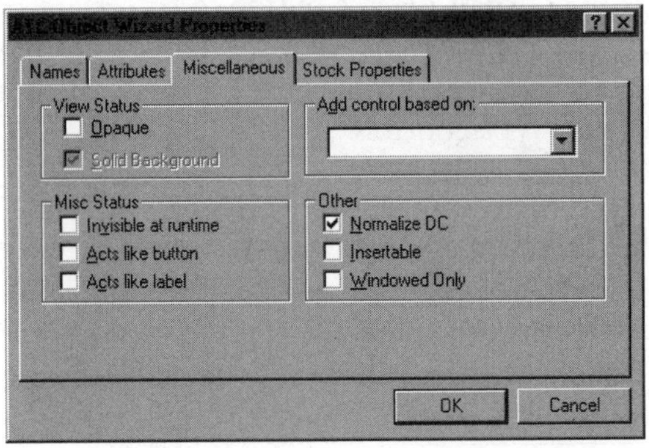

Figure 7.7
Object Wizard's
Miscellaneous Tab.

render your control more quickly. We discuss transparent controls later in the chapter.

NOTE: *The NoteIt control on the CD-ROM implements the BackStyle property. In other words, it supports drawing in both the opaque and transparent modes.*

MiscStatus Bits

When a control is initially embedded within a container, a negotiation process occurs between the two entities. As the control and container negotiate, the control provides the container with a set of bits that describes certain characteristics of the control. There are a number of these MISC_STATUS bits, but only a few of them pertain directly to ActiveX controls and their containers. Table 7.11 provides a list of those used by ActiveX controls.

Object Wizard's **MiscStatus** frame allow you to specify three of these bits. **Invisible at runtime** indicates that your ActiveX control will be invisible during the run phase. An invisible control typically provides some nonvisual service. A good example of this type of control is the timer control that we used back in Chapter 5 to provide a series of events. An invisible control, however, still provides some visual representation during the design phase.

The **Acts like button** and **Acts like label** bits are used by controls that provide functionality similar to that provided by buttons and labels. Since controls are small independent components that do not have knowledge of other controls in the container, they must rely on the container to provide container-wide information. For example, only the container knows if a button is the current default button. Also, certain controls, such as labels, indicate to the container that they should be treated specially in container's tabbing order. You will typically use these bits when implementing button-type and label-type controls.

Add Control Based On

The **Add Control Based On** option provides a skeletal project that superclasses an existing Windows control. You select the control to super-class from the drop down. You typically superclass a control because you

TABLE 7.11	Name	Purpose
Control OLEMISC Status Bits	ACTIVATEWHENVISIBLE	This bit is set to indicate that the control prefers to be active when visible. This can be very expensive when there are a large number of controls. The new Control '96 specification makes it possible for controls to perform most functions even when not active. This flag should be set so the control will work in containers that do not support the new specification.
	IGNOREACTIVATEWHENVISIBLE	Added by the Control '96 specification. If a control supports the new optimized control behavior it should set this flag to inform new containers that they can safely use the Control '96 specification enhancements.
	INVISIBLEATRUNTIME	Indicates that the control should be visible only during the design phase. When running, the control should not be visible. Any control that provides only nonvisual services will fit in this category.
	ALWAYSRUN	The control should always be running. Controls such as those that are invisible at run-time may need to set this bit to ensure that they are loaded and running at all times, so their events can be communicated to the container.
	ACTSLIKEBUTTON	The control is a button and so should behave differently if the container indicates to the control that it should act as a default button.
	ACTSLIKELABEL	The container should treat this control like a static label. For example, always set focus to the next control in the tab order.
	NOUIACTIVE	Indicates that the control does not support UI Activation. The control may still be in-place activated, but does not have a UI-Active state.
	ALIGNABLE	Indicates that the control would like for the container to provide a way to align the control in various ways. Usually along a side or top of the container.
	IMEMODE	Indicates that the control understands the Input Method Editor Mode. This is used for localization and internationalization within controls.
	SIMPLEFRAME	The control uses the `ISimpleFrameSite` interface (if supported by the container). `ISimpleFrameSite` allows a control to contain

TABLE 7.11
(Continued)

Name	Purpose
	instances of other controls. This is similar to group box functionality.
SETCLIENTSITEFIRST	Controls set this bit to indicate to the container that they would like their site within the container to be set up prior to the control's construction. This enables the control to use information from the client site (particularly ambient properties) during loading.

need functionality that is similar to that provided by a standard Windows control. For example, an edit field that accepts only numbers, a Windows 95 Tree View that allows multiple selections, a listbox that contains icons and text, and so on. By superclassing an existing control, some of the drawing code and control structures are already implemented for you. Of course, if you owner-draw the control, you still have to do most of the drawing yourself.

NOTE: *When developing ActiveX controls using MFC, you can instead subclass an existing Windows control. The techniques are very similar. Both subclassing and superclassing allow you to modify the behavior of an existing window class. Superclassing gives the developer a bit more control over the process, but it also requires more work to implement.*

Other

The **Other** section allows you to customize certain aspects of your control. Each of the three options is described in Table 7.12.

The Stock Properties Tab

When adding an ActiveX control component with Object Wizard, an additional tab is provided to set up the control's initial properties. The potential properties and their descriptions were provided in Table 7.5 earlier in the chapter.

As we described in Chapter 5, properties are characteristics of the control that map to an attribute or data member of the underlying component implementation. The ATL provides stock implementations for

TABLE 7.12

Other Options

Option	Description
Normalized DC	Checking this option will cause ATL to pass a normalized device context to your control. This makes drawing easier, but is less efficient.
Insertable	By checking this option, ATL will add the **Insertable** registry entry for your control. This indicates that the control can be embedded within standard OLE containers such as Microsoft Word.
Windowed Only	Controls created using the ATL will behave as windowless controls whenever possible. Windowless controls are more efficient than controls that create a window. However, older containers (e.g., Visual Basic 4.0) were created before the newer control specifications and do not support windowless controls. By default the ATL will create a window for controls when embedded in older containers and will not create a window when dropped in containers that support windowless control. By checking this option, you are specifying that your control *always* requires the existence of a window.

several standard properties. The term *stock* indicates that the implementation for the property is provided by ATL.

For our Note control, we'll add the majority of the properties so that we can demonstrate how they are used. In Object Wizard's **Stock Properties** tab, add the following properties to the control. The resulting dialog is shown in Figure 7.8.

■ Appearance

■ Background Color

■ Background Style

Figure 7.8
Adding Stock
Properties.

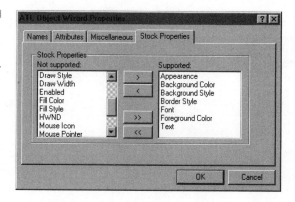

- Border Style
- Font
- Foreground Color
- Text

NOTE: *ATL vs. MFC: Compared to MFC's implementation, the stock property support provided by ATL is limited. MFC's COleControl class provides class members like the ATL does; however, it also provides a decent implementation of what the property should do. For example, the stock* Appearance *property is used to inform the control if it should draw either flat or 3D. In ATL, you must implement all of the drawing code yourself. With COleControl, the drawing code is provided. Just one other item to consider.*

ATL Object Wizard—Created Files

The Object Wizard created or modified several files in our Note project. The implementation for our control is provided via the NOTECTL.H and NOTECTL.CPP files. Also, the Object Wizard added a definition for our control's dual interface to the project's NOTE.IDL file. (See Table 7.13.)

Okay, we now have a basic control whose functionality is provided by the ATL classes. Our job now is to enhance this basic functionality by adding drawing code, overriding existing ATL class methods, and so on. However, as we do this, we discuss the various areas of functionality that an ActiveX control can provide. Before we begin, though, let's build our new project and insert the control into an ActiveX container. Figure 7.9 shows our ATL control embedded in Visual Basic.

Our control isn't very functional right out of the box, but that gives us an opportunity to learn as we add functionality. The ATL Object Wizard

Figure 7.9
Our Control on a
Visual Basic Form.

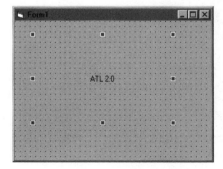

File	Description
NoteCtl.h	Contains most of the implementation of our control's C++ class CNoteCtl.
NoteCtl.cpp	Contains the implementation of certain CNoteCtl methods.
NoteCtl.rgs	An ATL Registrar file containing the registry script used to register the control.

TABLE 7.13

Object Wizard
Control files

created a control that implements 16 interfaces. As we've described, a control that implements the majority of these control interfaces should work in just about any container that supports ActiveX controls. However, a control developer doesn't have to implement all of these interfaces. The new control standards stipulate that a control must implement only those interfaces that it needs to supply its functionality. This is just fine, but most of today's containers *expect* a number of them to be there, and that's why we've chosen to implement a control that implements them all.

Before we begin, let's look at the files that the ATL Object Wizard generated for us. Here's a look at NOTECTL.H. Notice that the ATL provides an implementation class for each of our control's interfaces. The interface identifiers are then added to the control's `QueryInterface` implementation through the COM_INTERFACE_ENTRY macro.

```
//
// NoteCtl.h : Declaration of the CNoteCtl
//
...
class ATL_NO_VTABLE CNoteCtl :
      public CComObjectRootEx<CComSingleThreadModel>,
      public CComCoClass<CNoteCtl, &CLSID_NoteCtl>,
      public CComControl<CNoteCtl>,
      public CStockPropImpl<CNoteCtl, INoteCtl, &IID_INoteCtl, &LIBID_NOTEITLib>,
      public IProvideClassInfo2Impl<&CLSID_NoteCtl, NULL, &LIBID_NOTEITLib>,
      public IPersistStreamInitImpl<CNoteCtl>,
      public IPersistStorageImpl<CNoteCtl>,
      public IQuickActivateImpl<CNoteCtl>,
      public IOleControlImpl<CNoteCtl>,
      public IOleObjectImpl<CNoteCtl>,
      public IOleInPlaceActiveObjectImpl<CNoteCtl>,
      public IViewObjectExImpl<CNoteCtl>,
      public IOleInPlaceObjectWindowlessImpl<CNoteCtl>,
      public IDataObjectImpl<CNoteCtl>,
      public ISpecifyPropertyPagesImpl<CNoteCtl>
{
public:
      CNoteCtl()
      {
      }
```

```
DECLARE_REGISTRY_RESOURCEID(IDR_NOTECTL)


BEGIN_COM_MAP(CNoteCtl)
      COM_INTERFACE_ENTRY(INoteCtl)
      COM_INTERFACE_ENTRY(IDispatch)
      COM_INTERFACE_ENTRY_IMPL(IViewObjectEx)
      COM_INTERFACE_ENTRY_IMPL_IID(IID_IViewObject2, IViewObjectEx)
      COM_INTERFACE_ENTRY_IMPL_IID(IID_IViewObject, IViewObjectEx)
      COM_INTERFACE_ENTRY_IMPL(IOleInPlaceObjectWindowless)
      COM_INTERFACE_ENTRY_IMPL_IID(IID_IOleInPlaceObject, IOleInPlaceObjectWindowless)
      COM_INTERFACE_ENTRY_IMPL_IID(IID_IOleWindow, IOleInPlaceObjectWindowless)
      COM_INTERFACE_ENTRY_IMPL(IOleInPlaceActiveObject)
      COM_INTERFACE_ENTRY_IMPL(IOleControl)
      COM_INTERFACE_ENTRY_IMPL(IOleObject)
      COM_INTERFACE_ENTRY_IMPL(IQuickActivate)
      COM_INTERFACE_ENTRY_IMPL(IPersistStorage)
      COM_INTERFACE_ENTRY_IMPL(IPersistStreamInit)
      COM_INTERFACE_ENTRY_IMPL(ISpecifyPropertyPages)
      COM_INTERFACE_ENTRY_IMPL(IDataObject)
      COM_INTERFACE_ENTRY(IProvideClassInfo)
      COM_INTERFACE_ENTRY(IProvideClassInfo2)
END_COM_MAP()


BEGIN_PROPERTY_MAP(CNoteCtl)
      // Example entries
      // PROP_ENTRY("Property Description", dispid, clsid)
      PROP_PAGE(CLSID_StockColorPage)
END_PROPERTY_MAP()



BEGIN_MSG_MAP(CNoteCtl)
      MESSAGE_HANDLER(WM_PAINT, OnPaint)
      MESSAGE_HANDLER(WM_SETFOCUS, OnSetFocus)
      MESSAGE_HANDLER(WM_KILLFOCUS, OnKillFocus)
END_MSG_MAP()


// IViewObjectEx
      STDMETHOD(GetViewStatus) (DWORD* pdwStatus)
      {
            ATLTRACE(_T("IViewObjectExImpl::GetViewStatus\n"));
            *pdwStatus = 0;
            return S_OK;
      }

// INoteCtl
public:
      HRESULT OnDraw(ATL_DRAWINFO& di);

      CComPtr<IFontDisp> m_pFont;
      OLE_COLOR m_clrBackColor;
      OLE_COLOR m_clrForeColor;
      CComBSTR m_bstrText;
      long m_nBackStyle;
      long m_nBorderStyle;
      long m_nAppearance;
};
```

And here's a look at our NOTECTL.CPP file:

```
//
// NoteCtl.cpp : Implementation of CNoteCtl
//
#include "stdafx.h"
#include "NoteIt.h"
#include "NoteCtl.h"
///////////////
// CNoteCtl
///////////////
HRESULT CNoteCtl::OnDraw(ATL_DRAWINFO& di)
{
      RECT& rc = *(RECT*)di.prcBounds;
      Rectangle(di.hdcDraw, rc.left, rc.top, rc.right, rc.bottom);
      DrawText(di.hdcDraw, _T("ATL 2.0"), -1, &rc, DT_CENTER | DT_VCENTER |
DT_SINGLELINE);
      return S_OK;
}
```

Note much there, just a basic implementation of our control's drawing method.

The CComControl Class

ATL provides a lot of its ActiveX control functionality via the CComControl class. If you've developed controls using MFC, this class is very similar to MFC's COleControl implementation. By deriving our control class from CComControl we get support for the stock control properties described earlier plus a lot of other functionality. Speaking of stock properties, let's take a look at them first.

When we added our control's stock properties through the ATL Object Wizard, it basically did one thing. It created data members within our class to hold the values of our properties. Here's a look at the code:

```
// INoteCtl
public:
    HRESULT OnDraw(ATL_DRAWINFO& di);

    CComPtr<IFontDisp> m_pFont;
    OLE_COLOR m_clrBackColor;
    OLE_COLOR m_clrForeColor;
    CComBSTR m_bstrText;
    long m_nBackStyle;
    long m_nBorderStyle;
    long m_nAppearance;
};
```

However, that's all it did. We still need to set the initial values for the properties as the default ATL implementation doesn't do that for us. A good place to do this is in the control's constructor in NOTECTL.H:

```
CNoteCtl()
{
    // Initialize our stock properties
    static FONTDESC _fontDesc =
      { sizeof(FONTDESC), OLESTR("MS Sans Serif"), FONTSIZE( 12 ), FW_BOLD,
        ANSI_CHARSET, FALSE, FALSE, FALSE };
    OleCreateFontIndirect( &_fontDesc,
                           IID_IFontDisp,
                           (void **)&m_pFont);
    m_nAppearance = 1;
    m_nBorderStyle = 0;
    m_nBackStyle = 1;
    m_clrBackColor = RGB( 0, 255, 255 );
    m_clrForeColor = RGB( 0, 0, 0 );
}
```

We initialize our stock font property to "MS Sans Serif" by creating a FONTDESC structure and passing it to the OleCreateFontIndirect API. COM implements a special font object that provides a mechanism to persist and marshal fonts. ActiveX controls use these fonts through the IFontDisp interface. Our control maintains an IFontDisp pointer to the current font object.

Initialization of the other properties is more straightforward. Table 7.14 describes the different values for the numeric properties. The background color is set to blue, and the foreground color is initialized to black.

CComControl::OnDraw

Most ActiveX controls provide some sort of visual representation. Our NoteIt control is basically an expensive Windows label control. The

TABLE 7.14

Property Values

Property	Values
Appearance	0—Flat 1—3D
BorderStyle	0—None 1—Single Line
BackStyle	0—Opaque 1—Transparent

majority of its functionality is provided by drawing text on the screen. However, it demonstrates much of what you might do within an ActiveX control.

When our control is embedded, the container instantiates the control instance, loads up any property values and tells the control to render itself. Anytime the control's region needs to be redrawn, the contain again tells the control to render itself. The nice thing about all of this is that the control is always notified through the `CComControl::OnDraw` method. However, the default code provided by the Object Wizard doesn't do much. Here it is:

```
HRESULT CNoteCtl::OnDraw(ATL_DRAWINFO& di)
{
    RECT& rc = *(RECT*)di.prcBounds;
    Rectangle(di.hdcDraw, rc.left, rc.top, rc.right, rc.bottom);
    DrawText( di.hdcDraw,
              _T("ATL 2.0"),
              -1,
              &rc,
              DT_CENTER | DT_VCENTER | DT_SINGLELINE );

    return S_OK;
}
```

The first thing we need to do is add some drawing code. When the container asks the control to render itself, the container provides a device context on which to render. In most cases, the container will provide a DC that is part of its own window. With older tools, such as MFC, a control would get its own window. Today, though, that is rarely the case. It's not a big deal anyway; all we need is a device context to draw on anyway. Replace the previous code with this:

```
HRESULT CNoteCtl::OnDraw(ATL_DRAWINFO& di)
{
    // Need this macro for the ATL Unicode macros
    USES_CONVERSION;
    COLORREF  colBack, colFore;
    HBRUSH    hOldBrush, hBackBrush;
    HDC       hdc = di.hdcDraw;
    RECT& rc = *(RECT*)di.prcBounds;

    // Translate the color from an OLE_COLOR to a COLORREF
    OleTranslateColor( m_clrBackColor, NULL, &colBack );
    OleTranslateColor( m_clrForeColor, NULL, &colFore );

    // Create and select the background brush into the DC
    hBackBrush = (HBRUSH) CreateSolidBrush( colBack );
    hOldBrush = (HBRUSH) SelectObject( hdc, hBackBrush );
```

```
      // If the back style is opaque, fill the drawing rectangle
      // and set the back mode to OPAQUE
      // If were transparent, leave the rectangle along and
      // set the back mode to TRANSPARENT
      if ( m_nBackStyle == 0 )
      {
         SetBkMode( hdc, OPAQUE );
         FillRect( hdc, &rc, hBackBrush );
      }
      {
      SetBkMode( hdc, TRANSPARENT );
   }


   // Set the foreground text color
   SetTextColor( hdc, colFore );


   // If the Appearance property is set, draw a 3D
   // edge around our bounding rectangle. Then, adjust
   // the rectangle for the 3D edge.
   if ( m_nAppearance )
   {
      DrawEdge( hdc, &rc, EDGE_SUNKEN, BF_RECT );

      // Adjust our rectangle
      rc.left += 2;
      rc.top += 2;
      rc.bottom -= 2;
      rc.right -= 2;
   }


   // Check to see if we're in design mode or
   // runtime mode. If an design mode, get the ambient
   // font and ambient display name and draw them within
   // the control.
   BOOL bUserMode = FALSE;
   GetAmbientUserMode( bUserMode );
   if ( bUserMode == FALSE )
   {
      // Get the ambient font
      HFONT hOldFont = 0;
      IFont* pFont = 0;
      if ( SUCCEEDED( GetAmbientFont( &pFont )) && pFont )
      {
         HFONT hFont;
         pFont->get_hFont( &hFont );
         hOldFont = (HFONT) SelectObject( hdc, hFont );

         pFont->Release();
      }

      // Draw the ambient display name
      BSTR bstr;
      if ( SUCCEEDED( GetAmbientDisplayName( bstr )))
      {
         DrawText( hdc,
```

```
                OLE2A( bstr ),
                -1,
                &rc,
                DT_TOP | DT_SINGLELINE );
    }
}


// Set the stock font. We have to QI for the
// IFont interface to get a handle to the font
CComQIPtr<IFont, &IID_IFont> pFont( m_pFont );
HFONT hOldFont = 0;
if ( pFont )
{
    HFONT hFont;
    pFont->get_hFont( &hFont );
    hOldFont = (HFONT) SelectObject( hdc, hFont );
}


// If there is text in our Text property draw it centered
if ( m_bstrText.Length() )
{
    DrawText( hdc,
              OLE2A( m_bstrText ),
              -1,
              &rc,
              DT_CENTER | DT_VCENTER | DT_WORDBREAK );
}


// Delete any drawing objects before returning
if ( hOldFont )
    DeleteObject( hOldFont );
if ( hOldBrush )
    DeleteObject( hOldBrush );

    return S_OK;
}
```

Admittedly, this is a lot of code, but I've commented it liberally so that we don't have to go over every line. Basically, we're using the stock properties that we set up to render the control. After adding this code, rebuild the project, insert the control in Visual Basic, and voila! a pretty functional control.

After experimenting with the control, you should notice that if you set up a property value in design mode, and then run the application, the properties don't persist. In other words if you set the background color to red and hit F5 (run) in Visual Basic, the control's background isn't red. Why? Because we haven't actually persisted the property values. Whenever the control is destroyed and reinstantiated, it uses the defaults that we set in the constructor. In order to maintain state between design-mode and run-time mode, we need to implement property persistence.

Persisting Your Control's Properties (Property Maps)

To persist your control's properties, they must be added to ATL's property map. The ATL Object Wizard doesn't do this automatically, so you have to do it yourself. However, it's rather easy. For each property that you want to make persistent, add a PROP_ENTRY macro with a textual description of the property, the property's DISPID, and any associated property page. Our control doesn't have any property pages yet, so we use CLSID_NULL instead.

```
//
// NoteCtl.h : Declaration of the CNoteCtl
//
...
class ATL_NO_VTABLE CNoteCtl :
      public CComObjectRootEx<CComSingleThreadModel>,
...
BEGIN_PROPERTY_MAP(CNoteCtl)
    PROP_ENTRY( "Text", DISPID_TEXT, CLSID_NULL )
    PROP_ENTRY( "Appearance", DISPID_APPEARANCE, CLSID_NULL )
    PROP_ENTRY( "Border Style", DISPID_BORDERSTYLE, CLSID_NULL )
    PROP_ENTRY( "Background Color", DISPID_BACKCOLOR, CLSID_NULL)
    PROP_ENTRY( "Background Style", DISPID_BACKSTYLE, CLSID_NULL )
    PROP_ENTRY( "Foreground or Text Color", DISPID_FORECOLOR, CLSID_NULL )
    PROP_ENTRY( "Font", DISPID_FONT, CLSID_NULL)
END_PROPERTY_MAP()
```

After entering this code, rebuild the control and add it to a simple Visual Basic application that uses it. You should notice that the property values persist as you toggle between design- and run-time mode. But wait, we can make it even better.

Adding Stock Property Pages

The ATL provides three stock property pages for those standard, often used properties such as font, color, and picture. The stock property pages have standard CLSIDs and we can use them directly within our control. Change our control property map to this:

```
BEGIN_PROPERTY_MAP(CNoteCtl)
    PROP_ENTRY( "Text", DISPID_TEXT, CLSID_NULL )
    PROP_ENTRY( "Appearance", DISPID_APPEARANCE, CLSID_NULL )
    PROP_ENTRY( "Border Style", DISPID_BORDERSTYLE, CLSID_NULL )
    PROP_ENTRY( "Background Color", DISPID_BACKCOLOR, CLSID_StockColorPage)
    PROP_ENTRY( "Background Style", DISPID_BACKSTYLE, CLSID_NULL )
    PROP_ENTRY( "Foreground or Text Color", DISPID_FORECOLOR, CLSID_StockColorPage )
```

```
   PROP_ENTRY( "Font", DISPID_FONT, CLSID_StockFontPage)
   PROP_PAGE(CLSID_StockFontPage)
   PROP_PAGE(CLSID_StockColorPage)
END_PROPERTY_MAP()
```

Now rebuild the control, insert into a container, and finally launch the control's custom property sheet. You should see something resembling Fig. 7.10.

As we discussed in the property page section earlier, controls should implement a custom property page for its properties. We have default property pages for three of our seven properties, but we need a custom page for the remaining four. Let's do that next.

Adding a Property Page to Our ATL Control

Early in this chapter when we added the NOTEIT control to our project using the ATL Object Wizard, only the control component was added. As we now understand, a property page is an independent COM object used by the container to interact with a control. To add a custom property page to our control, we need to use the Object Wizard. Fire it up with the **Insert/New ATL Object...** menu item. Select **Controls** and **Property Page** option and click the **Next** button and you'll see something resembling Fig. 7.11.

Enter a short name of **NotePpg** and take the defaults for the rest of the **Names** dialog. Also take the defaults for the **Attributes** dialog, and enter whatever you feel is appropriate for the **Strings** dialog. When you're finished, click **OK,** and the ATL Object Wizard will create the files listed in Table 7.15.

Figure 7.10
Stock Property Pages.

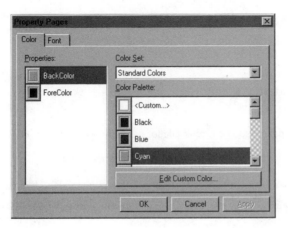

Figure 7.11
Property Page
Properties.

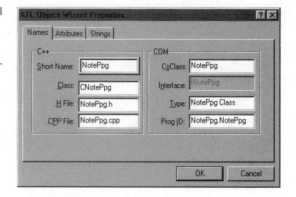

The ATL Object Wizard added several new files to support the custom property page for our control. The first thing to do is edit the dialog resource and add controls for each of our four properties. Table 7.16 details the control type and identifier. Figure 7.12 shows building the dialog with the Visual C++ resource editor.

After the dialog is built, we need to populate the controls with valid property values. Then, as the property page is loading we need to retrieve the current property values from the control instance. The best place to do this is when the dialog is being created. Override WM_INITDIALOG by adding the following to NOTEPPG.H.

```
// NotePpg.h : Declaration of the CNotePpg

#include "resource.h" // main symbols

#include "NoteIt.h"

class ATL_NO_VTABLE CNotePpg :
    public CComObjectRootEx<CComSingleThreadModel>,
    public CComCoClass<CNotePpg, &CLSID_NotePpg>,

...
```

TABLE 7.15

Property Page Files

File	Description
NotePpg.h	The header file for our new property page class: CNotePpg.
NotePpg.cpp	The CNotePpg class implementation.
NotePpg.rgs	The registry script for our property page object.
NoteIt.rc	A resource was added for the property page dialog.

TABLE 7.16

Property Page
Controls

Control Type	Identifier
Multiline Entry Field	IDC_TEXT
Drop-List Combobox	IDC_APPEARANCE
Drop-List Combobox	IDC_BORDERSTYLE
Drop-List Combobox	IDC_BACKSTYLE

```
BEGIN_MSG_MAP(CNotePpg)
    MESSAGE_HANDLER( WM_INITDIALOG, OnInitDialog )
    CHAIN_MSG_MAP(IPropertyPageImpl<CNotePpg>)
END_MSG_MAP()
```

```
LRESULT OnInitDialog( UINT, WPARAM wParam, LPARAM lParam, BOOL& )
{
    ATLTRACE(_T("CNoteProp::OnInitDialog\n"));
    USES_CONVERSION;

    if ( m_nObjects > 0 )
    {
        // QI for our INoteCtl dual interface and retrieve
        // the current property values
        CComQIPtr<INoteCtl, &IID_INoteCtl> pNoteCtl( m_ppUnk[0] );
        BSTR bstrText;
        if SUCCEEDED( pNoteCtl->get_Text( &bstrText ))
            SetDlgItemText( IDC_TEXT, W2A( bstrText ));

        // Initialize the Apearance combobox
        SendDlgItemMessage( IDC_APPEARANCE,
                            CB_ADDSTRING,
                            0,
                            (long) "0 - Flat" );
        SendDlgItemMessage( IDC_APPEARANCE,
                            CB_ADDSTRING,
```

Figure 7.12
Building the Property
Page.

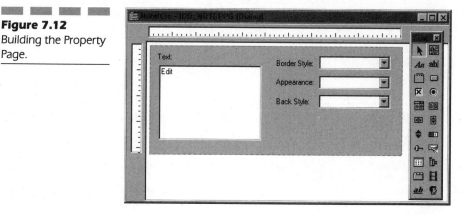

```
                                 0,
                                 (long) "1 - 3D" );
          // Get the current value of the Appearance property
          long lAppearance;
          if SUCCEEDED( pNoteCtl->get_Appearance( &lAppearance ))
             ::SendMessage( GetDlgItem( IDC_APPEARANCE ),
                            CB_SETCURSEL,
                            lAppearance,
                            0 );
...
          }
       return 1;
    }
...
};
```

When the dialog (property page) is initially created, we are doing two basic things. First, we query for the control's Vtable interface, `INoteCtl`. Once we have a pointer to this interface, we can pull property values from the control. Also, we're populating our drop-list comboboxes with valid property values. Once the comboboxes are populated, we retrieve the value from the control and set the current selection. The preceding code shows what we're doing only for the Text and Appearance properties. The code for the others is basically the same. Of course, the CD-ROM has the full implementation.

The previous code initially sets up the property page. However, if a user changes a value on the property page, we have to pass the new value to the associated control. We also have to enable the **Apply** button on the property sheet whenever a value has been changed. First, we need to trap the CBN_CHANGE event so that we're notified every time one of the comboboxes is modified.

```
BEGIN_MSG_MAP(CNotePpg)
    COMMAND_HANDLER( IDC_TEXT, EN_CHANGE, OnPropertyChange )
    COMMAND_HANDLER( IDC_APPEARANCE, CBN_SELCHANGE, OnPropertyChange )
    COMMAND_HANDLER( IDC_BORDERSTYLE, CBN_SELCHANGE, OnPropertyChange )
    COMMAND_HANDLER( IDC_BACKSTYLE, CBN_SELCHANGE, OnPropertyChange )
    MESSAGE_HANDLER( WM_INITDIALOG, OnInitDialog )
    CHAIN_MSG_MAP(IPropertyPageImpl<CNotePpg>)
END_MSG_MAP()
```

The following snippet of code sets the dirty flag for the page (thus enabling the Apply button) and notifies any attached property browsers (e.g., Visual Basic) that the property value has changed.

```
LRESULT OnPropertyChange( WORD wNotify, WORD wID, HWND hWnd,
                          BOOL& bHandled )
{
   SetDirty( TRUE );
```

```
    m_pPageSite->OnStatusChange( PROPPAGESTATUS_DIRTY | PROPPAGESTATUS_VALIDATE );
    return 0;
}
```

All that is left is to actually implement the functionality of the **Apply** button. ATL has helped us a bit, as it at least provided a do-nothing implementation of Apply in NOTEPPG.H. Here's what we need to add to it:

```
STDMETHOD(Apply)(void)
{
    ATLTRACE(_T("CNotePpg::Apply\n"));
    USES_CONVERSION;
    for ( UINT i = 0; i < m_nObjects; i++ )
    {
        CComQIPtr<INoteCtl, &IID_INoteCtl> pNoteCtl( m_ppUnk[i] );
        BSTR bstrText;
        if ( GetDlgItemText( IDC_TEXT, bstrText ) )
        {
            if FAILED( pNoteCtl->put_Text( bstrText ))
            {
                HandleError();
                return E_FAIL;
            }
        }
        long lAppearance;
        lAppearance = SendDlgItemMessage( IDC_APPEARANCE,
                                          CB_GETCURSEL,
                                          0, 0 );
        if FAILED( pNoteCtl->put_Appearance( lAppearance ))
        {
            HandleError();
            return E_FAIL;
        }
...
        m_bDirty = FALSE;
        return S_OK;
    }
}
```

Again, I've shown the implementation of only the Text and Appearance properties; BackStyle and BorderStyle are similar. All that's left in our property page implementation is the definition of `HandleError`. Here it is:

```
void HandleError()
{
    USES_CONVERSION;

    CComPtr<IErrorInfo> pError;
    CComBSTR strError;
    GetErrorInfo( 0, &pError );
    pError->GetDescription( &strError );
    MessageBox( OLE2T(strError),
                _T("Error"),
                MB_ICONEXCLAMATION );
}
```

However, we now have to go back to the code for our control to tell it about our new property page. We need to update our property map with the CLSID of our custom property page like this:

```
BEGIN_PROPERTY_MAP(CNoteCtl)
    PROP_ENTRY( "Text", DISPID_TEXT, CLSID_NotePpg )
    PROP_ENTRY( "Appearance", DISPID_APPEARANCE, CLSID_NotePpg )
    PROP_ENTRY( "Border Style", DISPID_BORDERSTYLE, CLSID_NotePpg )
    PROP_ENTRY( "Background Color", DISPID_BACKCOLOR, CLSID_StockColorPage)
    PROP_ENTRY( "Background Style", DISPID_BACKSTYLE, CLSID_NotePpg )
    PROP_ENTRY( "Foreground or Text Color", DISPID_FORECOLOR, CLSID_StockColorPage )
    PROP_ENTRY( "Font", DISPID_FONT, CLSID_StockFontPage)
    PROP_PAGE(CLSID_StockFontPage)
    PROP_PAGE(CLSID_StockColorPage)
END_PROPERTY_MAP()
```

Okay, we've made a lot of changes. Go ahead and rebuild the project. Fire up Visual Basic and check out our new functionality. The custom property page will allow you to change any of the control's properties. As soon as you hit the **Apply** button, the control will redraw.

Adding Control Methods

Adding a custom method to an ATL control is rather easy. However, it's not nearly as easy as using Visual Basic or MFC. First, you need to add the method declaration to your control's IDL file. As an example, we're going to implement the standard `Refresh` method for our NOTEIT control. Here's a look at the additions to NOTEIT.IDL.

```
interface INoteCtl : IDispatch
{
    [propput, id(DISPID_BACKCOLOR)]
    HRESULT BackColor([in]OLE_COLOR clr);
    [propget, id(DISPID_BACKCOLOR)]
    HRESULT BackColor([out,retval]OLE_COLOR* pclr);
...
    [id(DISPID_REFRESH)]
    HRESULT Refresh();
};
```

The refresh method takes no parameters and returns the standard HRESULT. Next, we need to add the declaration to our header file like this:

```
// INoteCtl
public:
    HRESULT OnDraw(ATL_DRAWINFO& di);
...
```

```
    STDMETHOD(Refresh)();
};
```

The actual implementation of the `Refresh` method is straightforward thanks to the `CComControl` class. It provides the `FireViewChanged` method which informs the container, through its `IAdviseSink` interface, which eventually calls our `OnDraw` method. Add the following code at the bottom of NOTECTL.CPP.

```
HRESULT CNoteCtl::Refresh()
{
    // Tell the container to force a redraw
    FireViewChange();
    return S_OK;
}
```

Adding IPropertyBag Persistence Support

So far, our control is using the ATL default `IPersistStreamInit` and `IPersistStorage` persistence interfaces. These interfaces need to be supported, but when working in a Web environment your controls also should support the new `IPersistPropertyBag` interface. Using ATL this is easy. Before we do this, however, let's look at what it initially provides. If you were to use our control as it is in ActiveX Control Pad, when you save the control, the resulting HTML will look something like this:

```
<OBJECT ID="NoteCtl1" WIDTH=192 HEIGHT=192
  CLASSID="CLSID:1176742F-BA90-11D0-A75A-56FED0000000"
  DATA="DATA:application/xoleobject;BASE64,L3R2EZC6nWlb+0AAAA
  //+AAAMAAQAAABMAAA1LjC5GPzhGd4wCqAEu4UQEATZXJpZg==">
</OBJECT>
```

By default, the ATL control doesn't provide support for `IPersistProp-ertyBag`. So, ActiveX Control Pad has to persist the control's properties using its `IPersistStreamInit` interface. If you recall, `IPersistProp-ertyBag` provides support for the HTML PARAM element, which is much easier to work with because it provides textual persistence. All that you have to do to provide support for `IPersistPropertyBag` is to add the ATL implementation to your control like this:

```
//////////////////////////////////////////////////////////////////
// CNoteCtl
class ATL_NO_VTABLE CNoteCtl :
    public CComObjectRootEx<CComSingleThreadModel>,
    public CComCoClass<CNoteCtl, &CLSID_NoteCtl>,
    public CComControl<CNoteCtl>,
```

```
...
   public IPersistPropertyBagImpl<CNoteCtl>
{
public:
     CNoteCtl()

...
BEGIN_COM_MAP(CNoteCtl)
   COM_INTERFACE_ENTRY(INoteCtl)
   COM_INTERFACE_ENTRY(IDispatch)
...
   COM_INTERFACE_ENTRY_IMPL(IPersistPropertyBag)
END_COM_MAP()
```

Those two lines of code give our control property bag support. So, now when we load up ActiveX Control Pad and add our control to an HTML page, the properties are saved like this:

```
<OBJECT ID="NoteCtl1" WIDTH=192 HEIGHT=192
  CLASSID="CLSID:1176742F-BA90-11D0-A75A-56FED0000000">
     <PARAM NAME="Text" VALUE="Hello World">
     <PARAM NAME="Appearance" VALUE="1">
     <PARAM NAME="Border Style" VALUE="0">
     <PARAM NAME="Background Color" VALUE="8454143">
     <PARAM NAME="Background Style" VALUE="1">
     <PARAM NAME="Foreground or Text Color" VALUE="0">
     <PARAM NAME="Font" VALUE="MS Sans Serif">
</OBJECT>
```

Much more readable wouldn't you say.

Adding Component Categories

Now that our control is about finished, let's add the appropriate component categories. Our control is a **Control** and supports Automation so it is **Programmable.** This means we should add these as "Implemented Categories" to the registry. Edit the NOTECTL.RGS file and add the highlighted lines:

```
ForceRemove {1176742F-BA90-11D0-A75A-56FED0000000} = s 'NoteCtl Class'
{
   ProgID = s 'NoteCtl.NoteCtl.1'
   VersionIndependentProgID = s 'NoteCtl.NoteCtl'
   ForceRemove 'Programmable'
   InprocServer32 = s '%MODULE%'
   {
      val ThreadingModel = s 'Apartment'
   }
...
   'Implemented Categories'
```

```
{
    '{40FC6ED4-2438-11cf-A3DB-080036F12502}'
}
'Implemented Categories'
{
    '{40FC6ED5-2438-11cf-A3DB-080036F12502}'
}
}
```

The next time the control is registered, these entries will be added to the registry.

Marking Your Control as Safe

Controls that operate in the Web environment have to be marked as safe for scripting and safe for initializing before they can be used in Internet Explorer (with security enabled). A control can be marked as such in one of two ways—either through component categories or by implementing the `IObjectSafety` interface.

CATID_SafeForScripting

ActiveX controls have complete access to the machine on which they are executing. This capability gives them the ability to explicitly harm the local system or in other cases expose capabilities that allow the control user to cause harm. Within Web browsers, such as Internet Explorer, a control's capabilities can be used by the scripting language of the browser (e.g., VBScript). The control may be safe when executing under normal circumstances, but what about when the control's capabilities are used by an untrusted or malicious script?

For example, say you develop a control that exposes a `CreateObject` function that allows a script writer to create instances of automation objects within VBScript. The control is not safe. It would be easy for someone to use the `CreateObject` method to instantiate an external application (e.g., Microsoft Word) and use it to delete local files, install a virus, and so forth.

If your control, in any way, exposes functionality that can be used by a malicious script to harm the local system it is not safe for scripting. If the control does not expose potentially malicious functionality, it can register the **SafeForScripting** component category or by implementing the `IObjectSafety` interface within the control. If a control is safe for scripting it can be used within ActiveX browsers with their security level set to high.

CATID_SafeForInitializing

In a browser environment, a control can also cause damage to a local system if the data it downloads is from a malicious or untrusted source. When the control is instantiated on the local machine, it is provided with an IPersist* interface by the container to initialize any persistent data. The data, since its location is provided by the script writer, is also a potential security problem. If a control's persistent data, even when coming from a unknown source, cannot harm the local machine, it can indicate that it is safe for initializing by registering the **SafeForInitializing** component category or by implementing the IObjectSafety interface.

```
IObjectSafety : public IUnknown
{
public:
    virtual HRESULT GetInterfaceSafetyOptions( REFIID, DWORD, DWORD ) = 0;
    virtual HRESULT SetInterfaceSafetyOptions( REFIID, DWORD, DWORD ) = 0;
};
```

Here's some code to implement IObjectSafety within your ATL control. By implementing this interface, you won't have to mess around with registering the two safety component categories.

```
//////////////////////////////////////////////////////////////////////
// CNoteCtl
class ATL_NO_VTABLE CNoteCtl :
    public CComObjectRootEx<CComSingleThreadModel>,
    public CComCoClass<CNoteCtl, &CLSID_NoteCtl>,
...
    public IObjectSafety,
    public IPersistPropertyBagImpl<CNoteCtl>
{
public:
    CNoteCtl()
...
BEGIN_COM_MAP(CNoteCtl)
    COM_INTERFACE_ENTRY(INoteCtl)
...
    COM_INTERFACE_ENTRY(IObjectSafety)
    COM_INTERFACE_ENTRY_IMPL(IPersistPropertyBag)
END_COM_MAP()
...
// IObjectSafety
STDMETHODIMP GetInterfaceSafetyOptions( REFIID riid,
                                        DWORD *pdwSupportedOptions,
                                        DWORD *pdwEnabledOptions )
{
    ATLTRACE(_T("CNoteCtl::GetInterfaceSafetyOptions()\n"));
```

```
    *pdwSupportedOptions = INTERFACESAFE_FOR_UNTRUSTED_CALLER |
                           INTERFACESAFE_FOR_UNTRUSTED_DATA;
    *pdwEnabledOptions = *pdwSupportedOptions;
    return S_OK;
}

STDMETHODIMP SetInterfaceSafetyOptions( REFIID riid,
                                        DWORD dwOptionSetMask,
                                        DWORD dwEnabledOptions )
{
    ATLTRACE(_T("CNoteCtl::SetInterfaceSafetyOptions\n"));
    return S_OK;
}
    ...
```

Debugging the Control

Visual C++ makes it fairly easy to debug ActiveX controls. To step through the code of our NoteIt controls, all we have to do is set a breakpoint on a particular line that we would like to debug and select **Build/Start Debug** from the menu.

This will bring up a dialog asking for **Executable for Debug Session.** Enter the path and filename for a control container such as the Test Container or Visual Basic. The container application will execute, place your control in the container and, depending on where you placed the breakpoint, execution should stop. Go ahead, debug through that ATL code. There's a lot there to learn.

Signing Your Control

If you want to use controls that you develop within the Web environment, you need to sign your controls. Internet Explorer will not download and install ActiveX controls that are not digitally signed unless the security is turned off. A personal certificate is available from Verisign (www.verisign.com) for $20.00 per year. The following steps describe the control signing process.

The Code Signing Wizard

To sign a control you use the signcode executable that is part of the ActiveX/Platform SDK. Signcode operates as a command line utility.

However, if you don't enter all of the parameters, it will step you through the code signing process. Figure 7.13 displays the initial dialog.

When signing your controls you must specify the path to the actual OCX file, a name for the control, and a URL where you can be contacted. This information is shown in Fig. 7.14.

You then need to provide a path to both your credentials file and your private key file. You get both of these from a digital signing vendor such as Verisign. Figure 7.15 shows the final steps.

If you don't want to use the Wizard method of signing your controls, here's a simple batch file that does the trick:

```
REM - SIGN.BAT
REM - Sign a control
REM - First parameter is the control
REM - Second parameter is the name of the control

signcode -prog %1 -spc WidgetWare.spc -pvk widgetware.pvk -name %2 -info
http://www.widgetware.com

REM - Check the sign

chktrust -c %1
```

Testing Your Control on the Web

Okay, we've got our control marked as safe and have digitally signed it. Now it's time to give it a real-world test. Using ActiveX Control Pad create

Figure 7.13
Code Signing Wizard,
Step One.

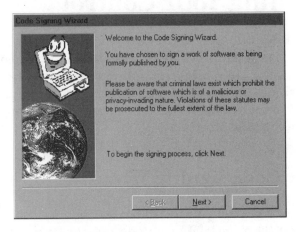

Developing ActiveX Controls with ATL

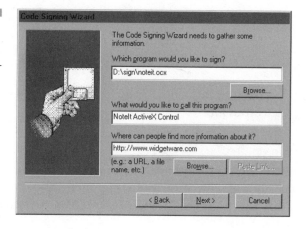

Figure 7.14
Signing Wizard, Step Two.

a simple test page like the following. Copy this file up to a Web server along with our NOTEIT.OCX file.

```html
<HTML>
<HEAD>
<TITLE>NoteIt Control Test Page</TITLE>
</HEAD>
<BODY>

<OBJECT ID="NoteCtl1" WIDTH=192 HEIGHT=192
CLASSID="CLSID:1176742F-BA90-11D0-A75A-56FED0000000"
CODEBASE=http://www.widgetware.com/noteit.ocx>
    <PARAM NAME="Text" VALUE="Testing 1,2,3,4,5">
    <PARAM NAME="Appearance" VALUE="1">
    <PARAM NAME="Border Style" VALUE="0">
    <PARAM NAME="Background Color" VALUE="16776960">
    <PARAM NAME="Background Style" VALUE="0">
    <PARAM NAME="Foreground or Text Color" VALUE="0">
```

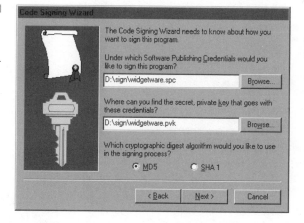

Figure 7.15
Signing Wizard, Step Three.

```
   <PARAM NAME="Font" VALUE="MS Sans Serif">
</OBJECT>

</BODY>
</HTML>
```

Next, make sure the control is no longer registered on your machine by using the command:

```
REGSVR32 /U NOTEIT.OCX
```

Launch Internet Explorer and navigate to your test page. Internet Explorer should download the component and eventually display the digital certificate like that in Fig. 7.16. You have written and deployed your own ActiveX control.

Summary

ActiveX controls have been around for several years now. They were initially specified in early 1994 and have garnered widespread industry support. ActiveX controls can be developed with several different tools. Microsoft provides three C++ frameworks: MFC, ATL, and the ActiveX

Figure 7.16
ActiveX Control
Digital Certificate.

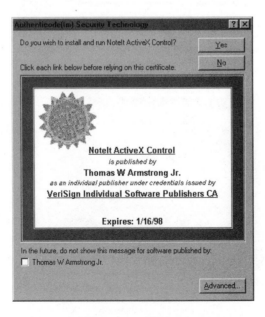

Control Framework that is part of the SDK. Other tools such as Visual Basic and Delphi 97 make developing controls even easier.

ActiveX controls are controlled by two specifications, one written in 1994 and the other written in 1996. Initially controls had to support a large number of COM-based interfaces. However, with the release of the '96 specification and its accompanying control guidelines, controls are now required to implement only those interfaces that they need. Today, any component that implements IUnknown and supports self-registration can be classified as an ActiveX control.

ActiveX controls provide functionality by implementing defined COM interfaces. Control containers also implement a defined set of interfaces and this standardization and cooperation provides the rich, vendor-independent environment. All controls are required to implement IUnknown and to support self-registration. Most ActiveX controls provide a run-time representation. To do so, they must support a number of OLE Document interfaces. The OLE Document interfaces allow the control to render itself within the container.

Most ActiveX controls expose properties and methods through the standard Automation interface: IDispatch. The control guidelines recommend that controls implement a dual interface if practicable. A control container will usually expose its own Automation interface. Through this interface, controls have access to certain container characteristics called *ambient properties*. ActiveX controls can also fire events using a COM technology called *connectable objects*. Connectable objects use two standard interfaces to set up a reverse IDispatch. Using this mechanism the control can call methods implemented by the container. Controls that expose properties should also provide one or more property pages to allow control users to modify its properties. A property page is an independent COM object that is instantiated by the container.

One of the more powerful features of controls is that they can persist their internal state. Controls persist their properties by implementing one of the OLE IPersist interfaces. The container passes a handle to a persistence storage, and the controls save its state. Controls should implement the IPersistPropertyBag interface if they will be used in the Web environment. IPersistPropertyBag allows a control to persist its properties as text.

The Active Template Library is a new template-based C++ framework for developing efficient COM objects. With the release of version 2.0, it supports building full-function ActiveX controls. The ATL COM Wizard creates the initial project. You then use the ATL Object Wizard to add components such as ActiveX controls and property pages. Component categories provide a mechanism for COM objects to specify their high-level behavior.

ActiveX controls have complete access to a machine. To deploy ActiveX controls on the Web they need to be digitally signed. A digital signature verifies the creator of a component and to run the Web environment; a control must also be marked as "Safe for Scripting" and "Safe for Initializing." A control can indicate that it is safe by adding some keys to the registry or by implementing the `IObjectSafety` interface.

CHAPTER **8**

Building ActiveX Controls with Visual Basic

With the release of Visual Basic version 5.0, Microsoft has added the capability to produce ActiveX controls. Microsoft has also elected to make a special version of Visual Basic 5.0, called the Control Creation Edition (CCE for short), available free on the Web. With this slimmed-down version of Visual Basic, you can build ActiveX controls along with projects that test the controls you build. You can compile the ActiveX controls you create into .OCX files; however, you cannot compile the test projects into true executable files.

To support the building of ActiveX controls using Visual Basic, a couple of Wizards have been provided that can substantially reduce the amount of code that has to be written by hand. The ActiveX Control Interface Wizard is similar to the Control Wizard found in Visual C++. The Property Page Wizard provides a good head start to producing fully functional property pages for your controls. There is also a new object type called the UserControl object that serves as the base object for any ActiveX controls you create. Like a form object, the UserControl object has a code module and a visual designer and it inherently supports many properties, methods, and events found in most ActiveX controls.

Over the course of this chapter we plan to develop an ActiveX control that will allow us to explore a majority of the new features introduced in VB 5.0. We'll use the Wizards to generate some code but we'll also do some coding the old-fashioned way so you can get a good picture of what's going on. Toward the end of the chapter, we discuss the important aspects to be aware of when using ActiveX controls on Web pages. The main concern of this chapter is to introduce you to the concepts of building ActiveX controls. We will assume the reader has a general understanding of the Visual Basic language and the Visual Basic development environment.

WEB RESOURCES:

URL	Description
http://www.microsoft.com/vbasic	Microsoft's Visual Basic site. Check here for the latest edition of the Control Creation Edition.

The MathProblem Control

For purposes of demonstrating the many ActiveX-related features of Visual Basic 5.0, we will develop a control that presents a graphical math problem to the end user. The control will implement several stock properties as well as some custom properties for setting the difficulty level, problem type, and so on. The control will also fire an event, alerting the container that a correct answer has been keyed in by the control user. We'll use a couple of Wizards to quickly implement stock and custom properties, control events, and create property pages. Figure 8.1 shows the completed Math control and its property pages within a container.

Starting a New Project

One of the neat new features in Visual Basic 5.0 is the ability to work with more than one project from within the same development environment. In other words, you can create a master project that really consists of two or more subprojects. When you're developing ActiveX controls, this feature is very handy because it allows you to develop a test project right along with the ActiveX control. In this way, you can easily build and test the design time *and* run time behavior of your control without having to switch to another instance of Visual Basic and back again.

Start up Visual Basic 5.0 and choose **New Project** from the **File** menu. Select the **ActiveX Control** option. The **Project Explorer** window will

Figure 8.1
The MathProblem
Control and Its
Property Pages.

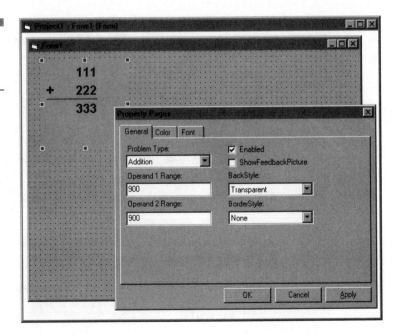

show a tree view containing the new ActiveX Control project. To establish a project for testing the control as we develop it, select **File/Add Project...** and choose **Standard EXE.** The next step is to set some properties for each project. In the **Project Explorer,** right-click on **PROJECT1.VBP** and select **Project1 Properties...** to bring up the dialog box shown in Fig. 8.2. The **Project Name** is the most important item here. The **Project Name** along with the control class name form a Programmatic ID that identifies the control in the Windows registry. We discussed the concept of a Programmatic ID back in Chapter 6—the ProgID provides a mapping from a human-readable identifier into the control's actual CLSID. It is important that this ProgID be unique to avoid a collision with previously registered controls.

The **Project Description** is used by the control container when referring to the control so it should contain an English-readable description of the control. The **Require License Key** option tells VB to create a **.VBL** file that will serve as the license file for the control. The license file would then be required on any machine using the control for development purposes. Click the OK button after ensuring your dialog box looks like Fig. 8.2.

Next, we set the class name of our control to establish its ProgID. We've already established the left-hand side of the ID when we set the **Project Name** to "MathControl." To set the right side, double-click on **UserControl1** in the **Project Explorer** window. The visual designer window will

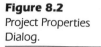

Figure 8.2
Project Properties
Dialog.

MathControl - Project Properties

General | Make | Compile | Component

Project Type:

ActiveX Control

Startup Object:

(None)

Project Name:

MathControl

Help File Name:

Project Help
Context ID:

0

Project Description:

Math Problem Control

☐ Unattended Execution

☑ Upgrade ActiveX Controls

☐ Require License Key

○ Thread per Object

○ Thread Pool   1   threads

OK   Cancel   Help

appear and the **Properties** window will display the properties for the UserControl class. Set the **Name** property to "MathProblem." We have now established that our control can be found in the registry under the name "MathControl.MathProblem." It won't show up there, however, until the first time we build the control.

Right-click on **Project2** and select **Project2 Properties.** Since this is just a project to test our control, it's not really important that we modify any of the properties; but we'll set the **Project Name** to "MathTest" just so we can easily identify it in the project window.

Now we need to save our projects. Right-click on the MathControl project and select **Save Project.** Create a root directory for the project and save the files with the following names: **MathProblem.ctl** and **Math-Control.vbp.** Repeat this procedure on **Project2** using the names **Math-Test.frm** and **MathTest.vbp.** You should use a different root directory for the test project so that the files that make up the two projects will be segregated. Finally, we need to save the master project. Click on the **File** menu and select **Save Project Group.** Use the name **MathControl.VBG** and save the file in the root directory of the math control. This is the project file you will want to open when working on this project in the future.

Designing the Control

Now that we have our project all set up, it's time to build the control. Before we jump right into that, however, we need to establish what exactly it is that our control is supposed to do and how it will be manipulated by the control user.

Purpose

As was mentioned earlier, the control we develop presents a mathematical problem to the end user. The control has the following characteristics:

- The problem type: either addition, subtraction, multiplication, or division will be configurable.
- The operand ranges will be configurable.
- The font and font color will be configurable.
- A property will be exposed that will indicate whether the keyed answer is correct.

- A method will be exposed for dynamically generating a new problem.
- A picture, whose visibility is configurable, will display one of two bitmap images based on the current solution provided by the user.
- A new problem will be generated when the picture is clicked.
- An event will be fired when a correct answer is keyed in to the control.
- When our control has focus, we will display an edit field to receive input from the end user. When focus leaves the control, the edit field will be hidden and static text will be used to display the current input.

After reading this description of the control, take a look back at Fig. 8.1. It should be apparent that we're providing a simple control that can be used to build a page of math problems—something akin to what we did back in elementary school.

Properties

We've described our control, so now let's define the properties that our control will expose. Certain properties are nearly always present in any ActiveX control. They are often referred to as standard, or stock, properties. Table 8.1 lists the standard properties that are present by default when using the ActiveX Control Interface Wizard that we encounter later.

Besides the stock properties, we will obviously need some custom properties to achieve the goals we have set for our control. Table 8.2 lists the custom properties that we want to implement.

TABLE 8.1

Standard Control Properties

Property	Purpose
BackColor	The background color of the control.
BackStyle	Indicates whether the background of the control is transparent or opaque.
BorderStyle	Determines whether the control will be drawn with a border.
Font	The font used by any text in the control.
ForeColor	The color of any text used in the control.
Enabled	Indicates whether the control can accept input.

TABLE 8.2

Custom
MathControl
Properties

Property	Purpose
CorrectAnswerColor	The color of the static text displaying a correct answer.
WrongAnswerColor	The color of the static text displaying an incorrect answer.
ProblemType	Indicates which problem operator (+, −, *, /) will be used when a new math problem is generated.
Operand1Range	Indicates the maximum value possible when generating the first problem operand.
Operand2Range	Indicates the maximum value possible when generating the second problem operand.
ShowFeedbackPicture	Indicates whether to display a picture showing a Happy Face when the correct answer is entered and a Sad Face when an incorrect answer is entered. This picture will also respond to the click event by generating a new math problem.
Correct	Indicates whether the current user input is the correct answer to the math problem. This property will be read-only and will not be visible in the property browser of our control.

Methods

Just as there are certain properties that most controls should support, there are also certain methods that should be supported as well. The ActiveX Interface Control Wizard selects only one method by default, the **Refresh** method. When this method is called on your control, you should force a complete repaint of the control. We also need a custom method for our control and it is listed in Table 8.3.

Events

If you haven't guessed by now, there is a set of stock events that most controls should support. The ones selected by default by the ActiveX Control Interface Wizard are listed in Table 8.4.

TABLE 8.3

Custom
MathControl
Methods

Method	Purpose
GenerateProblem	Tells the control to generate and display a new math problem.

TABLE 8.4

Standard Control
Events

Event	Purpose
Click	Fired when the user clicks anywhere within the control boundaries.
DblClick	Fired when the user double-clicks anywhere within the control boundaries.
KeyDown	Fired when the user presses a key when the control has focus.
KeyPress	Fired when the user presses and releases an ANSI key when the control has focus.
KeyUp	Fired when the user releases a key when the control has focus.
MouseDown	Fired when the user presses a mouse button when the control has focus.
MouseMove	Fired when the mouse is moved over the control.
MouseUp	Fired when the user releases a mouse button when the control has focus.

We will need to implement a custom event that is fired whenever the correct answer is input to the control. Table 8.5 shows our custom event.

Building the Control

We've established the blueprint for our control so now it's time to dig in and do some work. You are probably familiar with Visual Basic forms. An entity similar to a form is used when building ActiveX controls. All ActiveX controls are composed of a UserControl object which, like a form, has a designer window and a code module. The UserControl object has an interface that supports a large number of properties, methods, and events. Using this interface, you can get a lot of functionality with very little work simply by delegating to the appropriate UserControl member.

The first thing we need to do is place the controls that will make up our math problem control on the UserControl designer window. In VB

TABLE 8.5

Custom
MathControl
Events

Event	Purpose
CorrectAnswerEntered	Fired when the user enters a correct answer to the math problem.

parlance, controls that are used to construct a larger control are called *constituent* controls. For our purposes we will use some Label controls, a Text Box control, a Line control, an Image control, and an Image List control. To use the Image List control, you'll need to make sure the **Microsoft Windows Common Controls 5.0** component is available to your project. Do this by selecting the **Components...** option from the **Project** menu and selecting the appropriate component. Table 8.6 lists the controls that comprise the math control and the configuration information that should be applied to them.

To begin placing the controls, simply double-click on the **MathProblem.ctl** control in the **Project Explorer** window. This will bring up a window showing an empty UserControl designer window. Adjust the User-Control height property to 1275 and width property to 1335. By double-clicking on the appropriate control in the **Toolbox** window, place each control listed in Table 8.6 on the form and assign the properties accordingly. This should be pretty straightforward but the Image List control needs a little explanation. After you have placed the Image List control on the MathProblem control, click the **Custom** property to bring up the property page for the control. Switch to the **Image** tab and click the **Insert Picture** button. If you did a complete install when installing Visual Basic 5.0 you should find a \bitmaps\assorted\ directory in the VB installation directory. Here you will find the bitmaps HAPPY.BMP and SAD.BMP. Insert these bitmaps into the Image List control and assign the **Keys** "HAPPY" and "SAD" accordingly. If you can't find these bitmaps, just make a couple of bitmaps using Microsoft's **Paint** application that are 24 by 22 pixels in size.

Figure 8.3 shows a snapshot of the control with all the constituent controls placed on the UserControl designer window. Make sure the Label control lblAnswer is behind the TextBox control txtAnswer.

Okay, we've got all the constituent controls placed on our control. Let's go ahead and test it. Obviously it won't do anything yet, but this is a good opportunity to learn the difference between an active and inactive control. With the UserControl designer window still visible, double-click **Form1** in the **MathTest** project. This will bring up the MathTest designer window that will serve as the container for our control. Notice that our control in the Toolbox (it's the picture that looks like the icon for **MathProblem** in the **Project Explorer**) is currently disabled and thus we can't place an instance of it on our form. That's because as long as the UserControl designer window is visible the control is considered *active*. Now close the UserControl designer window and put focus to the Form1 designer window. The toolbox icon for our control has now become

TABLE 8.6

MathControl
Constituent
Controls

Control	Nondefault Property Settings		Purpose
Label	Name	lblOperand1	Displays the first problem
	Caption	111	operand.
	Alignment	Right Justify	
	Autosize	True	
	BackStyle	Transparent	
	Font	MS SansSerif/Bold/12	
	Top	60	
	Left	780	
Label	Name	lblOperand2	Displays the second problem
	Caption	222	operand.
	Alignment	Right Justify	
	Autosize	True	
	BackStyle	Transparent	
	Font	MS SansSerif/Bold/12	
	Top	480	
	Left	780	
Label	Name	lblAnswer	Displays the user input.
	Caption	333	
	Alignment	Right Justify	
	Autosize	True	
	BackStyle	Transparent	
	Font	MS SansSerif/Bold/12	
	Top	900	
	Left	780	
Label	Name	lblOperator	Displays the problem operator.
	Caption	"+"	
	Alignment	Right Justify	
	Autosize	True	
	BackStyle	Transparent	
	Font	MS SansSerif/Bold/12	
	Top	480	
	Left	60	
Line	Name	ProblemLine	The math problem under bar.
	X1	60	
	X2	1260	
	Y1	840	
	Y2	840	
Text Box	Name	txtAnswer	Accepts the user input.
	Text	(none)	
	Visible	False	
	Height	285	
	Width	1215	
	Top	900	
	Left	60	

TABLE 8.6
(Continued)

Control	Nondefault Property Settings		Purpose
Image	Name	imgFeedback	Shows a happy or sad face
	Height	375	depending on the user input.
	Width	375	
	Top	60	
	Left	60	
ImageList	Name	lstFeedbackImages	Contains the happy and
	Top	240	sad face images.
	Left	360	

enabled indicating that our control is now *inactive*. Now you can place as many instances of the control as you like. Go ahead and put a couple side by side on the test form by double-clicking on the control icon in the **Toolbox.** After you have done this, click the **Run** menu and select **Start** to launch the MATHTEST application. We still have a lot of work to do but, nonetheless, you have just created your first ActiveX control using Visual Basic!

ActiveX Control Interface Wizard

Now it's time to implement all the properties, methods, and events that our control will require. The code we will write is placed in the User-Control code module and the public procedures will form the interface of our control. We could type all the procedures out by hand but why do that when Visual Basic is willing to do a large majority of that work for us. The ActiveX Control Interface Wizard is a great tool that will generate the procedure templates and a good portion of the code for all of our properties, methods, and events. Also, the Wizard will generate the code

Figure 8.3
Math Control with
Constituent Controls.

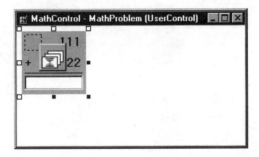

needed to persist and restore the properties we define for our control. Let's get started.

Click the **Add Ins...** menu and select **ActiveX Control Interface Wizard.** If this is the first time you have used the Interface Wizard, you'll be presented with an introduction dialog and you can simply press the **Next** button. The next screen, entitled **Select Interface Members,** is shown in Fig. 8.4. This screen allows you to create a list of all the standard members that your control will implement. Notice that the standard properties, methods, and events we discussed earlier are currently selected for our control. You can always add or remove members later but for our purposes we don't need to alter anything on this screen so click the **Next** button.

The next screen, displayed in Fig. 8.5, allows us to create custom interface members (properties, method, or events) for our control.

Let's create the custom properties first. Click on the **New...** button to bring up the dialog shown in Fig. 8.6. Type "CorrectAnswerColor" in the **Name** field and select **Property** as the member type then click the **OK** button. Repeat this procedure for each of the custom properties defined in Table 8.2 except for the "Correct" property. We'll implement that one by hand a little later. Now that you've got the hang of it, create the custom methods and events by referring to Tables 8.3 and 8.5. When you've finished entering in the custom members, click the **Next** button. This will

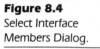

Figure 8.4
Select Interface
Members Dialog.

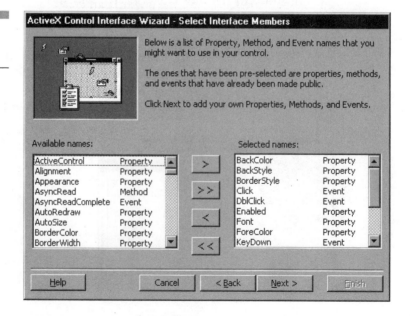

Figure 8.5
Create Custom
Interface Members
Dialog.

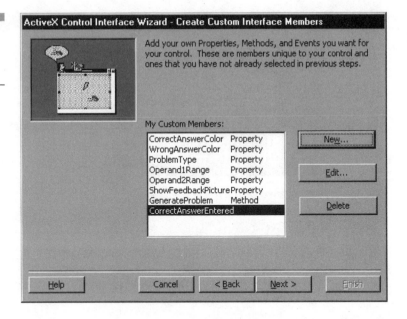

bring up the **Set Mapping** screen displayed in Fig. 8.7. This screen allows us to map our control members directly to one or more constituent controls and their corresponding members. We also have the choice of mapping a custom member to the entire control in general. By establishing these mappings, the Interface Wizard can create the code necessary to do the work of the control members, thus reducing the amount of work we must do as control developers.

For our control, we need only create mappings for the standard, or noncustom members. Map each standard member to the UserControl object. By default, the Interface Wizard will select the appropriate control member to complete the mapping. The custom properties that we have

Figure 8.6
Add Custom Member
Dialog.

Figure 8.7
Set Mapping Dialog.

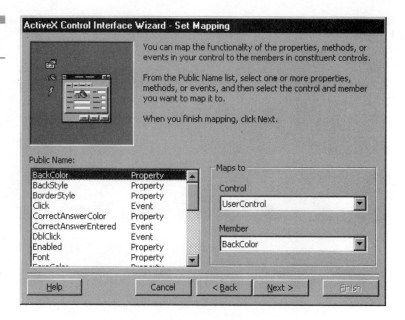

created for our control do not directly map to any constituent controls but rather dictate how the control will behave so we do not need to set any mappings for these.

Click the **Next** button to bring up the **Set Attributes** screen displayed in Fig. 8.8. This screen allows us to set the attributes of any unmapped members of our control. Table 8.7 lists each control member and the attributes to set for each one.

NOTE: *Visual Basic uses the term "attribute" to describe the combination of a property's data type (e.g., long), its default value (e.g., zero), and its run-time and design-time behavior. The attributes of an automation method are its return value and the number and types of its parameters. The attributes of an event are its parameters.*

The ProblemType member is special. We'll leave it as returning a variant for now, but later we will modify the code to accept and return a special enumeration type. After you have finished entering all the information from Table 8.7, press the **Next** button. This will bring up the final screen and you can now click the **Finish** button. The Interface Wizard will now create a substantial bit of code that we examine in the next section.

Figure 8.8
Set Attributes Dialog.

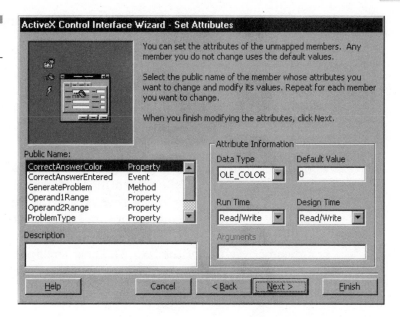

The Wizard of Code

Now it's time to take a look at the code that the ActiveX Interface Wizard created for us. Right-click on the MathProblem.ctl object in the **Project Explorer** and select **View Code.** This will bring up the UserControl code module. Let's start from the top.

TABLE 8.7

MathProblem
Member Attributes

Property/ Event/Method	Datatype	Default Value	Design Time	Run Time
CorrectAnswerColor	OLE_COLOR	0	Read/Write	Read/Write
CorrectAnswerEntered	N/A	N/A	N/A	N/A
GenerateProblem	Empty	N/A	N/A	N/A
Operand1Range	Integer	10	Read/Write	Read/Write
Operand2Range	Integer	10	Read/Write	Read/Write
ProblemType	Variant	0	Read/Write	Read/Write
ShowFeedbackPicture	Boolean	0	Read/Write	Read/Write
WrongAnswerColor	OLE_COLOR	0	Read/Write	Read/Write

The following code can be found in the Declarations section of the UserControl code module:

```
'Default Property Values:
Const m_def_CorrectAnswerColor = 0
Const m_def_WrongAnswerColor = 0
Const m_def_ProblemType = 0
Const m_def_Operand1Range = 10
Const m_def_Operand2Range = 10
Const m_def_ShowFeedbackPicture = 0
```

Here, the Interface Wizard has created some constants that define default values based on the information we provided when using the Interface Wizard's **Set Attributes** page. Notice the Microsoft coding standard of prefixing class members with "m_". This makes it easy when reading code to determine whether a variable is local to a particular procedure or a member variable of the class. The next few lines of code are the declarations of the custom properties that we created using the **Create Custom Interface Members** page:

```
'Property Variables:
Dim m_CorrectAnswerColor As OLE_COLOR
Dim m_WrongAnswerColor As OLE_COLOR
Dim m_ProblemType As Variant
Dim m_Operand1Range As Integer
Dim m_Operand2Range As Integer
Dim m_ShowFeedbackPicture As Boolean
```

The last bit of code in the declarations section consists of the Event declarations for the control:

```
'Event Declarations:
Event Click() 'MappingInfo=UserControl,UserControl,-1,Click
Event DblClick() 'MappingInfo=UserControl,UserControl,-1,DblClick
Event KeyDown(KeyCode As Integer, Shift As Integer)
'MappingInfo=UserControl,UserControl,-1,KeyDown
Event KeyPress(KeyAscii As Integer) 'MappingInfo=UserControl,UserControl,-1,KeyPress
Event KeyUp(KeyCode As Integer, Shift As Integer) 'MappingInfo=UserControl,UserControl,
-1,KeyUp
Event MouseDown(Button As Integer, Shift As Integer, X As Single, Y As Single)
'MappingInfo=UserControl,UserControl,-1,MouseDown
Event MouseMove(Button As Integer, Shift As Integer, X As Single, Y As Single)
'MappingInfo=UserControl,UserControl,-1,MouseMove
Event MouseUp(Button As Integer, Shift As Integer, X As Single, Y As Single)
'MappingInfo=UserControl,UserControl,-1,MouseUp
Event CorrectAnswerEntered()
```

This is interesting. Similar to Visual C++, VB 5.0 requires that you declare event procedures in the declarations section of a UserControl code module. You'll also notice some comment lines included with the code. These comments are used exclusively by the Interface Wizard to accurately display the current state if the Wizard is used again during the lifetime of the project. In other words, removing these comment lines does not affect the execution of the control; it simply means the Interface Wizard will not be entirely accurate and in fact, without our removing a single line of code, the Wizard will already display inaccurate information. For instance, start the Interface Wizard right now and navigate to the Set Attributes page and select the custom property "Operand1Range." Notice that the Default Value does not reflect the data we originally entered on this page. Because of this limitation, the Interface Wizard is typically used to get the code base rolling for a new project, but tweaking the code is done the old-fashioned way.

The next several lines of code represent the "get" and "let" property procedures for the standard members we included in our control. Rather than list all of the generated code here, let's take a look at the BackColor property as an example:

```
'WARNING! DO NOT REMOVE OR MODIFY THE FOLLOWING COMMENTED LINES!
'MappingInfo=UserControl,UserControl,-1,BackColor
Public Property Get BackColor() As OLE_COLOR
  BackColor = UserControl.BackColor
End Property

Public Property Let BackColor(ByVal New_BackColor As OLE_COLOR)
  UserControl.BackColor() = New_BackColor
  PropertyChanged "BackColor"
End Property
```

There's that Interface Wizard comment line again this time accompanied with a warning comment above it. The property procedures themselves are pretty straightforward. Each generated procedure simply delegates the property value to the appropriate UserControl property. By using the OLE_COLOR data type, we get a neat little piece of functionality for free. When Visual Basic displays this property in the property browser, it will automatically provide the standard color selection palette when the user wants to modify the property. The property browser will always do this when it recognizes the data type used by a property procedure. For example, if the data type is Boolean, the property browser will display a drop-down list providing the choices "True" and "False." Later we will see how to define our own enumeration type that we can use as a data type for property procedures. Just as you might expect, Visual Basic will provide the enumerated values as choices in the property browser.

The other interesting thing going on in this code is the use of the PropertyChanged method. This method in turn fires an event that notifies any associated property browsers that a property value has changed.

As a consequence of not invoking this method, a property value modified on a custom property page would not be simultaneously updated in the container's standard property browser. This may not be an issue in a container environment such as Visual C++ because the control property page is the only way of examining control properties. But since we want to write a robust control that can be used by many different containers, we should make use of the `PropertyChanged` method whenever applicable.

If you examine more of the code created by the Interface Wizard, you'll find the following:

```
Private Sub UserControl_KeyDown(KeyCode As Integer, Shift As Integer)
  RaiseEvent KeyDown(KeyCode, Shift)
End Sub
```

I've shown the `KeyDown` event for illustrative purposes. The rest of the generated event code is very similar. All that's going on here is that the `RaiseEvent` method is being used to fire an event when the UserControl object receives the event. We're simply piggybacking on top of the UserControl event that is trapped inherently. The `RaiseEvent` method takes as a parameter an event name and a corresponding argument. The parameters are type-checked against the event declarations that we saw in the Declarations section and an error will be raised if there is a type mismatch.

If you further examine the generated code, you'll find the "get" and "let" property procedures for our custom properties. I'll not list that code now but you can see for yourself that it's just like the procedures generated for the standard properties. Finally, if you examine the remainder of the code generated by the Interface Wizard, you'll see the `InitProperties`, `ReadProperties`, and `WriteProperties` events. These events, along with the `Initialize` event, are key to understanding how a custom control acts at design-time and run-time. Let's take a look at each of these events in detail.

InitProperties

The `InitProperties` event is an odd fellow. Under normal circumstances, it is called only once during the entire life cycle of an ActiveX control. When a developer first places your control in a container (in other words, when the control is instantiated for the first time), the `InitProperties` event is called. Thereafter it will never be called again. What is this event for, you ask? The `InitProperties` event provides you with a way to establish the default values for the properties exposed by your control. Let's look at the `InitProperties` event code that was generated for us:

```
'Initialize Properties for User Control
Private Sub UserControl_InitProperties()
  Set Font = Ambient.Font
  m_CorrectAnswerColor = m_def_CorrectAnswerColor
  m_WrongAnswerColor = m_def_WrongAnswerColor
  m_ProblemType = m_def_ProblemType
  m_Operand1Range = m_def_Operand1Range
  m_Operand2Range = m_def_Operand2Range
  m_ShowFeedbackPicture = m_def_ShowFeedbackPicture
End Sub
```

Here we see those default constants put into action. Each of our custom properties is being set to a default value that we established using the Interface Wizard. You'll also notice that the font property is being set to `Ambient.Font`. This is our first encounter with the Ambient object and we talk about it in the next section.

Initialize

Unlike the `InitProperties` event, the `Initialize` event is called every time an instance of your control is created in either design-time or run-time mode. It is always the first event that is called in the control. You can use the `Initialize` event for executing any startup code that may be necessary for the control. Be aware that the Ambient and Extender objects (we see these later) are not available at the time the `Initialize` event is called, so any attempt to access these objects will result in an error being raised.

ReadProperties

The `ReadProperties` event is called the second and all subsequent times the control is created. The event is used to restore property values from a persisted state. The following code shows the `ReadProperties` event code that was generated for us by the Interface Wizard:

```
'Load property values from storage
Private Sub UserControl_ReadProperties(PropBag As PropertyBag)
  UserControl.BackColor = PropBag.ReadProperty("BackColor", &H8000000F)
  UserControl.ForeColor = PropBag.ReadProperty("ForeColor", &H80000012)
  UserControl.Enabled = PropBag.ReadProperty("Enabled", True)
  Set Font = PropBag.ReadProperty("Font", Ambient.Font)
  UserControl.BackStyle = PropBag.ReadProperty("BackStyle", 1)
  UserControl.BorderStyle = PropBag.ReadProperty("BorderStyle", 0)
```

```
m_CorrectAnswerColor = PropBag.ReadProperty("CorrectAnswerColor", _
                                 m_def_CorrectAnswerColor)
m_WrongAnswerColor = PropBag.ReadProperty("WrongAnswerColor", _
                                 m_def_WrongAnswerColor)
m_ProblemType = PropBag.ReadProperty("ProblemType", m_def_ProblemType)
m_Operand1Range = PropBag.ReadProperty("Operand1Range", m_def_Operand1Range)
m_Operand2Range = PropBag.ReadProperty("Operand2Range", m_def_Operand2Range)
m_ShowFeedbackPicture = PropBag.ReadProperty("ShowFeedbackPicture", _
                                 m_def_ShowFeedbackPicture)
End Sub
```

Note the `PropertyBag` object that is passed in as a parameter to this event. This is a nice little object provided by Visual Basic that completely insulates the control developer from having to know the internals of persisting are retrieving property values. This "black box" provides only two methods: `ReadProperty` and `WriteProperty`. The `ReadProperty` method takes two parameters. The first parameter is a string containing the name of the Property whose value is to be queried. The second parameter is a default value for the property in case the property value is not retrieved from the persisted state. It is a good idea to use error-handling code when reading values using the PropertyBag object as the retrieved values could have been modified by users editing the container's storage files (e.g., by directly editing Visual Basic's .FRM files).

NOTE: *When the Interface Wizard generates code for the ReadProperties event, it assigns the retrieved values directly to the class member variables. In general it makes more sense to assign the retrieved values using the "Let" procedures that encapsulate the member variables since you may have added additional code to these procedures.*

WriteProperties

The WriteProperties event is called every time a *design-time* instance of the control is destroyed *and* at least one property has been modified. Obviously, this event is used to store the current values of the control properties. The following code was generated by the Interface Wizard:

```
'Write property values to storage
Private Sub UserControl_WriteProperties(PropBag As PropertyBag)
  Call PropBag.WriteProperty("BackColor", UserControl.BackColor, &H8000000F)
  Call PropBag.WriteProperty("ForeColor", UserControl.ForeColor, &H80000012)
  Call PropBag.WriteProperty("Enabled", UserControl.Enabled, True)
  Call PropBag.WriteProperty("Font", Font, Ambient.Font)
  Call PropBag.WriteProperty("BackStyle", UserControl.BackStyle, 1)
  Call PropBag.WriteProperty("BorderStyle", UserControl.BorderStyle, 0)
  Call PropBag.WriteProperty("CorrectAnswerColor", m_CorrectAnswerColor, _
                  m_def_CorrectAnswerColor)
```

```
Call PropBag.WriteProperty("WrongAnswerColor", m_WrongAnswerColor, _
                           m_def_WrongAnswerColor)
Call PropBag.WriteProperty("ProblemType", m_ProblemType, m_def_ProblemType)
Call PropBag.WriteProperty("Operand1Range", m_Operand1Range, m_def_Operand1Range)
Call PropBag.WriteProperty("Operand2Range", m_Operand2Range, m_def_Operand2Range)
Call PropBag.WriteProperty("ShowFeedbackPicture", m_ShowFeedbackPicture, _
                           m_def_ShowFeedbackPicture)
End Sub
```

Again, we see the `PropertyBag` object is passed to the event and, you guessed it, we will use the `WriteProperties` method to persist the property values. Inspection of this code reveals that the `WriteProperty` method takes three parameters. The first two are expected: a string containing the name of the property and the property's current value. The third parameter is the default value of the property. It may seem odd that we should have to supply a default value when we have already supplied the actual property value. There is a good reason for this, however. When the control container prepares to persist the property values of its child controls, it compares the actual property value to the default value. If it finds these two values to be the same, it does not actually persist the property value. This allows the container to keep its storage files to a minimal size. As we saw previously, the `ReadProperty` method is told what the default property value should be and so the value will always be restored correctly.

The Ambient and Extender Objects

Visual Basic provides two objects to the control designer that allow interaction with the control container—the `AmbientProperties` object and the `Extender` Object.

The `AmbientProperties` object exposes certain properties of the parent container. It can be accessed by using the Ambient property provided by the `UserControl` object. Armed with ambient property information, you can make your control's appearance stay consistent with its parent. For example, in the `InitProperties` event code that we saw in the last section, the font property of the Ambient object is queried so that the control will initially use the font of the parent container. The ActiveX Control standard defines the ambient properties that all containers should provide. A container, however, is not required to implement these properties and in the case when the property is not implemented, the `AmbientProperties` object will return a default value. The standard Ambient properties and their default values are listed in Table 8.8.

TABLE 8.8

AmbientProperties
Object Standard
Properties

Property	Description	Default Value
BackColor	Suggested interior color of the contained control.	System color for a window background.
DisplayAsDefault	Specifies whether control is the default control for the container.	False.
DisplayName	The name the control should display for itself.	An empty string (" ").
Font	Suggested font for contained control.	MS Sans Serif 8.
ForeColor	Suggested foreground color for the contained control.	System color for window text.
LocaleID	Specifies the language and country of the user.	Current system locale ID.
MessageReflect	Specifies whether the container supports message reflection.	False.
Palette	Suggested palette for the contained control.	Current system palette.
RightToLeft	Specifies the text display direction.	False.
ScaleUnits	Specifies the coordinates units being used by the container.	An empty string (" ").
ShowGrabHandles	Specifies whether the container handles the showing of grab handles.	True.
ShowHatchings	Specifies whether the container handles the showing of hatching.	True.
SupportsMnemonics	Specifies whether the container handles access keys for the control.	False.
TextAlign	An enumeration that specifies how text is to be aligned.	0—General Align.
UserMode	Specifies if the current environment is the design mode or end-user mode.	True.
UIDead	Specifies if the User Interface is nonresponsive.	False.

Because the `Ambient` object supplies defaults for all of the standard methods, you do not need to use error-handling code when accessing standard ambient properties. Control containers can, at their discretion, provide additional ambient properties to the control designer. Be sure to use error handling code when accessing these properties as you cannot always be sure whether the container your control is eventually placed in will support these custom ambients.

The `UserControl` object supports an event procedure called AmbientChanged. This event is fired by the container every time one of its ambient properties changes. The argument passed into this event is a string containing the name of the property that changed. You can place code in this procedure to immediately update your control's appearance whenever the change occurs.

Another useful object provided by Visual Basic is called the `Extender` object. When you eventually place our MathProblem control on a Visual Basic form, you will see several properties in the property browser window that we did not implement ourselves. Examples include Visible, Name, Top, Left, and so on. These control properties are actually provided by the container but are seamlessly integrated with our own properties. All of these additional properties can be accessed using the Extender object. For example, the Name property of the Extender object is often queried so that a design-time representation of a control can display the name it has been given by the user. Typically, you will only read these properties and rarely ever set them although some are read/write properties. The ActiveX control specification defines the minimal set of extender properties that all containers should provide and these are listed in Table 8.9.

Containers do not have to implement these properties so you should always use error-handling code when accessing extender properties. As

TABLE 8.9

Extender Object
Standard Properties

Property	Description	Access
Name	The name the user has given the control.	Read Only
Visible	Specifies whether the control is visible.	Read/Write
Parent	Returns the control's parent object.	Read Only
Cancel	Specifies whether the control acts as the Cancel button for the container.	Read Only
Default	Specifies whether the control acts as the Default button for the container.	Read Only

with the ambient properties, containers may provide additional extender properties not listed in Table 8.9. Again, use error-handling code when accessing custom extender properties.

The Custom Code

Finally! Now *we* get to write some code instead of having Visual Basic do all of the work for us. The Interface Wizard has given us a good start but our control still doesn't *do* anything yet. That's about to change. First, let's start by creating an enumeration type that defines the type of mathematical problem the control should generate. Open up the UserControl code module for our control and type the following code at the end of the Declarations section:

```
Enum ENUM_PROBLEM_TYPE
  mcAddition
  mcSubtraction
  mcMultiplication
  mcDivision
End Enum
```

This enumeration simply assigns the values 0 through 3 to the four enumerated strings respectively. The real advantage of using this enumeration type is seen when you make the following code changes:

```
Public Property Get ProblemType() As ENUM_PROBLEM_TYPE
  ProblemType = m_ProblemType
End Property
```

```
Public Property Let ProblemType(ByVal New_ProblemType As ENUM_PROBLEM_TYPE)
  m_ProblemType = New_ProblemType
  PropertyChanged "ProblemType"
End Property
```

Here, we are modifying the "get" and "let" properties for Problem-Type to accept and return the ENUM_PROBLEM_TYPE enumeration instead of the Variant data type. Because we have defined an enumeration type, the Visual Basic property browser now understands exactly what to present as choices when the control user wants to modify the ProblemType property. Also, if a developer wants to set the Problem-Type dynamically at run-time using code, the string values mcAddition, mcSubtraction, mcMultiplication, and mcDivision are available to the developer as constants.

Next, we will add code to the project that restricts the values that can be assigned to the Operand1Range and Operand2Range properties. We will restrict the values to a minimum of 1 and a maximum of 999. We do this simply because we are not going to code any sophisticated resizing algorithm that will enlarge our control whenever the operands in question become very large. Modify the properties in your code as shown:

```
Public Property Let Operand1Range(ByVal New_Operand1Range As Integer)
  If New_Operand1Range > 999 Or New_Operand1Range < 1 Then
    Err.Raise 380  ' Invalid property value
    Exit Property
  End If
  m_Operand1Range = New_Operand1Range
  PropertyChanged "Operand1Range"
End Property


Public Property Let Operand2Range(ByVal New_Operand2Range As Integer)
  If New_Operand2Range > 999 Or New_Operand2Range < 1 Then
    Err.Raise 380  ' Invalid property value
    Exit Property
  End If
  m_Operand2Range = New_Operand2Range
  PropertyChanged "Operand2Range"
End Property
```

Here, we are simply using the Visual Basic Err object to raise error number 380, whose textual translation is "Invalid property Value," whenever an illegal property value is assigned to the range properties. Because we used the `Integer` data type for these properties, Visual Basic is kind enough to automatically handle validating that the input is numeric when the values are changed via the Visual Basic property browser. This will, however, be our responsibility when we build the custom property page for our control.

The following code implements the functionality behind the feedback picture. Remember, the feedback picture visibility can be configured by the control user. When the picture is visible, it will display a "happy" or "sad" face depending on the current problem solution keyed in by the user. In addition, when the feedback picture is clicked, a new problem will be generated. Take a look at the following code:

```
Private Sub UserControl_Initialize()
  ' Initially set the feedback picture to the Sad face
  ' since no problem solution could have been entered yet
  Set imgFeedback.Picture = 1stFeedbackImages.ListImages("SAD").Picture
End Sub
```

We've found a use for the Initialize event in our control. We're simply defaulting the picture to be a "Sad" face since the initial problem solution, an empty text field, is always incorrect. Next, we'll toggle the visibility of the feedback picture based on the value received by the Let property for ShowFeedbackPicture:

```
Public Property Let ShowFeedbackPicture(ByVal New_ShowFeedbackPicture As Boolean)
  m_ShowFeedbackPicture = New_ShowFeedbackPicture
  ' Show or hide the feedback picture accordingly
  imgFeedback.Visible = New_ShowFeedbackPicture
  PropertyChanged "ShowFeedbackPicture"
End Property
```

Finally, we need to modify the InitProperties and ReadProperties events so that the ShowFeedbackPicture property value is assigned to the control property rather than directly to the class member variable that is accessed by the property. We do this for the obvious reason that we want to toggle the visibility of the control whenever the property value changes, not just assign a new value to a variable. That's the whole reason for encapsulation of class member variables via "get" and "let" properties. When you write future code using the Interface Control Wizard, you'll find that you convert most, if not all, of the code generated in the InitProperties and ReadProperties events to use property procedures rather than class members directly.

```
'Initialize Properties for User Control
Private Sub UserControl_InitProperties()
  ...
  m_Operand2Range = m_def_Operand2Range
  ' Assign the value to the property rather than
  ' the member variable directly. This way we don't have
  ' to duplicate code to show or hide the picture control
  ShowFeedbackPicture = m_def_ShowFeedbackPicture
End Sub
```

```
'Load property values from storage
Private Sub UserControl_ReadProperties(PropBag As PropertyBag)
  m_Operand2Range = PropBag.ReadProperty("Operand2Range", m_def_Operand2Range)
  ' Assign the value to the property rather than
  ' the member variable directly. This way we don't have
  ' to duplicate code to show or hide the picture control
```

```
ShowFeedbackPicture = PropBag.ReadProperty("ShowFeedbackPicture", _
                              m_def_ShowFeedbackPicture)
End Sub
```

Slowly but surely, we're adding real functionality to our control. The next thing we will tackle is the Font and ForeColor properties. If you look at the code that has been generated for the "let" and "set" properties you will see that the new font or forecolor value is assigned to the corresponding UserControl property. This effectively does nothing since the UserControl object itself is not displaying any text. What we want instead is to have the new values applied to the three Label controls and the Line control that make up the math problem. The following code demonstrates the needed modifications:

```
Public Property Get ForeColor() As OLE_COLOR
    ' Return the ForeColor for lblOperand1 since all
    ' of the labels use the same ForeColor.
    ForeColor = lblOperand1.ForeColor
End Property


Public Property Let ForeColor(ByVal New_ForeColor As OLE_COLOR)
    ' Assign the font to the label controls
    lblOperand1.ForeColor = New_ForeColor
    lblOperand2.ForeColor = New_ForeColor
    lblOperator.ForeColor = New_ForeColor
    ProblemLine.BorderColor = New_ForeColor
    PropertyChanged "ForeColor"
End Property


Public Property Set Font(ByVal New_Font As Font)
    ' Assign the font to the label controls
    Set lblOperand1.Font = New_Font
    Set lblOperand2.Font = New_Font
    Set lblAnswer.Font = New_Font
    Set lblOperator.Font = New_Font
    PropertyChanged "Font"
End Property


Public Property Get Font() As Font
    ' Return the font for lblOperand1 since all
    ' of the labels use the same font.
    Set Font = lblOperand1.Font
End Property
```

We also need to modify the WriteProperties and ReadProperties events so that we access the ForeColor property rather than the UserControl member variable directly:

```
'Write property values to storage
Private Sub UserControl_WriteProperties(PropBag As PropertyBag)
```

```
Call PropBag.WriteProperty("BackColor", UserControl.BackColor, &H8000000F)
Call PropBag.WriteProperty("ForeColor", ForeColor, &H80000012)
Call PropBag.WriteProperty("Enabled", UserControl.Enabled, True)
...
End Sub


'Load property values from storage
Private Sub UserControl_ReadProperties(PropBag As PropertyBag)
  UserControl.BackColor = PropBag.ReadProperty("BackColor", &H8000000F)
  ForeColor = PropBag.ReadProperty("ForeColor", &H80000012)
  UserControl.Enabled = PropBag.ReadProperty("Enabled", True)
...
End Sub
```

One of the requirements of our control is that the Textbox control should be displayed only when the control has focus. When focus leaves our control, the Textbox should be hidden and a Label control should be used to display the current user input. When we placed the Textbox control on the UserControl, we specified that the Visible property should be False so that when the control is initially shown, only the answer label will be visible. In order to toggle the visibility of the Textbox and Label controls, we will use the EnterFocus and ExitFocus events provided by the UserControl object. Take a look at the following code:

```
Private Sub UserControl_EnterFocus()
  ' The control has recieved focus.
  ' Hide the answer label and show the
  ' textbox control
  txtAnswer.Visible = True
  txtAnswer.SetFocus
  lblAnswer.Visible = False
End Sub

Private Sub UserControl_ExitFocus()
  ' The control has lost focus.
  ' Hide the textbox and show the
  ' answer label
  txtAnswer.Visible = False
  lblAnswer.Visible = True
End Sub
```

This is simple stuff. You may have noticed that the UserControl object also supports the events GotFocus and LostFocus and wondered why we didn't implement the toggling code in these events. The reason is this. When you create an ActiveX control from constituent controls, as in our MathProblem control, the UserControl object will never receive the Got-Focus and LostFocus events as long as at least one of the constituent controls can receive focus. Instead, the constituent control will receive these focus events. Since, in our control, the Textbox control is the only type of control that can receive focus and it is not visible until *after* the control has received a focus event, the GotFocus event is always fired for our control. However, when focus leaves our control, the Textbox control is visible and so the LostFocus event is fired for the Textbox control but not the UserControl object. Confusing, I know. To make a long story short, use the EnterFocus and ExitFocus events which will always be fired when you expect regardless of what type of constituent controls you have used.

We're getting close to wrapping this control up. Now it's time to implement the code that generates the math problem. We need to declare a variable that will hold the answer to the math problem that we generate. This is so that it will be easy to validate the user input later. Put the m_Answer variable declaration in the UserControl Declarations section:

```vb
' Holds the answer to the current math problem
dim m_Answer as integer
...
Public Sub GenerateProblem()
  Dim oper1, oper2 As Integer

  ' Generate the problem operands
  Randomize
  oper1 = Int((Operand1Range * Rnd) + 1)
  oper2 = Int((Operand2Range * Rnd) + 1)

  ' Generate the correct answer and set the
  ' problem operator
  Select Case ProblemType
    Case mcAddition
      m_Answer = oper1 + oper2
      lblOperator = "+"
    Case mcSubtraction
      ' Use absolute value in case the operands
      ' are displayed in reverse order
      m_Answer = Abs(oper1 - oper2)
      lblOperator = "-"
    Case mcMultiplication
      m_Answer = oper1 * oper2
      lblOperator = Chr$(215) ' multiplication symbol
    Case mcDivision
      ' Make sure the answer always comes out even
      oper1 = oper1 * oper2
      m_Answer = oper1 / oper2
      lblOperator = Chr$(247) ' division symbol
  End Select

  ' Always display the larger number on top
  If oper1 >= oper2 Then
    lblOperand1 = oper1
    lblOperand2 = oper2
  Else
    lblOperand1 = oper2
    lblOperand2 = oper1
```

```
    End If

    ' Clear out the answer label and answer textbox
    lblAnswer = ""
    txtAnswer = ""
End Sub
```

We've commented the code pretty well so I'm not going to go over each line. We've made sure to always display the larger operand on top since that's the way we're used to seeing math problems like these. Because of this, we have to use the absolute value when generating a subtraction problem answer since the real **oper1** could be smaller than **oper2**.

`GenerateProblem` is a public method that can be called at run-time by the control user, but we'll also call the method in our own code in a couple of different places. First, we want the control to display a new problem when the control is seen for the first time by the end user. At design-time, however, we want the control to always present the same look to the application designer. Look at the following code placed in the User-Control's show method:

```
Private Sub UserControl_Show()
    ' When the control is being displayed for the
    ' first time in end user mode, generate a
    ' new problem
    If Ambient.UserMode = True Then
        GenerateProblem
    End If
End Sub
```

Here we're using the `UserMode` property of the `AmbientProperties` object to determine what mode our control is in. If the `UserMode` is true then the control is being used by the end user. False means the control is being used in design mode. The code simply generates a new problem when the control is shown to the user for the first time. You might think we should put this code in the `Initialize` event but remember, the `AmbientProperties` object is not available in the `Initialize` event and so we would be unable to determine the current UserMode value.

The other time that we need to call `GenerateProblem` is when the feedback picture is clicked. This is another behavior that was defined in the control specification. We simply call the method from the `imgFeedback` click event:

```
Private Sub imgFeedback_Click()
    ' The feedback picture was clicked so
    ' we need to generate a new math problem
    GenerateProblem
End Sub
```

Run-Time- and Design-Time-Only Properties

Way back when we used the ActiveX Interface Control Wizard to create the custom members of the control, I said that we would implement the "Correct" property without the use of the Wizard. I wanted to do this so I could demonstrate some other neat features that VB provides. To implement this property, we first need to declare the appropriate member variable in the Declarations section:

```
' Signals whether the current input is the correct problem solution
dim m_Correct as Boolean
```

Now take a look at the public "get" and "let" properties for this class member:

```
Public Property Get Correct() As Boolean
   Correct = m_Correct
End Property

Public Property Let Correct(ByVal New_Correct As Boolean)
   ' Raise an error if the control user attempts to set
   ' this property at run time
   If Ambient.UserMode = True Then Err.Raise 382
End Property
```

There's nothing magic going on in the get property. Remember that we said that we wanted the "Correct" property to be unavailable at design-time and read-only at run-time? In the "Let" property, we are enforcing the second half of this requirement. When we determine that the end user is using the control, we raise an error if the "Let" property is called. This is the standard way of enforcing this rule. Another way we could have done it is to make the let property private, but that would raise an error stating "The property or method is not found" whenever this property is set by the control user. It would also prevent the property from appearing in Visual Basic's object browser. This behavior is not desirable since the property does exist; it just can't be set at run-time.

Our implementation of the code does present us with a problem, though. When the user does finally enter a correct answer (at run-time, of course) we are going to want to set the "Correct" property accordingly. We will not be able to call the "Let" property, however, because that would raise an error. Instead, we will simply set the class member `m_Correct` directly, avoiding the "Let" property entirely. You can see then that, if the control is used correctly, the let property for the control will never be called. We've simply implemented the property to be consistent.

Procedure Attributes

What about making the "Correct" property unavailable at design-time? Visual Basic provides a Procedure Attributes dialog for setting requirements just like this. Click the **Tools** menu and select **Procedure Attributes...** then press the **Advanced** button. In the **Name** combobox, select "Correct" to bring up the dialog shown in Fig. 8.9.

There are many attributes that can be set on this dialog, but we're interested in the checkbox options in the **Attributes** frame. The first option, **Hide this member,** sounds like what we're after but it actually does more than we are looking for. When this option is checked, the property will not show up in the container's property browser *or* the container's object browser. For our control, we simply don't want the property visible in the property browser, so click the option labeled **Don't show in Property Browser.** The other option, **User Interface Default,** simply makes the property the default property for the control. We visit this dialog again later when building an AboutBox for our control. Ensure your dialog looks like Fig. 8.9 and click the **OK** button.

We're just about finished with the custom code. We just need to react to a correct answer input from the end user. We'll do this by using the Change event of the answer Textbox control to call a method called ValidateAnswer:

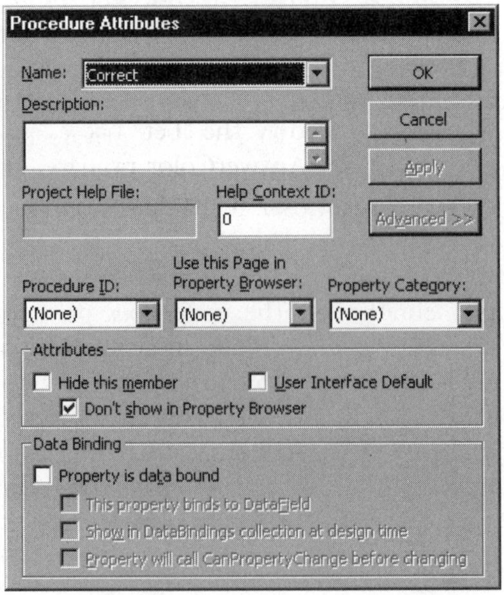

Figure 8.9
Procedure Attributes
Dialog.

```
Private Function ValidateAnswer() As Boolean
    ' Move the contents of the textbox to the answer label control
    ' This is the label control that will be visible when the control
    ' loses focus.
    lblAnswer = Val(txtAnswer)

    ' Compare the user input to the correct answer
    If m_Answer = Val(txtAnswer) Then
        ' Set the "correct" property
        m_Correct = True

        ValidateAnswer = True
    Else
        ' Set the "correct" property
        m_Correct = False

        ValidateAnswer = False
    End If
End Function

Private Sub txtAnswer_Change()
    If ValidateAnswer = True Then
        ' Set the feedback picture
        imgFeedback.Picture = 1stFeedbackImages.ListImages("HAPPY").Picture

        ' Set the answer label fore color
        lblAnswer.ForeColor = CorrectAnswerColor

        ' Raise the event signalling a correct answer
        RaiseEvent CorrectAnswerEntered
    Else
        ' Set the feedback picture
        imgFeedback.Picture = 1stFeedbackImages.ListImages("SAD").Picture

        ' Set the answer label and its fore color
        lblAnswer.ForeColor = WrongAnswerColor
    End If
End Sub
```

Finally, we need to modify the "Let" procedures for the CorrectAnswerColor and the WrongAnswerColor properties so that the new color values are applied immediately if necessary.

```
Public Property Let CorrectAnswerColor(ByVal New_CorrectAnswerColor As OLE_COLOR)
    m_CorrectAnswerColor = New_CorrectAnswerColor
    PropertyChanged "CorrectAnswerColor"

    ' Update the the color of the answer text
    ' if were in run mode
    If Ambient.UserMode = True Then
        If ValidateAnswer = True Then
            lblAnswer.ForeColor = m_CorrectAnswerColor
        End If
    End If
End Property

Public Property Let WrongAnswerColor(ByVal New_WrongAnswerColor As OLE_COLOR)
```

```
    m_WrongAnswerColor = New_WrongAnswerColor
    PropertyChanged "WrongAnswerColor"

    ' Update the color of the answer text
    ' if were in run mode
    If Ambient.UserMode = True Then
        If ValidateAnswer = False Then
            lblAnswer.ForeColor = m_WrongAnswerColor
        End If
    End If
End Property
```

Testing the Control

That should do it. You can now play with the control in the test project. Put several of the controls on the test form so you can see the behavior when the controls get and lose focus. There are still some things we could do to spruce it up such as writing code to allow numeric-only input in the answer Textbox or preselecting the Textbox data when the control receives focus. This is simple stuff and there is no need to go into that much detail here. The source code provided on the CD-ROM implements things of this nature so you can see how it is done.

At this point, the control can be used effectively but we still haven't implemented any property pages for our control. Also, we still need to provide an about box and an appropriate Toolbox icon. This is all covered in the following sections.

Property Pages

Now it's time to create the property pages that can be used to change property values of our control. Not all containers will support a standard property browser like the one provided by Visual Basic. Many containers rely on property pages exclusively for setting properties at design-time. Because you can't know in advance what container will house your control, it is important to include all your control's properties on property pages. Visual Basic has a built in Wizard to help you generate property pages for your controls. Of course, you can also build them yourself from scratch if you like. The **Project** menu contains a selection labeled **Add Property Page** which, when selected, will add a file to your project with a .PAG extension. After you have created a property page, you can assign it to the control by using the PropertyPages property of the UserControl object.

The Property Page Wizard

For our control, we're going to demonstrate the use of the Property-Page Wizard. Click on the **Add Ins…** menu and select the **Property Page Wizard…** option. This should bring up a dialog similar to Fig. 8.10.

When the dialog first comes up, your only property page options are StandardColor and StandardFont. These are built-in property pages that Visual Basic provides for free. Later, you will simply assign certain properties to use these pages and for those properties your work will be finished. We'll need a page to house some of our custom properties though, so click the **Add** button and use the name **General.** After you have created the new page, use the sorting buttons on the right to move the General property page to the top of the list. That way, the property page we're going to build will be the first one shown when the container displays the property pages for the MathProblem control. This is the typical behavior for an ActiveX control. Ensure your dialog looks like Fig. 8.10 and click the **Next** button.

The next dialog, shown in Fig. 8.11, allows us to assign our control's properties to the correct property pages. If you click on the Standard-Color and StandardFont tabs, you'll notice that the Wizard has already put certain properties on these pages and they cannot be removed. It was able to do this because it recognizes the property type. Any property that uses the **OLE_COLOR** data type will automatically be placed on the StandardColor page and properties using the **Font** data type will be placed on the StandardFont page. Additionally, any property using the **Picture** data type will automatically be placed on the Stan-

Figure 8.10
Property Page
Wizard, Page 1.

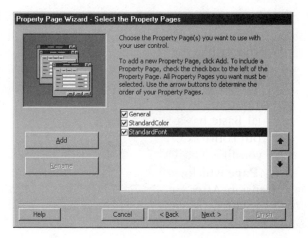

dardPicture property page. The properties that remain in the Available Properties list can be placed on the General property page. Do this by selecting the General tab and pressing the double-arrow right button. Curiously, the Property Page Wizard does not recognize properties that use user-defined data types. That's why the ProblemType property is not listed in the Available Properties list. We'll have to implement this property by hand. When you're finished with this dialog, click the **Next** button.

We're done. The last dialog allows you to view a summary report. Click the **Finish** button and you should see an additional file in the **Project Explorer** window for the General property page. Double-click on this object and you'll see the property page designer window with several controls already placed on it. The text for the label controls is taken directly from the property names so we'll need to do a little cleanup to make the page presentable. We also need to place a control for setting the ProblemType property. For that we'll use a Label control and a ComboBox control named cmbProblemType with a style of Dropdown List. The Wizard created Textbox controls for BorderStyle and BackStyle but we will want to use comboboxes with a style of Dropdown List instead. Put these controls on the property page and make the page look like the one shown in Fig. 8.12.

Figure 8.11
Property Page
Wizard, Page 2.

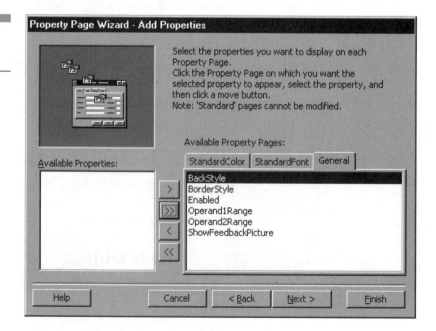

Figure 8.12
General Property
Page.

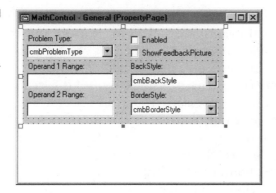

We'll write some custom code in a moment, but first let's just take a look at the code the Property Page Wizard generated for us.

If you right-click on the **General** object and select **View Code,** you will see the code window for the "General" property page. The Property Page Wizard, unlike the Interface Wizard, doesn't do a whole lot of work for us. The main benefit of using the Wizard is the creation of the Apply-Changes and SelectionChanged event code. For our control, this doesn't amount to a whole lot, but for bigger projects the generated code could be substantial:

```
Private Sub PropertyPage_ApplyChanges()
   SelectedControls(0).ShowFeedbackPicture = (chkShowFeedbackPicture.Value = vbChecked)
   SelectedControls(0).Operand2Range = txtOperand2Range.Text
   SelectedControls(0).Operand1Range = txtOperand1Range.Text
   SelectedControls(0).Enabled = (chkEnabled.Value = vbChecked)
   SelectedControls(0).BorderStyle = txtBorderStyle.Text
   SelectedControls(0).BackStyle = txtBackStyle.Text
End Sub

Private Sub PropertyPage_SelectionChanged()
   chkShowFeedbackPicture.Value = (SelectedControls(0).ShowFeedbackPicture And_
               vbChecked)
   txtOperand2Range.Text = SelectedControls(0).Operand2Range
   txtOperand1Range.Text = SelectedControls(0).Operand1Range
   chkEnabled.Value = (SelectedControls(0).Enabled And vbChecked)
   txtBorderStyle.Text = SelectedControls(0).BorderStyle
   txtBackStyle.Text = SelectedControls(0).BackStyle
End Sub
```

The SelectedControls Object

The ApplyChanges event is fired by the container whenever the user presses the **OK** or **Apply** buttons on the property page container *and* at least one property has changed. Notice the use of the SelectedControls object that is used to access the properties for our control. The Selected-Controls object is a collection of all the controls currently selected by the developer. Certain containers, including Visual Basic, show only a control's property page when a single control is selected. An index of zero is being used with the SelectedControls object in the ApplyChanges event code since only one control can exist in the SelectedControls collection. If the container does show property pages when more than one control is selected, you would need to iterate over the collection and set the properties accordingly. When doing this, you'll need to use appropriate error handling routines to protect yourself from attempting to set a property that the control does not support.

The SelectionChanged event is fired by the container each time the property page is displayed for the control and this event is used to initialize the controls with the current property values. Again, we're using the SelectedControls object to gather the values to be displayed on the property page. The SelectionChanged event is also called when the number of selected controls changes but, since Visual Basic only displays property pages when individual controls are selected, this will never happen with our test project.

The rest of the code generated by the Wizard is very rudimentary. It simply sets the Changed property whenever a property page setting has changed. The Changed property is monitored by the container so that it can enable the Apply button when necessary and, of course, it uses this property to determine whether to fire the ApplyChanges event.

Now let's add some custom code to get the property page to work correctly. First, we'll populate the comboboxes with the appropriate choices in the Initialize event:

```
Private Sub PropertyPage_Initialize()
  ' Fill the ProblemType combo box
  cmbProblemType.AddItem "Addition"
  cmbProblemType.AddItem "Subtraction"
  cmbProblemType.AddItem "Multiplication"
  cmbProblemType.AddItem "Division"

  ' Fill the BackStyle combo box
  cmbBackStyle.AddItem "Opaque"
  cmbBackStyle.AddItem "Transparent"

  ' Fill the BorderStyle combo box
  cmbBorderStyle.AddItem "None"
```

```
    cmbBorderStyle.AddItem "Fixed Single"
End Sub
```

Make sure that the Sorted property is false for the combobox controls as we will be relying on the positional index of the items when converting the choices from strings to integers. The next thing to do is to remove the Change event procedures for the Textbox controls that we replaced with ComboBox controls and code the Click event procedures for the new ComboBox controls. We use the click event since the Change event is never fired when the combobox style is Dropdown List:

```
Private Sub cmbProblemType_Click()
   Changed = True
End Sub
Private Sub cmbBackStyle_Click()
   Changed = True
End Sub
Private Sub cmbBorderStyle_Click()
   Changed = True
End Sub
```

The last thing to do is to modify the code in the ApplyChanges and SelectionChanged events:

```
Private Sub PropertyPage_ApplyChanges()
  ' Enforce that the operand ranges must be in the range 1-999
  If Val(txtOperand1Range) > 999 Or Val(txtOperand1Range) < 1 Then
    MsgBox "Invalid property value. Range value must be between 1 and 999.", _
    vbCritical
    Exit Sub
  End If
  If Val(txtOperand2Range) > 999 Or Val(txtOperand2Range) < 1 Then
    MsgBox "Invalid property value. Range value must be between 1 and 999.", _
       vbCritical
    Exit Sub
  End If

  SelectedControls(0).ShowFeedbackPicture = (chkShowFeedbackPicture.Value = vbChecked)
  SelectedControls(0).Operand2Range = txtOperand2Range.Text
  SelectedControls(0).Operand1Range = txtOperand1Range.Text
  SelectedControls(0).Enabled = (chkEnabled.Value = vbChecked)
  SelectedControls(0).BorderStyle = cmbBorderStyle.ListIndex
  SelectedControls(0).BackStyle = cmbBackStyle.ListIndex
  SelectedControls(0).ProblemType = cmbProblemType.ListIndex
End Sub

Private Sub PropertyPage_SelectionChanged()
    chkShowFeedbackPicture.Value = (SelectedControls(0).ShowFeedbackPicture And_
               vbChecked)
```

```
txtOperand2Range.Text = SelectedControls(0).Operand2Range
txtOperand1Range.Text = SelectedControls(0).Operand1Range
chkEnabled.Value = (SelectedControls(0).Enabled And vbChecked)
cmbBorderStyle.ListIndex = SelectedControls(0).BorderStyle
cmbBackStyle.ListIndex = SelectedControls(0).BackStyle
cmbProblemType.ListIndex = SelectedControls(0).ProblemType
End Sub
```

Here we are enforcing the legal range for the Operand range properties. If you like you can add code to allow numeric only characters in the text. The other modifications simply reference the new ComboBox controls instead of the original Textbox controls.

We now have a fully functional property page for our math control. We don't have to write any code at all for the properties that appear on the StandardFont and StandardColor pages. The Property Page Wizard took care of all this for us. Go ahead and try it out by bringing up your test project form, right-click on the MathProblem control, and select **Properties.**

Adding an AboutBox

Most ActiveX controls support an AboutBox for themselves and Visual Basic makes it very easy to implement one. Select the **MathControl** project in the **Project Explorer** window. Click the **Project** menu and select **Add Form.** In the **Project Explorer** window, double-click the new Form that has been added to the MathControl project to bring up the designer window for the form. Name the form frmAboutBox (the name is not unique; you could name it anything you like) and make it look like the dialog shown if Fig. 8.13.

Be sure to place code in the Click event of the AboutBox OK button that will unload the form. Now that we have built the AboutBox, we need to add a procedure in the MathControl code to display it:

```
Public Sub ShowAboutBox()
  frmAboutBox.Show vbModal
```

Figure 8.13
MathControl
AboutBox Dialog.

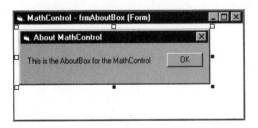

```
    set frmAboutBox = Nothing
End Sub
```

Again, the name of the procedure is not unique. Now all we have to do is figure out a way to notify the parent container that this control supports an AboutBox window. Visual Basic supports the concept of procedure IDs for just this situation. A procedure ID, also called a DISPID, is an identification number that is attached to every property or method that is written to an ActiveX control's type library. In general, Visual Basic assigns a unique procedure ID to each property or method without your doing any work at all. For certain procedures, however, you will want to assign a predefined procedure ID to a procedure in order to communicate to a control container that the procedure performs some well-defined function.

For example, when an ActiveX control is placed on a Visual Basic form, the control's type library is checked to see if the procedure ID "AboutBox" has been defined for the control. If the procedure ID is found, Visual Basic will add the AboutBox property to the control's property browser window and the control method referenced by the procedure ID will be called when the "AboutBox" property is queried. This cross-referencing of procedure IDs and procedure names gives you, the control developer, the flexibility to name procedures any way you see fit. You simply assign the procedure IDs accordingly.

The Interface Wizard assigned several ProcedureIDs when it created the original code for our control. Procedures such as ForeColor and Enabled had the appropriate IDs assigned to them. To assign the About-Box procedureID to the ShowAboutBox method, bring up the **Procedure Attributes** dialog and select ShowAboutBox in the Name field. Click the **Advanced** button to see the entire dialog. Ensure that your dialog looks like the one shown in Fig. 8.14 and then press **OK.**

In addition to assigning the procedure ID, the option "Hide this member" has been selected because we don't want this method to show up in VB's object browser.

That was simple. The last thing we have to do to finish up the control is provide an appropriate Toolbox icon.

Adding a Toolbox Icon

Now we're in the home stretch and this part is really easy. Simply use your favorite image editor to create a toolbox bitmap that is 16 pixels wide

Figure 8.14
Procedure Attributes
for ShowAboutBox.

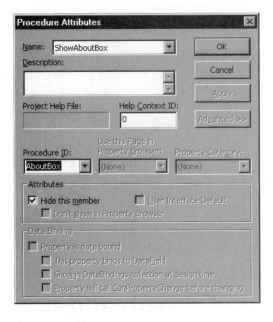

by 15 pixels high (the standard dimensions for toolbox icons.) After you have created the bitmap, bring up the property browser for the Math-Problem object. If you scroll down through the properties you'll find a property named ToolboxIcon. Simply set this property to the bitmap you've just created and you're done. Now you have a fully functioning ActiveX control created with Visual Basic.

Using the Control

Now that we've built this wonderful control, we ought to do something useful with it. In addition to the complete source code for the MathControl project that we have been developing in this chapter, you will also find a test project on the CD-ROM. This test project uses our MathProblem control to generate a 12-problem math test of varying difficulty. Figure 8.15 shows the entry screen you will see when you run the MathTest application.

After you've customized the test, press the "Create Test" button to take the test. Figure 8.16 shows a sample test that can be generated.

As you can see, this is a simple application, but if you examine the code it demonstrates the use of nearly all of the custom features of the Math-

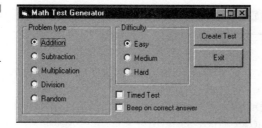

Problem control. You can do some fun things with this application to make it more fun for the kids—such as recording goofy .wav files that can be played when correct or incorrect answers are entered. Kids are easily entertained.

ActiveX Controls and the Web

Now that we have finished building the Math control, we need to do some work so that it can be used on HTML pages. First we will discuss some Internet features that are available to the control designer via the Visual Basic language. Then we will discuss CAB files and how they are used by Internet aware containers when they display pages that contain ActiveX controls.

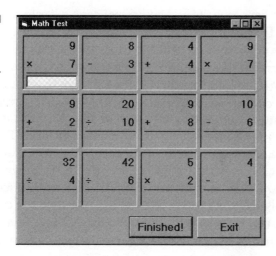

Asynchronous Downloading and the Hyperlink Object

Visual Basic provides a method and event pair, `AsyncRead` and `Async-ReadComplete`, that can allow your ActiveX control to asynchronously download property values. In other words, when a user sets a control property, rather than assigning the new value to the appropriate class member variable, you simply use the `AsyncRead` method to begin a process that will execute in the background so that the property procedure can return immediately. When the property has eventually been completely received, the `AsyncReadComplete` event is fired to notify the control that the download is complete. At this point, you can use the `AsyncProperty` object to retrieve the loaded property value and apply it to the control. The ability to download property values asynchronously is handy when the control is receiving potentially large amounts of information through a property such as a bitmap. Your control could display a temporary picture until the entire bitmap data has been retrieved.

The Hyperlink object, available via the `UserControl` Hyperlink property, allows an ActiveX control to request its hyperlink-aware parent container to navigate to a specified URL. The Hyperlink object contains the methods `NavigateTo`, `GoForward`, and `GoBack`. Be sure to use error-handling code when using these methods, as errors will be raised when the URL is invalid or when there are no URLs in the container's history list.

The Visual Basic Setup Wizard

You don't have to write any additional code to make your ActiveX control work on HTML pages. You do, however, have to create a special Internet distribution package for your control called a cabinet file or CAB file for short. A CAB file is a compressed file that contains your control's compiled .OCX file as well as any other dependent files that your control must have installed in order for it to work properly. The CAB file also contains information concerning the "safety" level of the .OCX file. A control's CAB file is accessed by a browser whenever it loads an HTML page that contains the ActiveX control. The browser then determines which, if any, of the compressed files within the CAB file need to be downloaded to the local workstation. This way, the workstation will have to suffer only through the potentially lengthy download time the first time the control is seen. After that, loading HTML pages containing the ActiveX control will be very fast because the necessary files already exist on the workstation.

Of course, Visual Basic does most of the work of creating a CAB file for you through the Application Setup Wizard (Fig. 8.17). The Setup Wizard can be used to create a setup program for your ActiveX control so that it can be easily installed on a development machine or it can be used to create CAB files for your ActiveX controls. After completing the Setup Wizard steps for creating a CAB file, five different file types will be created and these are described in Table 8.10.

One of the steps of the Setup Wizard allows you to specify the safety level of your control. You can select to mark your control as "Safe for Scripting" and "Safe for Initialization." What this basically means is that your control cannot be made to do damage to a user's computer when it is accessed on an HTML page. This is a wide-ranging statement, but as long as your control doesn't write to a file or the system registry using files or keys that are received via an HTML script your control is probably safe. Outside the scope of the Setup Wizard, you can choose to have your ActiveX control digitally signed. This is a method whereby you purchase a digital signature from a third-party certificate authority and attach the signature to your control. This establishes that you in fact created the control and thus gives any users recourse should there be a problem with the control. If you are seriously considering creating ActiveX controls for commercial distribution, digitally signing your controls is a must.

Figure 8.17
Setup Wizard.

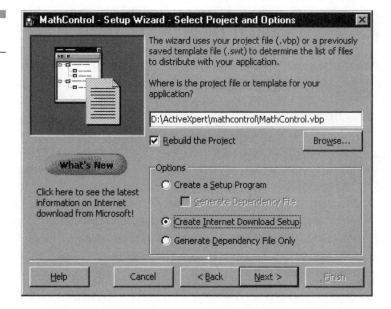

TABLE 8.10

Setup
Wizard–Generated
Files

Extension	Description
.cab	The cabinet file. It contains the .ocx file, the .inf file, and any other dependent files.
.inf	The setup information file. It tells the container how the files in the CAB file are to be installed.
.ocx	The compiled ActiveX control file in its uncompressed form.
.ddf	The Diamond Directives file. It is the project file for building the CAB file.
.htm	A sample HTML file that uses the ActiveX control.

Summary

We got through quite a bit of information in this chapter so let's go over some of the key points. Microsoft will make the Control Creation Edition of Visual Basic 5.0 freely available on the Web, finally making one of the most popular development environments available to ActiveX control developers. One of the key features in this edition is the ability to load multiple projects simultaneously, making debugging of controls quite easy.

The addition of two code generating Wizards—the ActiveX Interface Wizard and the Property Page Wizard—make development of ActiveX controls quick and painless. The ActiveX Interface Wizard allows you to choose which stock properties, methods, and events will be supported by your control. In addition, the Wizard allows you to create and customize your own control members as well. The Property Page Wizard, as its name implies, allows you to quickly generate custom property pages for your control.

The AmbientProperties object is available for examining the many ambient properties provided by the control container. The Ambient-Changed event is fired to alert the control when an ambient property has changed and thus the control's appearance can be made to be consistent with its parent. The Extender object is also available so that a control can query the container's extender properties—those control properties provided by the container such as Name and Visible. Both the Ambient-Properties object and the Extender object are not available in the control's Initialize event.

Public enumerations can be defined and used as property data types so that a container's inherent property browser can display the appropriate choices to the control user. Procedure IDs are assigned to certain control procedures to communicate to the control container that the procedure will act in some defined manor. Procedure IDs such as "AboutBox" make it possible for the container to know which procedure to invoke when the AboutBox property is queried from the control's property browser.

Cabinet, or CAB, files are used by HTML browsers for downloading ActiveX controls when they are accessed by an HTML page. A CAB file is a compressed file that contains the .OCX file as well as any files the ActiveX control needs to function properly on the workstation. A CAB file also contains information about the "safety" level of the ActiveX control. All ActiveX controls intended for commercial use on the Web should be digitally signed.

Active Scripting

Active Scripting is a technology that Microsoft released with the ActiveX SDK in late 1996. At first, it was called ActiveX Scripting, but like almost everything else, the "X" was eventually dropped and became part of the Active Desktop and Active Server architectures. Active Scripting is a series of COM-based interfaces that allow applications to either implement or access basic scripting capabilities. Script languages have two basic characteristics: they are interpreted and use a very high-level syntax (i.e., simple statements that encapsulate a lot of functionality). An example of a script-type language is Visual Basic.

Like most COM-based technologies, Microsoft has not only defined the standard Active Script interfaces, but has also provided a basic implementation. A complete implementation of an Active Script engine is shipped with Internet Explorer. The engine provides scripting support for VBScript and JScript languages. Internet Explorer uses the Active Script engine to provide its support for VBScript and JScript. However, other applications can use the basic scripting engines as well, and that's what we are covering in this chapter.

Active Script Engines

Active Scripting is comprised of two basic pieces: an Active Script engine and an Active Script host. The engine actually implements the scripting functionality through support for parsing and execution of the script language (e.g., VBScript). The Active Script specification requires the script engine to implement two or three COM-based interfaces. Developers can develop an engine based on these standard interfaces and they can be "plugged in" to applications that support Active Scripting, thus providing an extensible scripting architecture.

However, as mentioned earlier, Microsoft provides a fully functional engine that developers can use for free in their applications. It currently ships with Internet Explorer and provides support for the two languages we covered in Chapter 4: VBScript and JavaScript. To use this free functionality, though, you have to become an Active Script host.

Active Script Hosts

An Active Script host accesses the functionality of an Active Script engine by implementing and using a number of COM-based interfaces. Internet Explorer was the first Active Script host, providing its internal script support by acting as an Active Script host. What does it mean to be an Active Script host and what functionality does it provide? That's mostly what we discuss in this chapter.

Why Should I Care?

Good question. Every time I go off on one of my rants explaining how cool Active Scripting is, I get blank stares from my fellow developers. They are basically saying, "Tom, who cares?" and "What can we use it for?" The power of what Microsoft has provided with Active Scripting isn't evident at first glance, but with a little thought (and a demonstration) it becomes clear. Shortly after they've actually implemented and used the technology, they're singing a different tune. Something more like: "Active Scripting is neat."

Microsoft has basically given us a free license to integrate a subset of the Visual Basic language into our own applications. Microsoft's Office 97 applications all use Visual Basic for Applications (VBA) as a macro language. Now, with a few lines of code your editor, email package, or even your simulation game can use VBScript or JavaScript as your very own application macro language.

An Application Object Model

Before we get into the details of using Active Scripting, let's take a quick look at what we're trying to achieve. As we discussed in Chapter 4, VBScript is a subset of both Visual Basic and Visual Basic for Applications because it does not supply all of their syntactic features. However, this isn't necessarily a problem, because with Active Script we can add our own functionality to the language.

VBScript by itself provides only basic language parsing and evaluation. This basic capability allows you to perform simple operations like this:

```
sum = 1 + 2 + 3
MsgBox "Hi There"
```

This is nice, but a scripting language for an application needs to do more. To do more, the scripting language must operate on application-specific data and functionality. In other words, your application must expose an object model to the script. For example, Microsoft Excel exposes a rich object model through VBA. You can do things like this in Excel:

```
' Place the value 100 into the active cell
ActiveCell.FormulaR1C1 = "100"
' Select and copy it to the clipboard
Range("A1").Select
Selection.Copy
' Select a range of cells and paste the value
Range("B1:D17").Select
ActiveSheet.Paste
```

What makes scripting so powerful is that an application's functionality can be accessed programmatically. The trick to doing this, though, is to build and expose an Automation-based object model. In our Excel example, the application's object model is a series of hierarchical objects that represent user-level items—items such as spreadsheets, worksheets, cells, ranges, and so on. To effectively support Active Scripting in your application, it must expose an object model just as Excel and other Automation-enabled applications do.

Automation and IDispatch

Programmatic access to an application is provided by implementing an IDispatch interface for your application. Actually, most applications will wrap every important "object" with Automation. Just as we did in Chapters 6 and 7, Automation servers and ActiveX controls expose their capabilities through an implementation of the IDispatch interface. A typical application will wrap and expose a number of "objects." The application's object model is then described by the relationships of these objects.

Basic Scripting Architecture

In this section we discuss the basic architecture of Active Scripting with particular emphasis on what is required to act as an Active Script host. Hosting support is provided by implementing the IActiveScriptSite interface. Optionally, the host can implement the IActiveScript-SiteWindow as well.

An Active Script engine must implement IActiveScript and a script persistence interface, which can be one of the standard OLE persistence interfaces (IPersist*) or the new `IActiveScriptParse`. Figure 9.1 depicts the Active Script engine and host relationship.

Once the basic interfaces are implemented, the steps required to connect the Active Script engine to the host goes something like this:

Host/Engine Startup

■ The host application creates an instance of the script engine. The standard COM API, `CoCreateInstance`, is typically used.

■ The engine component is instantiated and an `IActiveScript` interface pointer is passed back to the host.

■ The host then passes a pointer to its implementation of `IActive-ScriptSite` by calling the `IActiveScript::SetScriptSite` method.

■ If the script has been persisted (say, to a *.BAS file), the host can load the script into the engine by querying for and calling through one of the `IPersist` interfaces. If the host is adding pieces of script code dynamically (à la Internet Explorer), then it should initialize the script engine by calling the `InitNew` method of `IActiveScript-Parse` before doing so. Once called, the host can add *scriptlets,* small pieces of script code via the `ParseScriptText` method.

■ At this point the host should load its object model into the engine. This is done by passing `IDispatch` interface pointers for each top-level object within the application. `IActiveScript::AddNamedItem` takes the textual name of the item and its associated `IDispatch`.

Figure 9.1
Active Script
Interfaces.

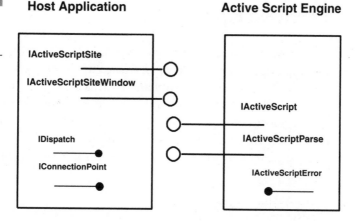

Host Application

IActiveScriptSite

IActiveScriptSiteWindow

IDispatch

IConnectionPoint

Active Script Engine

IActiveScript

IActiveScriptParse

IActiveScriptError

- Once everything is set up, the host will inform the engine that scripts can run by calling `IActiveScript::SetScriptState` with a state of SCRIPTSTATE_CONNECTED. Any script loaded into the engine will execute at this point.

- As the script executes, the engine will call through the host's site interface to get information about named items as they are encountered.

- If the host supports the scripting event model through the `IConnectionPoint` interface, the engine will attempt to establish an outgoing event interface. As events are fired within the script, the host's event dispatch will be invoked.

- Finally, as the script executes it will access the host functionality through its defined object model. In other words, as properties and methods are encountered in the script, the engine will use the `IDispatch` to access the functionality.

Active Script Engines

An Active Script engine is a COM-based component that supports two or three standard interfaces. `IActiveScript` is the primary Active Script interface that provides basic script support. The engine must also support a persistence interface. Either one of the standard OLE interfaces (`IPersist`) or the new `IActiveScriptParse` interface. The persistence interface provides a way to save and load a script into the engine.

IActiveScript

An Active Script engine must implement `IActiveScript`. The engine hosting application will then retrieve this interface to access the engine's capabilities. The engine implements this interface and the host application calls the interface methods to load and execute scripts. Table 9.1 provides a short description of each method. We discuss them in more detail later when we develop the example application.

To give you an idea of how everything gets started, here's some code from the example:

```
// Get the CLSID of the VBScript engine
hr = CLSIDFromProgID( A2W("VBScript"), &clsid );
```

```
if ( FAILED( hr))
{
    AfxMessageBox( "VBScript is not installed on your system!", MB_OK );
    return;
}

// Create new script engine and retrieve IActiveScript
hr = CoCreateInstance( clsid,
                       NULL,
                       CLSCTX_INPROC_SERVER,
                       IID_IActiveScript,
                       (void**) &m_pActiveScript );
```

This creates an instance of the Active Script engine component and returns a pointer to its `IActiveScript` interface implementation.

TABLE 9.1

IActiveScript
Methods

Method	Description
SetScriptSite	Called by the host to pass its `IActiveScriptSite` interface to the script engine.
GetScriptSite	Retrieves the `IActiveScriptSite` interface.
GetScriptState	Returns the current state of the script engine.
SetScriptState	Sets the current state of the engine. A number of different states are supported. SCRIPTSTATE_INITIALIZED SCRIPTSTATE_STARTED SCRIPTSTATE_CONNECTED SCRIPTSTATE_DISCONNECTED
Close	Shut down the script engine. This unloads any scripts and releases all interfaces.
AddNamedItem	Adds a top-level item to the engine's name space. The host uses this method to load its object model.
AddTypeLib	Adds a type library for a named item.
GetScriptDispatch	Returns an `IDispatch` for the actual running script. You can execute scriptlets directly through this dispatch.
GetCurrentScriptThreadID	Returns the thread ID of the currently executing thread.
GetScriptThreadID	Returns the thread ID of the currently executing thread.
GetScriptThreadState	Returns the state of a specific thread.
InterruptScriptThread	Stops execution of a script thread.
Clone	Clones the current scripting engine.

Engine States

After creating an instance of the script engine, the host application will force transitions in the engine's state. The engine will internally transition from the initial states, but the host can control these states through the `IActiveScript::SetScriptState` method. The various states are described in Table 9.2.

To give you an idea of how the engine moves from the uninitialized to started states, here is some code from our forthcoming example. The steps below occur after the engine is created with `CoCreateInstance`. We haven't discussed all of the constructs shown below, but I want you to get a view of the flow:

```
// Pass our host interface to the engine
hr = m_pActiveScript->SetScriptSite( &m_xActiveScriptSite );

// Query for the engine's persistence interface
IActiveScriptParse* pParse;
hr = m_pActiveScript->QueryInterface( IID_IActiveScriptParse,
                                      (void**) &pParse);

// Initialize the parser. This should only be called once.
hr = pParse->InitNew();

// Release the interface
pParse->Release();

// Start up the script engine
hr = m_pActiveScript->SetScriptState( SCRIPTSTATE_STARTED );
```

IPersistStreamInit

An Active Script engine must support one of the standard OLE persistence interfaces (e.g., `IPersistStorage` or `IPersistStream`) or the new `IActiveScriptParse` interface that we describe next.

An engine supports a persistence mechanism to allow script code to be loaded and executed. COM's `CoCreateInstance` API creates an instance of a *type* of object. Specific component instances are handled through OLE's `IPersist` interfaces. So, an engine can implement one of these interfaces to allow a host to persist its scripts. In other words, the host can then manage script files like Visual Basic's .FRM, .BAS, and .CLS files.

An Active Script engine does not have to support persistence through one of the `IPersist` interfaces, and Microsoft's current VBScript and JScript engines do not. However, if the engine does not, it must support the `IActiveScriptParse` interface. `IActiveScriptParse` provides a way to

	State	Description
TABLE 9.2 *Script Engine States*	Uninitialized	The engine has been created, but its state has not been initialized.
	Initialized	The engine has been initialized. Initialization is completed by initializing the engines persistent state through one of the persist interfaces (e.g., IActiveScriptParse::InitNew), and by setting the host's script site. If script is passed to the engine while in this state, it is queued.
	Started	As the engine transitions to this state, any code loaded in the initialize step will execute. However, Automation objects added through AddNamedItem will not have their outgoing event sinks set up until transition to the next state. The host forces the transition to the started state by calling SetScriptState(SCRIPTSTATE_STARTED).
	Connected	The engine will set up event sinks for any host-defined Automation objects. At this point the engine is completely ready.
	Disconnected	By setting the state to disconnected, the host forces the engine to disconnect any event sinks within the host. However, the script is still loaded. Setting the state back to connected reestablishes the event connections.
	Closed	All interfaces are released and any script is unloaded. The script engine should be closed before exiting a host application.

load scripts at run-time. In other words, any persistence is provided directly by the host.

IActiveScriptParse

An Active Script engine implements IActiveScriptParse to provide a way for the host application to dynamically load raw script code into the engine. Not all hosts can provide a rich script development environment that supports the previously described IPersist interfaces. An example of such a host is Internet Explorer. As Internet Explorer loads a Web page, it identifies the scriptlets via the HTML SCRIPT tag. The scripts are passed to the Active Script engine via the IActiveScriptParse interface. After the script is loaded into the engine, it is executed. In this environment, there isn't an explicit need for engine-based persistence. (See Table 9.3.)

IActiveScriptError

Certain errors encountered when parsing and executing will generate a call through the host's IActiveScriptSite::OnScriptError

TABLE 9.3

IActiveScriptParse
Methods

Method	Description
InitNew	InitNew is called to initialize the engine. It should be called only once.
AddScriptlet	Adds a piece of script code to the engine's code space.
ParseScriptText	How are these different?

method. One of the parameters to this method is an object that implements the `IActiveScriptError` interface. The host can then retrieve verbose error information to use internally or to display to the user. Table 9.4 provides an overview of the `IActiveScriptError` methods. We describe using it in the example.

Component Categories

Active Script engines should indicate what interfaces it supports by registering the appropriate component categories. Engines that support `IActiveScript` and one of the standard OLE persistence interfaces (e.g., `IPersistStreamInit`) should register the CATID_ActiveScript category. If an engine supports both `IActiveScript` and `IActiveScriptParse` it should register the CATID_ActiveScriptParse category. The two engines provided with Internet Explorer are shown in Fig. 9.2.

Active Script Hosts

To add scripting capabilities to our application, we have to become an Active Script host, which, as always, means we need to implement one or more COM-based interfaces—in particular, `IActiveScriptSite` and

TABLE 9.4

IActiveScriptError
Methods

Method	Description
GetExceptionInfo	Retrieves an EXCEPINFO structure with detailed error information.
GetSourcePosition	Retrieves the location of the error within the source code.
GetSourceLineText	Retrieves the actual line of code where the error occurred.

■ ■ ■ ■
Figure 9.2
Script Engines in
OLEVIEW.

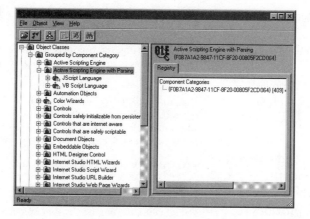

IActiveScriptSiteWindow. And, as we discussed earlier, our application also needs to expose an IDispatch-based object so that the script write has something to operate on.

IActiveScriptSite

The most important step in enabling an application to use Active Scripting internally is the implementation of the IActiveScriptSite interface. A pointer to the host's implementation of this interface is passed to the engine after it is created. Cooperation between the engine and host is then accomplished through the two major scripting interfaces: IActive-Script and IActiveScriptSite. IActiveScriptSite contains a number of methods that must be implemented. However, many of them can just return S_OK. Table 9.5 briefly describes each method. We go into more detail later as we implement each one.

IActiveScriptSiteWindow

The IActiveScriptSiteWindow interface should be implemented by hosts that provide a user interface. The primary purpose of this interface is to allow the engine to correctly pop up GUI elements during execution. One method returns a window handle that the engine can use as a parent window, and the other controls the state of the host's main window. This allows the engine to pop up modal windows. Table 9.6 describes these two methods.

Method	Description
GetDocVersionString	Returns a string that uniquely identifies the current host document. This is primarily for any engine-side persistence mechanism.
GetItemInfo	The host adds named item through `IActiveScript::AddNamedItem`. The engine can later call this method to obtain additional information about the item. Information such as the items `IUnknown` interface or type information.
GetLCID	Returns the locale ID of the host's user interface.
OnEnterScript	Called when the engine begins executing the script code.
OnLeaveScript	Called when the engine finishes executing the script code.
OnScriptError	Called whenever the engine encounters an error while executing the script code.
OnScriptTerminate	Called when the script has completely terminated.
OnStateChange	Called whenever the current state of the engine changes.

IDispatch

Active Scripting can't do much without an external set of objects. As we discussed earlier, the application itself needs to expose an Automation-based set of components that can be accessed within the script code. The script engine allows you to add these items to its global name space through the `AddNamedItem` method. Here's an example:

```
m_pActiveScript->AddNamedItem( OLESTR("POLY"),
                               SCRIPTITEM_ISSOURCE |
                               SCRIPTITEM_ISVISIBLE |
                               SCRIPTITEM_ISPERSISTENT |
                               SCRIPTITEM_GLOBALMEMBERS );
```

This informs the engine that it may encounter an object with the name "POLY." The host application also implements, on its `IActive-`

Method	Description
EnableModeless	Tells the host to enable or disable modeless operation.
GetWindow	Returns an HWND that will act as the parent of any of the engine's windows. This is typically the main host application window.

ScriptSite interface, a method through which the engine can obtain additional information about the item, something like this:

```
HRESULT CScriptDlg::XActiveScriptSite::GetItemInfo( LPCOLESTR pstrName,
                                                    DWORD dwMask,
                                                    LPUNKNOWN* ppunkItem,
                                                    LPTYPEINFO* ppTypeInfo )
{
...

   IUnknown* pUnknown = 0;
   CString strItemName( pstrName );
   if ( strItemName.CompareNoCase( "POLY" ) == 0 )
   {
       pUnknown = pThis->m_PolyCtl.GetControlUnknown();
       pUnknown->AddRef();
   }
...
}
```

The engines calls the `IActiveScriptSite::GetItemInfo` method to get the "POLY" object's `IUnknown` interface (through which it can query for `IDispatch`) and other information such as the object's type library. This allows script code like the following to be written:

```
Sub Test( x )
   POLY.Sides = x
   POLY.FillColor = &HFF0000
End Sub

' Call our procedure
Test( 3 )
```

The POLY object is part of our application's object model. It exposes properties, methods, and events, and as you can see, Active Scripting allows you to treat your application objects as if they are part of the language.

IConnectionPoint (Events)

Automation objects support properties and methods through the `IDispatch` interface. Automation objects can also support the concept of an "event." Events provide a basic callback—or asynchronous notification—mechanism. COM implements events using its Connectable Object specification that we discussed back in Chapter 7.

The Active Script host application does not necessarily have to support the `IConnectionPoint` interfaces itself. Only those objects that need to expose an event set need to. Also, the engine provides basic event support.

As named items are added to the engine's name space, the `ICon-nectionPointContainer` interface is queried for, and the event sink is established. This all occurs as the engine transitions to the SCRIPT-STATE_CONNECTED state.

The syntax for coding events in your script follows the form *Object-Name_EventName*. So if our POLY object supports a *ClickIn* event, you add code to the event like this:

```
Sub POLY_ClickIn( x, y )
    msg = "x = " & x & " y = "  & y
    MsgBox msg
End Sub
```

Okay, enough talk about the basics; let's get to some real coding.

An Example Application

The rest of this chapter deals with the development of a simple application that acts as an Active Script host. It is written in C++ and uses MFC. The application is basically a dialog with an embedded ActiveX control, a multiline edit box, and an execute button. Figure 9.3 shows the completed application.

The example uses the POLYGON ActiveX control. This control is provided as part of Visual C++ in the ATL samples directory. The POLYGON control is simple, but provides what we need to understand Active Scripting. Before starting the project, be sure to build the POLYGON control example.

Figure 9.3
Our Script
Application.

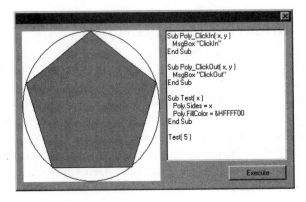

The embedded control comprises our applications object model. By entering script in the edit box and pressing the **Execute** button, we will affect the appearance and behavior of the control. The example demonstrates what is required for your application to act as a Active Script host. The example uses the VBScript engine (VBSCRIPT.DLL). However, by changing one line of code, it can use the JavaScript engine (JSCRIPT.DLL) instead.

Creating the Project

To create the initial project, start up Visual C++ and choose **File/New.** Then, from the **New** dialog, select the **Projects** tab. Select the **MFC App-Wizard (EXE)** project type, enter a project name of "**Script**". This step is shown in Fig. 9.4.

Click the **OK** button and use the settings below as you step through the AppWizard dialogs.

- ■ MFC AppWizard Step 1 of 4—Select **Dialog based** application.
- ■ MFC AppWizard Step 2 of 4
  —Select **3D controls** and **ActiveX Controls** support. The defaults.
  —Change the **Dialog title** to "Active Script Application."
- ■ MFC AppWizard Step 3 of 4—The default of **Shared DLL** is fine.
- ■ MFC AppWizard Step 4 of 4—Use the default names.

Finally, press the **Finish** button and the **New Project Information** dialog should be very similar to Fig. 9.5.

Figure 9.4
New Project Screen.

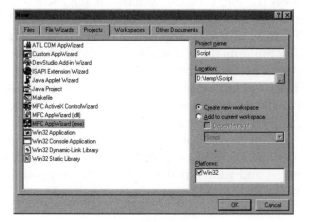

Figure 9.5
Project Settings.

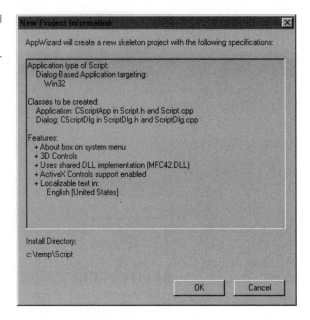

New Project Information

AppWizard will create a new skeleton project with the following specifications:

Application type of Script:
    Dialog-Based Application targeting:
        Win32

Classes to be created:
    Application: CScriptApp in Script.h and Script.cpp
    Dialog: CScriptDlg in ScriptDlg.h and ScriptDlg.cpp

Features:
    + About box on system menu
    + 3D Controls
    + Uses shared DLL implementation (MFC42.DLL)
    + ActiveX Controls support enabled
    + Localizable text in:
        English [United States]

Install Directory:
c:\temp\Script

OK   Cancel

Building the Dialog

Before we add any code, let's build the main dialog. First, make the dialog a bit larger, and remove the **OK** and **Cancel** buttons. Then, add the POLYGON control to the dialog by right-clicking on the resource editor. Select **Insert ActiveX Control...** and choose the "PolyCtl Class." Give the control an ID of IDC_POLYCTL. Next, add a multiline entry field to the right of the control. Set the ES_MULTILINE and ES_WANTRETURN styles on the entry field and name it IDC_SCRIPT. Finally, add a push button with a caption of "**Execute**" and an ID of IDC_EXECUTE. When you're finished, you should have something resembling Fig. 9.6.

After building the dialog, we next need to map the controls to member variables within our `CDialog`-derived class. Using ClassWizard, go to the **Member Variables** tab and add variables for the POLYGON control, call it **m_PolyCtl**; and the multiline entry field, call it **m_Script**. When you try to add a member variable for the POLYGON control, you will get a dialog asking if you would like a C++ wrapper class generated for the control. Choose **OK** and two files: POLYCTL.H and POLYCTL.CPP will be generated and added to the project. The finished ClassWizard dialog is shown in Fig. 9.7.

Figure 9.6
The Application's
Dialog.

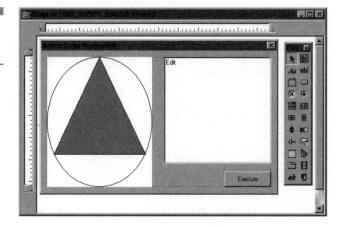

Implementing IActiveScriptSite

Implementing the `IActiveScriptSite` interface is the primary requirement for making an application an Active Script host, and so that's what we're going to focus on first. However, the default MFC implementation does not include the main Active Scripting header file: ACTIVSCP.H. The ACTIVESCP header file contains the definitions of the Active Script interfaces and data structures. We need it in our main dialog class, `CScriptDlg`, so add it to SCRIPTDLG.H like this:

Figure 9.7
ClassWizard Member
Variables.

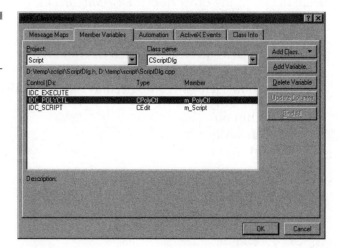

```
//
// ScriptDlg.h : header file
//


// Active Script include
#include <Activscp.h>

//{{AFX_INCLUDES()
#include "polyctl.h"
//}}AFX_INCLUDES

#if !defined(AFX_SCRIPTDLG_H__7E5A8AE8_AAAC_11D0_A6DF_0000837E3100__INCLUDED_)
#define AFX_SCRIPTDLG_H__7E5A8AE8_AAAC_11D0_A6DF_0000837E3100__INCLUDED_

#if _MSC_VER >= 1000
#pragma once
#endif // _MSC_VER >= 1000
```

MFC's COM-based Interface Support

MFC provides basic COM support in classes that derive from CCmdTarget. All window classes derive from CCmdTarget so we have built-in support for the two most important COM interfaces: IUnknown and IClassFactory. In order to support IActiveScriptSite, we just need to add the interface to something MFC calls its *interface map*.

MFC uses C++ class nesting to support multiple COM interfaces (i.e., Vtables). A C++ class is nested inside the main class for every interface that is supported. However, this detail is hidden by the use of a number of MFC-specific macros. The technique is rather complicated and I've covered it in detail in one of my other books: *Designing and Using ActiveX Controls*.

Basically, we need to first declare an interface map using MFC's DECLARE_INTERFACE_MAP macro. Next, we will use MFC's INTER-FACE_PART macros to create a nested class for each interface that we implement. The macros use the standard COM macro STDMETHOD in their implementation. Here's what we need to add to SCRIPTDLG.H.

```
//
// ScriptDlg.h : header file
//

// Active Script include
#include <Activscp.h>
...
class CScriptDlg : public CDialog
{
...
    // ClassWizard generated virtual function overrides
    //{{AFX_VIRTUAL(CScriptDlg)
```

```
    protected:
    virtual void DoDataExchange(CDataExchange* pDX);
    //}}AFX_VIRTUAL
```

```
    //*** Active Script Implementation
    DECLARE_INTERFACE_MAP()

    BEGIN_INTERFACE_PART( ActiveScriptSite, IActiveScriptSite )
        STDMETHOD(GetLCID)( LCID* plcid );
        STDMETHOD(GetItemInfo)( LPCOLESTR pstrName,
                                DWORD dwMask,
                                LPUNKNOWN* ppunkItem,
                                LPTYPEINFO* ppTypeInfo );
        STDMETHOD(GetDocVersionString)( BSTR* pbstrVersion );
        STDMETHOD(OnScriptTerminate)( const VARIANT* pvarResult,
                                      const EXCEPINFO* pexcepinfo );
        STDMETHOD(OnStateChange)( SCRIPTSTATE State );
        STDMETHOD(OnScriptError)( IActiveScriptError* pError );
        STDMETHOD(OnEnterScript)();
        STDMETHOD(OnLeaveScript)();
    END_INTERFACE_PART( ActiveScriptSite )

    BEGIN_INTERFACE_PART( ActiveScriptSiteWindow, IActiveScriptSiteWindow )
        STDMETHOD(GetWindow)( HWND* phWnd );
        STDMETHOD(EnableModeless)( BOOL fEnable );
    END_INTERFACE_PART( ActiveScriptSiteWindow )
...
};
```

This code declares the two new interfaces that we will add to our dialog class. We also need to add a few macros to our SCRIPTDLG.CPP file. Here they are:

```
//
// ScriptDlg.cpp : implementation file
//

#include "stdafx.h"
#include "Script.h"
#include "ScriptDlg.h"

#ifdef _DEBUG
#define new DEBUG_NEW
#undef THIS_FILE
static char THIS_FILE[] = __FILE__;
#endif
```

```
// Unicode/ANSI conversion macros
#include <afxpriv.h>

// Added to support QI for our new interfaces
BEGIN_INTERFACE_MAP( CScriptDlg, CDialog )
    INTERFACE_PART( CScriptDlg, IID_IActiveScriptSite, ActiveScriptSite )
    INTERFACE_PART( CScriptDlg, IID_IActiveScriptSiteWindow, ActiveScriptSiteWindow )
END_INTERFACE_MAP()
...
```

The first few lines include the MFC's private Unicode/ANSI conversion macros. This file gives us several simple macros that allow us to go back and forth between ANSI and Unicode strings. You can read more about this topic in MFC Tech Note 59. The INTERFACE_MAP macros build a table of interface IDs that facilitate MFC's implementation of our applications `QueryInterface` method. What follows next is the step-by-step implementation of each `IActiveScriptSite` and `IActiveScriptSiteWindow` method.

The IUnknown Methods

MFC's macros hide the fact that there were declarations for the three `IUnknown` methods. However, we still have to implement them, though it's rather easy. The most important part is understanding what the METHOD_PROLOGUE macro does.

MFC's nested class idiom saves space by not requiring the implementing classes to maintain back pointers to the interface implementation classes. Instead, it uses the C `offsetof` operator to calculate the offset from the outer class implementation to the nested instance of the interface implementation. The METHOD_PROLOGUE macro uses the `offsetof` macro to calculate and assign an outer class pointer called **pThis.** You can then use this pointer to access data and methods in the nesting class. Complicated, yes, but it's easy if you forget about these details. Here are the implementation of the `IUnknown` methods for both of our new interfaces:

```
/////////////////////////////////////
// ActiveScriptSite implementation
/////////////////////////////////////
STDMETHODIMP_(ULONG) CScriptDlg::XActiveScriptSite::AddRef()
{
   METHOD_PROLOGUE( CScriptDlg, ActiveScriptSite )
   return pThis->ExternalAddRef();
}

STDMETHODIMP_(ULONG) CScriptDlg::XActiveScriptSite::Release()
{
   METHOD_PROLOGUE( CScriptDlg, ActiveScriptSite )
   return pThis->ExternalRelease();
}

STDMETHODIMP CScriptDlg::XActiveScriptSite::QueryInterface( REFIID iid, void** ppvObj )
{
   METHOD_PROLOGUE( CScriptDlg, ActiveScriptSite )
   return pThis->ExternalQueryInterface( &iid, ppvObj );
}
```

```
/////////////////////////////////////
// ActiveScriptSiteWindow implementation
/////////////////////////////////////
STDMETHODIMP_(ULONG) CScriptDlg::XActiveScriptSiteWindow::AddRef()
{
   METHOD_PROLOGUE( CScriptDlg, ActiveScriptSiteWindow )
   return pThis->ExternalRelease();
}

STDMETHODIMP_(ULONG) CScriptDlg::XActiveScriptSiteWindow::Release()
{
   METHOD_PROLOGUE( CScriptDlg, ActiveScriptSiteWindow )
   return pThis->ExternalRelease();
}

STDMETHODIMP CScriptDlg::XActiveScriptSiteWindow::QueryInterface( REFIID iid, void**
ppvObj )
{
   METHOD_PROLOGUE( CScriptDlg, ActiveScriptSiteWindow )
   return pThis->ExternalQueryInterface( &iid, ppvObj );
}
```

As you can tell, there's something else going on here. Because the implementing classes are nested, you have to use multiple C++ scoping operators to implement the methods. Also, we're calling MFC's `ExternalQueryInterface` method. MFC manages the details of reference counting through the nested class macros on these internal methods.

IActiveScriptSite:GetLCID

The `GetLCID` method should return the local identifier associated with the host's user interface. The engine will use this whenever it displays an interface element such as a message box. If you just want to use the local system default, you can return E_NOTIMPL, which is what we do.

```
STDMETHODIMP CScriptDlg::XActiveScriptSite::GetLCID( LCID* plcid )
{
   *plcid = 0;
   return E_NOTIMPL;
}
```

IActiveScriptSite:GetItemInfo

The `GetItemInfo` method is the longest and most complicated method to implement. It's also the most important. The `GetItemInfo` method is

called whenever the engine needs information about our application-specific objects. These objects are added through the `IActiveScript:`
`:AddNamedItem` method, which we haven't yet added to our example. In the next section, we will add an item named "POLY." The following code will return information about the "POLY" object.

The `GetItemInfo` method has four parameters. The first two are incoming parameters. They provide the name of the item and a mask value which specifies what information the engine needs. The mask basically specifies if the engine needs the item's `IUnknown` or `ITypeInfo` interfaces, or both. Take a look at it and then we'll discuss it.

```
STDMETHODIMP CScriptDlg::XActiveScriptSite::GetItemInfo( LPCOLESTR pstrName,
                                                         DWORD dwMask,
                                                         LPUNKNOWN* ppunkItem,
                                                         LPTYPEINFO* ppTypeInfo )
{
  METHOD_PROLOGUE( CScriptDlg, ActiveScriptSite )
  HRESULT hr;

  IUnknown* pUnknown = 0;
  CString strItemName( pstrName );
  if ( strItemName.CompareNoCase( _T("POLY")) == 0 )
     pUnknown = pThis->m_PolyCtl.GetControlUnknown();

  if ( pUnknown == 0 )
     return TYPE_E_ELEMENTNOTFOUND;
  else
     pUnknown->AddRef();
  // Support for ITypeInfo is important
  // if the object supports events
  ITypeInfo* pti = 0;
  if ( dwMask & SCRIPTINFO_ITYPEINFO )
  {
     IProvideClassInfo* ppci = 0;

     hr = pUnknown->QueryInterface(IID_IProvideClassInfo, (void**) &ppci);
     if ( SUCCEEDED( hr ))
     {
        hr = ppci->GetClassInfo( &pti );
       ppci->Release();
     }
     else
     {
        IDispatch* pDispatch;
        hr = pUnknown->QueryInterface( IID_IDispatch, (void**) &pDispatch );
        if ( SUCCEEDED( hr ))
        {
           hr = pDispatch->GetTypeInfo( 0, LOCALE_SYSTEM_DEFAULT, &pti );
           pDispatch->Release();
        }
     }

     if ( SUCCEEDED( hr ))
        *ppTypeInfo = pti;
```

```
        else
            *ppTypeInfo = 0;
    }

    if ( dwMask & SCRIPTINFO_IUNKNOWN )
        *ppunkItem = pUnknown;
    else
        pUnknown->Release();

    return S_OK;
}
```

The first thing we do is compare the incoming name with POLY. If it matches, we use the CWnd::GetControlUnknown method to retrieve our POLY control's IUnknown interface. We call AddRef through the returned interface because GetControlUnknown does not, and we will eventually pass this interface pointer to the engine. If we don't recognize the name, we indicate that the element was not found.

The second parameter contains a mask value that specifies what type of information is needed. We first check to see if the engine needs the object's type information. If the SCRIPTINFO_TYPEINFO bit is set, we try two different techniques of obtaining a pointer to the object's IType-Info interface. If the object supports the IProvideClassInfo interface (most controls do), we grab the interface and use its GetClassInfo method to get the ITypeInfo pointer. If the object doesn't support IProvideClassInfo (e.g., a simple Automation server), we see if the object has implemented the IDispatch::GetTypeInfo method. Finally, if one of these methods works, we assign the return interface to the return parameter, and if not, we set it to zero.

We then continue processing because the mask value may also indicate that the IUnknown value is required. If it is, we assign the value; if is not, we release the IUnknown pointer before returning.

IActiveScriptSite:GetDocVersionString

The GetDocVersionString method provides a way for the host to store a document version along with the script. This is useful only for engines that support persisting scripts. The default VBScript engine does not provide this capability. Even if it did, our application has only one document, so it isn't necessary. If the host doesn't support the notion of a document version, it should return E_NOTIMPL, which is what we do.

```
STDMETHODIMP CScriptDlg::XActiveScriptSite::GetDocVersionString( BSTR* pbstrVersion )
{
    return E_NOTIMPL;
}
```

IActiveScriptSite:OnScriptTerminate
IActiveScriptSite:OnStateChange
IActiveScriptSite:OnEnterScript
IActiveScriptSite:OnLeaveScript

These four methods provide the host with the ability to perform certain functions based on the state of the executing script. The method names pretty much explain what's going on. For our implementation, we just need to return S_OK.

```
STDMETHODIMP CScriptDlg::XActiveScriptSite::OnScriptTerminate( const VARIANT* varResult,
                                                               const EXCEPINFO* )
{
    return S_OK;
}

STDMETHODIMP CScriptDlg::XActiveScriptSite::OnStateChange( SCRIPTSTATE State )
{
    return S_OK;
}

STDMETHODIMP CScriptDlg::XActiveScriptSite::OnEnterScript()
{
    return S_OK;
}

STDMETHODIMP CScriptDlg::XActiveScriptSite::OnLeaveScript()
{
    return S_OK;
}
```

IActiveScriptSite:OnScriptError

The OnScriptError method is very useful. If the engine encounters an error while executing the script, this method is called. The engine passes a pointer to an object that implements the IActiveScriptError interface that we described earlier in this chapter. The object contains information about what exactly caused the script execution error. Here's our implementation:

```
STDMETHODIMP CScriptDlg::XActiveScriptSite::OnScriptError( IActiveScriptError* pError )
{
    METHOD_PROLOGUE( CScriptDlg, ActiveScriptSite )

    DWORD dwCookie;
    long lChar;
    ULONG ulLineNo;
    BSTR bstrSource;
    EXCEPINFO ei;
```

```
    pError->GetSourcePosition( &dwCookie, &ulLineNo, &lChar );
    pError->GetSourceLineText( &bstrSource );
    pError->GetExceptionInfo( &ei );

    CString strMessage;
    strMessage.Format( "Script Error:\n %s at character %d\n in line: %s",
                    CString( ei.bstrDescription ),
                    lChar,
                    CString( bstrSource ));

    AfxMessageBox( strMessage, MB_OK );

    SysFreeString( bstrSource );
    SysFreeString( ei.bstrSource );
    SysFreeString( ei.bstrDescription );
    SysFreeString( ei.bstrHelpFile );

    return S_OK;
}
```

IActiveScriptError provides three methods that return specific error information. GetSourcePosition provides the line number and exact character position of the error; GetSourceLineText retrieves a BSTR containing the actual text of the offending source line; and GetExceptionInfo retrieves an Automation EXECPINFO structure, which contains even more detailed information.

```
typedef struct FARSTRUCT tagEXCEPINFO {
    unsigned short wCode;              // An error code describing the error.
    unsigned short wReserved;
    BSTR bstrSource;                   // Source of the exception.
    BSTR bstrDescription;              // Textual description of the error.
    BSTR bstrHelpFile;                 // Help file path.
    unsigned long dwHelpContext;       // Help context ID.
    void FAR* pvReserved;
    // Pointer to function that fills in Help and description info.
    HRESULT (STDAPICALLTYPE FAR* pfnDeferredFillIn)
            (struct tagEXCEPINFO FAR*);
    RETURN VALUE return value;         // A return value describing the error.
} EXCEPINFO, FAR* LPEXCEPINFO;
```

We gather up the most important information and display it to the user. When we're finished, we have to explicitly de-allocate any memory allocated by the engine. We use the COM SysFreeString to do this.

Well, that finishes the implementation of IActiveScriptSite. All that's left: two methods in IActiveScriptWindow.

Implementing IActiveScriptSiteWindow

Our host provides a standard Windows interface and so needs to provide an implementation of the IActiveScriptSiteWindow interface. The purpose of this interface is give the engine a parent HWND when it needs to pop up GUI elements during execution. The `GetWindow` method returns a window handle that the engine can use as a parent window, and `EnableModeless` controls the state of the host's main window. This allows the engine to pop up modal windows. Here's our implementation:

```
/////////////////////////////////////////
// ActiveScriptSiteWindow implementation
/////////////////////////////////////////
STDMETHODIMP_(ULONG) CScriptDlg::XActiveScriptSiteWindow::AddRef()
{
    METHOD_PROLOGUE( CScriptDlg, ActiveScriptSiteWindow )
    return pThis->ExternalRelease();
}


STDMETHODIMP_(ULONG) CScriptDlg::XActiveScriptSiteWindow::Release()
{
    METHOD_PROLOGUE( CScriptDlg, ActiveScriptSiteWindow )
    return pThis->ExternalRelease();
}

STDMETHODIMP CScriptDlg::XActiveScriptSiteWindow::QueryInterface( REFIID iid, void**
pvObj )
{
    METHOD_PROLOGUE( CScriptDlg, ActiveScriptSiteWindow )
    return pThis->ExternalQueryInterface( &iid, ppvObj );
}


STDMETHODIMP CScriptDlg::XActiveScriptSiteWindow::GetWindow( HWND* phWnd )
{
    METHOD_PROLOGUE( CScriptDlg, ActiveScriptSiteWindow )

    HWND hWnd = pThis->GetSafeHwnd();
    if ( hWnd == 0 )
        return E_FAIL;

    *phWnd = hWnd;
    return S_OK;
}

STDMETHODIMP CScriptDlg::XActiveScriptSiteWindow::EnableModeless( BOOL fEnable )
{
    METHOD_PROLOGUE( CScriptDlg, ActiveScriptSiteWindow )

    pThis->EnableWindow( fEnable );
    return S_OK;
}
```

We've already explored the implementation of the `IUnknown` support methods, and remember, every COM-based interface must implement these methods. The code for the `GetWindow` and `EnableModeless` methods is straightforward. We use the METHOD_PROLOGUE method to access the nesting, CDialog-derived class, and from there we call the appropriate MFC methods to retrieve the HWND and set the dialog's enabled state.

Creating an Instance of the Active Script Engine

At this point, the application should compile and run. However, it still won't do much. Next, we need to create an instance of the Active Script engine. Since we'll be using the script engine throughout the lifetime of our application, the best place to create it is when the dialog is first created via the WM_INITDIALOG message.

```
BOOL CScriptDlg::OnInitDialog()
{
   CDialog::OnInitDialog();
...
   // Set the icon for this dialog. The framework does this automatically
   //   when the application's main window is not a dialog
   SetIcon(m_hIcon, TRUE);      // Set big icon
   SetIcon(m_hIcon, FALSE);     // Set small icon

   //*** Active Script support
   m_pActiveScript = 0;
   InitializeEngine();

   return TRUE;  // return TRUE unless you set the focus to a control
}
```

As you can see, we need a member variable that will hold our IActiveScript pointer. Here's its declaration along with a declaration for the InitializeEngine method.

```
//
// ScriptDlg.h : header file
//
...
class CScriptDlg : public CDialog
{
...
   // ClassWizard generated virtual function overrides
   //{{AFX_VIRTUAL(CScriptDlg)
   protected:
      virtual void DoDataExchange(CDataExchange* pDX);
   //}}AFX_VIRTUAL

   //*** Active Script Implementation
public:
   void InitializeEngine();
protected:
   IActiveScript* m_pActiveScript;

   DECLARE_INTERFACE_MAP()
...
};
```

The `InitializeEngine` method does most of the work of creating an instance of the engine and setting its initial state. Let's go through it a piece at a time.

```
void CScriptDlg::InitializeEngine()
{
  USES_CONVERSION;
  HRESULT hr;
  CLSID clsid;

  // Get the CLSID of the VBScript engine
  hr = CLSIDFromProgID( A2W("VBScript"), &clsid );
  if ( FAILED( hr ))
  {
     AfxMessageBox( _T("VBScript is not installed on your system!"), MB_OK );
     return;
  }
```

The two Active Script engines provided by Microsoft can be located by their programmatic identifiers (or ProgIDs). The VBScript engine is identified with the string "VBScript" and the JScript engine with "JavaScript." So, if you want to convert the example to parse and execute JavaScript instead of VBScript, all you have to do is change the preceding lines to:

```
// Get the CLSID of the JScript engine
hr = CLSIDFromProgID( A2W("JavaScript"), &clsid );
if ( FAILED( hr ))
{
   AfxMessageBox( _T("JScript is not installed on your system!"), MB_OK );
   return;
}
```

The `CLSIDFromProgID` converts the ProgID into the engine's unique CLSID. Once we have that we can call COM's `CoCreateInstance` function to create an instance of the component. We also ask COM to return the `IActiveScript` interface from the engine instance.

```
hr = CoCreateInstance( clsid,
                       NULL,
                       CLSCTX_INPROC_SERVER,
                       IID_IActiveScript,
                       (void**) &m_pActiveScript );

if ( FAILED( hr ))
{
   AfxMessageBox( _T("Unable to initialize the VBScript engine."), MB_OK );
   return;
}
```

If all goes well, we pass a pointer to our `IActiveScriptSite` implementation, and then query for the `IActiveScriptParse` interface.

Where did `m_xActiveScriptSite` come from? Well, those MFC macros that we used to add the script interfaces to our class actually create embedded instances. `m_xActiveScriptState` is actually an instance of our `IActiveScriptSite` class embedded within `CScriptDlg`. If you bust apart the END_INTERFACE_PART macro, you'll find the declaration:

```
hr = m_pActiveScript->SetScriptSite( &m_xActiveScriptSite );

IActiveScriptParse* pParse;
hr = m_pActiveScript->QueryInterface( IID_IActiveScriptParse,
                                      (void**) &pParse);

if ( SUCCEEDED( hr ))
{
    // Initialize the parser. This should only be called once.
    hr = pParse->InitNew();

    // Add our named item
    m_pActiveScript->AddNamedItem( A2W("POLY"),
                SCRIPTITEM_ISSOURCE |
                SCRIPTITEM_ISVISIBLE |
                SCRIPTITEM_ISPERSISTENT |
                SCRIPTITEM_GLOBALMEMBERS );

    // Release the interface
    pParse->Release();
}
}
```

After we get the `IActiveScriptParse` interface, we call its `InitNew` method. These two steps—setting the script site and initializing the `IActiveScriptParse` component—move the engine from the uninitialized to the initialized state. Once the engine is initialized, we can add our named item.

This is an important step. The `AddNamedItem` method adds those user-defined objects that we will support through the `IActiveScriptSite::GetItemInfo` method. We've already coded that, and here is how we tell the engine the names of our application-specific objects. In our example, we have just utilized the POLYGON control that we added earlier. The `AddNamedItems` method takes the name of the object and a set of flags that tell the engine a little about the object. Table 9.7 details each of the possible flags.

We use the four flags that indicate to the engine that our object supports events, is directly visible to the script writer, that we would like the name to persist between engine state transitions, and that it should be treated as a global variable within the script.

We perform all of these steps only once, as the application is starting up.

Flag	Description
TABLE 9.7

AddNamedItem Flags | |
SCRIPTITEM_ISPERSISTENT	Setting this flag tells the engine to save the item if the script is persisted. It also indicates that in the case of a transition to the initialized state, the engine will maintain the item's name and type information. We set the flag for the latter case.
SCRIPTITEM_ISSOURCE	This flag indicates that the item being added supports events. Our control supports events so we set this flag.
SCRIPTITEM_ISVISIBLE	This flag indicates that the item's name is available from within the script. In other words, we can now use script syntax like this: POLY.Sides = 10
SCRIPTITEM_GLOBALMEMBERS	Indicates that the item is part of the global name space of the script engine. In certain cases, there may be naming conflicts with global members, and by setting this flag, the host is taking responsibility for their resolution.
SCRIPTITEM_CODEONLY	Indicates that the item represents code and not a specific object instance. The host has only a name for this object and no information available through GetItemInfo.
SCRIPTITEM_NOCODE	Indicates that the item is just a name that is being added to the engine's name space. There is no code associated with the item. By default, the engine will create a separate code module for each named item.

Loading and Executing the Script

Once we have the engine created and initialized, we can now execute scripts. Before we add code to do that, we need to use ClassWizard to add a handler for our **Execute** button. Start up ClassWizard, go to the **Message Maps** tab, select the IDC_EXECUTE **Object ID**, and add the handler. This is shown in Fig. 9.8. Finally, click the **Edit Code** button and add the following code.

Whenever the user of our application clicks the **Execute** button, we will pass the script code in the edit box to the script engine for execution. Again, we'll go through the OnExecute code step-by-step.

Figure 9.8
Adding the
OnExecute Handler.

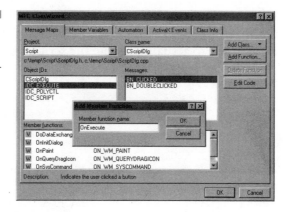

```
void CScriptDlg::OnExecute()
{
    USES_CONVERSION;
    HRESULT hr;

    // Start up the script engine
    hr = m_pActiveScript->SetScriptState( SCRIPTSTATE_STARTED );
    if ( FAILED( hr ))
    {
        AfxMessageBox( _T("Unable to start the scripting engine."), MB_OK );
        return;
    }

    // Allow the engine to make any event connections
    hr = m_pActiveScript->SetScriptState( SCRIPTSTATE_CONNECTED );
    if ( FAILED( hr ))
    {
        AfxMessageBox( _T("Unable to connect the scripting engine."), MB_OK );
        return;
    }
```

The first thing we do is transition the engine from the initialized to the started state. Any queued code will execute as the engine moves to the started state. However, scriptable objects that support outgoing events will not be able to fire the events until the engine connects their event sinks. The engine does this only when in the connected state. After starting the engine, we next transition it into the connected state. At this point the engine is ready to execute script code and handle events from the objects.

```
// Grab the script text from the edit box
CString strScript;
m_Script.GetWindowText( strScript );

IActiveScriptParse* pParse;
hr = m_pActiveScript->QueryInterface( IID_IActiveScriptParse,
                                      (void**) &pParse);
if ( FAILED( hr ))
{
    AfxMessageBox( _T("Engine does not support IActiveScriptParse"), MB_OK );
    return;
}
```

Next, we grab all of the text in the edit window. We then use Query-
Interface to get a pointer to the engine's IActiveScriptParse interface, which we'll use to actually execute the script.

```
EXCEPINFO ei;
hr = pParse->ParseScriptText( A2W( strScript ),
                              0,
                              0,
                              0,
                              0,
                              0,
                              SCRIPTTEXT_ISVISIBLE,
                              0,
                              &ei );

pParse->Release();
}
```

The ParseScriptText method parses the script, and either adds the
code to the engine's name space or immediately executes the code. Procedure code like the following isn't executed; instead it is added as a code
module to the engine's name space.

```
Sub Test( x )
   Poly.Sides = x
End Sub
```

This code is a procedure declaration. To execute the procedure, a script
must actually invoke the procedure, something like this:

```
Sub Test( x )
   Poly.Sides = x
End Sub

Test( 10 )
```

Passing this to ParseScriptText will set the number of sides in the
polygon to 10. The engine does this in two steps. First, the Test procedure
is parsed and added to its module definitions. Then as the engine parses the
Test(10) call, the module is called with a parameter of 10, and the
Poly.Sides statement is executed.

ParseScriptText takes a number of parameters, each of which is
detailed in Table 9.8. In our previous code, we're just filling out three. The
first is the script code itself, after being converted to Unicode. The seventh
parameter tells the engine that the script is visible and can be called, and
the ninth parameter is a standard Automation EXCEPINFO structure for
returning any error information.

TABLE 9.8

ParseScriptText
Parameters

Parameter	Description
LPCOLESTR *pstrCode*	The actual script code.
LPCOLESTR *pstrItemName*	A named item that describes the context in which the script should be executed. If this parameter is NULL, the script is evaluated in the global context.
IUnknown *punkContext*	This parameter is reserved for provision of a debugging context. Should be NULL, until debugging is documented.
LPCOLESTR *pstrEndDelimiter*	A character that delimits the end of the script. If NULL, the host has not delimited the script.
DWORD dwSourceContextCookie	A cookie that will describe the context of the script.
ULONG ulStartingLineNumber	The starting line number to use for this script.
DWORD *dwFlags*	Flags associated with the scriptlet. One or more of the following: SCRIPTTEXT_ISEXPRESSION—The statement should executed as an expression. The default is to interpret script's as a series of statements. SCRIPTTEXT_ISPERSISTENT—For those engines that can persist scripts, this flag indicates that the specific script should be persisted. SCRIPTTEXT_ISVISIBLE—The script should be visible and callable by name as a global method.
VARIANT *pvarResult*	If the script is an expression, this parameter will return the result of the evaluation. If the ISEXPRESSION flag is not set, this should be NULL.
EXCEPINFO *pexcepinfo*	The address of a standard Automation exception information structure for returning any errors.

When we're finished with the `IActiveScriptParse` interface pointer, we release it.

Shutting Down

That's it. All that is left is to shut down the engine correctly. Our application keeps the engine instance around throughout its lifetime, so we just need to close the engine and release our `IActiveScript` interface pointer as the application shuts down.

One of the last messages a dialog window receives is WM_DESTROY. Add a handler for this message using ClassWizard, and add the following code:

```
void CScriptDlg::OnDestroy()
{
    // Clean up and release the script engine
    if ( m_pActiveScript )
    {
        m_pActiveScript->Close();
        m_pActiveScript->Release();
    }

    CDialog::OnDestroy();
}
```

Building and Testing the Application

After typing in all of the preceding code (or you've loaded the example from the CD-ROM), build it, and finally, start it up. The next two sections give you some simple scripts to exercise our new scriptable application.

Simple Scripts

Our POLY object doesn't do a lot. It has two properties and two events. Our first script is shown as follows:

```
Poly.Sides = 6
Poly.FillColor = &HFFFFFF
```

Type in this code and press the **Execute** button. What happens? The polygon in our control should redraw with six sides and its color should be white. Our POLY object is a global object, so the engine knows what POLY is and executes the code. VBScript has a number of global objects that are built in. Functions like InputBox, MsgBox, and Trim, standard operators, statements, and so on. By using the VBScript engine, we can use all of this functionality in our application. So you can do things like this:

```
x = InputBox( "Enter the number of sides:")
Poly.Sides = x
MsgBox "The polygon should now have " & x & " sides"
MsgBox "Today's date is " & Date
```

Pretty cool, huh? We're using VBScript as a macro language for our application! Everything VBScript can do we can now do. All the statements work too.

```
For i = 3 to 10
  Poly.Sides = i
  MsgBox "The polygon should have " & i & " sides"
Next
```

All of the previous examples demonstrate immediate execution of code that uses global objects. You can also declare your own functions and procedures like this:

```
Function Sum( x, y )
  Sum = x + y
End Function

Sub SetPolySides( Sides )
   Poly.Sides = Sides
End Sub

MsgBox "Answer is " & Sum( 10, 77 )
SetPolySides( 5 )
```

Declaring a function or procedure places it into the engine's global name space. You can then call the function or procedure later, as the example demonstrates. If you type something incorrect when you try this example, you should get something like Fig. 9.9. We get such useful

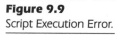

Figure 9.9
Script Execution Error.

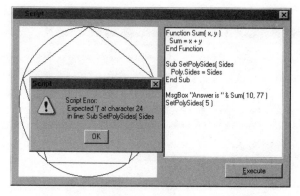

information because of our implementation of the `IActiveScript-Site::OnScriptError` method.

Handling events adds another dimension to what you can do.

Handling Events

Writing script code to handle events from your application's objects is just a matter of syntax. The engine maps an event to an object by looking for a procedure name of the form: *ObjectName_EventName*. So, our POLY control object fires two events: *ClickIn* and *ClickOut*. Both of the events return two parameters, the *x* and *y* coordinates of the mouse. To write some script that executes when the event fires, you do something like this:

```
Sub Poly_ClickIn( x, y )
   MsgBox "ClickIn Fired! x = " & x & " y = " & y
End Sub

Sub Poly_ClickOut( x, y )
   MsgBox "ClickOut Fired! x = " & x & " y = " & y
End Sub
```

Clicking within and outside the polygon will bring up one of the message boxes; you should see something resembling Fig. 9.10.

Licensing VBScript

Licensing VBScript and JScript for use in your application is easy and it doesn't cost anything. All you have to do is acknowledge Microsoft in

Figure 9.10
Handling Object
Events.

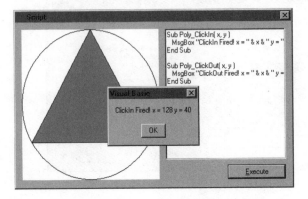

Figure 9.11
Our Application's
About Box.

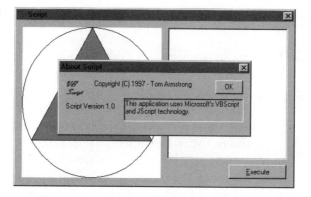

your application's about box. Fair enough. The final step in building our sample application is to add some text to the About Box. Figure 9.11 shows what the one on the CD-ROM says.

Extending a Scripting Engine's Capabilities

An Active Script engine, such as the VBScript one that we've focused on in this chapter, can be enhanced by adding application-specific objects. Script engines can also be enhanced to provide general capabilities that they may not intrinsically support. For example, for security reasons, VBScript does not support the Visual Basic `CreateObject` function, but with a little work, we can add this capability (and just about anything else) to VBScript.

All that is required is to add an object to your application that represents system-level functionality. For example, to add a method that would allow the creation of Automation objects within your scripts, you could add an object called SYSTEM. The system object could be implemented directly within your application or you could write a simple ActiveX control that provided the functionality. You would then dynamically create an instance of the control and add it to the engine's name space through `IActiveScript::AddNamedItem`. Once done, your application's script language could do something like this:

```
AutoServer = SYSTEM.CreateObject( "Automation.Server" )
```

If the scripting language doesn't have something that you need, you can add just about anything using this technique.

Summary

Active Scripting is a series of COM-based interfaces that allow applications to either implement or access basic scripting capabilities. Script languages have two basic characteristics: they are interpreted and use a very high-level syntax (i.e., simple statements that encapsulate a lot of functionality). An example of a script-type language is Visual Basic. Microsoft has defined the Active Script interfaces and has also provided two functional implementations. Internet Explorer uses Active Scripting technology internally, and by using Active Scripting in your application, you can add this high-powered technology to your own applications.

Active Scripting is comprised of two basic pieces, an Active Script engine and an Active Script host. The engine actually implements the scripting functionality through support for parsing and execution of the script language. Microsoft provides two engines, one for VBScript and another for JScript, Microsoft's implementation of JavaScript. An Active Script host accesses the functionality of an Active Script engine by implementing and using a number of COM-based interfaces.

Applications that act as scripting hosts should expose an application-specific object model so that script developers can access the functionality of the application. Examples of applications that make effective use of this approach are Microsoft's Office suite. An application implements an object model by exposing its functionality through an `IDispatch`-based, Automation interface.

An Active Script engine supports two or three standard interfaces. `IActiveScript` is the primary Active Script interface that provides basic script support. The engine must also support a persistence interface, either one of the standard OLE interfaces (`IPersist*`) or the new `IActiveScriptParse` interface. The persistence interface provides a way to save and load a script into the engine.

An Active Script host must implement the `IActiveScriptSite` interface, and optionally the `IActiveScriptSiteWindow` interface. The application will typically implement an IDispatch interface as well, to expose its object model. If the default Active Script engine doesn't provide everything that an application needs, it can easily be extended by adding function-specific Automation-based components.

Java and ActiveX

Java seems to have taken the programming world by storm. With the promise of "write once, run everywhere," Sun Microsystems makes Java sound very appealing. No longer do you have to worry about what platform to target for an application; instead you can be assured that any platform that can run the Java Virtual Machine will execute your Java program unaltered!

Microsoft has jumped on the Java bandwagon as well. Microsoft's Visual J++ development environment for Java is an excellent tool for producing pure Java applications. And if you are planning on targeting only the Windows operating systems for your Java applications you can take advantage of the ActiveX support for Java provided by Visual J++.

This chapter begins with a general discussion about Java, comparing it to C++. Then there is a getting acquainted session with Visual J++. Then it's time to get into the meat of the topic and look at the three ways Java and ActiveX/COM fit together. The first two exercises discuss how to use an ActiveX component from Java. The techniques for using ActiveX controls and Automation are both covered. Then Java will be used to implement an Automation server. The chapter wraps up with a general discussion about handling COM errors in Java.

Java and C++

To compare Java and C++ does Java a great deal of injustice. Java was developed from scratch as an extensible, pure object-oriented language. It is true that Java has similar syntax, keywords, and statements. However, Java is not C++, and architecturally it is very different. Yet, if you are a C++ programmer, most of the knowledge that you have about the language and its object-oriented techniques will help you quickly learn Java.

Java is both a language and an operating subsystem. The operating subsystem, known as the Java Virtual Machine (JVM), emulates a virtual CPU. The JVM has been ported to most major operating systems, and this is what gives Java its multiplatform support. The JVM also has been implemented within most major Web browsers, allowing them to download and execute Java applications over the Web.

You can develop applications in Java a number of ways. The most basic is to download the Java Development Kit (JDK) from Sun Microsystems. This will provide you with a compiler, debugger, and a Windows 32-bit implementation of the Java Virtual Machine. Microsoft also distributes its version of the JDK, known as the Software Developers Kit (SDK) for Java. This implementation of the JDK has been enhanced by Microsoft to run more efficiently on Windows and to offer accessibility to Micro-soft's technologies, such as COM and ActiveX. There are also a number of development environments for Java available, such as Visual J++, that pro-vide a GUI wrapper (an IDE) around the JDK/SDK command line tools.

Programming in Java is similar to most other programming languages. You type your source code in and save it as a source file. The source file is compiled and then may be executed. In C++, the source files are typi-cally .H and .CPP files. These are compiled to .OBJ files which are linked to produce executable (EXE) or .DLL files. In Java, there are just two file types. Source files have an extension of .JAVA, which are compiled to cre-ate Java class files with an extension of .CLASS. Java class files contain Java byte-code that can be read and executed by the JVM.

Java, like C++, uses classes to define objects. Java classes, like C++ classes, support many of the same concepts: single inheritance, abstract classes, and constructors and destructors. However, the definition and imple-mentation of a class is quite different. Let's take a look at a simple class def-inition for comparison to C++.

```
class HelloWorld
{
    /*
     * Instance variables
     */
    private int iCount;
    private String strHello = "Hello World!";

    /*
     * Methods
     */
    public void SayHello()
    {
        for( iCount = 0; iCount < 10; iCount++ )
        {
            System.out.println( strHello ); // Java's printf()
        }
    }
}
```

At first glance, it's hard to tell the difference between Java and C++. They seem to have the same statement syntax, comment structures, scope modifiers, types, and so forth. But there are some differences that should be pointed out.

- The variable *strHello* is of type *String*. This is one of the basic types provided by Java, along with *byte, short, int, long, float, double, boolean, char,* and *Object*.

- There is no constructor or destructor in the class definition. In Java, constructors and destructors are not required to be defined. However, if they are defined in a class definition, the constructor would be specified as *public <classname>()* and the destructor, as with all Java classes, would be *public void finalize()*.

■ The method *SayHello()* is implemented within the class definition. In C++, the class definition and the implementation are typically separated. Any methods defined within the class definition are called in-line methods. However, in Java, methods must be defined and implemented within the class definition itself.

■ The semicolon is left off of the ending brace of the class definition. As you can see, the use of the semicolon in Java for the most part is identical to C++. The reason the semicolon is left off of the ending brace of the class definition is that no executable statements can appear outside of a class definition. Therefore, it is not necessary to separate the class definition from other executable statements as it is in C++.

This class will compile, but it cannot be executed. Java class files, like C++ executables, must have a known entry point to begin execution. To run a Java application, the class name is passed to the Java Virtual Machine. The Java Virtual Machine then attempts to load a static, public method called *main()*. The following code snippet must be added to enable execution of the class file by the Java Virtual Machine:

```
class Hello
{
    // Main entry point
    static public void main( String args[] )
    {
        // Create an instance of the HelloWorld object
        HelloWorld obj = new HelloWorld();

        // Call the SayHello() method
        obj.SayHello();
    }
}
```

Once compiled, two Java class files would be produced, HelloWorld.class and Hello.class. Since Hello.class has the *main()* method, it would be the class file specified to be run by the JVM.

```
<JVM> Hello.class
```

NOTE: *The JVM provided by Sun for Windows is named Java.exe. The JVM provided by Microsoft is named Jview.exe.*

The class name specified on the command line is the class searched for in the class file. The search performed is case-sensitive, so you must specify the class on the command line in the same case as it would be found in the class file.

When the Java Virtual Machine loads the Hello class, it will execute the static, public method *main()*. The *main()* method uses the *new* keyword to create an instance of the HelloWorld class and then calls the *SayHello()* method. This type of Java program is called a stand-alone Java application, because it doesn't require a Web browser to execute. The other type of Java program—and the most publicized—is the Java applet.

Just as a stand-alone Java application has to implement a *main()* method, Java applets are required to implement certain methods. These methods are encapsulated in a class known as Applet. In order to create a custom applet, all you have to do is inherit from the Applet class and override the methods that you want to customize. Let's take a look at the Java code necessary to create a simple applet:

```java
import java.applet.*; // include the Applet class(es)
import java.awt.Graphics; // include the Graphics classes

class HelloWorldApplet extends Applet // inherit from Applet
{
    // Override the init() method:
    // This method is called by the browser
    // to allow the class to set aside the
    // screen real estate required by the applet
    public void init()
    {
        resize( 100, 50 );
    }

    // Override the paint() method:
    // This method is called by the browser
    // to tell the class to paint itself
    public void paint( Graphics g )
    {
        g.drawString("Hello World!", 10, 20);
    }
}
```

In order for the HelloWorldApplet class to inherit from, or extend, Applet, the Applet class must be included into the Java source file. This is done by using the *import* statement. Similar to the *#include* statement in C++, the *import* statement is used to bring external classes into the source file. The name specified after the import statement represents what is known as a package. A *package* is a directory that contains a class or collection of classes. If an "*" is specified at the end of the package name, then all of the classes in the package are to be imported. Packages should exist along a search path environment variable named CLASSPATH. Take for example the statement *import java.applet.**. The compiler will traverse the directories specified in the CLASSPATH looking for <CLASSPATH element>\java\applet and import all the classes in that directory.

The *extends* keyword is used to tell the compiler that the *HelloWorldApplet* class should inherit the functionality of the *Applet* class. Once the *HelloWorldApplet* inherits from *Applet* it can override the methods that need to be customized for this particular applet.

After compilation, this Java program can be added to an HTML document using the <APPLET> element so that it can execute within a browser. We plan to do more with applets in the next few sections.

There is a great deal more that could be discussed about Java, and there are many excellent books that do so, but for the purposes of this chapter, enough has been covered in order to discuss Java and ActiveX. However, knowledge of Visual J++ is almost a requirement in order to integrate Java and ActiveX, so let's get acquainted with the Visual J++ development environment.

WEB RESOURCES:

URL	*Description*
http://www.javasoft.com/	Download the latest Java Development kit here.
http://www.microsoft.com/java	Get Microsoft's latest Java SDK here.
http://www.microsoft.com/visualj	Information on Visual J++.

Introduction to Visual J++

Visual J++, a member of Microsoft's Developer Studio, is Microsoft's entry into the ever growing Java development tool market. It is good at creating "pure" Java applications, and a must for seamlessly integrating Java and ActiveX.

To begin development of a Java application or applet, you will probably use the Java Applet Wizard (see Fig. 10.1). The Java Applet Wizard, like the MFC AppWizard in Visual C++, walks you through a series of screens, querying for the features that you would like to include in your Java applet. It takes care of the details of setting up the project, and generates a skeleton applet, allowing you to focus on the job of writing code.

The Java Applet Wizard can be launched through the **File/New** menu option in Visual J++. The **Projects** tab on the **New** dialog displays a list of the types of projects that can be created in Developer Studio. To launch the Java Applet Wizard, you must select it from the list and give

Figure 10.1
Java Applet Wizard.

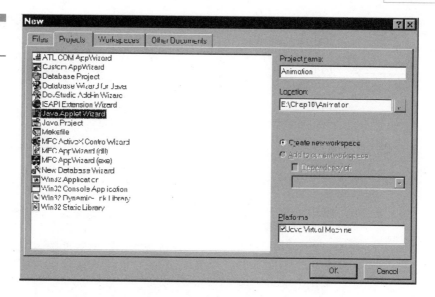

the new project a name and a location to store project files. For this exercise, give the project the name of '**Animation**' and set the location to a directory of your choice. When all the information has been entered, click the **OK** button and the Java Applet Wizard will start. You must complete five steps before the source can be viewed, compiled, and then executed.

In step one, we define the type of program we want, the name of the Java class, and whether we want comments generated with the initial source code (see Fig. 10.2).

There are two types of Java programs to choose from: applets and applications. Applets are programs that are designed to be downloaded by an HTML document, and can run only within the context of a Web browser. Since applets are downloaded from a server to the client, they are considered "untrusted," and therefore there are restrictions placed on applets. These restrictions are enforced by the browser, and do not allow an applet to access the hardware of the client computer. This ensures that an applet cannot perform any destructive acts on the client, such as formatting the hard drive. However, these restrictions also limit the functionality that an applet can provide, such as saving data or printing. A Java application, on the other hand, is similar to a standard operating system executable. Java applications run stand-alone within the context of the Java Virtual Machine. Since a Java application is stored on and executed from the local machine, it is considered to be "trusted" and is therefore allowed access to the hardware.

Figure 10.2
Applet Wizard,
Step 1.

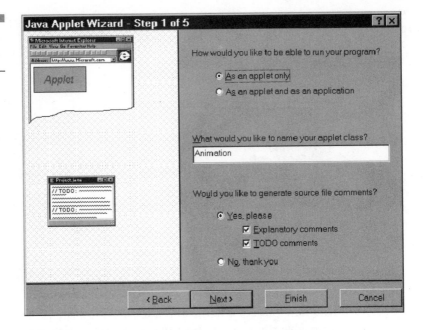

For this exercise, we will create an applet. The Java Applet Wizard will default the name of the initial Java class to the name of the project which is fine for this exercise. Also, let the Wizard add the initial source code comments. Once you have chosen the correct options, navigate to the next step in the Wizard by choosing the **Next** button.

In step two, we tell the Wizard whether we want it to create a sample HTML file, and what we would like for the default size of the applet. (See Fig. 10.3.) We take the defaults provided by the Wizard for this dialog. The Wizard will create a sample HTML file that will already contain the <APPLET> tag to load our applet into a browser. It also defaults the size of the applet to 320 × 240 pixels. Choose **Next** to continue.

A great deal of functionality can be added automatically to our applet by the Wizard in step three. (See Fig. 10.4.) In this step, we can add multiple thread support, animation, and mouse event handlers.

If your applet or application is graphical or will interact with the user, it should be multithreaded. This allows the user interface to be responsive to the user while more time-consuming tasks are performed in a background thread. In this exercise, we want the applet to be multithreaded, support animation, and support the MouseDown(), and MouseUp() events. Select the options and click **Next.**

Step four allows us to define parameters for the applet. (See Fig. 10.5.) Any parameters that you define here will be contained within the <APPLET>

Figure 10.3
Applet Wizard,
Step 2.

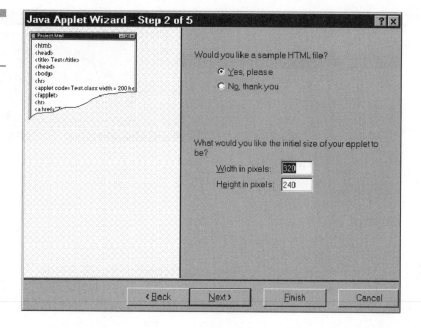

Figure 10.4
Applet Wizard,
Step 3.

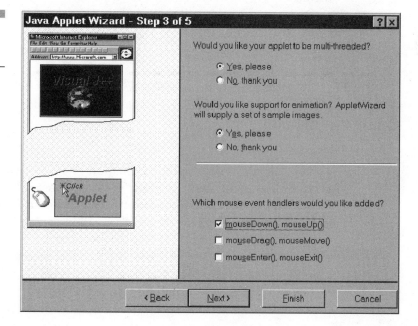

Figure 10.5
Applet Wizard,
Step 4.

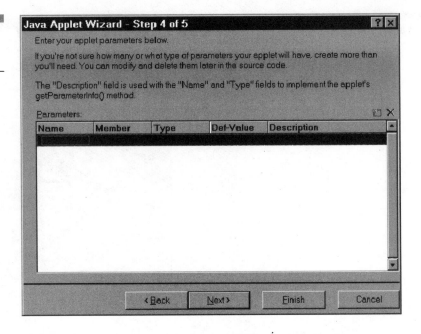

block of the sample HTML file. If you are creating a Java application, you can skip this screen since applications are not loaded via HTML documents.

Our sample applet will not have any special parameters in this exercise. Click **Next** to continue.

NOTE: *Applet parameters are not accessible by Applications. Parameters are specified in the <APPLET> block of an HTML document and applications are not loaded by HTML documents.*

Step five allows copyright information to be defined. (See Fig. 10.6.) This is equivalent to an about box that is stored internally in the applet class. Other Java applets and applications that create an instance of our class can call a public method of the class called getAppInfo() to retrieve the copyright information.

For our exercise, we will use the defaults provided by the Wizard. Choose Finish to complete the Java Applet Wizard.

Before any files are actually generated, a summary of the information gathered is displayed for review. (See Fig. 10.7.) This gives you a chance to

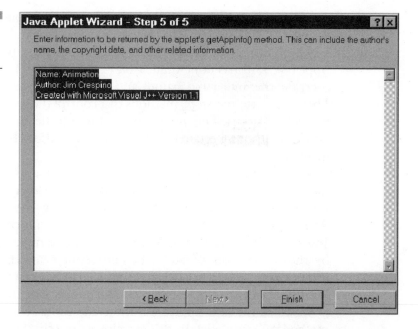

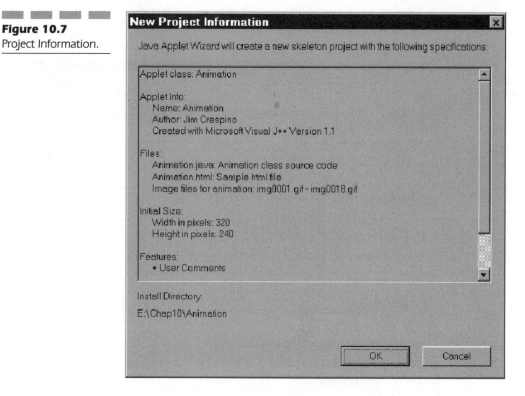

cancel and restart the project if necessary. Unless you have an objection, choose OK and let's see what Microsoft's Java Applet Wizard produces.

As you can see by expanding the Animation class in ClassView, the Java Applet Wizard has done quite a bit of work for us. Our Animation class overrides the init(), run(), paint(), and destroy() methods of the Applet class. There are start() and stop() methods that control the secondary thread. Also, we will get notified of mouse events through the MouseUp() and MouseDown() methods. Certain other supporting methods have also been implemented.

Without having to add a line of code, our applet is already pretty impressive. To see the results, choose **Build/Build Animation** from the menu. When the applet has built successfully, choose **Build/Execute Animation.** Developer Studio (Fig. 10.8) will launch Internet Explorer and load ANIMATION.HTML, which is the sample HTML file created by the Java Applet Wizard. The end result is an animated applet that shows a graphic of the earth rotating, a snapshot of which can be seen in Fig. 10.9. To return to Developer Studio, simply exit Internet Explorer.

We asked the Java Applet Wizard to add MouseUp() and MouseDown() methods to our applet. In this exercise, we use the MouseDown() method to toggle the animation state of the applet off and on. Four lines of code is all we have to add to implement this functionality.

Figure 10.8
Developer's Studio.

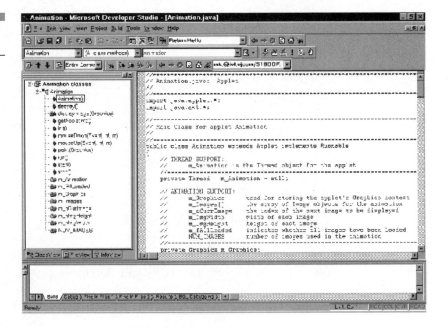

Figure 10.9
Applet in Internet
Explorer.

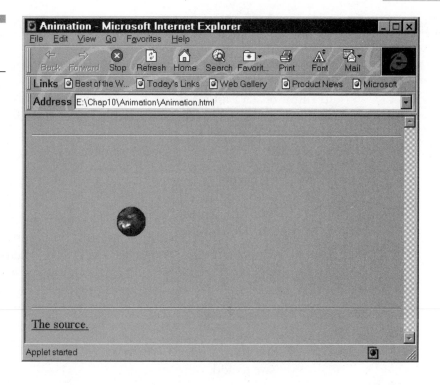

From ClassView, double-click on the MouseDown() method to go to that code, and enter the following statements:

```
public boolean mouseDown(Event evt, int x, int y)
{
        // TODO: Place applet mouseDown code here
        if (m_Animation == null)
                start();
        else
                stop();

        return true;
}
```

Again, build and execute the applet. This time, after the applet has started executing, click on the globe to stop the animation, and again to restart it.

As you can see, Visual J++ and the Java Applet Wizard are two very powerful tools that allow the Java developer to concentrate on writing code, instead of worrying about project details. We make use of this applet later in the chapter when we interact with an ActiveX control.

Integrating Java and COM

Although Java and COM are very different technologies, and were developed independently of one another, they integrate very well. Many seem to think of Java and ActiveX as two competing technologies. However, COM is a language-independent architecture, while Java is actually a programming language. But the two do share many of the same concepts, which makes Java an excellent language for using and implementing COM objects.

All the changes necessary to allow Java to integrate with COM were done by Microsoft in its implementation of the Java Virtual Machine. Since the Java language already had the constructs necessary for implementing COM objects, such as supporting multiple interfaces, nothing had to be added to the language itself. The Microsoft Java Virtual Machine takes on the responsibility of locating and allocating the COM object, marshaling the calls, and managing object lifetimes. As far as Java is concerned, COM objects are Java objects. Programming COM objects in Java allows you to forget about the more obscure and error-prone aspects of COM programming.

Java Applets and ActiveX Controls

In this section, we make use of the Animation applet and sample HTML file from the previous exercise. We will add an ActiveX control to the HTML file, specifically a command button. We will use the command button to control the animation state of the Java applet. As the applet changes animation states, it will set the Caption property of the button to either "Start" or "Stop," depending on the current state of the animation. To accomplish this, we will employ some of the scripting techniques that were covered in Chapter 4, as well as make use of Microsoft's ActiveX support for Java.

The first issue that must be overcome is the fact that, currently, Java applets do not have the ability to directly receive events generated by an ActiveX control. To notify the applet that a "click" event from the command button has occurred, we will have to forward the events produced by the control to the applet with a small amount of VBScript.

To begin we will add the ActiveX control and the VBScript to our sample HTML file (see Fig. 10.10). For this, we will use ActiveX Control Pad. Start ActiveX Control Pad and open the sample HTML file, ANI-

MATION.HTML, from the directory that contains the Animation project. To place the button under the applet, position the cursor at the front of the line following the </APPLET> tag, and then choose **Edit/Insert ActiveX Control** from the menu. Select the **Microsoft Forms 2.0 CommandButton** from the list of controls and then select **OK.**

The button will be displayed in a grid layout along with a properties dialog. For this exercise, we are not interested in altering any of the control's properties. Even a caption doesn't need to be entered because ultimately the applet is going to set the caption. Instead, simply close the **Edit ActiveX Control** dialog to be returned to the HTML editor. The following HTML block shows what was added to the ANIMATION.HTML file:

```
<html>
<head>
<title>Animation</title>
</head>
<body>
<hr>
<applet
  code=Animation.class
  name=Animation
  width=320
  height=240 >
</applet>

<OBJECT ID="CommandButton1" WIDTH=120 HEIGHT=40
 CLASSID="CLSID:D7053240-CE69-11CD-A777-00DD01143C57">
  <PARAM NAME="Size" VALUE="2540;846">
  <PARAM NAME="FontCharSet" VALUE="0">
  <PARAM NAME="FontPitchAndFamily" VALUE="2">
  <PARAM NAME="ParagraphAlign" VALUE="3">
  <PARAM NAME="FontWeight" VALUE="0">
</OBJECT>
<hr>
<a href="Animation.java">The source.</a>
</body>
</html>
```

Figure 10.10
Inserting an ActiveX Control.

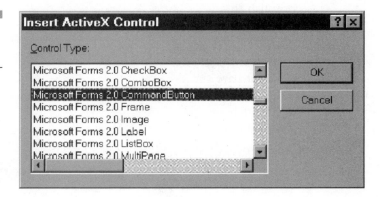

A small amount of script now needs to be added that will forward the click events, generated when the command button is pressed, to the applet. As in Chapter 4, use the Script Wizard provided with ActiveX Control Pad to add the script. To be sure that VBScript is the language generated by the Script Wizard, select **Tools/Options/Script** from the menu. Verify that Visual Basic Scripting Edition is set to the Default Script Language. Once the language has been verified, invoke the **Script Wizard** from the **Tools** menu.

In the Script Wizard, expand the CommandButton1 item in the Select an Event list. Only one VBScript statement, *document.Animation.handle-Click,* as seen in Fig. 10.11, needs to be added to the CommandButton1_Click subroutine. This line accesses the Animation applet by name within the HTML document and calls a public method that will soon be added to the Animation class. When the statement has been added to the body of the subroutine choose OK on the Script Wizard dialog to return to the HTML document in ActiveX Control Pad.

The entire HTML document should look as follows:

```
<html>
<HEAD>
<title>Animation</title>
</HEAD>
<BODY>
<hr>
```

Figure 10.11
Script Wizard.

```
<applet
  code=Animation.class
  name=Animation
  width=320
  height=240 >
</applet>
  <SCRIPT LANGUAGE="VBScript">
<!--
Sub CommandButton1_Click()
        document.Animation.handleClick
end sub
-->
  </SCRIPT>
  <OBJECT ID="CommandButton1" WIDTH=120 HEIGHT=40
   CLASSID="CLSID:D7053240-CE69-11CD-A777-00DD01143C57">
    <PARAM NAME="Size" VALUE="2540;846">
    <PARAM NAME="FontCharSet" VALUE="0">
    <PARAM NAME="FontPitchAndFamily" VALUE="2">
    <PARAM NAME="ParagraphAlign" VALUE="3">
    <PARAM NAME="FontWeight" VALUE="0">
  </OBJECT>
<hr>
<a href="Animation.java">The source.</a>
</BODY>
</html>
```

Next, we need to add the handleClick() method to our applet. Reopen the Visual J++ Animation project in Developer Studio. In ClassView, expand the Animation class. Invoke the ClassView shortcut menu by right-clicking on the Animation class and choose Add Method. To define the handleClick() method, fill out the Add Method dialog as seen in Fig. 10.12. The definition of the method is very easy because it will take no

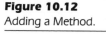

Figure 10.12
Adding a Method.

parameter and will not return any values. However, it does have to be declared as public so that the script can access it. After completing the dialog, select **OK** to let Visual J++ generate the code for the method.

NOTE: *Any public method of an applet class is automatically exposed by Internet Explorer to the Script engine.*

The handleClick() method will implement the functionality of the mouseDown() method from the first exercise. Depending on the state of the m_Animation member variable, either start() or stop() will be called. So as not to duplicate code, the mouseDown() method should be modified to call the handleClick() method. The completed handleClick() and modified mouseDown() methods should appear as:

```
public void handleClick()
{
        if (m_Animation == null)
        {
                start();
        }
        else
        {
                stop();
        }
}

public boolean mouseDown(Event evt, int x, int y)
{
        // TODO: Place applet mouseDown code here
        handleClick();

        return true;
}
```

Now it's time to build the project and execute it. When Internet Explorer loads the Web page, you should be able to click on the applet as well as the button to toggle the animation state of the applet. (See Fig. 10.13.) When you have finished testing your work, exit Internet Explorer and return to Visual J++ because we are only halfway there.

The second part of this exercise is to have the Java Applet update the caption of the button to reflect the action that will be performed if the button is pressed. For example, if the globe is spinning, then the button should say "Stop" and vice versa. This can be accomplished by using Microsoft's ActiveX/COM classes for Java.

Figure 10.13
Internet Explorer with Our Button Control.

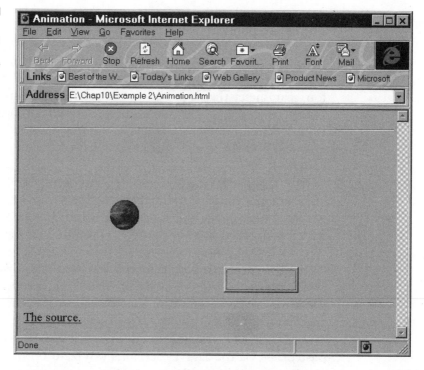

Currently, the button control and the applet have no knowledge of one another. They operate in a vacuum within the Web page. In order for the applet to access the properties and/or methods of the button control, it must be made aware of the existence of the control. This can be accomplished by passing a reference of the button control, via VBScript, as a parameter to yet another public method that must be defined in the applet. The applet will receive the button control as a native Java object and can then access its properties and methods just as it would any other Java object.

The VBScript that needs to be added to the HTML file is quite simple and can be done directly from Visual J++. From the File View, open ANI-MATION.HTML. Add the following to the SCRIPT block:

```
<SCRIPT LANGUAGE="VBScript">
<!--
Sub window_onLoad()
      document.Animation.setControl CommandButton1
end sub

Sub CommandButton1_Click()
      document.Animation.handleClick
```

```
end sub
-->
  </SCRIPT>
```

Again the Animation applet is referenced by name as it exists in the document. The public method, setControl(), is called. The CommandButton1 parameter that is passed to the method is simply the name of the button control as it is referenced by the document. When the HTML file is loaded by Internet Explorer, the window_onLoad() subroutine will be executed and the applet will be notified of the existence of the button control.

Now that a reference to the control has been passed to the applet, a Java class wrapper must be defined so that the applet knows what properties and methods are available for the command button. A tool provided with Visual J++, called JavaTLB, is used to produce a Java class wrapper for any ActiveX/COM control type library. JavaTLB reads the type library of an ActiveX component and generates Java class files that describe the control's properties and methods as native Java properties and methods. Once the class wrappers have been produced, they are simply included in the Java source file using the *import* statement.

JavaTLB is a command line tool, but it can be accessed from within Visual J++ via the Java Type Library Wizard on the **Tools** menu. From the Java Type Library Wizard, an ActiveX component can be chosen, and a Java class wrapper will be produced.

Activate the Java Type Library Wizard. The button control used in the exercise is part of the Microsoft Forms 2.0 Object Library, so select Microsoft Forms 2.0 Object Library from the list and choose OK. Output from the Wizard will be displayed in the Java Type Library Wizard tab of the Output window. The output should include the line that is used to import the class(es) into the source code. Following is an example of the output from the Wizard:

```
Microsoft (R) Visual J++ Java Typelib Conversion Utility Version 1.01.7022
Copyright (C) Microsoft Corp 1996. All rights reserved.

import fm20.*;
...
C:\WINDOWS\java\trustlib\fm20\summary.txt(1): Class summary information created
C:\WINDOWS\java\trustlib\stdole2\summary.txt(1): Class summary information created
Tool returned code: 0
```

The classes created from the Microsoft Forms 2.0 Object Library are contained in the fm20 package in the <windows>\java\trustlib\fm20 directory. All Java class wrappers will be stored in the trustlib directory since only trusted applets may access these classes. The class definitions for the Microsoft Form 2.0 components can be included into the source code by using the blanket statement *import fm20.*; at the beginning of the ANIMATION.JAVA source file. To find out the names of the Java classes and interfaces in the Java class file(s) produced by JavaTLB, edit the SUMMARY.TXT file(s) produced. In this exercise, we are interested in the `CommandButton` class and its `ICommandButton` interface.

NOTE: *It's important to check the summary.txt files produced by JavaTLB because the names of the classes and interface may not always be what you expect.*

When using an ActiveX component in Java, whether it's an ActiveX control or Automation server, it is accessed through its COM interface. In this exercise the object that is received as a parameter in the setControl() method will be cast to the COM interface, ICommandButton, and stored in a member variable of the same type. So now that the Java class wrappers for the command button control have been produced, it's time to add the code to access the control from our applet.

We begin by adding the import statement to the code. In the current project, if fm20.* is added to the code, an ambiguous reference error will be received from the compiler. That is because the fm20 package contains a class named image and the Animation class in this project has a member variable named image that holds the array of pictures for the animation. The compiler has no way to know what image reference is being made in the code. If it were necessary to use the image class from the fm20 package, the name of the image member variable in the Animation class would have to be changed. However, only the `ICommandButton` interface is of interest in this exercise. So instead of importing everything using the statement *import fm20.*;, only the `ICommandButton` will be imported by using the *import fm20.ICommandButton;* statement. This statement can be added after the other import statements that already exist in the source code.

```
import java.applet.*;
import java.awt.*;
import fm20.ICommandButton;
```

Next the member variable that will hold the reference to the command button control, received from the setControl() method, needs to be added to the Animation class. Using the ClassView shortcut menu on the Animation class choose Add Variable. The variable should be called `m_CommandButton` and its type must be `ICommandButton` as defined in the fm20 package. Also, give the variable an initial value of *null.* Figure 10.14 shows how the Add Variable screen should be filled out. Once the `m_CommandButton` has been defined, choose **OK** to have the variable added to the code.

Now the setControl() method must be defined. Use the same procedure we used earlier to define the handleClick() method. The method should be public, return a void, and accept a parameter named objActiveXCtrl that has a type of Object. Figure 10.15 shows the Add Method screen for the setControl() method definition. Once the necessary information has been entered, choose **OK** to generate the method in the source code.

Within the setControl() method, the generic Object parameter, `objActiveXCtrl`, is checked to verify that we only receive an object that implements the `ICommandButton` interface. Assuming that the correct type of object is received, `objActiveXCtrl` must be cast to its `ICommandButton` type and assigned to the `m_CommandButton` member variable. Once `m_CommandButton` is assigned the reference to the command button control, the properties and methods of the control can be accessed. However, properties are not directly supported by COM. Instead, properties are implemented as put*property*() and get*property*() methods. Therefore, in

Figure 10.14
Adding a Variable.

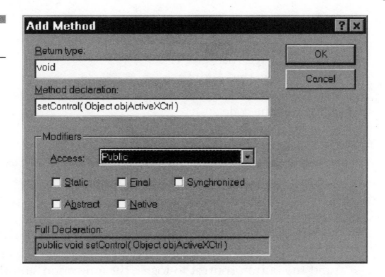

order to set the Caption property of the command button control, use the putCaption() method. The text to be used as the caption for the button is sent as a parameter to the putCaption() method. During the setControl() method, the caption of the button should to be "Stop!" because the animation should currently be active. The entire setControl() method follows:

```
public void setControl( Object objActiveXCtrl )
{
    // Assure that we only accept CommandButton objects
    if ( objActiveXCtrl instanceof ICommandButton )
    {
        m_CommandButton = (ICommandButton) objActiveXCtrl;
        m_CommandButton.putCaption( "Stop!" );
    }
}
```

■ ■

NOTE: *The Java* instanceof *keyword actually performs a COM QueryInterface call on the object. This is just one example of where Java keywords map almost directly to underlying COM support.*

The call to the putCaption() method must occur in two other places in the code. The handleClick() method needs to set the caption button based on the current state of the animation. The additions to the handleClick() method are:

```
public void handleClick()
{
    if (m_Animation == null)
    {
        start();
        // Animation has started pressing the button
        // again will stop the animation
        m_CommandButton.putCaption( "Stop!" );
    }
    else
    {
        stop();
        // Animation has stopped pressing the button
        // again will start the animation
        m_CommandButton.putCaption( "Start!" );
    }
}
```

At this point, the project should be complete. Build and execute the Animation project. The user should be able to click on both the applet and the button control to toggle the animation, and the caption of the button should be updated appropriately. The finished result should look something like Fig. 10.16.

Figure 10.16
Internet Explorer Again.

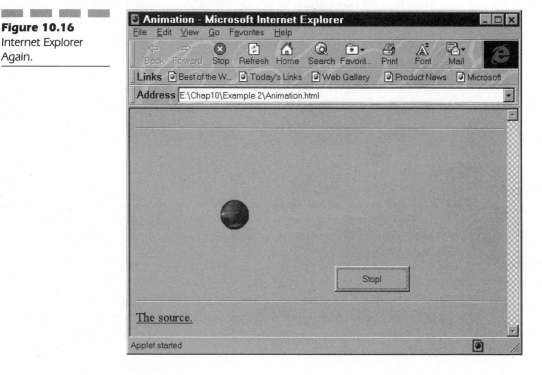

There are a few things to note from this exercise. First, once an applet is given a reference to an ActiveX Control, it can access the properties and methods of that control regardless of where the event is generated. This is proven by the fact that the caption of the button changes whether the event occurs internally to the applet, in the case of the mouseDown event, or externally, in the case of an event from the button. In both cases, the caption of the command button control is altered.

Second, this example currently executes only under the context of the Visual J++ environment. If Internet Explorer were launched from outside of Visual J++ and attempted to load this project's HTML file, the applet would not be allowed to change the caption of the button. This stems from the fact that Java applets are "untrusted" and are not allowed to access the client machine or native code. The Java class wrappers created by the JavaTLB tool make calls to native Windows DLLs, which is not allowed in the Java security model. The Visual J++ development environment disables this security feature of the Java Virtual Machine in Internet Explorer so that applications can initially be developed. To run this project outside of Visual J++, the applet must be placed in a Microsoft cabinet file (.CAB) and digitally signed so that it can be verified as trusted by Internet Explorer when downloaded from a server.

Finally, the fact that the Java class wrappers make native calls to Windows DLLs make this applet nonportable. In particular, this applet can run only within Internet Explorer on a Windows operating system unless and until the ActiveX libraries are ported to other operating systems. And on top of that, the Java Virtual Machine supported within Internet Explorer must be a current release. You must ensure that the Java Virtual Machine for Internet Explorer supports Java and COM integration. This can be done by inserting the following HTML into the page that contains the applet and ActiveX control.

```
<OBJECT
CLASSID="clsid:08B0E5C0-4FCB-11CF-AAA5-00401C608500"
CODEBASE="http://www.microsoft.com/java/IE30Java.cab#Version=1,0,0,1">
</OBJECT>
```

This tag causes Internet Explorer to check the version of its Java support. If it is not up-to-date, Internet Explorer will download the latest version and update itself.

The tools and methods used to integrate an ActiveX control with a Java applet are also used to access an Automation server from a Java. An example of this is discussed in the next section.

Accessing an Automation Server from Java

Most productivity applications that are written for Windows today expose some sort of Automation interface. As stand-alone Java applications become more prevalent, they will be expected to coexist and interact with these applications. Fortunately, Microsoft makes accessing an Automation server in Java easy and natural.

First, we have to develop an Automation server to use. One can easily be created using Visual Basic's ActiveX DLL project template. For this exercise, name the project '**Chap10ex3**' and the class that will be implemented '**MathAXS.**' The following code shows the one property and four methods that the automation server will be exposing. Once coding for the project has been completed, it must be built as a DLL. Visual Basic will automatically register the automation server as Chap10ex3.MathAXS in the Window's registry. Once it's registered, the Java Type Library Wizard will be able to read the type library of the automation server and create the Java class wrappers.

```
Public Error As String


Public Function Add(ByVal Op1 As Long, ByVal Op2 As Long) As Long
  Add = Op1 + Op2
  Error = ""
End Function


Public Function Subtract(ByVal Op1 As Long, ByVal Op2 As Long) As Long
  Subtract = Op1 - Op2
  Error = ""
End Function


Public Function Multiply(ByVal Op1 As Long, ByVal Op2 As Long) As Long
  Multiply = Op1 * Op2
  Error = ""
End Function


Public Function Divide(ByVal Op1 As Long, ByVal Op2 As Long) As Long
  If Op2 <> 0 Then
    Divide = Op1 / Op2
    Error = ""
  Else
    Divide = 0
    Error = "Attempt to divide by zero"
  End If
End Function
```

In order to effectively use the Automation server in Java, a trusted applet or a stand-alone application must be created. For this exercise, we'll use a stand-alone Java application. Java applications are trusted within the Java Virtual Machine because they are stored and executed directly on the local machine instead of being downloaded from a server. Java applications are allowed to access services of the local client without any special packaging. It's just as if it were written in Visual Basic or Visual C++.

Using Visual J++, create a new Java Applet Wizard project with the following options.

- Give it a name of **JavaClient.**

- In Step 1 of 5 indicate that the finished program should run as both an applet and an application.

- In Step 2 of 5 take the default values.

- In Step 3 of 5 indicate that the project should be multithreaded, but do not select animation or mouse event handlers.

- Click **Finish** to take the defaults on the remaining dialogs and create the project.

Since the Visual Basic Automation server will be used within this Java project, Java class wrappers must be created using the Java Type Library Wizard. From the list of registered ActiveX components, find Chap 10ex3 as seen in Fig. 10.17 and choose OK.

The Output window will display the import statement that needs to be used in the source code as well as the name of the summary file produced. Following is an example of the output from the Java Type Library Wizard:

```
Microsoft (R) Visual J++ Java Typelib Conversion Utility Version 1.01.7022
Copyright (C) Microsoft Corp 1996. All rights reserved.

import chap10ex3.*;
C:\WINDOWS\java\trustlib\chap10ex3\summary.txt(1): Class summary information created
Tool returned code: 0
```

SUMMARY.TXT should be viewed to determine the name of the interface that was created for the Chap10ex3.MathAXS Automation server.

```
public class chap10ex3/MathAXS extends java.lang.Object
{
}

public interface chap10ex3/_MathAXS extends com.ms.com.IUnknown
{
  public abstract int Subtract(int, int);
```

Figure 10.17
Java Type Library
Wizard.

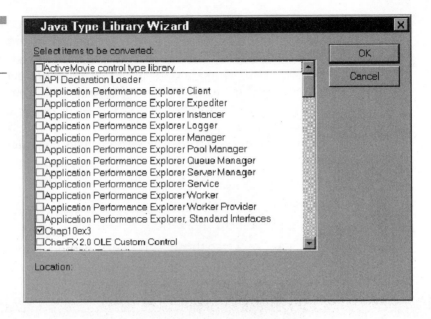

```
    public abstract int Add(int, int);
    public abstract int Multiply(int, int);
    public abstract int Divide(int, int);
    public abstract java.lang.String getError();
    public abstract void putError(java.lang.String);
}
```

For this project, an object of type MathAXS will be created and cast to the _MathAXS interface. Remember, ActiveX/COM objects can be created, but their properties and methods are exposed only through their COM interface.

In order to create the MathAXS automation server, the import statement defined by the Java Type Library Wizard must be included in the Java source file. Importing chap10ex3.* includes the definitions of both the Java class and interface of the MathAXS automation server.

```
import java.applet.*;
import java.awt.*;
import JavaClientFrame;
import chap10ex.*;
```

The method used to create a COM object and reference its properties and methods can be a bit confusing, so we will take a moment to discuss how COM objects are created and accessed.

COM objects are not dissimilar from the Microsoft Foundation Classes Document/View architecture. In the MFC Document/View architecture, document objects hold raw, unformatted data. The data in the document object is accessed and displayed via different views. As an example, imagine a class that holds data that should be displayed in a graph. The views are interfaces to the document object and implementations of the graphs: a pie chart view, a bar chart view, a line chart view. You do not access the data of the document object directly, but rather through its views.

COM objects, like document objects, hold raw, unformatted data. The interfaces that the COM objects implement and expose are the views of that COM object. A COM object is never accessed directly, but rather through one of its implemented interfaces.

Take, for example, a COM class, CComClass, that implements two interfaces, IView1 and IView2. Perhaps IView1 has only one method, displayView1(), and IView2 has only one method, display View2(). In Java, two variables would be created, each one with a type of one of the interfaces implemented by the COM object.

```
IView1 myView1; // IView1 view of CComClass
IView2 myView2; // IView2 view of CComClass
```

The *new* statement is used to create an instance of CComClass and then that object is cast to the IView1 interface and assigned to myView1. Once the COM object has been cast to the IView1 interface, the myView1 object can access the method displayView1.

```
myView1 = (IView1) new CComClass()
myView1.displayView1();
```

MyView1, even though it can see only the properties and methods exposed by the IView1 interface, still holds a full reference to CComClass. That fact can be taken advantage of to set the myView2 variable. To get to the IView2 interface of CComClass, we can simply cast the myView1 object to IView2 and assign it to myView2.

```
myView2 = (IView2) myView1;
myView2.displayView2();
```

Notice that we did not have to create another instance of the CComClass. We just had to look at the current instance differently. Since the myView1 object holds a full representation of the CComClass object, it is only necessary to cast the myView1 variable to the IView2 interface to be able to access the displayView2() method.

In this exercise, the MathAXS object only implements one interface _MathAXS. Therefore, it is only necessary for us to create one instance variable of type _MathAXS to access the properties and methods of the MathAXS object.

From the ClassView of the JavaClient project, use the shortcut menu to add a variable to the JavaClient class. The variable should be named m_MathAXS with a type of _MathAXS, initial value of null, and a scope of private. Figure 10.18 shows an example of the Add Variable dialog.

Once the variable to hold the reference of the COM class has been defined, an instance of the MathAXS automation server can be created in the JavaClient() class constructor.

```
// JavaClient Class Constructor
//----------------------------------------------------------------
public JavaClient()
{
        // TODO: Add constructor code here
        m_MathAXS = (_MathAXS) new MathAXS();
}
```

It is just about time to run a preliminary test of the application. First, it is necessary to tell Visual J++ that this project should be run as an application instead of an applet. That change must be made to the project's settings. In Visual J++ choose **Project/Settings** to bring up the Project Settings dialog. On the **Debug** tab, set the radio button that tells Visual J++ to run the project using the Stand-alone interpreter. Once the changes have been made, as shown in Fig. 10.19, build and execute the application.

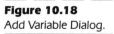

Figure 10.18
Add Variable Dialog.

Add Variable [?] [X]

Variable type:

_MathAXS

Variable name:

m_MathAXS

Initial value

null

Modifiers

Access: Private

☐ Static   ☐ Final

☐ Volatile   ☐ Transient

Full Declaration:

private _MathAXS m_MathAXS = null

OK

Cancel

Figure 10.19
Project Settings.

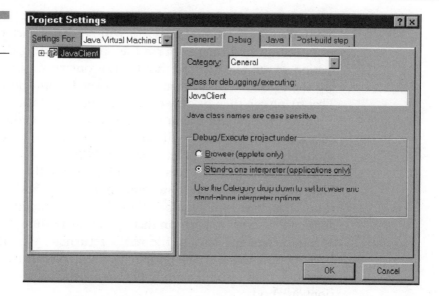

If the applet executes properly, and the MathAXS automation server is created, then the application should display a "Running" message and random numbers. This is default behavior that the Java Applet Wizard generated. The application is shown in Fig. 10.20.

If the application ran, then the MathAXS automation server could be created, but this application should display calculations made using the

Figure 10.20
Java Client
Application.

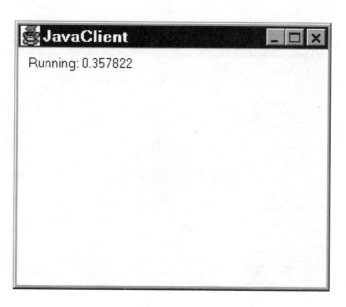

Automation server instead of random numbers. We need to add a new method to the JavaClient class that will randomly pick two numbers and an operation, and then perform the operation using the MathAXS automation server. The method should also construct a Java String representing the operation and the answer returned from the automation server. That string can then be drawn to the client area of the JavaClient window.

Using the shortcut menu in ClassView, add a method named DoCalculation(). The method will take no parameters, return a String, and should have a scope of private. (See Fig. 10.21.)

The DoCalculation() method will perform three major operations. First, it must generate the two random operands and the random operation. Then based on the operation chosen, it should call the MathAXS automation server to perform that operation, passing in the two operands as parameters and storing the result returned. After the operation has been performed, a string should be built consisting of the operands, operation, and result. Example 10.x shows the source for the DoCalculation() method.

```
private String DoCalculation()
{
        String strReturn;

        // Check that the MathAXS automation server was created
        if ( m_MathAXS != null )
        {
                int iOp1 = (int)( Math.random() * 100 ); // number between 9 and 99
                int iOp2 = (int)( Math.random() * 100 ); // number between 0 and 99
```

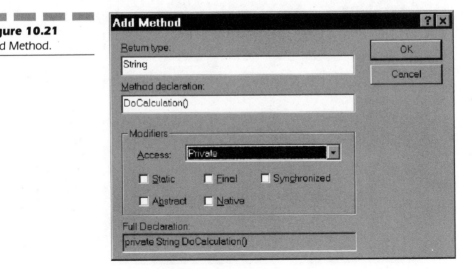

Figure 10.21
Add Method.

```
int iOperation = (int)( Math.random() * 4 ); // number between 0 and 4
char chOperation; // operation performed
int iAnswer; // answer

// perform a random mathematical operation
switch ( iOperation )
{
case 0: // Add
        chOperation = '+';
        iAnswer = m_MathAXS.Add( iOp1, iOp2 );
        break;

case 1: // Subtract
        chOperation = '-';
        iAnswer = m_MathAXS.Subtract( iOp1, iOp2 );
        break;

case 2: // Multiply
        chOperation = '*';
        iAnswer = m_MathAXS.Multiply( iOp1, iOp2 );
        break;

case 3: // Divide
        chOperation = '/';
        iAnswer = m_MathAXS.Divide( iOp1, iOp2 );
        break;
}

// Create a string representation of the operation
strReturn = iOp1 + " " + chOperation + " " + iOp2 + " = ";

// If an error occurred, display that instead of the answer
if ( m_MathAXS.getError().length() != 0 )
        strReturn += m_MathAXS.getError();
else
        strReturn += iAnswer;
}
else
{
        strReturn = "MathAXS automation server unreachable";
}

return strReturn;
}
```

The code looks pretty straightforward. However, there are at least three items of interest that should be pointed out.

First, note the Error property of the MathAXS automation server. In Visual Basic, Error is simply a public string variable, similar to a property. But in the Java source, Error is accessed through the getError() method call. This is not a Java convention but is instead a COM convention. COM does not directly support class properties; instead it implements them as get*property*() and put*property*() method calls.

Second, the length of the Error property is checked by using *m_ MathAXS.getError().length()* statement. This statement was possible because strings in COM are automatically converted to the Java String class of which length() is a method. Once the getError() method was resolved to a string, the length() method could then be called.

The last item of interest is the mapping of types between COM and Java. Table 10.1 shows a list of comparable IDL and Java types. Remember, the Visual Basic implementation of the ActiveX server defined the operands and return types from the methods as *LONGs*. However, in the Java source code, the operands and the return types are defined as *ints*. This is because of the COM to Java-type conversion that must take place. It may seem odd that a *LONG* in Visual Basic doesn't map to a *long* in Java. However, the Java Virtual Machine is implemented as a 64-bit environment, while Microsoft's Windows is currently a 32-bit environment; therefore long decimals in the two systems do not map to each other.

NOTE: *To obtain the definitive answer on the Java-type to use for a COM class or variable, refer to the SUMMARY.TEXT file produced by the Java Type Library Wizard.*

The last bit of coding necessary to complete the application is to call the DoCalculation() method and display the results on the screen. That is done in the paint() method of the Java application.

```
// JavaClient Paint Handler
//------------------------------------------------------------
public void paint(Graphics g)
{
      // TODO: Place applet paint code here
      g.drawString( DoCalculation(), 10, 30 );
}
```

Now that the code to test the MathAXS automation server exists, build and execute the JavaClient. The result should produce something similar to Fig. 10.22.

As you can see from the execution of the application, calling a COM automation server from Java is quite fast. In order to slow down the display, modify the run() method of the JavaClient, and increase the time that the thread sleeps before repainting the display. The value passed to the sleep() method is in milliseconds. To increase the delay between calculations to 2 seconds, change the value of the sleep parameter to 2000.

TABLE 10.1

Java Type to IDL
Type Mapping

IDL Type	Java Type
boolean	boolean
char	char
double	double
int	int
int64	long
float	float
long	int
short	short
unsigned char	byte
BSTR	java.lang.String class
CURRENCY/CY	long (the original currency value can be returned by dividing by 10,000)
DATE	double
SCODE/HRESULT	int (com.ms.com.ComException)
VARIANT	com.ms.com.Variant class
Iunknown*	com.ms.com.IUnknown class
Idispatch*	java.lang.Object class
SAFEARRAY	com.ms.com.SafeArray
typename*	single-element array of type typename on [out], not valid on [in]
void	void

```
public void run()
{
      while (true)
      {
            try
            {
                  repaint();
                  // TODO: Add additional thread-specific code here
                  Thread.sleep(2000);
            }
            catch (InterruptedException e)
...
```

Figure 10.22
Java Client.

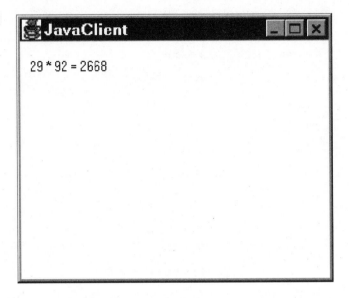

Using an Automation server in Java is just as simple as using an ActiveX control. The only difference is that ActiveX controls are typically passed into a public method of the Java class already instantiated, and Automation servers must be explicitly created.

These last two exercises can be modified to make use of any ActiveX control or automation server. In the next Java/ActiveX topic, we will reverse the implementation of the last exercise.

Using a Java Class as an Automation Server

In this exercise, the previous exercise will be reproduced. However, this time the Automation server will be written in Java, and the client in Visual Basic. This exercise begins by generating the same interface provided by the MathAXS automation server from the previous exercise but using Java to implement the COM object.

The first step is to define the COM interface that the Java class should implement. To describe a COM object, an IDL file is used. This file defines the guid, classes, interfaces, properties, and methods, that will be implemented by the COM object. The interface definition language used to create an IDL file can be quite involved. Instead of creating the IDL from scratch, Visual J++ can create and manage the details of the file allowing the developer to focus on simply implementing the properties and methods of the automation server.

To begin, create a Java project in Visual J++. Unlike the last two examples, the Java Applet Wizard will not be used; instead, just a blank Java Project needs to be created. To do this, choose **File/New** from the menu. Select **Java Project** from the list of projects and give it a name of 'MathJXS' as shown in Fig. 10.23. When finished, choose **OK** to create the workspace.

With an empty Java project workspace, it is up to the developer to create the files necessary for the project. The first file that needs to be produced is MathJXS.java. Choose **Project/New** from the menu and select **Java Source File** from the list of file types. Use MathJXS as the name for the Java source file and choose **OK** (see Fig. 10.24).

Once the MathJXS.java file has been added to the project, the MathJXS class must be defined within that file. For now, only the initial class definition needs to be created.

```
class MathJXS
{
}
```

In order for Visual J++ to create an IDL file, a Java class file must first exist. With a simple class definition, the MathJXS project will build successfully and create the class file. Once the compiler has run and the

Figure 10.23
Java Project.

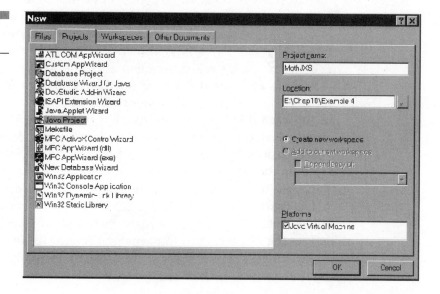

Figure 10.24
Adding a Java Source
File.

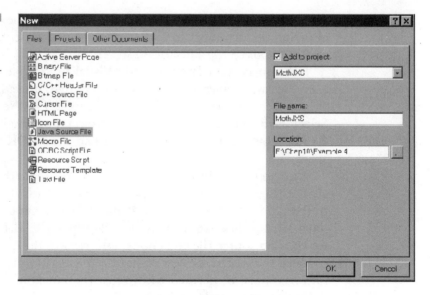

MathJXS.class file has been built, the ActiveX Wizard for Java can be run
to create the IDL file.

The ActiveX Wizard for Java can be launched from the **Tools** menu in
Visual J++. The Wizard has three screens that must be traversed. The first
screen, shown in Fig. 10.25, asks which class to convert to an ActiveX component, and whether an IDL file produced. Verify that the class name is
MathJXS.class and that an IDL file will be produced, then choose **Next.**

The second screen of the Wizard will generate a class identifier (CLSID)
for the automation server and register it in the Windows registry. (See Fig.
10.26.) Verify that a new class id will be created and that the class will be
registered as an ActiveX component, then choose **Next.**

The last screen of the Wizard queries the type of interface(s) that the
ActiveX component should support and whether a type library should
be produced. (See Fig. 10.27.) IDispatch is the type of COM interface most
commonly implemented by ActiveX components. However, Visual J++
and the Microsoft Java Virtual Machine allow Java ActiveX components
to also implement a dual interface. A dual interface implements both an
IDispatch interface as well as exposing the virtual function table of the
COM object directly. The difference between the two is simply performance. If the client can access the virtual function table directly, then it's
as if that COM object was implemented as a native language class. For the
purpose of this example, choose the **Dispinterface** option to implement
just the IDispatch interface.

Figure 10.25
ActiveX Component
Wizard.

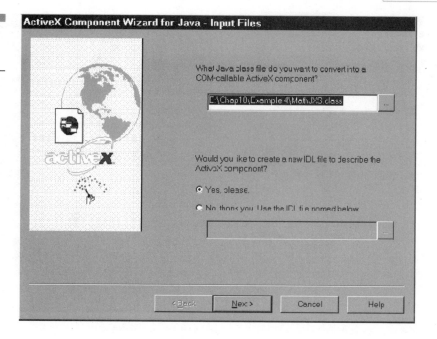

Figure 10.26
ActiveX Component
Wizard, CLSID.

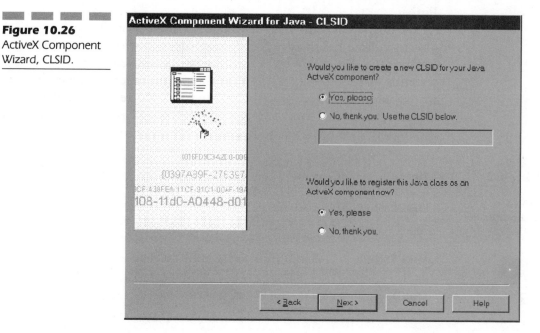

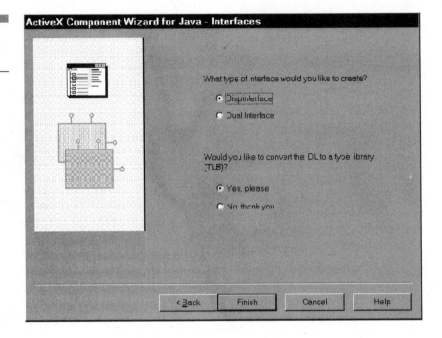

Figure 10.27
ActiveX Component
Wizard, Interfaces.

Also, a type library needs to be produced so that the automation server can be accessed later from Visual Basic. Once the Wizard has been set to implement the **Dispinterface** and to have a type library produced, choose **Finish.**

The ActiveX Wizard for Java produces a number of files in our project directory. Table 10.2 shows a list of those files and what they represent.

Once the ActiveX Wizard for Java has completed its tasks, one last screen is displayed (Fig. 10.28) giving the programmer a snippet of code that should be included into the existing Java source file as well as some project settings that should be altered. The code snippet, which provides the import statement, a modified class definition, and an instance vari-

TABLE 10.2

Component
Wizard–Produced
Files

File	Contents
MathJXSlib.idl	IDL (interface definition language) file that describes the COM interfaces, classes, properties, and methods implemented by the ActiveX component.
MathJXSlib.tlb	A compiled version of the MathJXSlib.idl file produced by the MIDL compiler.
MathJXS.reg	A text file that lists the Windows registry entries that were made for the ActiveX component.

able containing the CLSID should be copied to the clipboard and pasted into the Java source file. The project settings must be altered so that the Java class file produced by the project is placed in the Java CLASSPATH so that it can be loaded and executed when an instance of the automation server is requested to be created.

After the changes to the Java source file have been made, it should look like this:

```
import mathjxslib.*;

public class MathJXS
  implements mathjxslib.IMathJXS
{
  private static final String CLSID =
   "ca6005a0-b3fe-11d0-b5f9-444553540000";

}
```

Now, the IDL file needs to be added to the project. Once added, Visual J++ will manage the modifications that we must make to the IDL file to define the properties and methods of the COM interface. To add the IDL file to the MathJXS project, choose **Project/Add** from the menu. Add MathJXSlib.idl to the project and choose **OK.** Visual J++ will then parse the IDL file and add the IMathJXS class to the ClassView of the project. From ClassView, the shortcut menu can be used to easily add properties and methods to the IDL file without having to learn the IDL syntax.

The first element to be added to the IMathJXS inteface is the Error property. To add this property to the IMathJXS interface, use the Class-

Figure 10.28
ActiveX Component
Wizard, Additional
Steps.

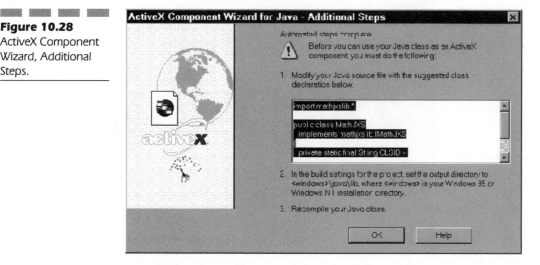

View shortcut menu and choose Add property. The **Add Property to Interface** dialog will display.

When defining both properties and methods for the COM interface in the IDL file, COM types must be used. As you can see from the Add Property dialog, the default return type is set to HRESULT. This is because typically all return types for COM properties and methods should be of type HRESULT. For the Error property, HRESULT is fine for the return type.

The Error property will ultimately store a string that will be defined as a java.lang.String class. Since a COM type must be used in the interface definition of the property, use Table 10.1 to determine the proper Java/COM type mapping for java.lang.String. As can be seen in the table, types of java.lang.String are mapped to BSTR in COM. Therefore, BSTR must be used as the COM type for the Error property.

Lastly, the Error property should also be marked as read-only, and should implement only the Get Function for this property.

Figure 10.29 shows how the Add Property to Interface dialog should be filled out for the Error property. When finished, choose OK to have Error

Figure 10.29
Add Property to Interface.

listed as a property within the IMathJXS interface and added to the IDL file.

After the Error property has been added to the IMathJXS interface, the methods must be added. Again, use the ClassView shortcut menu for the IMathJXS interface and choose Add method. The Add Method to Interface dialog will display.

Here the method, its parameters, and its return type are defined. The name of the first method to be added should be Add.

As was stated earlier, COM expects the return type from COM methods to be of type HRESULT. But for the methods of the MathJXS automation server, a 32-bit value needs to be returned with the result of the arithmetic operation. In IDL, implementation return types for an interface method are defined as a special tagged method parameter. Actually, when defining parameters to a COM interface method, all parameters are tagged either as input, output, or return values. Valid tag values for COM parameter are [in], [out], [in, out], and [out, retval] tags. In the case of the Add method, the two input parameters have a COM type of long, as is the return value. Return values in COM are also defined as pointers, even if they may not implemented as such. The Parameters entry field for the interface definition of the Add method should be formatted as:

```
[in] long, [in] long, [out, retval] long*
```

Figure 10.30 shows the completed Add Method to Interface dialog for the Add method interface definition. When finished, choose OK to have the method definition added to the IMathJXS interface, and in the IDL file.

Figure 10.30
Add Method to
Interface.

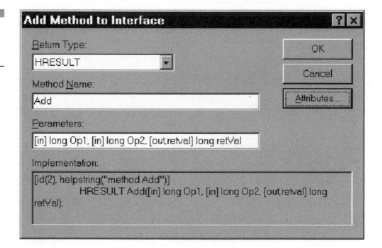

The other three methods, Subtract(), Multiply(), and Divide() also need to be defined. Repeat the process used for the Add() method to define the other methods. When the property and method definitions for the MathJXS automation server have been defined in the IMathJXS interface, the IDL file will contain the following entries:

```
[
  uuid(ca6005a2-b3fe-11d0-b5f9-444553540000),
  helpstring("MathJXSLib Type Library"),
  version(1.0)
]
library MathJXSLib
{
  importlib("stdole32.tlb");


  [
   uuid(ca6005a1-b3fe-11d0-b5f9-444553540000),
   helpstring("IMathJXS Interface")
  ]
  dispinterface IMathJXS
  {
  properties:
  methods:
          [propget, id(1), helpstring("property Error")]
                     HRESULT Error([out, retval] BSTR *pVal);
          [id(2), helpstring("method Add")]
                     HRESULT Add([in] long, [in] long, [out,retval] long* );
          [id(3), helpstring("method Subtract")]
                     HRESULT Subtract([in] long, [in] long, [out,retval] long* );
          [id(4), helpstring("method Multiply")]
                     HRESULT Multiply([in] long, [in] long, [out,retval] long* );
          [id(5), helpstring("method Divide")]
                     HRESULT Divide([in] long, [in] long, [out,retval] long* );
  }


  [
   uuid(ca6005a0-b3fe-11d0-b5f9-444553540000),
   helpstring("CMathJXS Object")
  ]
  coclass CMathJXS
  {
  [ default ]
  dispinterface IMathJXS;
  };

};
```

Now that the definition of the COM interface for the Automation server has been completed, the IDL file must be recompiled to produce an updated type library. The type library will then be reconverted into a Java class wrapper that can be imported into the Java source so that the class can implement the methods defined by the COM interface. All of this can be done automatically via the ActiveX Wizard for Java.

Start the ActiveX Wizard for Java once again. The last time the Wizard produced a basic IDL template that we used to define the properties and methods for the COM interface. This time the Wizard will be directed to use the updated IDL file, instead of creating a new one. On the first screen of the Wizard, specify MathJXS as the class and MathJXSlib as the IDL file as seen in Fig. 10.31.

When Next is pressed, the ActiveX Wizard for Java will analyzed the IDL file, and prompt for verification of the coclass and interface from the IDL file that should be processed to create the Java class wrappers. Figure 10.32 shows the screen that should be displayed by the Wizard after analyzing the IDL file. Verify that the CMathJXS coclass and IMathJXS interface are specified, and select Finish to allow the Java class wrappers to be produced.

When the Wizard has completed, it will again display the steps required to use the Java class wrappers that were produced. These are the same suggestions that were made the first time that the Wizard was run. Since the requested actions were performed the first time, there is no reason to repeat them, so simply choose OK.

The ActiveX Wizard for Java automatically ran the JavaTLB tools to produce the Java class wrappers and the summary.txt file that lists the Java class, interface, and methods that were created from the IDL file. The

Figure 10.31
ActiveX Component
Wizard Input Files.

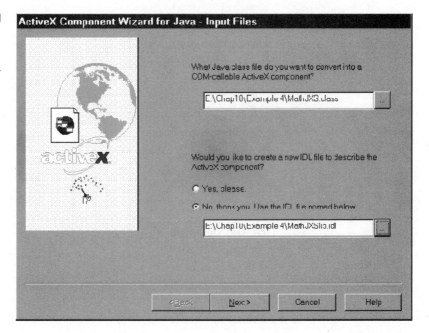

Figure 10.32
ActiveX Component
Wizard Select Coclass.

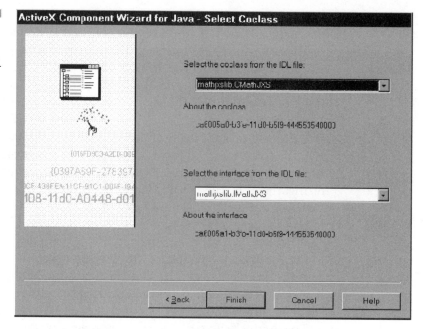

methods defined in the mathjxslib/IMathJXS interface are the abstract
methods that must be implemented in the MathJXS class.

```
public class mathjxslib/CMathJXS extends java.lang.Object
{
}
public interface mathjxslib/IMathJXS extends com.ms.com.IUnknown
{
    public abstract int Subtract(int, int);
    public abstract int Add(int, int);
    public abstract int Multiply(int, int);
    public abstract int Divide(int, int);
    public abstract java.lang.String getError();
}
```

As you can see, the read-only Error property is implemented as the
getError() method. Remember, COM does not directly support properties
and instead implements them as get*property*() and put*property*() methods.
Following is the full listing of the MathJXS class and the Java code necessary to implement the IMathJXS interface.

```
import mathjxslib.*;

public class MathJXS
    implements mathjxslib.IMathJXS
{
    private static final String CLSID = "ca6005a0-b3fe-11d0-b5f9-444553540000";
```

```
    private String Error = "";

    public MathJXS()
    {
    }

    public String getError()
    {
        return Error;
    }

    public int Add( int Op1, int Op2 )
    {
        Error = "";
        return Op1 + Op2;
    }

    public int Subtract( int Op1, int Op2 )
    {
        Error = "";
        return Op1 - Op2;
    }

    public int Multiply( int Op1, int Op2 )
    {
        Error = "";
        return Op1 * Op2;
    }

    public int Divide( int Op1, int Op2 )
    {
        if ( Op2 != 0 )
        {
            Error = "";
            return Op1 / Op2;
        }
        else
        {
            Error = "Attempt to divide by zero";
            return 0;
        }
    }
}
```

As expected, the code is very similar to the Visual Basic implementation of the MathAXS automation server from the previous exercise. Once the methods have been added to support the IMathJXS interface, the project can be compiled. The resulting MathJXS.class file should now reside in the <windows>\java\lib directory as per the project settings changes that we were asked to make by the ActiveX Wizard for Java. Since the class lives in the <windows>\java\lib directory, the Microsoft Java Virtual Machine will be able to find it when requested to instantiate the MathJXS Automation server.

The second part of this exercise is to implement the Visual Basic client that will access the newly created MathJXS automation server. A standard Visual Basic application can be used for this exercise. The project can be named VBClient. In order to re-create the JavaClient from the previous exercise in Visual Basic, a form that contains a timer control and a label field will be needed. The timer can keep its default name of Timer1, and the interval property should be set to 2000 so that the timer fires every 2 seconds. The label field can also keep its default name of Label1, and will be used to display a string representing the operation and the result returned from the MathJXS automation server.

In order to use the MathJXS automation server, Visual Basic has to be made aware of its existence. Choose **Project/References** from the menu. The **References** dialog lists all the components registered with Windows. The MathJXS automation server was not registered by name, so the type library will have to be explicitly read to determine the functionality provided by the MathJXS automation server.

From the References dialog choose the browse button. Navigate to the directory that contains the MathJXS project and select the MathJXSlib.tlb type library. Visual Basic will then add MathJXSlib to the list of ActiveX components. Assure the MathJXSlib is checked, as shown in Fig. 10.33, so that it will be included in the VBClient project.

Figure 10.33
Visual Basic
References.

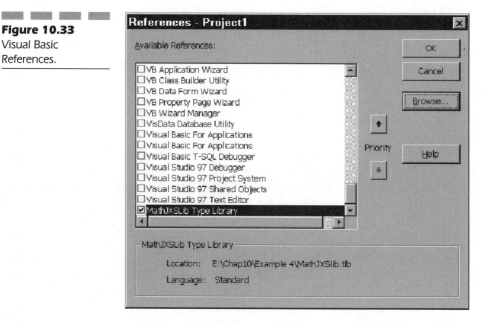

At this point, code can be added to create and access the MathJXS automation server. Typically, the following statements are used to create an automation object in Visual Basic:

```
Dim obj as Object 'allocate a reference object
set obj = CreateObject( "Word.Basic" ) 'instantiate the Word Basic automation server
```

However, the MathJXS automation server implements a custom interface, IMathJXS, and is not named. Therefore, the CMathJXS COM class must be explicitly defined and created. In order to create an instance of the MathJXS automation server the following statements must be used:

```
Dim obj as CMathJXS
set obj = new CMathJXS
```

You might notice that the type of CMathJXS was used as the Visual Basic type for the *obj* variable. When the ActiveX Wizard for Java in Visual J++ created the MathJXSlib.idl file, it created the COM interface that defines the properties and methods exposed by the COM class, or coclass. That coclass was given a name of CMathJXS in the IDL file and it is that name that is referred to now. Remember, Visual Basic has no idea that the automation server was implemented in Java, and therefore does not care what the Java class name is that implemented the server. Instead, the language-independent COM class is created, which in turn is responsible for determining how to instantiate the object.

The rest of the Visual Basic code need to implement the VBClient is fairly simple.

```
Dim obj As CMathJXS 'Reference to automation server
Dim lOp1 As Long 'Operand 1
Dim lOp2 As Long 'Operand 2
Dim lOperation As Long 'Operation
Dim strOperation As String 'string Operation type
Dim lAnswer As Long 'Answer from operation
Dim strDisplay As String 'String to display in label

Private Sub Form_Load()
  Randomize 'initialize the random number generator
  Set obj = New CMathJXS 'instanciate the class
End Sub

Private Sub Form_Unload(Cancel As Integer)
  Set obj = Nothing
End Sub

Private Sub Timer1_Timer()

  Timer1.Interval = 0 'Disable the timer
```

```
'Generate random numbers
lOp1 = Rnd * 100 '0 to 99
lOp2 = Rnd * 100 '0 to 99
lOperation = Rnd * 4 '0 to 3

Select Case lOperation
  Case 0: 'Add
    strOperation = "+"
    lAnswer = obj.Add(lOp1, lOp2)
  Case 1: 'Subtract
    strOperation = "-"
    lAnswer = obj.Subtract(lOp1, lOp2)
  Case 2: 'Multiply
    strOperation = "*"
    lAnswer = obj.Multiply(lOp1, lOp2)
  Case 3: 'Divide
    strOperation = "/"
    lAnswer = obj.Divide(lOp1, lOp2)
End Select

'Format display string
strDisplay = Str(lOp1) + " " + strOperation + " " + Str(lOp2) + " = "

'Append answer or error
If Len(obj.Error) = 0 Then
  strDisplay = strDisplay + Str(lAnswer)
Else
  strDisplay = strDisplay + obj.Error
End If

'Display
Label1.Caption = strDisplay

Timer1.Interval = 2000 'start the timer again
End Sub
```

Figure 10.34 shows the finished, running result of the VBClient. As you can see, the results are very similar to the JavaClient from the previous exercise.

With Microsoft's optimized Java Virtual Machine, they have made Java a very viable alternative to C++ and Visual Basic for creating fast and efficient Automation servers.

COM Errors and Java

There will be times when errors occur using COM objects. Those errors are usually communicated via the HRESULT return code of a COM method. Microsoft provides a Java package named com.ms.com.ComException that wraps the HRESULT in a Java class.

Figure 10.34
VB Client.

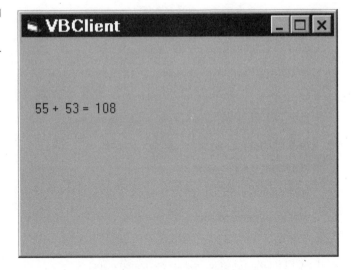

When a Java class wrapper is produced for a COM object, the methods are defined with an implicit *throws* clause. Even though the summary.txt file produced by the Java Type Library Wizard tool doesn't show it, all of the methods can be assumed to be defined as:

```
void method() throws com.ms.com.ComException;
```

ComException is derived from the Java class RuntimeException, and therefore the *throws* clause is not strictly required by the compiler in method definitions. And for the same reason, try/catch blocks are not required when making calls to COM methods in your Java source code.

Since ComException wraps the HRESULT value, it provides a method to retrieve the error code. The method getHResult() returns the error code as a Java *int* that describes the specific error. ComException also implements the Throwable interface and thus provides the method getMessage() to get a detailed message.

There are two subclasses derived from ComException. ComSuccessException is used by the COM method to indicate success. ComFailException is used to indicate a failure and should be caught by a try/catch block in order to determine if an error occurred.

The following code snippet shows how to use a try/catch block along with the ComFailException class:

```
import "com.ms.com.*";

...
```

TABLE 10.3

COM Error Codes

Error	Value
E_UNEXPECTED (Unexpected failure)	0x8000FFFF
E_NOTIMPL (Not implemented)	0x80004001
E_OUTOFMEMORY (Ran out of memory)	0x8007000E
E_INVALIDARG (One or more arguments are invalid)	0x80070057
E_NOINTERFACE (No such interface supported)	0x80004002
E_POINTER (Invalid pointer)	0x80004003
E_HANDLE (Invalid handle)	0x80070006
E_ABORT (Operation aborted)	0x80004004
E_FAIL (Unspecified error)	0x80004005
E_ACCESSDENIED (General access denied error)	0x80070005
E_NOTIMPL (Not implemented)	0x80000001
DISP_E_UNKNOWNINTERFACE (Unknown interface)	0x80020001
DISP_E_MEMBERNOTFOUND (Member not found)	0x80020003
DISP_E_PARAMNOTFOUND (Parameter not found)	0x80020004
DISP_E_TYPEMISMATCH (Type mismatch)	0x80020005
DISP_E_UNKNOWNNAME (Unknown name)	0x80020006
DISP_E_NONAMEDARGS (No named arguments)	0x80020007
DISP_E_BADVARTYPE (Bad variable type)	0x80020008
DISP_E_EXCEPTION (Exception occurred)	0x80020009
DISP_E_OVERFLOW (Out of present range)	0x8002000A
DISP_E_BADINDEX (Invalid index)	0x8002000B
DISP_E_UNKNOWNLCID (Memory is locked)	0x8002000C
DISP_E_ARRAYISLOCKED (Memory is locked)	0x8002000D
DISP_E_BADPARAMCOUNT (Invalid number of parameters)	0x8002000E
DISP_E_PARAMNOTOPTIONAL (Parameter not optional)	0x8002000F
DISP_E_BADCALLEE (Invalid callee)	0x80020010
DISP_E_NOTACOLLECTION (Does not support a collection)	0x80020011

```
try
{
        IComClass obj = (IComClass) new CComClass();

        obj.setProperty( 1 );
        obj.Method();
}
catch( ComFailException e )
{
        System.out.println( "COM Exception occurred:" );
        System.out.println( e.getHResult() ); // display error code
        System.out.println( e.getMessage() ); // translate error message
}

...
```

Table 10.3 shows some common system-defined errors that can be returned in the HRESULT of a COM method.

Summary

To use existing ActiveX components from Java and to implement them using Java lends a great deal of credibility to this fledgling language. Since Windows is the desktop operating system of choice for most PC users, Java will be expected to integrate seamlessly with existing applications. Users do not care what language a program is written in, just that their applications integrate seamlessly together.

Microsoft has taken great care not to intrude on the philosophy of Java. Developers are moving to Java because of its purity and portability. Microsoft understands this and that is why there were no changes made to the language to support ActiveX components. By modifying only the Java Virtual Machine, Microsoft is able to support both "pure" Java applications as well as ActiveX-enabled ones.

INDEX

A

SOFTWARE AND INFORMATION LICENSE

The software and information on this diskette (collectively referred to as the "Product") are the property of The McGraw-Hill Companies, Inc. ("McGraw-Hill") and are protected by both United States copyright law and international copyright treaty provision. You must treat this Product just like a book, except that you may copy it into a computer to be used and you may make archival copies of the Products for the sole purpose of backing up our software and protecting your investment from loss.

By saying "just like a book," McGraw-Hill means, for example, that the Product may be used by any number of people and may be freely moved from one computer location to another, so long as there is no possibility of the Product (or any part of the Product) being used at one location or on one computer while it is being used at another. Just as a book cannot be read by two different people in two different places at the same time, neither can the Product be used by two different people in two different places at the same time (unless, of course, McGraw-Hill's rights are being violated).

McGraw-Hill reserves the right to alter or modify the contents of the Product at any time.

This agreement is effective until terminated. The Agreement will terminate automatically without notice if you fail to comply with any provisions of this Agreement. In the event of termination by reason of your breach, you will destroy or erase all copies of the Product installed on any computer system or made for backup purposes and shall expunge the Product from your data storage facilities.

LIMITED WARRANTY

McGraw-Hill warrants the physical diskette(s) enclosed herein to be free of defects in materials and workmanship for a period of sixty days from the purchase date. If McGraw-Hill receives written notification within the warranty period of defects in materials or workmanship, and such notification is determined by McGraw-Hill to be correct, McGraw-Hill will replace the defective diskette(s). Send request to:

Customer Service
McGraw-Hill
Gahanna Industrial Park
860 Taylor Station Road
Blacklick, OH 43004-9615

The entire and exclusive liability and remedy for breach of this Limited Warranty shall be limited to replacement of defective diskette(s) and shall not include or extend to any claim for or right to cover any other damages, including but not limited to, loss of profit, data, or use of the software, or special, incidental, or consequential damages or other similar claims, even if McGraw-Hill has been specifically advised as to the possibility of such damages. In no event will McGraw-Hill's liability for any damages to you or any other person ever exceed the lower of suggested list price or actual price paid for the license to use the Product, regardless of any form of the claim.

THE McGRAW-HILL COMPANIES, INC. SPECIFICALLY DISCLAIMS ALL OTHER WARRANTIES, EXPRESS OR IMPLIED, INCLUDING BUT NOT LIMITED TO, ANY IMPLIED WARRANTY OF MERCHANTABILITY OR FITNESS FOR A PARTICULAR PURPOSE. Specifically, McGraw-Hill makes no representation or warranty that the Product is fit for any particular purpose and any implied warranty of merchantability is limited to the sixty day duration of the Limited Warranty covering the physical diskette(s) only (and not the software or in-formation) and is otherwise expressly and specifically disclaimed.

This Limited Warranty gives you specific legal rights; you may have others which may vary from state to state. Some states do not allow the exclusion of incidental or consequential damages, or the limitation on how long an implied warranty lasts, so some of the above may not apply to you.

This Agreement constitutes the entire agreement between the parties relating to use of the Product. The terms of any purchase order shall have no effect on the terms of this Agreement. Failure of McGraw-Hill to insist at any time on strict compliance with this Agreement shall not constitute a waiver of any rights under this Agreement. This Agreement shall be construed and governed in accordance with the laws of New York. If any provision of this Agreement is held to be contrary to law, that provision will be enforced to the maximum extent permissible and the remaining provisions will remain in force and effect.